Terrific Majesty

TERRIFIC MAJESTY
The powers of Shaka Zulu and the limits of historical invention

Carolyn Hamilton

HARVARD UNIVERSITY PRESS
Cambridge, Massachusetts
London, England
1998

Library of Congress Cataloging-in-Publication Data

Hamilton, Carolyn.
Terrific majesty : the powers of Shaka Zulu and the limits of historical
invention / Carolyn Hamilton.
p.   cm.
Includes bibliographical references and index.
ISBN 0-674-87445-5 (cloth)
ISBN 0-674-87446-3 (pbk.)
1. Chaka, Zulu Chief, 1787?–1828. 2. Zulu (African people)—History.
3. Zulu (African people)—Kings and rulers—Biography. 4. Inkatha Freedom Party.
5. Nationalism—South Africa. I. Title.
DT1768.Z95H36   1998
968.4′039′092—DC21
[B]
98-10551

" The Government of the Zoolas. – It would almost puzzle a DeLolme,
or any of the ancient writers on governments, to define that of the
Zoolas; and I may assert, without the least apprehension of its being
controverted, that it is indisputably the most incomprehensible
government with which any known nation on the face of the earth
is conversant. In one part of this work I have, from not being able
to find anything approximating to it, among the ancient or modern
states, designated it a Zoolacratical government—an appellation to which,
from its inexplicability, I thought it entitled. Its outline, however, may be
said to be perfectly simple—namely, despotic. "

(Nathaniel Isaacs, *Travels and Adventures in Eastern Africa*, 1836)

Contents

Acknowledgements

In 1986 Shula Marks passed on to me a photocopy of David William Cohen's paper prepared for the Fifth Roundtable in Anthropology and History, held in Paris that year. With typical sensitivity she had drawn out of my own earlier work efforts to edge towards some of the same kinds of perspectives that David was at that time developing with such effect around questions of the "production of history." Instead of going to London to study with Shula, as had many of my own earlier teachers and those of my peers, I followed her directions toward the Johns Hopkins University, Baltimore, to join in David's exploration of the practice of history both within and beyond the academy, and to undertake the Ph.D. research on which this book is based. But if I was never directly trained by Shula, the reader of this book will be left in no doubt as to how profoundly her work has influenced me and how great my intellectual debt to her is. Yet, perhaps of even more value to me has been the warm and stimulating comradeship Shula has extended to me over the years and the great pleasure of staying with her and Yitz.

At the Johns Hopkins University my characteristically South African parochialism was sharply challenged by the wide-ranging and demanding scholarship of Philip Curtin, who also took the time to teach me how to write. I valued greatly his close criticism of my work and the pleasure of engagement with so astute a scholar. For me, the challenge of the day was to get the innovations of a Cohen-inspired argument past the rigor of Curtinesque criticism!

Working with David William Cohen has been one of the most demanding and rewarding experiences of my life, and has been a great privilege. In retrospect, I understand that David's supervisory role in my doctoral research took a form that simultaneously freed, empowered, and challenged me to think. Still more importantly it has positioned me to take that freedom, empowerment, and challenge beyond the thesis into all the aspects of my life concerned with intellectual engagement, always asking that such movements be accompanied by attention to questions of integrity. It would seem to be impossible to ask more of a mentor, but it has been followed by a rich friendship which offers all those same things in new contexts.

Foremost amongst my other intellectual debts is that owing to John Wright. It was in my undergraduate days in Pietermaritzburg that John first inspired in me an interest in the early Zulu kingdom and in the challenge of grappling with sources pertinent to its history, and he remains my harshest critic, closest collaborator, and cherished friend. Indeed, sections of this book owe so much to conversations and arguments with John, and draw so closely on aspects of his research, that no acknowledgement can do justice to the depth of our engagement.

In addition to those already mentioned, JoAnne Brown, David Bunn, Monica von Beusekom, Tim Burke, Garrie Dennie, Gillian Feeley-Harnick, Ran Greenstein, Martin Hall, David Hammond-Tooke, Adam Kuper, Paul Landau, Eleanor Preston-Whyte, Jon Sadowsky, Keith Shear, Gay Seidman, Michael Westcott, and Leslie Witz all read the manuscript or sections of it, at various stages in its evolution, and offered wonderful and imaginative suggestions for improvement. Jo Behrens, Geoff Blundell, Laura Cloete, Ronette Engela, Sue Eber, Anne Holliday, Megan Kearns, Caroline Jeannerat, Jeff Rice, and Graeme Rodgers assisted in various ways with the technical production of the manuscript. Richard Cope, Marcus Darwell, Graeme Dominy, Jan-Bart Gewald, Sue Kramer, David Lazar, Stephen Ramsay, Graeme Rodgers, Gay Seidman, and John Wright all provided important newsclippings, references, or notes from archival sources which were of great assistance. Acknowledgements are also due to the staff of the Killie Campbell Africana Library, and Bobbi Eldridge in particular, as well as the staff of the John G. Gubbins Library of Africana, University of the Witwatersrand, notably Margaret Northey.

Funds from the Johns Hopkins University, the Institute for Advanced Study and Research in the African Humanities at Northwestern University, the University of the Witwatersrand and the Centre for Science Development assisted the research at various stages and facilitated its presentation at conferences and seminars. This financial support is gratefully acknowledged.

Portions of chapters 2, 5, and 6 are closely based on articles which have already been published and the permission of the *Journal of African History* (33, 1, 1992, pp. 37–63), *Radical History Review* (44, Spring 1989, pp. 5–31) and *Social Dynamics* (21, 2, 1995, pp. 1–22) to reproduce these materials is acknowledged.

Orthographic and Terminological Notes

In South Africa today many place names continue to be officially rendered using incorrect orthography. Even the latest maps and official documents use the colonial form "Tugela" rather than "Thukela" for the major river in the KwaZulu–Natal region. I have retained the colonial orthography to refer to colonial institutions and settlements, as in "Tugela magistracy," but have used the correct orthography for physical features such as rivers or Zulu institutions and settlements. An improved orthography is also used for the names of persons except where personal names were rendered in an older orthographic form by the person concerned. It seems likely that the spellings of the names of the individuals interviewed by James Stuart reflected his usage rather than their own. In that case I have elected to use the spellings for the interviewees' names as used by the editors of the published version of the interviews, to avoid confusion. Thus where Stuart spelt the name of the son of Thimuni as "Ndhlovu," that man's testimony occurs in the published version of Stuart's text as the testimony of "Ndhlovu," and is cited in my notes as being the text of "Ndhlovu." In such instances the use of the older orthographic form continues to signal the extent to which the recorded text is a product of both Stuart and the son of Thimuni. Where I refer to the activities of the son of Thimuni, I use the correct orthography, that of "Ndlovu," as I do not know what spelling he himself would have employed. All quotations and book titles retain the original orthography.

"Zulu kingdom" refers to the independent polity in southeast Africa established by Shaka in the 1810s and ruled by his descendants until 1879. The term "Zululand" is used to refer to roughly the same area under colonial and, later, Union rule. Today the province that incorporates the old Zulu kingdom and the colony of Natal is called "KwaZulu–Natal." For the sake of clarity the correct orthographic rendering of "KwaZulu" has been used in the study to refer to the apartheid homeland of that name established in 1971, even though in the time of its existence the Europeanized form "Kwazulu" prevailed, while those who refused to recognize its existence chose various orthographic strategies to signal their stances, such as "kwazulu."

The term "native" was a key aspect of the discourse of nineteenth-century colonial administrators. It is part of the argument of this study that for at least some administrators, recognition of the indigenity of the local inhabitants whom they sought to rule underpinned their policies. The term was inherited by later administrations and acquired a distinctly pejorative inflection through its use in segregationist and racist discourses. The term is retained in this study to refer to specific policies and institutions which were labeled at the time of their existence as "native," and as a strategy to underscore the centrality of indigenous ideas in early colonial thinking.

Abbreviations

APS	Aborigines' Protection Society
ANC	African National Congress
BPP	British Parliamentary Papers
CO	Colonial Office Papers
Codesa	Convention for a Democratic South Africa
Cosatu	Congress of South African Trade Unions
C.P.	Colenso Papers
GH	Government House Papers
IFP	Inkatha Freedom Party
JSA	*James Stuart Archive*
KCAL	Killie Campbell Africana Library
NAD	Natal Archives Depot
NNC	Natal Native Congress
SABC	South African Broadcasting Corporation
SNA	Secretary for Native Affairs
Sh.P.	Shepstone Papers
S.P.	Stuart Papers
UDF	United Democratic Front

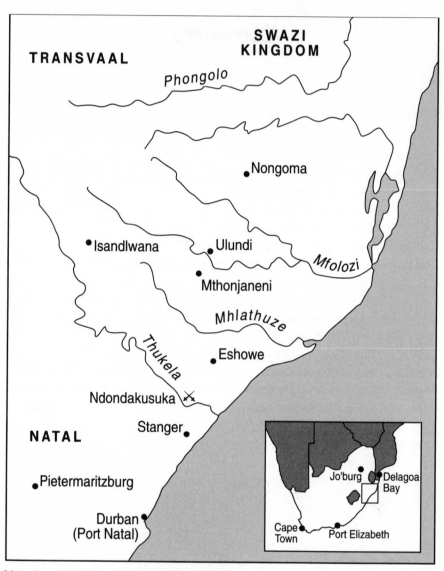

Natal and Zululand in the early 1880s

Introduction

On September 24, 1828 the founder of the Zulu kingdom, Shaka, son of Senzangakhona, was assassinated at his Dukuza residence. In the early 1970s the Zulu cultural organization, Inkatha, succeeded in getting September 24 proclaimed as "Shaka Day," and proceeded to make the figure of Shaka the centerpiece of an ideological campaign promoting Zulu nationalism. Every year since, Shaka Day rallies have been held across what is today the KwaZulu–Natal region of South Africa and in the migrant workers' hostels in and around Johannesburg.

The main celebration occurs at the supposed site of Shaka's Dukuza grave in the modern town of Stanger on the north coast of KwaZulu–Natal. Prior to South Africa's first democratic election in 1994 the present monarch, King Goodwill Zwelithini, dressed in traditional regalia, usually delivered an address approved in advance by his uncle and "traditional prime minister," Mangosuthu Buthelezi. The address typically extolled Shaka and contained some kind of affirmation of the "traditional prime minister." Buthelezi, also the leader of Inkatha (and later of its successor, the Inkatha Freedom Party [IFP], and, following the 1994 elections, the national minister of home affairs), would speak immediately afterwards. He normally responded by pledging his allegiance to the king and taking the opportunity to remind the audience of his qualifications for high office (both genealogical and as an anti-apartheid leader). In disquisitions liberally laced with analogies to the reign of Shaka, he characteristically went on to justify his most recent political activities and to launch attacks on his political opponents. In short, the annual Shaka Day celebrations, redolent with powerful historical associations, were, and still are, at once important arenas for political maneuvers and unique barometers of "Zulu-ist" politics.

In 1994, the newly installed ANC-dominated government ratified a preelection land deal which effectively placed large areas of the former homeland of KwaZulu under the direct control of the Zulu king. With this transfer, Zwelithini was, for the first time in his reign, freed from direct financial dependence on the local authority headed by Buthelezi or its predecessors. Long-simmering tensions between the king and his powerful minister began to bubble over. Things reached boiling-point when Zwelithini invited the new state president and ANC leader, Nelson Mandela, to attend the 1994 Shaka Day festivities in Stanger. Buthelezi, alarmed at this sign of rapprochement between the two protagonists on whose supposed long-time rivalry his personal political success had flourished, objected to the invitation extended without his clearance and threatened darkly that Mandela's safety could not be guaranteed at the rally.[1] Political tensions rose sharply in the KwaZulu–Natal region with speculation rife that Zwelithini was about to ditch his "traditional prime minister." When President Mandela traveled to the Zulu king's eNyokeni palace to discuss these developments, IFP supporters stormed the royal residence and threw stones at Mandela's helicopter. In a bid to defuse the situation, Mandela agreed not to attend the ceremonies. Zwelithini then canceled all Shaka Day events. Nevertheless, Buthelezi and his supporters went ahead with certain rallies on Saturday, September 24, at which the king and his supporters were conspicuously absent.[2]

Matters came to a dramatic head the next day when a member of the newly established royal committee advising Zwelithini, Prince Sifiso Zulu, appeared on the nightly television news program *Agenda* to discuss the Shaka Day dispute between the king and Buthelezi. In the live broadcast, Sifiso Zulu argued that in the history of the Zulu kingdom since Shakan times there had never been any such office as that of a "traditional prime minister," and effectively repudiated the special relationship between the royal family and Buthelezi that two decades of Shaka Day celebrations had affirmed. An enraged Buthelezi stormed out of a nearby suite where he had just completed a recording for another program on the Shaka Day conflict, and burst into the *Agenda* studio. In full view of a riveted nationwide television audience, the minister of home affairs and his bodyguards accosted Sifiso Zulu, berating him for daring to speak publicly on the king's behalf. Zulu was hustled out of his chair and his seat in front of the cameras was taken by Buthelezi, who then presented his version of the controversy.

In the weeks following, Buthelezi's act of "air piracy"[3] was raised in parliament and in the cabinet, was roundly condemned by press-freedom activists, and was extensively discussed on radio talk shows, in the press, and in other public forums. The 1994 Shaka Day conflict was a challenge to Buthelezi's capacity to use representations of the past in the service of current political needs, and the close-knit connections between the Zulu royal family as the direct bearers of the Shakan legacy and contemporary Zulu nationalist politicians began to unravel. By the time Shaka Day 1995 came around the Zulu king had clearly aligned himself with Mandela, against his erstwhile prime minister and diehard Zulu nationalists. Paradoxically then, the controversial Shaka Day celebrations had come to focus on a dispute between Zwelithini, Shaka's descendant (albeit through a fraternal line), and Buthelezi, who claimed the mantle of Shaka for the cause of Zulu national-ism. The only thing that both parties agreed on was that the Shaka legacy was the basis for uniting the people of KwaZulu–Natal.[4]

The post-election Shaka Day conflicts draw attention to the power of historical references in South Africa and to the ferocity of the contests over the control of such references. In 1992 the *Vrye Weekblad* newspaper announced in banner head-lines that "Shaka's Spirit Lives Again." It lives again in countless forms and multiple locations: in politics, the press, the academy, popular culture, novels, household items, and high art. This book examines key aspects of the historical processes that have invested one particular historical symbol, that of Shaka, with such po-tency and with a powerful and insistent contemporary presence.

Terrific Majesty is written against the background of political violence in South Africa, and the particular character given to that violence by the mobilization of a Zulu identity, by perceptions of the legacy of the military achievements of Shaka, and by the problems created by the invocation of Shaka and of Zulu militarism in the present. In part, the study is driven by the pressing need to gain insight into these historically linked elements of contemporary ethnic politics. The book does not seek to document or account for the rise of Zulu identity and the way in which it has been used by those exercising power. It is an examination rather of how cer-tain symbolic forms and forces were constituted historically, often through the ex-ercise of power, and came to be the founding ideas of a Zulu identity.[5] It looks at the processes by which various features of the precolonial world and of the colo-nial encounter came to be condensed into the figure of Shaka, as well as how, in the course of that condensation, they gathered power and conviction. It probes the ideas underpinning P.E. Zondi's claim made in 1996 that "an overemphasis on a Shakan tradition produces an 'impi mentality' which contributes to the violence in KwaZulu–Natal."[6]

Another context is provided by Mahmood Mamdani's recent study, *Citizen and Subject: Contemporary Africa and the Legacy of Late Colonialism*,[7] which addresses similar questions about the persistence and significance of "tribal" identities and customary law, both in South Africa and elsewhere in Africa. Central to Mamdani's argument concerning the division of African societies into "citizens" (those enjoy-ing civil liberties and usually located in urban settings) and "subjects" (those, mostly peasants, subject to customary law and "tribal" authorities) is the notion that the institutional framework of indirect rule enshrined in apartheid and late colonialism elsewhere in Africa was a creation of the colonial authorities. Recog-nition of this point, Mamdani suggests, is an essential pre- requisite for any reforms designed to move beyond deracialization to democracy. *Terrific Majesty* both pushes back in time Mamdani's discussion of the roots of institutional segregation in South Africa and suggests that the power and resilience of notions about "tribal" identity and custom among those whom he terms "subjects" is located in the complex historical entanglement of indigenous and colonial concepts in ways that his study does not consider.

This study is also driven by developments in another setting, the crisis over sources that confronts historians of precolonial times. A major historiographical development of the late 1980s and early 1990s in southern Africa was the debate over the "*mfecane,*" the name given to a period of turmoil—generally attributed to the rise of the Zulu power under Shaka—which prevailed across much of southern Africa in the early decades of the nineteenth century. Suggesting that the idea of Shakan agency was a fraudulent settler alibi to mask the illegal procurement of Africans' land and labor, the initiators of the debate have called into question the status of the sources of early nineteenth-century southern African history, most of which owe their capture in written form to colonial recording practices. Taken together with currently influential literatures on the invention of tradition, the "West's" definition of the colonial "Other," and the constructed nature of knowledge itself, these developments pose a serious challenge to historians seeking to reconstruct the history of Shakan times, particularly those scholars and activists interested in recovering something of the substance of precolonial African discourses and practices.

A host of recent studies have focused on the inventions, plagiarisms, and myths that characterize writings about Shaka and Shakan times. They have changed irrevocably the way scholars read the historical sources and have introduced into the historiography a new and valuable awareness of the extent to which such writings were shaped by colonial fears and desires. Benefiting from their insights, this study seeks now to qualify and temper them, by investigating the limits and constraints on the processes of invention and myth-making so as to grapple with the power of a historical idea such as the legacy of Shaka.

Terrific Majesty responds to the challenges faced by historians today through examination of the moment of first contact between the early Port Natal traders and the Zulu kingdom under Shaka. It probes how contemporary indigenous ideas about Shaka influenced the traders' perceptions and representations of the Zulu king. It goes on to trace the way in which, in the following decades, the secretary for native affairs in the new colony of Natal, Theophilus Shepstone, drew on conceptions of social order and sovereignty, and images of Shaka and Shakan rule, which were likewise available within African society, to provide a model for the Natal native administration. Shepstone's model was subsequently distorted by the British authorities in the course of events surrounding the 1879 Anglo-Zulu War. Struggles subsequently ensued over the form and aims of what was known as "native policy." One colonial official in particular, James Stuart, sought to bring about the reinstatement of what he understood to be the essential "Shakan" core of the Shepstone system and, to that end, committed himself to a vast task of research into the reign of Shaka.

Between 1897 and 1924, Stuart collected the testimonies of nearly two hundred informants on topics concerning the history of the Zulu and neighboring peoples. Stuart's collection is the primary source for African versions of the Shakan period available to historians. The present study examines Stuart in the context of his times, as well as through a more intimate biographical lens, establishing in the process something of his location in, and his sense of distance from, colonial society in Natal. It traces the legacy of Shepstone in Stuart's approach to the topic of Shaka and, through a close examination of his motivations and working methods, assesses the extent of Stuart's presence in the testimonies recorded about Shaka. Detailed historical investigation reveals that Stuart was no mere inventor of Zulu history, that his collection warrants, and bears, the close scrutiny of historians seeking to recover the traces of indigenous views of Shakan times. The extent of his commitment to the recording of detailed historical material in the words of his African informants raises questions about the nature and course of the development of knowledge of "native affairs." The focus on Stuart offers a perspective on the shaping of that expertise by its close coupling with the demands of "native administration," and the manner of its professionalization and transformation into the academic "sciences" of anthropology and Bantu studies. The study further examines the way in which the complex image of Shaka that emerged out of the writings of administrators such as Shepstone and Stuart was widely promoted in the novels of popular writers such as Henry Rider Haggard.

By the time the Zulu royal family, rural traditionalists, and the educated and Christianized African elite in Natal came to draw on images of Shaka in an attempt to forge a united identity as Zulu in the 1910s and 1920s, and segregationist and (later) apartheid ideologues sought to distinguish the basis of a Zulu homeland, the figure of the first Zulu king was already the product of a long and complex process of reworking. In particular it incorporated the understandings of Shaka in the later nineteenth century, developed by Shepstone and the Zulu king Cetshwayo, which were shaped by each other's interpretations not only of the past, but of the very nature of power and legitimacy: their enacted invocations of Shaka ensured that public apprehension of the first Zulu king was similarly complicated. Thus by the 1920s the figure of Shaka as discussed by constituencies as diverse as popular novelists, Zulu nationalists, academics, and the writers of serious literature was the product of a century of discussions about sovereignty and governance, and of enactments of power and resistance that defy neat categorization in terms of lineages such as white or black views. The interweaving of these discussions makes it impossible to draw clear distinctions between the versions of the colonized and the colonizers, or even between those of subjects of the Zulu king and non-subjects. What we discover, then, is a blurring of the familiar lines of alterity usually drawn crisply by scholars of the creation of tribalism. It is this blurring that has made the figure of Shaka a powerful metaphor in South African political life.

Because part of the rationale for the study lies in a desire to reassess the extent to which colonial constructions of Zulu history "invented" their own Shaka, this study is largely confined to a consideration of the constraints and limitations on white inventions and reinventions of Zulu history. In the process a clear view emerges of the various ways in which Africans engaged with, sometimes concurring with and sometimes challenging, colonial concerns with Shaka. A topic that awaits fuller investigation in its own right is the way in which ideas about the Zulu past have been taken up by African writers, and the way their works have affected and in turn been shaped by white writings. Nonetheless, this study shows that what the early travelers, missionaries, and colonial administrators found in the area that is today KwaZulu–Natal was not a clearly articulated and bounded culture, nor a singular identity, and was bolstered by no unargued Zulu history. The cultural ideas, historical notions, and identities that prevailed in the area were complex and powerfully articulated constructs with contested meanings and heterogeneous origins. The same is true of the ideas, notions, and identities imported into the area. And from their moments of first contact these highly varied bodies of material locked onto one another in a myriad of different ways effecting processes of continuous change, interaction, and imbrication. These processes of interchange marked not only the texts of the time, both oral and written, the many and varied forms of material culture, but even the performances and practices of power itself.

In the course of the nineteenth and early twentieth centuries, and in a variety of ways, the figure of Shaka was increasingly established as a central metaphor in South African politics. Much previous scholarship divides into works dealing either with representations of the Zulu, or with historical reconstructions of events and processes in Natal and the Zulu kingdom in the nineteenth century, such as the rise of the Zulu kingdom or the development of native policy. This study tries to bring together these previously distinct domains at the same time as it focuses on divisions within the Zulu kingdom and within the Natal native administration.

Finally, this historical perspective on the making of the image of Shaka facilitates readings of two more recent productions of Shaka—the television series *Shaka Zulu* and the holiday resort Shakaland—and of the post-election Shaka Day fracas. The strength of the historical perspective lies in its capacity to explain why and how Shaka and Shakan times have become potent metaphors for latter-day South African politics, as exemplified in these contemporary settings.

In sum, the power of the image of Shaka lies not, as most previous commentators have suggested, in its openness to manipulation, to invention, and to imaginative reworkings. Rather it is to be found in, or at least as much in, their very opposite, the historical limits and constraints attached to Shakan historiography (where historiography is broadly construed to include a wide range of forms of the production of history), and to the possible depictions of Shaka. In filling in the limits and constraints on the acts of inventing and imagining, the historian brings to a terrain currently dominated by anthropologists and literary theorists a crucial complementary method and perspective. This is achieved through consideration of the processes behind the making of the archive on which the history of Shaka is based and of the way that its constituent materials are a product of a complex interweaving of past events and previous concerns.

Painted chests, academic body servants and visions of modern airlines: Shaka in contemporary discourses

❝ *Without the metaphor of memory and history, we cannot imagine what it is to be someone else. Metaphor is the reciprocal agent, the universalizing force: it makes possible the power to envision the stranger's heart.* **❞**

(C. Ozick, *Metaphor and Memory*, p. 279)

Painted chests and popular consciousness

In 1992 in Johannesburg a migrant worker selected a wooden chest at the Mai-Mai market, located under the freeway and close to the hostel where he stayed. The worker imagined the chest occupying pride of place in the front room of his home in what was then the "independent" Xhosa homeland of the Transkei. There were two versions of the beautifully painted box. The first had an inset of the Virgin Mary in richly catholic colors of magenta, gold, and turquoise. The second was embellished with pictures of the Zulu kings surrounding a central oval featuring the first Zulu king, Shaka. Both versions were highly popular in 1992, the Shaka chest attracting as many non-Zulu-speaking buyers as Zulu speakers.[1]

At much the same time, billboards advertising the progressive Afrikaans newspaper *Vrye Weekblad* screamed the headline "*Shaka se Gees Herleef*" (Shaka's spirit lives again). The article to which the headlines referred depicted the leader of the Inkatha Freedom Party, Mangosuthu Buthelezi, in the delicate period of negotiations prior to the first democratic election, as returning to the "tribal politics of the warrior nation" ("*Die stampolitiek van die 'warrior nation'*")[2] and as following closely in the tracks of the founder of the Zulu kingdom, Shaka.

This was a view of Shaka, and of the relationship between the past and the present, actively propagated by contemporary Zulu nationalist politicians such as Buthelezi. Claiming throughout the 1980s and through into the 1990s that his "role is ordained by history,"[3] Buthelezi constantly invoked the image of Shaka and of Shakan times to explain the present. While appeals to the past were a characteristic feature of the Zulu nationalist movement, even Zulu speakers who distanced themselves politically from Inkatha asserted their pride in "the military exploits of the Zulu empire" and "the legend of Shaka."[4]

The 1980s saw an explosion of interest in Shaka in the media marked by the release in 1986 of the South African Broadcasting Corporation's multi-million-rand television series *Shaka Zulu*. The series reached an enormous audience at home and abroad, and received wide media coverage. It was hailed by some critics as a much-needed revision of Zulu history, and slated by others for the use of a white narrator and failure to escape the standard racist stereotypes. *Shaka Zulu* was followed closely by a second television series set in Shakan times, *John Ross: An African Adventure,* the story of a young Scot who was a member of the first party of Europeans to visit Shaka. This series, too, resulted in huge controversy, not least because author Stephen Gray published his novel *John Ross: The True Story* shortly afterwards. The novel, based on the published memoirs of Charles Rawden Maclean, alias John Ross, claimed to put forward "the true story" of John Ross and a new view of Shaka, versions of that period of history suppressed in the television series and in earlier writings.

At much the same time as Gray produced his alternative account of Shakan times, the Natal journalist and outspoken critic of the *Shaka Zulu* television series Louis du Buisson published a popular account of Shakan times that also claimed to demythologize and reconstitute the history of this period.[5] This was followed by yet another revision of Zulu history in popular form, Inkatha-linked academic Charles Ballard's *The House of Shaka*.[6] All three of these new texts were remarkable for their sharp, and self-conscious, reversal of the image of Shaka from villain to hero.[7]

Then in the late 1980s the holiday resort Shakaland opened its doors, offering tourists a forum for gaining familiarity with Zulu history and culture otherwise denied to non-Zulu speakers by the prevailing situation of civil war in KwaZulu and Natal, and on the Rand. Like the television series, the resort enjoyed phenomenal success, among black and white visitors alike.

South Africans did not only find Shakas on their television screens, in nonfiction, and in holiday resorts; they proliferated on stage, in art galleries, and novels.[8] Shaka was also firmly embedded in an unarticulated, private domain of their consciousness. This deeper awareness of the symbol of Shaka was revealed in a variety of ways. In 1989 in Ladysmith, Natal, a young white schoolboy held his classmates captive at gunpoint, claiming to be Shaka incarnate. In neighboring Namibia, a notice appeared in the local newspaper, advertising the arrival in Windhoek of Dr. Chaka, a "*wit Sangoma en twee van sy Swart Sangomas vanaf die Republic van*

South Africa [*sic*]" (a white sangoma [diviner, healer] and two of his black sangomas from the Republic of South Africa).[9]

The image of Shaka also had powerful resonances farther afield. In Kenya, an African-American man engaged in a court battle with the government to secure the rights of African-Americans to the citizenship of African countries in which they wish to live. "Our forefathers were Africans and because of the slave master's tricks got intermarried and lost their culture. So if any Black man from America wants to settle in Africa today why should he be denied the right to do so?" he asked. In an effort to emphasize his African connections this ex-Houston sociology student changed his name, to "Shaka Zulu Assegai." He is by no means the only foreigner to favor this choice of name. A son of James Forman, the long-time American civil rights activist, likewise bears the name Shaka.[10]

The choice of the name "Shaka" in these contexts was, and still is, an invocation of heroic resonances. In some cases, however, it connotes specifically "black" power or force, as in the name of the African-American Minneapolis group "Shaka's Zulu Warriors."[11] In the context of violence in contemporary South Africa, the image of Shaka was, and remains, ambiguous, at once fundamentally linked to that of Zulu militarism, and to notions of both order and chaos.

In a 1992 Shaka Day speech aimed at whipping up support for Inkatha in its deadly conflict with the supporters of the ANC, the Zulu king, while affirming commitment to a national peace process, made use of precisely this ambiguity by calling for discipline and order, and in the same breath using Shaka as a metaphor for war. He also claimed for Zulu valor and unity the status of a philosophy:

> We are a people who come from warrior stock . . . This was the philosophy of King Shaka, a philosophy passed on along the long line of illustrious Zulu kings who followed in his footsteps. It is this strength and courage in unity that flowed in the blood of the great warriors of King Shaka's armies, and that today flows in our blood—the great Zulu nation of Africa . . . We, as the Zulu people, are prepared to die for our principles today because that is the way we were founded. We share the convictions of King Shaka's great warriors who went forth to do battle, courageous men also prepared to die for their principles.[12]

Inkatha made the figure of Shaka—the creator of the powerful nineteenth-century Zulu kingdom—into the centerpiece of its ideology. The glorification of Shaka, centered on the annual celebration of Shaka Day, has been a key element in the creation of twentieth-century Zulu nationalism. Shaka Day speeches by Zulu leaders typically extolled Shaka in elevated terms:

King Shaka rose like a colossus in his day and age to make KwaZulu a place of Zulus . . . He made one people out of many peoples . . . King Shaka . . . was the greatest visionary of his time . . . That great King, with his deep sense of vision, started something that we must finish. There is unfinished business in Zulus seeing to it that Black and White live together to bring the great advantages of the union that King Shaka saw at the beginning of the nineteenth century. King Shaka did not only have a vision of somehow Whites coming in to benefit his people, King Shaka was ahead of his time. He had a vision of the future nobody could understand. He himself was totally mystified by his vision of great iron birds flying through the air. That great man, who can be confined to no generation, or even century, had visions of modern airliners at a time when the most other men could dream of was the manufacture of some kind of wings he could flap with his arms.[13]

While the language in which these claims were made is overblown and the ideological manipulations transparent, the press seized on the connections between Shaka and modern leaders, between events then and events in the late 1980s and early 1990s, favored by Buthelezi and the king. Journalists constantly made the same connections, using historical allusions to add flourish to their writings and employing the metaphor of Shaka to do the work of making the complexity of latter-day ethnic politics apparently simple and accessible for their readers.

In a *Weekly Mail* article on the bloody war between the ANC communities of Natal and the supporters of the IFP which raged through much of the 1980s and early 1990s, the journalist Mondli Makhanya—himself a Zulu speaker who identified with pride in the heritage of Shaka, but who did not support the IFP—ended his article with the thoughts of the Ezimeleni squatter-camp resident Leonard Mshinga. Mshinga quoted the curse that Shaka was reputed to have uttered after being stabbed by assassins: "You will never rule this land. It will be ruled by the swallows from across the sea, the ones with the transparent ears [an allusion to whites]." Mshinga suggested that the pre-election conflict showed that black South Africans would not rule the country: "Imagine what will happen when we have the country. We will wipe each other out."[14] In 1991 Bra Mzala, in his column in the *Natal Mercury*, described how male infants and toddlers were dressed up by their mothers as girls, "because certain elements are going around killing young boys because they will grow up to be comrades [ANC supporters]."[15] Mzala went on to draw an analogy from history: "This is a horrific reminder of the times of Shaka Zulu, who ordered that all boys in opposing groups be killed." Invoking the notion of the *mfecane*—the period of violence across the subcontinent that is understood to have flowed from the expansion of the Zulu kingdom under Shaka—Buthelezi too used images from Shakan times to discuss the conflict: "We know the meaning of Mfecane and Difaqane. We know the consequences of mass violence . . ."[16] Likewise, Piet "Skiet" [Shoot] Rudolph, leader of the ultra right-wing Afrikaner organization Ordeboerevolk, predicted a modern-day *mfecane* as "violence between Zulu and Xhosa . . . for control of power."[17]

Other commentators emphasized the ideas of discipline historically associated with Shaka. Barry Renfrew, bureau chief for the Associated Press in Johannesburg, said of a Zulu rally: "The discipline is extraordinary. I have heard three thousand of them *breathing* together. It sounds like the purring of a giant cat."[18] Some reports amalgamated the two images, but all seemed to find recourse to the metaphor of Shakan times irresistible as a means of explicating the present.[19]

Academic body servants

Journalists in the 1980s and early 1990s frequently drew on the research of historians to bolster the authority of their analyses of Zulu-ist politics, and a number of newspapers carried articles commissioned from historians. In October 1990, the British newspaper *The Independent on Sunday* published a lavishly illustrated four-page article by the historian R.W. Johnson on the historical bases for contemporary Zulu militarism. In the article Johnson first offered a short summary of Zulu history. He began with the figure of Shaka, "the inescapable central figure of Zulu history, perhaps even black history in South Africa" who "welded a disparate series of groups into a single unit by dint of ruthless wars of conquest" using "the awesome power of the Zulu impis—a force without parallel in Africa in their fearsome discipline and utter determination." He emphasized that this resulted in "pride in a warrior tradition" coupled with "strength in the face of adversity and injustice."[20] For Johnson, conflict between the Zulu and their Xhosa-speaking neighbors is a "tragic inevitability" rooted in history—in the Xhosa being unceremoniously flung out of the Zulu kingdom by Shaka—and underpinned by the power struggle between what he described as the Xhosa-dominated ANC and the Zulu nationalist organization Inkatha.

Johnson's analysis drew a penetrating response from the doyenne of southern African history and author of leading publications on the emergence of Zulu nationalism, the professor of Commonwealth history at the University of London, Shula Marks. Describing Johnson's article as a "travesty of Zulu history," Marks pointed out that the Xhosa were resident in country far south of the Zulu kingdom hundreds of years before Shaka's accession to power and were not pushed out of the Zulu territories by him. Marks criticized Johnson for an attempt to manipulate the historical evidence to suggest a "'traditional' and 'inevitable' enmity between the 'Zulu' and the 'Xhosa'." Marks went on to stress that many of the victims of Inkatha attacks were not Xhosa speakers, but fellow Zulu speakers, while contemporary Zulu nationalism was itself not simply an inevitable legacy of the past, but was largely built on foundations laid in the 1920s by the Zulu royal family in alliance with conservative Christian Africans, white businessmen, and the Natal Native Affairs Department.[21]

In some instances the initiative to join in discussion and debate lay within the academy. In 1992, an opinion piece appeared in the Pietermaritzburg newspaper the *Natal Witness,* written by John Wright, professor of history at the University of Natal, Pietermaritzburg. Wright, who has published widely on the history of Shakan times, commented on Inkatha's demand that the Zulu king be allowed to lead a delegation separate from that of Inkatha at Codesa, the primary negotiating forum in the run-up to the first general election. Noting that Inkatha's claims rested on "[s]haky historical claims," Wright argued that current research revealed that the Shakan kingdom was not as exceptional as had long been thought, that "it was not the only one of its kind, nor was it the first." Likewise, he suggested that the Zulu kingdom was "smaller and less united than commonly thought." He argued that the image of Shaka had been heavily mythologized and needed to be looked at critically. In summary, he challenged the assumption that a Zulu kingdom continuous with that of Shaka still existed in the present, and that it had a unique place in South African history.[22]

When the historians' work began to percolate through into publications with a grassroots readership in Natal, the debate escalated into open conflict. In 1989 the Zulu-language publication promoting cultural debate, *Injula,* carried an article by a Zulu-speaking teacher. Depicting the Zulu king as an illegitimate usurper, and a hated tyrant "whose hands were full of his people's blood," the writer queried whether Shaka really was the great unifier he had been made out to be, and a hero worthy of deep admiration.[23] The article prompted angry responses from readers "sick and tired of this poppycock about King Shaka."[24] One reader, Otto B. Kunene, deplored the influence on the article writer of "certain white historians who pose to be the champions of our cause [and who] write a distorted history of our kings with the aim of denigrating them . . . so that we might disown them and feel ashamed of them." Another reader railed against the "minority of Zulus and others who usually feel pleased when the Zulu culture and heritage is turned upside down." Yet another, who began by drawing a comparison between research on Shaka and the question of the literal truth of the story of Jesus Christ, commented: "Even this bloodshed which is facing us currently should not surprise those who are so proud of Shaka, for it is but the restoration of the custom upheld by Shaka."[25]

In late 1990–early 1991 the *Natal Witness* supplement, the *Echo,* ran a series entitled "The Making of our History." The authors of the series, Wright and Natal Museum archeologist Aron Mazel, presented the latest scholarship on the history of the Natal–Zulu kingdom area in an accessible and effective format that expressly eschewed the biases typical of apartheid history. The series was generally well received by the *Echo*'s largely African readership. With the publication of episodes concerning Shaka, however, controversy erupted.[26]

The authors noted, among other things, that some of Shaka's subjects viewed him as an "upstart," that the Zulu kingdom was never fully united, that it was smaller than people think, and that Zulu society under Shaka was highly stratified. These critical remarks drew the fire of the IFP's mouthpiece, the newspaper *Ilanga*. *Ilanga* launched its attack by describing Wright and Mazel as "academic body servants." "Body servants," in this context, is the English rendition of the Zulu term *izinsila* (singular *insila*). *Izinsila* were officers charged with the disposal of the potent bodily discharges of the royal Zulu. They enjoyed considerable influence because of their performance of this excessively intimate but most important task. In its article, *Ilanga* first sought to establish connections between the designers of the *Echo* series and the IFP's political rivals, the ANC, by describing the authors as "first and foremost Marxists." The article went on to designate them "secondly . . . [as] what one might call ANC nsilas," and cited an unnamed historian as calling them "academic hyenas of the left with a mission to diminish the accomplishments of King Shaka, the founder of the Zulu kingdom." Finally Wright and Mazel were likened to monkeys on a barrel organ. "As long as the Marxist organ grinder cranks the handle," *Ilanga* concluded, "they will dance his tune." The substance of the *Ilanga* article challenged Wright and Mazel's version of Shakan times, arguing that Shaka was not a usurper, that he enjoyed widespread support, that he established his rule over an enormous territory stretching from Mozambique in the north to the Drakensberg in the west and as far south as the Mzimvubu river, that he was a "military and political genius who brought relative stability, peace and order to the period of intermittent warfare, chaos and misery that had been endemic among the disunited Nguni peoples before Shaka's consolidation efforts commenced in 1816."[27] In support of these claims the *Ilanga* article cited as evidence the testimony of Zulu informants published in the *James Stuart Archive,* one of the editors of which is the academic body servant John Wright.[28]

The following week, *Ilanga* carried a letter from the managing editor of the *Echo* series demanding from *Ilanga* corrections of errors of fact and asserting the importance of publishing different views of Zulu history.[29] This drew yet another tirade from *Ilanga* against the "historical pornographers," in which *Ilanga* rejected a further feature of the original *Echo* series, its description of Shaka as a "warlord," this time citing a range of academic studies in support of the various historical points made. Wright and Mazel successfully sued *Ilanga* for defamation.

The attempt by ardent Zulu nationalists to remove the figure of Shaka from academic purview did not rest there. In a Shaka Day speech in 1991, Buthelezi attacked Shula Marks "for what she had to say about our Zulu commitment to our unity and to our culture which we experience today."[30] Buthelezi was reacting to a British Broadcasting Corporation (BBC) radio interview in which Marks discussed the issue of a modern Zulu identity, and its embeddedness in particular conceptions of history. Buthelezi was specifically stung by Marks' comments that the present-day conflict was about what it means to be Zulu. In high temper Buthelezi went on to grumble about

> the academic Anglo-Zulu war that is going on just now at most of the English Universities in South Africa, and which is backed by certain academics in the United Kingdom. There seems to be a campaign to scale down Zulus as Zulus, and concerted efforts to re-invent Zulu history. There is an effort to write what is now supposed to be a "Proper History" of the Zulu people, which is no more than propaganda against the Zulu people in favour of certain political parties and organisations.[31]

The essentials of the dispute between the academics—Marks, Wright, and Mazel—and the Zulu nationalists such as Buthelezi and *Ilanga* concerned the question of the size and power of the Zulu kingdom, the nature of Shakan rule, and the legitimacy of Shaka's accession. A number of the selfsame questions became the subject of an equally heated debate, although in a very different setting and between other protagonists. In 1991, the University of the Witwaters-rand hosted a colloquium on the so-called *mfecane* debate. In summary, the debate concerned the issue of whether there really was an "*mfecane*," by which is generally meant a period of upheaval across the subcontinent in the early nineteenth century caused by the rise of the Zulu kingdom under Shaka. The debate, widely covered at the time in the press, continued at a great rate in various academic journals and other publications.[32]

A crucial aspect of the debate was that it demanded a reassessment of the importance of the Shakan state. John Wright focused on this component of the debate and made a vigorous argument for the scaling down of the kingdom, both geographically and in terms of its impact on the wider region.[33] This development was, as we have noted above, strongly resisted by Zulu nationalists.

Shakan historiography

The *mfecane* debate also threw a spotlight on the historiography of Shakan times. Julian Cobbing, the initiator of the attack on the notion of the *mfecane*, argued that the same version of Zulu history in Shakan times extended unchanged from the early settler historians, if not before, into the present.[34] He claimed that all previous writers treated Zulu history, and the *mfecane* in particular, as something separate from the colonial history of South Africa, and presented the rise of the Zulu state as a self-generated internal revolution that caused disruption across the subcontinent. Cobbing's historiographical generalizations have come under fire for failing to trace accurately earlier shifts in representations of Shaka and Zulu history.[35]

Cobbing's understanding that there are few significant differences between the accounts of the earliest travelers and modern views of Shaka is one perspective on the historiography of Shakan times. It is a view shared by a number of other scholars including William Worger, Johannes Raum, Dan Wylie, and Mbongeni Malaba, and focuses on the biography of Shaka, seeing its ingredients as largely unchanging from earliest accounts to the present.[36] The second view, presented by Christopher Saunders, Wright and Hamilton, and Daphna Golan,[37] among others, emphasizes a significant shift in the historiography from a focus on the "Great Man" to a concern with wider social and economic changes. The different interpretations of the historiography of Shakan times lie at the heart of the *mfecane* debate, with the contending parties establishing the pedigree of the notion of *mfecane* in different ways.

The writing of history conceived of in disciplinary terms, that is, the production of professional history[38]—not necessarily by academy-trained historians or full-time historians, but by researchers who viewed their task as a scholarly and autonomous exercise—began in South Africa in the late nineteenth and early twentieth centuries with the work of George McCall Theal, George Cory, and Eric Walker. Largely concerned with the emergence of colonial society, these works treated African societies as peripheral to colonial history.[39] Despite their relatively curtailed handling of African history, the early settler historians were responsible for fixing in the historiography very particular and specific representations of African society. Saunders rightly insists, however, that there are important distinctions among these writers in their treatment of Shaka and Shakan times which resist their designation as typical "*mfecane* theorists," notably differences in their views of the causes and consequences of the *mfecane,* and in their treatment of the relationship between the *mfecane* and the history of colonization.[40] Nevertheless, these writers share some general characteristics. They tended to focus on the details of Shaka's rise to power, his reorganization of the Zulu army, the instillation of perfect obedience in his followers, and his military innovations. Shaka was generally depicted as aggressive and cruel, and his reign viewed as a period of vast destruction and devastation.

If Zulu history was cursorily represented in their works, it figured more fully in the writings of political thinkers in South Africa grappling with what they termed "the native question."[41] Both the historians and political thinkers drew heavily on the accounts of Zulu history recorded by early travelers, administrators, and missionaries, on the collections of historical documents compiled by John Bird and J.C.Chase, and (a point ignored by Cobbing) on African oral evidence. In missionary texts Shaka was frequently represented as "the noble savage"; whereas in travelers' accounts it was more often his "barbarism" that was emphasized, but this pattern was not as invariant as some reviews suggest. The collections of historical documents and the oral accounts alike offered negative and positive views of Shaka.[42]

By the 1920s, with the emergence of the discipline of anthropology and the creation of Bantu studies departments in the universities (at least partly in the service of what came to be known as Bantu administration), African societies in their own right became the focus of attention in academic studies. This occurred outside the discipline of history: African societies were mostly viewed as changeless; it was believed that there was little evidence on which historical research could be based. The history of the Shakan kingdom was thus relegated to short introductory chapters in ethnographies, marred by implicit structural–functional assumptions that the rural African societies of the early twentieth century studied by anthropologists differed little from rural societies a century earlier.[43]

The other area where research on precolonial southeast Africa occurred was in the writings of amateur scholars, many of them missionaries, and some later associated with universities. The most notable scholar in this respect was the Rev. A.T. Bryant, who was first a Natal-based missionary, then a research fellow in Zulu ethnology, and later a member of the department of Bantu studies at the University of the Witwatersrand. Bryant's publications, which are still today among the most influential works on precolonial Zulu history, added a mass of new, detailed information about the Shakan kingdom, but did so in a form close to the conceptual mold of the settler historians. His histories of the Zulu kingdom were cast in terms of Zulu invasions and devastations, and with causality attributed to the "Great Man" rather than to larger socio-economic forces.[44] Bryant's speculations about Shaka's sexuality and the size of his penis continued as a strong theme in the literature and were extended in studies that examined the "Shaka complex."[45]

By the 1920s, Zulu nationalists were constructing a Zulu ethnic identity manifest in a Zulu cultural revival which drew on the history of the Zulu kingdom and on the story of its establishment by Shaka. Paul la Hausse has revealed something of the different threads involved in this exercise. His study shows that while certain leaders of the 1923 Inkatha organization were looking for an alliance between

Zulu traditional authority and the conservative Christian African elite, the Rev. Petros Lamula, one subject of La Hausse's study, tried to construct a form of politics out of Zulu nationalism and Africanism.[46] This period saw the publication of a variety of writings about Zulu history through which black intellectuals began to contest the versions produced by missionaries and members of the colonial bureaucracy.[47]

With the development of apartheid ideology, the history of the African communities of South Africa received greater attention than ever before, as government policy makers sought historical grounds for the separation of the African population of southern Africa into different ethnic groups, as well as justification for the "retribalization" of urban Africans and for the occupation by whites of choice lands. In this period, the precolonial history of southern Africa was initially left in the hands of the early ethnographers, such as N.J. van Warmelo. The sustained treatment of African history by Afrikaner academics came later when conservative historians used new research on precolonial societies to provide an ethnic interpretation of South African history which justified the apartheid government's Bantustan ideology.[48]

This new work had begun in the 1960s with an Africanist initiative developed in the publications of the anthropologists Max Gluckman and Monica Wilson, as well as that of the Ibadan-based historian John Omer-Cooper.[49] These scholars sought to move beyond the earlier systematized and normative picture of the Zulu kingdom. They identified phenomena in the precolonial past such as the rise of states and the growth of interstate conflict, and tried to account for these developments. They conceptualized the Shakan kingdom as a creative and constructive response to regional changes. In positing that population pressure was the cause of such changes, Gluckman suggested that the changes were not attributable only to Shaka's leadership. In 1968 these initiatives led to a conference in Lusaka, and culminated in the publication of *African Societies of Southern Africa,* edited by Leonard Thompson, and *The Oxford History of South Africa,* edited by Monica Wilson and Thompson. E.V. Walters' study of political violence was also published at the same time. Walters argued that what was often seen as Shaka's madness—his autocratic and harsh rule—had to be seen as the effective use of terror as a principal means of government.[50] The net effect of these publications was the rescue of what Thompson called the "forgotten factor" in southern African historiography. African history was being drawn centerstage in southern African historiography.

The 1970s saw the more Africanist focus of these scholars develop in two new directions. The first of these, coinciding with the political growth of the Black Consciousness movement, presented a highly idealized view of life in precolonial southern Africa. Notions of communal ownership, social equality, responsive and responsible chiefship, and heroic and able leaders, were the characteristics of the period emphasized by writers on precolonial times.[51]

The other development of the 1970s was the infusion of early Africanist academic writings with materialist concerns. This provided historians with crucial new tools for the conceptualization of precolonial societies. The phenomenon of state formation—and most notably the emergence of the Zulu state—was the chief subject of this approach. The emphasis was away from a focus on Shaka, and on his abilities and achievements in creating the Zulu nation, and toward the generation of a much wider-ranging debate with contributions from both within and outside a Marxist perspective about explanations for the rise of the Zulu state. The explanations advanced included the further development in a number of ecological studies of the population pressure hypothesis, exploration of the impact of external mercantile capital and, most recently, consideration of the significance of trade in slaves through Delagoa Bay.[52] The thrust of these arguments was to suggest that demographic, ecological, or trading pressures, or a combination of all three, caused massive changes in the region that gave rise to states. Such change was conceptualized by Philip Bonner, among other historians, as a transition from a lineage mode of production to a new tributary mode of production, characterized by a new division of labor—notably in the form of the king's *amabutho* (the units that made up the army)—the interruption of homestead heads' control over production and reproduction, and the emergence of a new aristocratic class. In terms of these arguments, the role of Shaka in the making of the Zulu kingdom was significantly played down in favor of more fundamental causes.[53]

The 1980s were characterized by two major developments in academic historiography. Firstly, the *mfecane* debate, already mentioned, placed a spotlight on the hitherto neglected issue of the slave trade, suggesting that it, rather than the rise of the Zulu kingdom, was responsible for the upheavals known as the *mfecane*. The other important development of the 1980s was a shift away from the political economy approach of the materialist scholars to an examination of the ideological bases of the early states and a new concern with methodology. Influenced by literary theory, this approach raised fundamental questions about historians' reading of "sources," and in particular about the genealogies of those "sources." Both developments led to investigations as to how the received wisdoms came into place.[54] The late 1980s and early 1990s have seen renewed interest in the figure of Shaka and a new approach to the ways in which he has been represented in texts.

Renascent interest in the representation of Shaka was prefigured in an essay by William Worger published in 1979. In his article on the myth of Shaka, Worger attempted to examine the methodology of historians working on Shaka and the early Zulu state. He reviewed the main sources of evidence relating to Shaka in nineteenth-century texts, both European and African in derivation, "to see what it can tell us about the first Zulu king and what it can suggest about the motives of those who presented it." Worger argued that such a review is an essential prerequisite to any attempt to reinterpret the career of Shaka in relation to the origins of the Zulu state. Worger's argument made little impact when first published because he failed to offer a radically new perspective on the nature of evidence or on the process of the production of texts. His argument that most of the accounts of Shakan times are "partisan arguments rather than unbiased testimony" was not especially novel. In his interest in the stereotypes of Shaka, in assessing the arguments regarding the aberrance of Shaka's sexual behavior, his personal relations with people around him, and his cruelty (often used as proof of his psychotic nature), Worger was occupied with establishing what Shaka really was like at a time when there was, among historians, a waning interest in the doings of great leaders and a growing concern with the thoughts and actions of ordinary people, and the socio-economic forces affecting their lives.[55] In the late 1980s, with the renewed interest in representations of Shaka the aim has largely been not so much to distinguish reality from myth but rather to highlight processes of invention.

This approach characterized the work of Daphna Golan. Golan periodized the historiography of the Zulu kingdom into four phases. These she identified as defined by colonialist images, the first African images in written form, the anti-colonialist histories of the 1960s, and, more recently, liberation texts. Golan did not treat the oral texts as part of Shakan historiography. She acknowledged the impact of literary texts on the making of the image of Shaka, but did not examine the relationship between the historical and literary representations of Shaka.[56]

Shaka in literature

Literary reworkings of the Shaka story are legion.[57] The connections between the literary treatments and the historiography have, however, been little investigated. The novels, plays, and poetry that deal with Shaka, and the commentaries on them, are concerned largely with aspects of Shaka's life and personality. The first wave included the blood-and-thunder accounts by Henry Rider Haggard, Ernst Ritter, and Peter Becker, a near-obsessive interest in Shaka's sexuality, the heroic Shaka who featured in Roy Campbell's "Flaming Terrapin," the psychologically complex Shaka of F.T. Prince's poetry, and the profoundly ambiguous figure in the writings of Africans such as Thomas Mofolo, John Dube, Rolfes Dhlomo, and Herbert Dhlomo.[58]

A second wave crested in the late 1960s with the end of colonialism in much of Africa, and as African writers found in Shaka an ideal symbol of the nation builder coupled with a strong image of talent. Typically, this Shaka represented a distinguished African past, and provided an important symbol of African initiative and achievement. This occurred in South Africa but was especially the case among Francophone West African writers.[59] Anna Ridehalgh, in a review of more recent Francophone versions of the Shaka story, has distinguished two distinct phases in this second wave. Shaka was a great African hero in both phases but in the first period was often represented ambiguously, as "a figure of questionable authority." Ridehalgh discerned from about 1975 a new irreverence in the figure of Shaka, as he became more of a plebeian hero, and "a modern subversive."[60]

The endless reworkings of Shaka as symbol or myth in literature have attracted a number of academic commentators.[61] The first full-length study of this kind was Donald Burness' *Shaka, King of the Zulus in African Literature*.[62] Written in the heyday of Pan-Africanism and African nationalism, this focused on the treatment of Shaka in contemporary written African literature. For Burness, African literature is inescapably political, and he explored the way in which the figure of Shaka was used as a proud expression of Négritude. For Burness, Shaka was a mythical figure that could be reworked to explain the origin and destiny of a people.

The next full-length study, Malaba's 1986 doctoral dissertation, extended Burness' discussion of the treatment of Shaka to encompass African oral literature—notably, the praise poems of Shaka. Like Burness, Malaba focused mostly on literary texts—although he took limited cognizance of the historiography—seeing them as shaped by the twin heritage of Africa with its white and black lineages. Malaba's study included a review of popular texts conventionally excluded from literary comment. Essentially Malaba viewed himself as a literary critic whose task was "to evaluate the merits and demerits of the different interpretations of Shaka's significance."[63] He also sought to pick out the main themes in these interpretations. All this he accomplished with skill and, indeed, he went farther than this in making important connections between texts, tracing lineages, and, in particular, recognizing the influence of oral texts. For Malaba, Shaka is "all things to many Africans, but the mythopoeisis of Shaka is a largely African phenomenon."[64]

In 1991 the French literary scholar Jean Sévry published *Chaka Empereur des Zoulous: Histoire, Mythes et Légendes*. For Sévry, it is possible for one simply to choose one's own Shaka; the appropriation of Shaka is without limits. "Chacun son Chaka, parce que chacun le regarde a partir de son système de representations, en un lieu précis, a une périod historiquement datée."[65]

The most recent addition to the corpus of scholarship on literary representations of Shaka is the work of Dan Wylie. Wylie investigated the patterns of thought displayed by white writers in their literary portrayals of Shaka, and what they reveal about the quite specific attitudes held by whites toward the wider phenomenon of Africa. Wylie was concerned with the textual strategies pursued by, and the literary influences on, these writers. For Wylie the portrayals of Shaka in the texts he analyzed all ultimately had their origins in, and were shaped by, the seminal text of the early trader Nathaniel Isaacs, who was resident in southeast Africa during Shaka's reign, and whose account of his travels was published in 1836.[66]

Shaka as invention?

We see thus the presence of Shaka in a wide variety of settings. Representations of Shaka can be distinguished in three identifiable fields: the ideological, political, and cultural domains of the migrant worker and the Inkatha leaders; the arena of academic historical research; and finally, the field of literature. In all three areas, the image of Shaka is much reworked and considerable commentary exists on the nature of such reworkings. In general, the commentaries agree in identifying a genealogy for most reworkings that derives from the writings of the earliest white visitors to Shaka's court. Apart from this heritage, the general view is that writers have created or invented their own version of Shaka.

Embroilment of academic historians in debate over Shaka raises sharply the question of the nature of their project. If Shaka is but an invention, how do historians read texts as sources? Do accounts like those of the early traveler Isaacs, or the poet Mazisi Kunene, who published *Emperor Shaka the Great: A Zulu Epic* in 1979, have any value as historical sources? And what of the historians' own texts? Are they, too, simply imaginative reconstructions of a host of inventions? Finally, why does the figure of Shaka lend itself to so many reworkings in such varied contexts?

Increasingly today, historiographers are less confident of the "noble dream" of objectivity and are sensitive to the impact on historians of their political and social environments.[67] They are also beginning to acknowledge the contributions of amateur and popular historians to the development of historiographies.[68] There are those who suggest that the production of history is a fundamentally political act.[69] John Wright, for example, argued in his review of two publications on South African historiography that ". . . history is an intrinsically political discourse; . . . it is a site of constant struggle between dominant and dominated groups, for which control of the past is of central importance in establishing precedents, moral justifications, collective identities, and group cohesion."[70]

It is necessary to accept fully the political nature of the production of history: indeed, one of the tasks of this study is to rethink the nature of the relationship between politics and history in the making of the image of Shaka. Yet it is also possible to go beyond the generally recognized distinction between propaganda and serious research. At one level, this distinction is obviously useful, but as is revealed by the disputes between the academics and politicians, and the particular trajectory and timing of the *mfecane* debate, this simple distinction does not have the capacity to enable adequate conceptualization of these multifaceted contests. It does not, for example, explain why *Ilanga* chose to denigrate the university-based historians through powerful historical allusion to the concept of *izinsila*. This study shows that such debates, and their complex intertwining of history and politics, are by no means a recent phenomenon, but rather that they characterize the development of the image of Shaka from earliest times. One of the tasks of the book, then, is to tease out the historical relationship between historiography and politics as it concerns Shaka, and to use an understanding of that historical process to rethink the nature of their connection.

Consideration of the way in which politics and ideology affect representations of Africa began with Philip Curtin's seminal work, *The Image of Africa*. This study led the way in identifying the existence of stereotypes of Africa.[71] For Curtin these were largely preconceptions and prejudices—with origins in travelers' accounts, and missionary reports—of a popular mind that was not aware of the work of professional historians. For Curtin, "the most striking aspect of the British image of Africa in the early nineteenth century was its variance from the African reality, as we now understand it. There was also a marked lack of the kind of progress one might expect to find in a body of ideas that was constantly enlarged by accretions of new data."[72] Curtin suggested two explanations for this: he noted that commentators were responsive to data that confirmed their European preconceptions and that the image of Africa tended to shift in relation to changes in European thought. "In this sense," he noted, "the image of Africa was far more European than African."[73]

In the early 1980s the work of Edward Said[74] on the relationship between colonial power and knowledge of colonized peoples, as well as the new disciplinary and discursive self-consciousnesses of the period, influenced scholars such as Russell Martin to go back to the question of the images of Africa with a new set of conceptual tools. Focusing on British images of the Zulu, Martin queried whether such images were confined to the popular mind and whether they permeated, albeit in different forms, the perceptions of scholars as well. Martin examined the way in which such images were made up out of the interpretations of travelers and missionaries and were shaped or, as Martin put it, "deliberately created . . . designed to serve a variety of functions—to engage the British public in action, to rationalize imperial policies, to justify and conceal."[75] Martin's notion of "individuals and communities respond[ing] to, accommodat[ing] and re-creat[ing] the Zulu for themselves"[76] also characterizes the work of Burness, Malaba, Golan, Sévry, and Wylie.

While helpful in moving us beyond the simple idea that history is an objective account of the past, the fundamental assumption that histories are ideological texts, shaped by and reflective of power relations of their time, runs the risk of excluding from view numerous facets of the process of producing such texts. One of the objects of this book is to throw into relief the complexities of that process of production, to trace the influences on it of matters conventionally designated beyond, or outside, historiography, and to show that histories are not simply reinvented in terms of contemporary interests. This book also challenges the bipolar idea, reflected in a number of these works, that, as Golan puts it, for whites Shaka "symbolizes tyranny and the 'rule of fear', while for many blacks, he represents African power before colonialism and the belief in the capacity of blacks to lead themselves."[77] At certain stages, some whites viewed Shaka in a very positive light, while the view of Shaka as a tyrant has been shared by many black South Africans. This study aims to show how these texts influenced each other, and how they established, in the process, limits on the possible recreations of Shaka.

There are those who would argue that history is but text, and that history's subject is fundamentally implicated in textual processes.[78] Such a line of argument suggests the encompassing of politics and history within textual analysis. Interest in the literary aspects of historical texts has prompted a growing number of scholars to seek to overcome the disciplinary divide between history and literature, but the distinctions remain uncomfortably present.[79] This study is alert to the rhetoric of historical accounts, their fictionality and their subjectivity, and to the sources of these features.

In this area the work of Hayden White has been richly suggestive.[80] White has argued that the essentially poetic question of prefiguring a historical field as a domain of a particular kind constitutes an initial interpretative act. Before cognitive operations can be brought to bear, the historical field must be imagined in terms of particular kinds of data bearing certain kinds of relations to each other. Delimiting the field constitutes a second level of interpretation. Temporal boundaries are imposed and certain events made salient. Chronicle is transformed into complex story as some events are narrativized as inaugural, transitional, and concluding motifs. Emplotment, White continued, constitutes a third level of interpretation. Plot characterizes dynamic relations between events and drives the story forward, figuring events into a recognizable story type, thereby specifying how the narrative in its entirety should be read. White has thus offered a conception of narrative as a form of knowledge in itself, and a critique of positivist conceptions of historical practice.

In other words, White suggested that it is not enough to ask of a historical narrative whether the data are reliable, and the argument valid. We need to see that the rhetoric of the text is not merely a question of style, but embodies content and meaning. Part of what this study seeks to do is to establish historically the process by means of which the field of Zulu history, and more specifically Shakan times, came to be established. It tries to identify what data were brought to bear, when and why this happened, how temporal boundaries were created and certain events were made salient. It seeks to account historically for the emplotment of Shakan historiography. In addition, it extends a textual approach to the analysis of public events, ceremonies, holiday resorts, and television series that focus on Shaka.

The study goes on to use the classically anthropological methodology of making the familiar—in this case, history—strange, and in this way to seek a new understanding of its nature. The method is not limited to the synchronic act of making strange, but seeks to explore history-made-strange diachronically, charting change over time. It tries to establish something of what "history" may mean in African oral tradition. It explores as well the connections between the development of native administration and the novels of Rider Haggard and draws out their implications for Shakan historiography. It assesses furthermore the ways in which the television series *Shaka Zulu* and the Shakaland theme park function as forms of historiography. In so doing it seeks to go beyond the aim of recognizing the literary aspects of historical accounts, to reconstrue the idea of historiography itself.[81]

The limits of invention

Making history strange poses anew the question why it is that the past is important, why history is produced both professionally—either orally or in the universities—and in non-professional contexts. There are two stock answers to this question. The first is that knowledge of the past helps society to understand the present, and thus, by implication, assists in planning for the future. The second concerns the importance of memory and the role of history in the constitution of identity. Both answers are connected to the often-asserted claim that the past provides "justification" for the present status quo.[82]

The acts of manipulating and imagining that these answers imply are now generally accepted.[83] The central thrust of this study is to identify the constraints on these acts. The concern with limits on the manipulation of Shaka in politics and the imagining of Shaka in literature flows out of two reservations about the current theoretical literature on the making of the image of Africa. The first reservation concerns the ease with which students of ethnicity and nationalism have recourse to the notion of "the invention of tradition."

As originally formulated by the essays in Eric Hobsbawm and Terence Ranger's influential edited collection, *The Invention of Tradition,* the concept derived from examinations of the way in which new traditions were created in diverse political settings: by movements of cultural nationalism, imperialist states, and radicals seeking to challenge powerful conservative rituals with counter-traditions of their own. The book showed how these traditions play an important role in the construction of ideologies of nationalism, imperialism, and radicalism, and marked an important watershed in the development of our understanding of the complex relationship between history and ideology. This work in turn stimulated a host of other studies along similar lines.[84]

The Invention of Tradition, while oblivious neither of the processes that give rise to such traditions nor of the preexistence of some of the materials from which they are constructed, was concerned primarily with the artificial aspects of the traditions invoked in nationalist and other struggles. While Hobsbawm and Ranger admitted that "the actual process of creating such ritual and symbolic complexes has not been adequately studied by historians,"[85] they viewed that process as determined by what is politically expedient and as constrained by prevailing political necessities. Few historians have taken up the challenge to look more closely at such processes, and to go beyond explanations grounded in current political needs. Similarly, while acknowledging that invented traditions are often "adaptations" of old ones, the contributors to the volume tended to focus on the novel aspects of the new forms rather than concerning themselves with investigation of their residual continuities with the ancient materials. They, and a good number of the studies inspired by *The Invention of Tradition,* did not examine closely what it is that determines the material selected for adaptation, and how the process of adaptation actually takes place. They did not ask what materials are available, why they are available for adaptation, and what the limitations are on their use. Finally, they did not explain why it is that traditions that are obviously mythical are believed to be true. In other words, is it possible simply to "choose your Shaka," to paraphrase Sévry, or are there constraints on these processes of invention?

The notion of "invention" can all too easily lose sight of the history of the tradition, of the way in which the tradition's (or elements of the tradition's) own past shapes its present. It further places full control over content and form in the hands of the "inventors"—usually political elites—and ignores the way that their versions of history are shaped by contesting and conflicting versions of the past. It loses sight of the struggles between existing, often opposed, bodies of knowledge, and the ways in which such contests are related to the social conditions that prevail in the worlds inhabited by their promoters. It denies the possibilities of "subjugated knowledges,"[86] and the effects these subversive texts have on the versions of the past promoted by those with political power. It sets up a crude opposition between "myth" and "reality."[87] The argument of this study, by way of contrast, is that the image of Shaka is not an invention, either from scratch or from preexisting materials. Rather, it is an image established over time, through processes which can be charted historically and which set limits on the extent and form of its manipulation in the service of politics.

A second reservation concerns the idea of the "West's" creation of the "Other." Following Edward Said, it is now widely argued that "the West" invented a "primitive Other" in opposition to its "civilised self."[88] This perspective has been extremely useful in stimulating a critique of colonial modes of representation, in drawing attention to the way in which enduring power inequalities affect knowledge of dominated societies, and in highlighting the persistent tropes used to visualize the colonized.

The great virtue of Said's study—his powerful demonstration of "the sheer knitted-together strength"[89] of western discourse on the exotic—is also his argument's weakest point. His thesis, and the many studies that flow from it which focus on the process of "othering,"[90] can be criticized for presenting western discourse as fully systematic and invariant. As others have noted, Said's approach fails to make qualitative distinctions between a variety of texts produced under a range of circumstances for different audiences.[91] One of the tasks of this study is to distinguish between texts produced under different circumstances, to query the very notion of a "western" discourse on the Zulu, and, more specifically, the idea of a consistent representation of the Zulu king. The coming chapters demonstrate how "western" discourses changed over time, and show how their representations were shaped by preexisting indigenous discourses, themselves far from homogeneous. The notion of the West's construction of the Other loses sight of the historiographies of the people labeled "Other," and the ways in which they have shaped the "West's" knowledge of those communities. The argument presented here is that historically indigenous communities had a lot to say and spoke with many voices, and, more importantly, were heard.[92] Their words were not reflected in pristine form in colonial discourse, and it may not now be possible to recover their voices, but the sediments and influences of their speech can be discerned. In some cases, this study shows, colonial researchers succeeded in recording "hidden transcripts,"[93] having access to views opposed to those of the Zulu rulers. In other cases, it reveals traces in "public transcripts" of divergent views which have been absorbed and neutralized by elites.[94] These traces are present, I shall suggest, because the colonial worldview was not simply imported from the metropole and imposed on the colonized, nor was a new worldview suddenly "invented." Rather, it emerged out of the colonial experience, through a process of transformation and rearrangement. It was the hegemonic view because it articulated different versions of the world—including those of the colonized—in such a way that their potential antagonisms were neutralized.[95] In some instances, of course, those traces can be detected because opposition in the past was successful or because it was dramatic and noisy. In other instances, they remained hidden while contexts of unfavorable power relations prevailed, and later, in changed circumstances, became visible. In still other cases, the colonizers actively selected elements of the new world-view which they promoted from contemporary African ideas, not as a consequence of struggles from below, but because of the power and attractiveness of indigenous concepts.[96]

This study is critical of the crude we–they dichotomy that lies at the heart of many current discussions of colonial discourse. It does this (directly) through exploration of the complex moment when the colonial administrator Theophilus Shepstone "becomes Shaka" in order to oversee the installation of the independent Zulu king Cetshwayo, and (indirectly) through analyses of Rider Haggard's romantic African heroes and heroines. It qualifies Said's perception of an ontological and an epistemological distinction between the Orient and the Occident in "western discourse," or in this case, Africa and "the West," and acknowledges that historians' subjects' own representations have epistemological equality with those of the historians. It follows Gyan Prakash's injunction to "revisit the historical record, to push at the edges, to unsettle the calmness with which colonial categories and knowledges were instituted as the facts of history."[97] Finally, by highlighting colonial concerns with Shaka, and demonstrating their roots in indigenous discourses, this study charts the connection between questions of rule and the first Zulu king in a manner that begins to provide a perspective on the attachment of power to the image of Shaka.

While Valentin Mudimbe is correct to argue that the foundations of discourse about Africa lie in the colonial encounter,[98] this book stresses that we have to recognize that the origins of many of its components lie in indigenous African discourses.[99] In making this argument, I do not claim that it is possible for us today to recover intact those indigenous discourses. I suggest that we can identify their traces in colonial and Africanist discourses, and can reconstruct more of the process of their incorporation into their present situations.

This book takes up Christopher Miller's challenge to begin breaking down the barriers between the domains of "western theory" and "African sources."[100] Whereas Miller limits himself to an examination of the ways in which the cultural codes of "Africa" and the "West" began to play off one another in late and post-colonial times, however, this study asserts that indigenous intellectual endeavors were just as present in precolonial and first-contact times, and influenced the earliest colonial readings of Africa. The identity and desires of the colonizers were not simply projected or inscribed on Africa, nor was Africa drawn from the imagination.[101] My study shows there was a dialogic process in the making of the image of Shaka. While Miller claims this complex intermix of conflicting codes happened only when "Senghor and Césaire took pieces of their new Africa from Frobenius,"[102] a focus on the image of Shaka pushes back its origins to the moment of first contact. Rather than tracing small shifts in the representation of Shaka from one text to the next, and linking changes to changing politics and context—as do scholars such as Malaba, Golan, and Sévry—I seek to identify the events and historical developments that allow us to answer the question "why Shaka?" and that set the limits on "which Shakas?"

The view of colonial discourse as systematic and universal leads commentators such as Golan and Cobbing to decry white writings about Zulu history as distortions of the Zulu past, and to depreciate the historical value of the collections of materials made by colonial officials and missionaries.[103] Such judgments inhibit these scholars from coming to grips with the full complexity of the research efforts of a late nineteenth-century administrator such as James Stuart. As much as one ought to look at how Stuart's notion of civilization was imposed on the traditions he recorded, so too is it important to consider the way in which his ideas of "uncivilized" were shaped by the indigenous idea of *buzimuzimu,* translated by Stuart as "cannibalism," but glossed in other contexts by African writers as the opposite of civilized.[104] In advocating a reevaluation of the historical endeavors of a colonial official such as James Stuart, I am not reverting to the position of accepting Father Placide Tempels on his own terms.[105] Nor do I accept uncritically the idea of Tempels or Stuart, rejecting the role of bringers of light in favour of becoming receivers of native wisdoms. Yet, just as Andrew Apter feels that Tempels cannot be as easily dismissed as Mudimbe would like,[106] so, too, do I argue that Stuart should continue to command our attention, and that he offers a viable source of historical data, which, sensitively read, have a great deal to offer historians of Shakan times. To dismiss the writings of Stuart and Tempels as examples of "colonial discourse" is to close off the possibilities of recovering material about Africa's precolonial past, and ultimately to revert to a denial of that history. In cases where early African oral traditions only exist in forms recorded by white writers, then, as Greg Dening put it, "One can see beyond the frontier only through the eyes of those who stood on the frontier and looked out. To know the native one must know the intruder."[107]

Prompted by new methodological concerns about the nature of evidence, and by the crisis over the nature of "white" sources caused by the eruption of the *mfecane* debate, one of the main themes of this book is consideration of the many representations of Shaka in order to develop a view of how these texts might be read by historians and how they can be used as evidence about the past. In other words, it asks critical questions about the sources historians use in the reconstruction of Shakan times. It suggests that there is a far more complex relationship between indigenous narratives and colonial ones, and the processes of representation in which they engage, than Said, Martin, Malaba, Golan, and Sévry allow. It suggests that there is a historically conditioned dialectic of intertextuality between "western" models of historical discourse and indigenous traditions of narrative, and it seeks to identify some of the places where the indigenous narrative interpenetrates "modern" historical practice. This asserts the importance of history and of historicizing Shaka rather than Golan's relatively simplistic notion of the invention or reinvention of Shaka, and Sévry's idea that one can simply choose one's Shaka's or Wylie's idea that a single line of descent can be traced from Isaacs' 1836 text—the first full-length account of the early traders' contacts with Shaka—into the present.

This approach positions us to question not only the maintenance of distinctions between the fields of politics, history, and literature, but also challenge divisions implicit within each area. Chief among these is the distinction within political discourse between ideology—as in Buthelezi's Shaka Day speeches—and popular culture, as expressed, for example, in the Shaka chest. Another such distinction exists within academic historical writings between historical texts—the production of the guild-trained historians—and "sources"—notably oral traditions, but also the accounts of early travelers, missionaries, and colonial officials. Within the field of literature distinctions exist between the poetry, drama, and novels produced by scholars—*La Mort de Chaka,* or *Emperor Shaka the Great*—and the nineteenth-century praise poems of Shaka or even the popular 1980s television series *Shaka Zulu*. Each of these distinctions demands critical reassessment.

Writings on Zulu nationalism emphasize the way in which the image of Shaka is manipulated to suit current political ends. Such manipulations clearly resonate with popularly held views of Shaka, as expressed in the Shaka chest and other forms. Many commentators explain contemporary Zulu militarism associated with the image of Shaka as the result of ideological manipulations by Zulu nationalists and their supporters.[108] This perspective, while extremely useful in drawing attention to the constructed nature of identity, fails to explain why the ideas concerned are readily accepted by ordinary people, including some Zulu speakers who are opposed to Zulu nationalism. Many Zulu speakers today claim an awareness of themselves as existing and acting in a continuous context of social relationships that began with Shaka. One of the questions that concern this study is the history of that historical awareness. It seeks to make a contribution to the understanding of ethnic politics in arguing that historicization of the image of Shaka allows us to begin to understand something of the making of popular apprehensions of Shaka. It looks at the way in which, over time, meaning has accrued to the image of Shaka. The chapters that follow explore the ways in which that process of accrual serves to limit and constrain political and ideological manipulations of the past. They suggest that the contours of the history of the image of Shaka themselves give form and meaning to the story of Shaka, and limit the recasting of the image by political elites and their opponents alike.

The distinction between histories and sources is present in most historical reconstructions of Shakan times. Histories are understood to be the work of academy-trained professionals, while in the category "sources" are included the oral accounts of Zulu speakers and their neighbors alongside the writings of early travelers, traders, and officials. While it is obvious that professional historians tackle the reconstruction of the past in a very different way from oral historians, unquestioning acceptance of this division ignores what is similar or comparable in their work. It further blurs important distinctions within the category "oral historians," namely the differences between oral historians whose professional work it is, and was, to produce historical material, and oral historians who have been so labeled simply because they have been interviewed by researchers about the past. Indigenous oral histories demand historicization, have their own canons, and are governed by rhetorical strategies and narrative conventions that are in some respects similar to and in other ways different from those of guild historians.[109]

In terms of the third category, Kunene's epic poem *Emperor Shaka* is widely recognized as a "significant" component of the body of literature on the image of Shaka. Enacted texts, such as the television series *Shaka Zulu*[110] and the "total holiday resort" Shakaland, are not generally subjected to the same textual treatment, nor are they regarded as being part of the corpus of historiography. But both of these enterprises are complex texts that are enormously powerful in their impact on the envisioning of life under Shaka. As visual evocations of the past, they, along with pageants and plays about Shakan times, are highly authoritative and seductive productions of the past. Indeed, they have a powerful impact on all acts of imagining the Shakan era, including the work of professional historians. They, too, set limits on how the Shakan past is reconstructed in other arenas and in the future.

While concerned with the politics of representations of Shaka, the historiography of Shaka, and Shaka in literature, this study focuses less on the central texts in each of those fields, and explores rather what happens in the borderlands between these areas. It is concerned with texts and webs of connection on the boundaries between the oral and the written, between professional and popular history, between history and literature, and those that elude such categorizations. It also seeks to problematize the processes of declaring what is history and what is not; to look at texts whose status as history is contested and at locations denied the status of being "history." It looks beyond the colonial archive not only at oral texts, but also at history produced in household items, public events, in ceremony and display.

An understanding of historiographical practice in all these domains, as well as a clear picture of the history of the image of Shaka, is a precondition for the evaluation of sources for, and the conduct of research on, Shakan times. The ideas that early European sources are untrustworthy and should not be used by scholars, and that African sources on Shakan times are absent, are simply untenable.[111] However, the intention here is not limited to expanding the category of Shakan historiography and historicizing the image of Shaka. This study posits that "Shaka" is not simply a story that changes in the telling over time. It is also an image of highly compressed—and changing—meaning.

Shaka as metaphor[112]

The discovery of representations of Shaka in many and varied locations requires us to move beyond seeing each occasion as a historiographical exercise concerned with the reconstruction of the past. Rather, it seems, the figure of Shaka, and the system of government associated with his name, while the object of intense historiographical attention, are also deployed as metaphors and, as such, influence Shakan historiography in particular ways.

Metaphor allows a great deal of information to be compressed into a single utterance. Any given human experience—the reign of Shaka or present-day ethnic conflict—is complex. Metaphor telescopes its complexity without simplifying it. Metaphors are persuasive and attractive; they have a creative dimension. The aspect of metaphor that is poetically based resists translation into literal language. Literal language, likewise, cannot easily cope with the full complexity of that human experience, especially in so far as it is a changing complexity. So it hands those aspects over to vivid and forceful figurative language.[113] A great strength of metaphors is their capacity not to be true or false but to offer, or be seen to offer, insight.[114] In other words, one does not need to prove that contemporary African society is like Shakan society, or that a particular rendition of Shakan society is like it really was in the past. Rather, it is sufficient for the claim to be made that a particular way of thinking about Shakan society, which is not false, offers insight into how we think about African society in other contexts. JoAnne Brown has argued of metaphor that it is its

very vagueness and the multiplicity of metaphorical meaning that makes it a powerful social adhesive. Metaphor through its familar literal referent, appears to offer self-evident, socially shared meaning to the unfamiliar. Yet it invites each listener to interpret its meaning personally, even privately. Metaphor thus softens contradictions and differences because it encapsulates a whole social system of meanings in one term, while the comprehension of specific aspects of the metaphor nevertheless may remain a very private mental act.[115]

In some instances, it should be noted, the image of Shaka is polytropic,[116] in that it may embody metonymic or synecdochical principles. Thus we find instances where Shaka is the part that represents the Zulu whole or the Zulu political system. There are also instances where Shaka is represented as an exception—as different from all other Africans—or as the symbol of all Zulus, where Zulus are regarded as being exceptional and different from all other Africans.

This study examines the use of the figure of Shaka and the Shakan regime as metaphors in South African political discourse. It explores the questions of why, by whom, and how it was that the metaphor of Shaka was selected and agreed upon as the bearer of meanings, in preference to any other option. It tries to establish historically how the image of Shaka came to encapsulate a whole system of meanings.[117] The chapters that follow tease out what these meanings were and are, and, finally, show how the comprehension of specific aspects of the metaphor varied in time and space. They demonstrate that the metaphor of Shaka was open to different interpretations by various parties who nonetheless perceived their respective interpretations to be widely shared, without ever realizing, as Brown puts it, "that the consensus is created by the vagueness of the metaphor itself."[118]

The political function of metaphor is to take something that is formed in the past, project it into the future, and then fill in the blanks. Metaphor functions as a model of an imagined future. Thus the historical dimension of metaphor is crucial, and can be said to have a predictive aspect. At the same time, it also has a constraining function, since it sets the limits on the acts of imagining. In the Shaka case, Shaka often becomes the model for future race relations, but in so doing, by conferring on Zulus, for example, a notion of their own militarism, becomes part of the making of the future. Since analogy established by metaphor is often vague and imprecise, in the action of projecting the past into the future there is plenty of room for change, for the introduction of new materials. While there is scope for alterations, the possibilities of change are limited. Naomi Quinn has argued that, as meanings are culturally constituted, it is important to recognize that particular metaphors are selected by speakers and favored by listeners because they provide satisfactory mappings onto already-existing cultural understandings.[119] Thus, in contrast to the generally accepted position of George Lakoff and Mark Johnson,[120] who argue that metaphor is productive of meaning, Quinn suggests that metaphor is constrained by understanding. One of the tasks of this study will be to explore the way in which Shaka as metaphor is constrained by cultural understandings.

What are the implications of the use of one particular metaphor rather than another? In other words, what were the references to shared understandings and experience that were being claimed by the evocation of Shaka rather than alternative metaphors? For Kunene, for example, the answer is simple. Shaka is the choice because of what he was "in reality": "The one trait that has made the Shaka of both history and legend a universal conversation point and an inspiration of artistic creations, and sometimes even a symbol of African political aspirations, has been his Herculean temperament."[121]

This study suggests an alternative answer to the question, an answer located in the history of the image of Shaka. It explores first the emphasis in oral traditions on Shaka. An important explanation for their treatment of Shaka, it suggests, lies in the central concern of oral traditions with the issue of the Zulu succession, a matter hinged on the figure of Shaka. Shaka's legitimacy is understood to be founded, not on his birthright, but on his success and his achievements, which, in turn, depended on his army and its character as highly disciplined and effective. These emphases found in the oral traditions, I shall go on to show, were transferred into European written accounts of Zulu history in a variety of ways, but most decisively when the Natal native administration began to draw on Zulu history for a model of domination and control. The model became the core of what Mahmood Mamdani calls the system of "decentralised despotism" that was colonialism's legacy to the apartheid state. Finally, I look at how the model came to be made into a metaphor for South African politics.

Once the Shaka metaphor was accepted, alternative ways of thinking about African society become very hard to imagine. Shaka as metaphor for African society made a number of very specific notions about the nature of that society seem commonplace, self-evident, and historically validated. As whites became increasingly isolated from their black compatriots through apartheid and separate development and had less and less personal, first-hand, intimate knowledge of Africans, new pressures developed for gaining knowledge of "the native as he really is"—that is, was—before contact with Europeans. This led to the emergence of a small group of experts "qualified" to mediate, to translate, to pronounce on the essences of Zulu history. This book also seeks to investigate their impact on the making of the image of Shaka.

In summary, then, this study looks at aspects of the history of the image of Shaka and at some of the historical processes by means of which Shaka developed into a metaphor for contemporary politics. It shows how, in terms of both of these historical perspectives, certain data were preferred over others, how temporal boundaries were established, and selected events in the story of Shaka were made salient. It accounts for key aspects in the emplotment of Shakan historiography. It looks at the construction and production of the image of Shaka, but also discusses what was excluded, forgotten, or silenced. It is especially concerned with the constraints and limitations on the making of Shaka as image and metaphor, and the manner of their establishment. Historicization is invoked as an effective strategy for investigating these processes, but with the recognition that it does not provide a complete and unitary history.[122] This book does not seek to construct a continuous homogenizing narrative that "explains" the development of the image and the metaphor of Shaka.[123] Rather, it takes a number of consecutive, but separate, often pivotal moments—culminations that capture the major coordinates of power, resistance, and accommodation of a period—and interrogates them in an effort to comprehend the forces and pressures through which the image has developed and in which it is enraveled.

Chapter Two

The origins of the image of Shaka

“ *We are concerned to write the anthropology and history of those moments when native and intruding cultures are conjoined. Neither can be known independently of that moment.* ”

(G. Dening, *Islands and Beaches: Discourses on a Silent Land*, p. 43)

The origins of the image of Shaka are today open to our investigation primarily through exploration of the moment of first contact between the early European travelers and the Zulu kingdom and its immediately adjacent areas. This chapter examines the image of Shaka promoted in the Cape by the traders of Port Natal (present-day Durban) in the 1820s and distinguishes between the versions sponsored by different factions within the Port Natal community. It looks at the way that these representations shifted during the period under review in response to specific developments in the traders' commercial ventures, and in their relationships with the Zulu court and their African neighbors.

The argument presented here suggests that before the Zulu king's death in late 1828, the traders' presentation of Shaka was that of a benign patron. There were two exceptions to this, and these arose in response to the particular financial difficulties that one of the traders, James King, faced at two specific moments in time. The chapter shows that in the Cape, King came to be seen as manipulative and unreliable. His two negative depictions of Shaka were discredited in the eyes of the colonial administration and in the popular press, and did not, before 1829, succeed in establishing a negative image of Shaka in the colony.

As was the case with the traders' images of Shaka, different versions of Shaka were promoted by various interest groups within the Zulu kingdom and the neighboring Natal area, and these also shifted over time in response to changing circumstances. The origins of Shaka's image as a tyrant are located both in versions of Shaka current among disaffected elements in the Zulu kingdom in the 1820s and in the picture of a despot promoted by the Zulu authorities themselves. The traders' productions of Shaka were not simply manifestations of the view of Shaka that most directly suited their material interests, but were also shaped by the form and content of the various African views they encountered and with which they intersected during their stay in Natal. My proposition is that, at various times, the Shaka in different European perorations took cognizance of the many Shakas that were heard in African voices, and vice versa.

Earliest Cape intelligence of Shaka

In 1822, a young Englishman who had come out to the Cape in search of opportunity and a position, Henry Francis Fynn, joined the *Jane,* a vessel belonging to the Cape mercantile concern Nourse & Co., trading with Delagoa Bay (present-day Maputo). In a stay that overlapped with that of a British naval squadron under Captain W.F.W. Owen, Fynn spent some six months at Delagoa Bay, and undertook extensive exploration of its immediate surroundings. Fynn recorded that he heard of "the Zulu tribe, under Shaka, [who] were a very powerful nation." Intrigued, he arranged a visit to a Zulu homestead and would have continued on to Shaka's capital if the distance had not proved prohibitive. While much of Fynn's account of his visit to Delagoa Bay was written long after the event, and was extensively informed by subsequent information and attitudes that he acquired, it is evident that the impression of Shaka gleaned at Delagoa Bay excited his curiosity and promised good trading possibilities.[1]

By 1823, reports of the prospects of trade with the Zulu kingdom received from Nourse & Co. were so favorable that another Englishman, the trader and adventurer Lieutenant Francis Farewell (formerly of the Royal Navy), was able to secure significant financial backing from Cape merchants for an exploratory voyage to Delagoa Bay and Natal. Farewell chartered two ships, the *Julia* and the brig the *Salisbury,* under James King. When they arrived at Delagoa Bay, Owen's vessel, the *Leven,* was in port, and Farewell went aboard to interview Owen. The interview contained nothing to discourage him, and he and King immediately proceeded to the coast of Natal in an effort to open communications with Shaka.[2] They failed to land successfully, and in the attempt sustained damage to their ships, losing two boats and a considerable amount of their trade goods.[3]

Undaunted, Farewell returned to the Cape, negotiated new financing with Messrs. Hoffman and Peterssen, hired a large party to accompany him—including the young Fynn—and engaged two ships to transport the party and their cargo to Natal. In response to a request from the governor of the Cape for information regarding his activities, Farewell reported that the prospects of trade from a base at

Port Natal were excellent, the "natives hav[ing] requested that we come and traffic with them. . . ."[4]

By June 1824 both ships had landed their cargoes successfully, and Farewell and Fynn had traveled overland to meet Shaka themselves. In the first report from the new Port Natal settlement to the Cape, Farewell confirmed the expectations that Shaka would make a good trading partner. He depicted the Zulu king as enthusiastic about the settlement, and well disposed toward the British. He noted that his companions found the orderliness, manners, and customs of the Zulu both "astonish[ing] and pleas[ing]."[5] Cape opinion of Shaka at this time could not have been better.

The traders' Shaka, 1824–1827

The traders' commercial enterprises flourished as they acquired ivory directly from Shaka, from the Mpondo country to the south of Shaka's domain, and from the inhabitants in and around Port Natal.[6] It is possible that the traders were also interested in, or on occasion may have participated in, slaving activities of one sort or another, but as yet the evidence for this proposition is tenuous in the extreme.[7] In a report that was subsequently published in the *Cape Town Gazette and African Advertiser,* Lieutenant Hawes, the officer commanding the *York,* which called in at Port Natal in May 1825, observed that the traders were "living on the best terms of friendship with the natives and under the protection of king Inguos Chaka," who, he noted, "professes great respect for white people." As Hawes reported, "The success of the party in their mercantile speculations is believed to be the extent of their expectations."[8]

The traders were markedly less successful in turning Port Natal into a viable base camp for their activities. The small Port Natal community experienced repeated crises over the cultivation of agricultural products for their own consumption, as well as a shortage of labor more generally.[9] While there is nothing to indicate that the traders feared Shaka, Farewell was sensible of the small settlement's vulnerability, and of the need for the traders to operate from a secure and relatively self-sufficient base. It was on Farewell's agenda to establish clearly in the minds of the Zulu rulers the extent and nature of the traders' power and commercial interests.[10] Moreover, by September 1824, ten members of the original party had left Port Natal, and still another ten desired to go.[11] As part of a plan to maintain at Port Natal the infrastructure necessary for the prosecution of trade, Farewell attempted at this time not to induce the British to establish a colony, but rather to promote the more limited objective of the settlement at Port Natal of a "few families."

Lieutenant Hawes, who had reported in 1825 on the success of the traders' connections with Shaka, also commented on the traders' lack of a boat and supplies.[12] Since their arrival in Port Natal, the traders had only once been able to use the *Julia* to replenish their supplies and transport their ivory before the ship was lost off the Natal coast. The cargo lost in the wreck of the *Julia* was valued in excess of the amount for which it was insured. Coming on top of the previous losses, this latest disaster almost certainly meant that Farewell was beginning to experience financial pressures over and above his supply problems.[13]

It was at this point that James King reentered the picture. Although he had been on the earlier exploratory voyage with Farewell, he had done so in the latter's employ. He subsequently struggled to raise the necessary capital for a Port Natal venture independent of Farewell.[14] In the loss of the *Julia*, however, King saw an opportunity for entering into the trade at the port. The motivation for Cape capital to back him at this point consisted of two parts: the first was the commercial calculation that, by arriving with much-needed supplies and a vessel, King would be able to take over the sea-transport aspect of the trading venture initiated by Farewell, if not actually insert himself into the port trade itself; the second was the possibility of gaining the logistical support of the Cape government by representing the endeavor as the humanitarian succoring of Farewell's party supposedly cut off for some time from the colony.[15] In September 1825, King set sail in the *Mary,* with a good supply of trade beads, and sufficiently armed by the colonial government to be able, as he put it, "to put to effect the relief of Mr. Farewell and his party."[16]

King's expectations, rather like those of Farewell before him, were dashed when his vessel, the *Mary,* was wrecked on entering the bay at Port Natal in October 1825, and its cargo lost.[17] King's party suddenly found themselves entirely dependent on Farewell. Undaunted, King tried another tack. The new arrivals set up camp in a separate area of the bay and immediately began building a ship. It seems that their aim was not to enable them to quit the shores of Natal, which they could have done on any one of a number of ships that called in at Port Natal during their sojourn there. Rather, the building of the ship offered a means of recouping their financial losses, and of gaining a hold over Farewell, who still lacked access to a much-needed vessel.[18]

The building of a boat was a lengthy undertaking. The account of another of the traders, Nathaniel Isaacs, makes it clear that King's party, of which he was a member, soon began to run short of provisions. They had nothing much to trade for provisions or ivory, while Farewell's party—similarly without sources of resupply—was constrained to husband its resources. After King's first visit to Shaka, together with Fynn and Farewell, the traders came away with 107 head of cattle; one solution to the problem of supplies was to survive by Shaka's patronage. This King initially tried to do by salvaging gifts for the king such as the *Mary's* figurehead, but when ingenuity in this area ran out, his party was faced with a stark choice: either to be cut off from Shaka's patronage, or to become Zulu clients—a course of action that King quickly realized involved military services.[19]

While the party hesitated over this issue, their conditions declined still further. It was at this time that relations between Shaka and the traders became strained for the first time, with the Zulu monarch seizing the ivory collected—apparently without royal permission—by Fynn.[20] Thus when, in April 1826, the *Helicon* arrived at Port Natal, King took passage aboard in order to proceed to the Cape to obtain much-needed new cargo, leaving his comrades in what Isaacs described as a "miserable situation."[21]

Reports of the traders' circumstances which immediately preceded King's arrival in the Cape, and, indeed, his own initial remarks, continued to promote conditions in Natal and the Zulu kingdom as promising and contained no negative references to Shaka or the inhabitants of the Zulu kingdom.[22] "The natives" were described as "harmless" and as behaving "extremely well."[23] So satisfied was the colonial administration with the intelligence at its disposal for Natal, and the attractiveness of conditions there, that it had no hesitation in sanctioning proposed visits to Natal by botanists, missionaries, and the like.[24] Thus, when King arrived in Port Elizabeth in April 1826, both the general public in the Cape and the colonial authorities had heard substantial praise of the Zulu king, Shaka.[25] In his first public comments, contained in an article in the *South African Commercial Advertiser*, King continued in this vein, describing Shaka as obliging, charming, and pleasant, stern in public but good-humored in private, benevolent, and hospitable.[26]

In the meantime, however, King's attempts to raise money for another ship and a cargo failed.[27] He was thus forced to approach the colonial authorities for assistance. In his appeal he resuscitated the claim that he wanted to succor those left behind.[28] When he heard on June 7 that even this appeal had failed, King chose a new approach. In another article on June 11, 1826 in the *South African Commercial Advertiser*, King, for the first time, suggested that Shaka was a "despotic and cruel monster."[29] On the basis of the new claim about the threat posed by Shaka to the apparently vulnerable "castaways" at Port Natal, he succeeded in rallying sufficient support to fit out another vessel, the *Anne*, for a "rescue" mission, and King thereby returned to Port Natal with a cargo of trade items and Mrs. Farewell.[30] As Brian Roberts notes in a much-neglected study that focuses on the contradictions between the traders' pronouncements of Shaka's murderousness and their actions, Mrs. Farewell's inclusion in the party makes "one suspect the disparity between King's words and actions."[31]

Thus King's second article in the *South African Commercial Advertiser* differs markedly in content and style from his first article. The sudden demonization of Shaka and about-turn in the representation of Port Natal as under threat from Shaka formed a specific strategy pursued at a particular moment. This image of Shaka also stands in sharp contrast to King's own earlier statements, as well as to the reports of the other traders, notably Farewell. The Cape authorities, however, clearly set little store by King's latest intelligence on Shaka, and continued to sanction trips to Natal.[32] Indeed, within months, King himself was obliged to try and repair the damage by convincing his backers in Cape Town that Shaka, although a despot, "to do him justice, is for a savage the best-hearted of his race."[33]

With King's cargo-laden return to Port Natal, the situation of his party improved dramatically.[34] But conflict immediately erupted between Farewell and King. The tensions between the two groups that prevailed before King's first trip to the Cape, and the open conflict that ensued after his return, have implications for the specific views of the Zulu king that the traders subsequently promoted. Writers on the affairs of the traders who have taken note of the split between the two parties have failed to find a satisfactory explanation for it.[35] This is because the available evidence is not especially illuminating. Isaacs, one of the major sources on the quarrel, noted that it was over "matters of a pecuniary nature," and elaborated on a particular tussle between the two over the question of whose name would be used in sending trade goods to Shaka.[36] Farewell, in a letter to the *South African Commercial Advertiser* in January 1829, claimed that King had undermined him and attempted to exclude him from the trade.[37]

While it is difficult to say with any certainty what underlay the conflict, these remarks are consistent with the thesis that King had proceeded to the Cape on the understanding that he would there procure trade goods on Farewell's behalf, if not on his own as well. This enabled him to tap Farewell's superior credit at the Cape.[38] All along, it had been King's aim to enter the Port Natal trade on terms more advantageous to himself. Initially these had collapsed when he lost all his cargo in the wreck of the *Mary*. On his return to Port Natal in October 1826, however, King was in a position to hold Farewell to ransom over the question of supplies.

Farewell refused to cooperate with King, as did John Cane and Henry Ogle of his party, although Fynn, previously one of Farewell's party, now began to play a role increasingly independent of Farewell. Again, the reasons for this are not hard to find when the trading interests of the parties are examined. Fynn was one of the most active among the traders, particularly in the area south of Natal. His success in the collection of ivory, his relative independence from Shaka, and his own lack of connections to Cape capital meant that he would have had none of Farewell's objections to "buying" supplies from King, if not exchanging ivory for them, and, perhaps because of the dynamism of his operation, an even more urgent need for fresh supplies.

As has been argued above, the greatest difficulties experienced by the Port

Natal traders concerned the maintenance of a direct import–export route to and from the Cape. The traders needed a regular supply of goods from the Cape to exchange for ivory and for provisions. Likewise they needed to be able to transport the ivory collected back to the Cape. The seas between Natal and the Cape are unusually treacherous,[39] while the financing of ships for the task involved considerable expense, a problem exacerbated by the succession of losses experienced by the traders and the difficulty of negotiating the sand bar at the entrance to Port Natal.[40] One option investigated by King was the location of an alternative port. The other was the opening up of a route overland.[41] An overland route would reduce the necessary capital outlay in terms of ships and crews, and offered a generally more reliable means of resupply. For this to be a viable option, however, the traders needed secure routes through a variety of independent chiefdoms. It seems that at this time the traders approached Shaka with a plan to secure the overland route. King and Fynn (the trader with the most southerly base) began actively to pursue a plan to open up a direct southern overland connection with the Cape.[42] This was the logic underlying King's next journey to Port Elizabeth with two ambassadors from Shaka, and the attacks, at much the same time, by Shaka and Fynn on the communities of Africans living along the overland route in the area between the southern reaches of the Zulu kingdom and the colony.

This series of events has also been misinterpreted and little understood, largely because of the obfuscation caused by the argument that the traders desired to use Shaka's southern campaigns to generate fear at the Cape and in that way to push the British authorities into establishing a colony in Natal. Julian Cobbing has argued that from the moment of their arrival in Port Natal, it was in the interests of the traders and their backers at the Cape to see the establishment of a British colony there. To achieve this, he continues, the traders were concerned from the first to represent Shaka as a tyrannical despot so as to persuade the British authorities of the need to annex Natal. Cobbing suggests that ideas about Shaka's depredations were assiduously promoted by traders, among others, as part of the elaborate *mfecane* "alibi" designed to obscure the disruptive effects of their own activities, notably their participation in a local slave trade.[43] Likewise John Wright argues that King went to the Cape to get recognition for his latest land concession from Shaka, and "to agitate for the establishment of some kind of British authority at Port Natal to give his claims effect."[44] In fact, King did not raise the issue of the land grant until July 29, 1828, that is, more than two months after his arrival at the Cape and, significantly, at the lowest point in his negotiations with the authorities. He used the grant to claim for himself the power to negotiate on Shaka's behalf, something the authorities were expressly trying to avoid. Had King's primary objective been to obtain land-grant recognition, he would surely have brought the original (or a supposedly original) document of the agreement concluded with

Shaka with him, but he did not. Instead he made a copy from memory—or so he claimed: the existence of the document, and of an original land grant, was later strenuously denied by another of the traders, John Cane.[45]

King's plan, it seems, was less ambitious. A more likely reconstruction of his objectives at this time is that he aimed to have Shaka support Fynn in clearing the way between Port Natal and the Cape Colony, by establishing Zulu authority in the area—possibly at first through local chiefs forced to recognize a loose form of distant Zulu rule, and, if necessary, the extension over time of a more direct form of Zulu administration—thus creating conditions more conducive to the prosecution of trade and the maintenance of a secure route. But King knew, of course, that any attempt by Fynn and Shaka to subdue the intervening communities ran the risk of causing alarm at the Cape.

Shaka seems at this time to have started to work with the traders more closely than before, supplying them with ivory directly and easing the restrictions on their other trading initiatives.[46] He was interested in developing the southern reaches of his kingdom for other reasons. With the defeat of his northern Ndwandwe enemies in 1826, the bulk of the Zulu army was freed for redeployment in the south. Internal disaffection at this time placed Shaka in a position of wanting to cement and monopolize the relationship with the traders, themselves based in the south. When Shaka mooted a plan to send ambassadors to the Cape so as to consolidate his position within the kingdom, King immediately agreed.[47] The ambassadors would serve as a sign of the support from Shaka enjoyed by the traders, and would allay any fears regarding Shaka's intentions in venturing south. By brokering the establishment of relations between the Zulu kingdom and the Cape Colony, King hoped to gain sufficient influence with both parties to secure control over the trade for himself.

The Cape's Shaka, 1827–1828

The first move in the preparation of informed opinion at the Cape for the plan to open the overland route between the colony and Port Natal was the release by the traders' backers in Cape Town of a letter from Port Natal for publication in the *South African Commercial Advertiser*.[48] In the letter, King praised Shaka, spelt out his plan for a southern campaign, and stressed that Shaka's intentions toward the colony were peaceful. Thus, if anything, when King set sail in early 1828 in the recently completed *Elizabeth and Susan* for the Cape, he did so with the aim of promoting a very positive image of Shaka. On his arrival at Port Elizabeth on May 4 he continued to stress "the friendly disposition of Chaka towards our nation," and the absence of any threat to the colony from Shaka's latest campaigns.[49]

However, King had made a significant miscalculation. In the period between his first (1826) and second (1828) visits, the colonial administration's policy shifted from a concern with the opening up of new markets and strategic bases beyond the colony to one of stabilizing the independent frontier chiefdoms and containing expansion. By late 1827 the lieutenant-governor of the Cape, General Richard Bourke, stated that official policy was "to maintain those situated immediately on our front in possession of their country as long as by their friendly and peaceable conduct they prove themselves deserving of our protection. This will be the easiest and cheapest way of preserving the colony itself from plunder and disquietude. . . ."[50]

In terms of this policy, the colonial authorities could not countenance Shaka's campaigns on or near the borders of the colony.[51] By the time King came to compose a detailed written statement for the authorities on the purpose of the Zulu embassy, he was acquainted with the new policy, and was obliged to rethink his approach. In his statement he stressed the urgency of sending one of the ambassadors back to the Zulu kingdom as soon as possible to apprise Shaka and Fynn of this unexpected shift in colonial policy. To his injunctions for speed, King added the puzzling comment that he had left hostages in Shaka's hands to guarantee the safety of the Zulu ambassadors. It is clear from the operations at precisely this time in the Mpondo country between Port Natal and the colony of one of the claimed hostages, Fynn, that this was not the case.[52] However, King's claim lent an added impetus to the urgency of returning a messenger to Shaka, at the same time obscuring Fynn's role in a southern campaign that was increasingly showing the possibility of coming into direct confrontation with British interests in the area. The claim also contrived to suggest that the traders' role in Shaka's campaigns was forced upon them.[53] Once this report was submitted, King waited to see whether his communication regarding Shaka's peaceful intentions toward the colony would result in a change in policy.

King was also waiting for the registration of the homemade craft, the *Elizabeth and Susan*, to be completed by the Port Elizabeth port authorities. He anticipated that the boat, once registered, would either begin plying regularly between Port Natal and the Cape, thus alleviating the supply problem, or alternatively, if disposed of, would provide him with the necessary capital to obtain a new cargo and to transport it to Natal. During May, King was optimistic on both counts. His statement of Shaka's friendly intentions had filtered through to the frontier, while on the basis of his positive intelligence regarding Shaka, the authorities sanctioned the expedition of Messrs. Cowie and Green to the Zulu kingdom. Likewise, the press assured the public that there was nothing to fear from Shaka.[54]

When, however, it appeared that the registration of the boat might be in jeopardy, and the Cape authorities, already tardy in responding to the embassy, appeared to want Shaka to bring his campaign to a halt, King attempted, once again, to use the threat of Zulu hostility to achieve his ends. He declared that if his craft was not registered he would not risk sending it back to Natal with the one Zulu ambassador whose arrival Shaka was anxiously awaiting. If Shaka did not hear from his ambassador, he improvised, the safety of the colony could not be guaranteed.[55] The invocation of Shaka as a volatile tyrant was a desperate ploy to force the hand of the authorities. The threat fell on deaf ears.[56]

The colonial authorities refused to be drawn into what they recognized as King's machinations. A government representative, Major A.J. Cloete, was dispatched to Port Elizabeth to circumvent King and to deal directly with the Zulu ambassadors. Cloete was instructed to inform the ambassadors that King enjoyed no status in the eyes of the British authorities.[57] Although at this time intelligence from the frontier indicated that Shaka's army was advancing on the frontier chiefs, there were no fears in the official mind that the colony was the object of Shaka's attacks.[58] What they did fear was that a war north of the frontier would send large numbers of refugees streaming into the colony. Cloete's subsequent discussions with the Zulu envoys did not alter the picture of Shaka's intentions toward the colony as peaceful, and the tenor of the pertinent official correspondence over the next two months indicates that King's image of Shaka-as-villain had failed to take root. The policy of the colonial officials was to meet with Shaka at the first possible opportunity to explain their position with regard to the chiefdoms across the border, after which, they believed, he would withdraw.[59] Over the next two months, the Cape authorities only became more skeptical of King and of what Cloete described as his "determined perversion of facts."[60] Likewise, reports in the press questioned the idea that Shaka was vengeful, describing him as "amiable" and as a better diplomat than the British officials.[61]

King's strategies were by no means exhausted, and until his departure in August he tried a range of other ploys to extort money from the authorities and attempted to shore up his position in the eyes of the Zulu envoys, but all of these were blocked by the perspicacious Cloete. Cloete also put considerable effort into exposing King's manipulations to the ambassadors, indicating that the British government dissociated itself from King, and emphasizing the colony's favorable disposition toward Shaka.[62]

Perhaps King's most outrageous maneuver was to approach the chief commissioner for Uitenhage, J.W. van der Riet, in an attempt to circumvent Cloete, and on the basis of reports of Shaka's imminent advance on the Xhosa chief Hintsa, to offer to broker an accord between Shaka and the colony. With this ploy, King tried for the last time to invoke a threatening Shaka, claiming that, if he did not intervene, both the Port Natal settlement and the colony would be attacked by the Zulu. Once again the authorities remained unconvinced, with justification it seems, for in the same week King was again claiming Shaka as a "friend of nearly three years" to whose "humanity and kindness" he owed a great debt.[63] By August, as the situation on the frontier deteriorated, the colonial administration deemed it best to return the envoys to Shaka with assurances of friendship and a clear statement of their determination not to countenance his southern attacks. The embassy, including King, was returned to Natal aboard the naval vessel the *Helicon*. After their departure, the press continued to report favorably on Shaka. When British forces thought, mistakenly, that they had engaged the Zulu army, an editorial in *The Colonist* accused the commanding officer, Dundas, of "gross violation of the law of nations."[64]

In fact, so "civilized" did the press consider Shaka to be that it was speculated that he must be "of white extraction."[65] In the same edition one correspondent commented perceptively on the problem of interpreting Shaka:

> The character and objects of Chaka it is not to be expected should be favorably represented by the tribes he had ruined, or threatened to destroy, and considerable caution is therefore requisite in weighing the evidence only procurable through prejudiced channels; from sources of this kind the Invader is declared a determined, a systematic, and a practiced plunderer, raising no corn, breeding no cattle, and procreating no children.[66]

The same reservation was true for King's representation of Shaka and, indeed, was widely held.[67]

On the mission's return to Natal, Shaka received the reports of his ambassadors, including the chronicle of King's deceits and manipulations, as well as the messages from the British authorities. Incensed by King's duplicity and foolishness, and concerned that he had come close to provoking the British into battle, Shaka promptly dispatched a member of Farewell's camp, John Cane, overland to the Cape to affirm his peaceful intentions and his compliance with British requests. He also asked for an official British agent to the Zulu kingdom.[68] Through Cane Shaka stressed that he "was no longer disposed to molest the frontier tribes of Caffers" and that his aim was "free intercourse with the colony."[69] The Cape authorities were highly receptive to this latest embassy, and in November the *South African Commercial Advertiser* reported its belief that the "frightful stories" sometimes told about Shaka were "mere fabrications."[70] As far as informed opinion at the Cape was concerned, in 1828 Shaka was no villain. Nor, for that matter, had there been anywhere a call for Natal to be colonized.

Shaka posthumously

Unbeknown to the *South African Commercial Advertiser* and its readers, however, both James King, the opportunistic purveyor of rumors of a Zulu attack, and Shaka, the king-who-was-not-a-monster, were already dead. James King died mysteriously on September 7, and Shaka was assassinated on September 24. Cobbing argues on the basis of circumstantial evidence that Fynn was behind the assassination of the Zulu king.[71] The timing and circumstances of these deaths are odd, and Cobbing is correct to question the conventional interpretations. But his evidence for Fynn's involvement is not conclusive, and in his preoccupation with white agency and white sources, Cobbing fails to take account of Zulu oral tradition on the event, in which there is no hint of involvement by Fynn. Oral traditions are notoriously permeable to such information, while the succession practices of local northern-Nguni speakers—which preclude an assassin from succeeding to the office of his victim—would have placed a high premium on the revelation by the contenders for the succession of any involvement by Fynn and Farewell. It should be noted, moreover, that the traders' response to the assassination was defensive. They improved their fortifications at Port Natal and readied their boat for an emergency departure. Indeed, Farewell and Isaacs left soon thereafter for Port Elizabeth.

It was only after the death of Shaka that the traders began for the first time to talk about the colonization of Natal and to employ a rhetoric critical of Shaka.[72] Their monopoly over the Natal trade, which had prevailed since 1824, was finally coming to an end. Their successful promotion of conditions in Natal had stimulated others to follow in their footsteps.[73] The traders had not yet established relations with the new Zulu king in the way they had with the old, and circumstances in Natal, in early 1829, were more volatile and less predictable than before. The traders had attempted repeatedly to make a go of the Natal trade on their own, and had failed. By 1829, and under these circumstances, colonization offered the traders an excellent opportunity for making good what were by now quite considerable losses. It was at this time that Farewell raised capital against his land grant in expectation of the rapid development of Port Natal.

The vilification of Shaka that began at this time was as specific to the conditions that prevailed in early 1829 as King's remarks in 1826 and early 1828 were specific to his particular circumstances at the time. On his return to the Cape, Farewell faced accusations that he had fought in the Zulu armies—an allegation not without substance. The thrust of his defense, an argument subsequently taken up by Fynn and Isaacs, was that the traders had been threatened by Shaka and forced to participate in the campaigns.[74] At this point, precisely because the Zulu king was dead, the traders could malign Shaka to provide an "alibi" for their own actions without undermining their own representations of the stability of conditions in Natal. In support of their case against Shaka, they drew on a stock of stories with which they had become acquainted in Natal, stories garnered from African associates and informants.

Moreover, the traders were also aware that they could no longer monopolize the image of Shaka that prevailed at the Cape. The British authorities had resolved to send the agent requested by Shaka, and were highly suspicious of the traders. In addition, numerous other parties in the Cape announced their intention of proceeding north to the Zulu kingdom.

When these various groups arrived in Natal, they found that the image of Shaka as a tyrant that was gaining ground in the Cape in 1829 echoed strongly the images prevalent in the Zulu kingdom and in Natal. Shaka-the-monster was no more the "invention" of the traders in 1829 than it had been before then. Nor was a negative view of Shaka the only image that prevailed in Zulu society in 1829. Resistance to Shaka's assassin and successor, Dingane, ensured the continuity of positive images of Shaka. It is to an examination of the various African productions of Shaka that the next section of this chapter turns.

Domination and resistance in the Zulu kingdom under Shaka

Sometime before about 1820, in a controversial succession, Shaka kaSenzanga-khona took over the leadership of the Zulu chiefdom with the assistance of the neighboring Mthethwa paramount, Dingiswayo. Then, as a tributary of Dingi-swayo, Shaka was encouraged to establish a firm regional challenge to the Mthe-thwa's greatest rivals, the Ndwandwe. This was the beginning of Zulu power. The Ndwandwe subsequently defeated the Mthethwa, but the forces of the Zulu, which had not participated in the campaign, remained intact. Under threat of continued Ndwandwe aggression, the Zulu stepped into the gap left by the defeat of the Mthethwa paramount, and began to rally their neighbors into a defensive alliance. Over time, this was consolidated into Zulu domination over substantial territories. Sometime before the first traders arrived at Port Natal the Zulu forces, considerably enlarged and reorganized, repulsed a Ndwandwe attack, an act that heralded the collapse of the Ndwandwe kingdom. The Zulu were poised to become the predominant power in the region between the Phongolo and Thukela rivers.[75]

When the traders arrived in 1824, they entered a relatively new and highly heterogeneous polity which Shaka was in the process of welding into a centralized state. Divisions within the ruling house were rife. Shaka had isolated his close surviving male relatives, had placed distant male and female relatives in high positions, and surrounded himself with powerful generals and advisers who were not members of the royal house.[76] He declined to produce an heir. His controversial accession had divided the Zulu ruling house and provided fertile grounds for rebellion against him. Ultimately, these conflicts and tensions within the royal house were to culminate in his assassination in 1828 by two of his surviving brothers.[77]

As Shaka consolidated his position as ruler of the Zulu, dispute within the royal family was overshadowed by struggles between the Zulu rulers and both their subjects and neighbors. One of the ways in which the Zulu rulers sought to unify the new kingdom was through the *amabutho* system. The *amabutho* system drew young men together from different areas and socialized them into identifying with the Zulu king as their ritual leader and source of their welfare. At the same time, the king assumed the authority to decide when young men could set up households of their own. Unity within the kingdom was also fostered through the assertion of common origins for the disparate chiefdoms incorporated under Shaka in the early years of his reign. It seems that they were now obliged to think of themselves as being of common Ntungwa descent, and to speak "proper" Zulu.[78]

By the mid-1820s, however, this new ideology of state was not yet well entrenched; neither was the centralization of the kingdom complete. In particular, Shaka faced rebellion in three areas: in two of the chiefdoms subordinate to his rule—among the Khumalo in the north and the Qwabe in the south—and still further south, in the Lala chiefdoms close to Port Natal. In the later years of his reign, Shaka began to incorporate the inhabitants of newly subordinated chiefdoms south of the Thukela, not as "subjects" of the Zulu kingdom, but rather as despised "outsiders"—"those who sleep (*ukulala*) with their fingers up their anuses"[79]—who were regarded as being ethnically inferior to the subjects of the core Zulu kingdom. Their chiefly houses were required to maintain identities clearly distinct from that of the Zulu ruling house, and their leaders, although accorded a number of privileges which distinguished them from the bulk of their own subjects, were excluded from certain of the kingdom's central decision-making processes. Their young men were not permitted to join the king's *amabutho*, but were put to work at menial tasks such as herding cattle at outlying royal cattle-posts. In summary, members of these chiefdoms were oppressed by their Zulu rulers.[80] This situation was maintained by a combination of coercive and ideological measures. There were thus great inequalities within the Zulu kingdom, deep-seated divisions, and signs of considerable dissension.

Even after the defeat of the Ndwandwe and the collapse of Khumalo resistance in 1826, Shaka's position was by no means secure. In a subsequent battle against the Ngwane chief, Matiwane, the Zulu forces seized about 30,000 cattle, but only at the cost of the lives of some 3,000–4,000 warriors.[81] So serious was the disaffection in 1827 that Shaka was obliged to use the harsh restrictions imposed after the death of his mother, Nandi—involving the execution of anyone who was not perceived to have mourned sufficiently—to eliminate his enemies. Prior to his death Shaka had already survived one assassination attempt.

Ongoing resistance of this kind, and smaller outbreaks of rebellion elsewhere, prompted continued coercive and ideological responses from the Zulu king. These included merciless campaigns and stern sentences for individual rebels. The effect of these actions was to invest Shaka with a reputation for harsh and arbitrary action. On the one hand, he fostered this image through carefully managed displays of despotism and brutal justice at his court, using terror as a basis for absolute rule across a huge kingdom. These displays were not only designed to inspire obedience from his subjects; they were also meant to strike fear into the heart of his enemies and to impress outsiders, such as the traders, with his power. His despotism was justified in the minds of some of his subjects by the other component of Shaka's image, that of a leader of tremendous abilities, the great unifier, and the hero in battle. Both components of the image are reflected in his *izibongo* (praises). The Zulu king was reputedly one of the architects of his own image, collecting praises for himself that he liked. According to Mbokodo kaSokhulekile, Shaka took for himself the praise "The one whose fame resounds even as he sits," after he heard it used in respect of the Mbo chief, Sambela.[82] But as much as the reputation for harshness served Shaka's purposes, so too did it form the basis of opposition to his rule. Qwabe accounts of Shaka typically vilify him as a tyrant; Lala accounts often depict him as a marauder, a destroyer, and a "madman."[83]

Detailed review of the body of recorded traditions concerning Shaka allows us to identify accounts of Shaka that appear to date back in form and content to the time of his reign. The following analysis of three such productions, based as it is on a close reading of the history of the Zulu kingdom, may seem daunting to readers unfamiliar with Zulu names and to those wary of dense historical and cultural detail. Despite difficulties of this kind, gaining a perspective more interior to the logic of the narrators is crucial to the exegesis of the texts. Close analysis of this kind begins to make possible a nuanced reading of the meaning and significance of oral traditions about Shaka, and to reveal the way the dominant versions of the past took cognizance of, and were constrained by, opposition views. It shows that Shaka was portrayed in the 1820s as a tyrant and even as an inhuman monster both by oral historians who supported him and by those who opposed him. The traders encountered these different views of Shaka in many contexts ranging from his court—in circumstances of his making—to contacts with the rebellious Qwabe, Khumalo, Lala, and others. By 1826 the traders were firmly inserted in the Zulu kingdom, and were closely involved in the extension of Zulu rule south of the Thukela, which was by that time proceeding apace. They also heard reports of Shaka's depredations from the African community at Port Natal, many members of which had previously been driven out of their homes by Shaka.[84]

Listening for the voices of domination and resistance

Shaka's supporters and opponents had very different images of the Zulu king, although they drew on a shared stock of motifs and narrative devices. The existence of these diverse views, the struggles between them, and their shifting content in response to changing conditions, both during the reign of Shaka and subsequently, have been ignored by writers such as Golan and Cobbing. They are effectively precluded from consideration by current developments in the theoretical literature on colonial discourse discussed in chapter 1, which emphasize the colonial construction of Africa.

Although Golan fails to recognize the diversity of African views of Shaka, she is one of the few commentators on the representation of the Zulu king who consider the story of Shaka contained in oral traditions.[85] She includes in her historiographical overview of the Zulu literature a detailed structural analysis of an oral tradition, "the invariant core of Shaka's life story . . . a fiction,"[86] which is, she claims, the basis for all later, written versions. This structural investigation, she argues, reveals the stories to be symbolic representations of alternative worldviews rather than records of past times. For Golan, "the very basic story which most historians accept is but an invention."[87] She argues that the reason why, for example, Shaka is depicted as illegitimate in the oral traditions is not related to the actual circumstances of his birth, contested or otherwise, but that Shaka is used as a symbol of changing succession patterns—from a lineage inheritance basis to a merit basis— changes associated with the emergence of states. Golan's approach, which views the details of Shaka's story as the clichés typical of hero stories—common to the life stories of figures as diverse as Sundiata and Moses—suggests a new and useful way of reading such texts. Golan argues that while Shaka's birth and childhood "were recorded only in oral tradition and took place within a 'mythical' time, records of his death, on a known date and in a known place, are part of 'objective' history and come from non-mythical sources." While claiming to see oral traditions as a mixture of myth and history, Golan sets up what is effectively an opposition between pre-contact oral texts, which are myths subject to structuralist analysis that "do not even pretend to be factual," and post-contact written texts, which can be mined for "real" historical detail.[88]

An alternative approach might regard the stock features of the oral traditions as also being historical elements, or dramatic devices typical of oral narratives, onto which are hooked meanings and interpretations. This position draws in part on Harold Scheub's idea of a core of images lying at the heart of the storytelling tradition that narrators use as the basic materials for their accounts,[89] and extends it to argue that these forms are invested with particular core historical content. To reduce the content of the oral stories of Shaka to metaphor alone, such as a metaphor for succession, is to deny the historiographical status of these traditions. The rest of this chapter demonstrates their fundamentally historiographical nature, but does not exclude their metaphorical aspect.[90] While Golan is certainly right to point up the clichés and the significance of their similarity to stock elements in the stories of other "heroes," she does not probe sufficiently the connection between the use of clichés and personal narrative and public tradition.[91]

The mythical or cliché elements in oral traditions are narrations about the past and offer evidence of the past, but they are also a force in the present time of narration and are tied to the struggles of that present. Nowhere does Golan attempt to identify the interests such sources represented, or to specify the relationship between the writers and their informants, or between either of these two parties and the Zulu king. Also largely ignored in her account is the internal world of Zulu kingdom politics, ideological struggles, and culture in the early nineteenth century, and its impact on Zulu historiography, as well as the participation of European writers in that world. The assumption underlying Golan's idea of a generic life story of Shaka, which is a metaphor for the changing constitution of Zulu society, is that the ideological discourses reflected in history are peculiar to western society, and that Africans only participate in these ideological discourses when they begin to *write* their history. Except in its ahistorical representation as a single "oral tradition," oral Zulu historiography is absent in Golan's study.[92]

Cobbing is another scholar who collapses all the different, contending interpretations of Shaka in oral tradition into a single "Zulu voice," which presented a view of the Zulu past unchanged between 1820 and 1900, and which, in recorded form, he sees as being contaminated by the traders, who shaped the historical fantasies of all subsequent recorders of oral tradition, in particular those of the most energetic "transcriber," James Stuart.[93] Cobbing is undoubtedly correct to reiterate Jan Vansina's seminal points about the need for scholars using information contained in collections of oral traditions to come to terms with the presences in the traditions of the collectors. However, the recorders' interests are not as all-determining of their texts as Cobbing supposes. Recent advances in the theory of literary criticism have demonstrated the capacity of texts to say things over and above what their authors, their editors, and even their collectors intend. The context in which the tradition is recorded affects its content, as do any interests that the informant or the collector intends the text to advance, counter, avoid, or neutralize.

Oral traditions thus require the reconstruction of their own histories. We need to know under what circumstances oral texts came to be transcribed, and by whom.[94] We need to know all about the background, interests, and experiences of the transcribers. We also need to know who the informants were, their backgrounds, interests, and experiences. We need to establish how they gleaned the information provided, and we need to know the same things, in turn, about their original sources. On the basis of all this information we can begin to make judgments about the traditions, their periodization, and the extent of their faithfulness in written form to the oral versions. Where transmutations may have crept in over time we need to assess their likely content and scope. The extant traditions about Shaka differ significantly about key episodes in his life and fundamentally in their evaluation of the Zulu king. Oral texts, as much as written texts, reflect the biases and background of their composers and chroniclers, the intellectual currents of their time, and have debts to one another.[95]

The form of the traditions also requires attention. The traditions discussed here are loosely structured narratives, not readily divisible into clear genres.[96] Their status as literary forms with a life of their own outside the interview situation is not confirmed.[97] It may be that we still need to sensitize ourselves to the indigenous concepts and narrative conventions. One feature that is immediately identifiable, however, is—as Isabel Hofmeyr, following Karin Barber, puts it—"a clear sense of political and social struggle as a key determinant in African oral literature."[98] This discussion focuses on this central generic characteristic.

The rest of this chapter looks at three productions of Shaka contained in oral traditions, all of which were recorded by James Stuart. One possible approach would be to begin with Stuart himself in an attempt to evaluate his impact on the traditions. Instead, consideration of Stuart and his presence in the traditions is held over for treatment in a later chapter. This will have the advantage of following and building on discussions of the connections between the image of Shaka and the development of "native policy" in the decades before Stuart joined the colonial service.

The discussion of the three oral stories about Shaka is divided in two parts: an examination of the background and contexts of the narrators and their informants; and a discussion of the role of the productions of Shaka contained in the traditions in promoting, countering, avoiding, and neutralizing interests and counter-interests. The discussion utilizes material and information yielded up by both the form and the content of the narratives. The second part of the discussion returns thus to the central question of this section of the study, the nature and role of different African representations of Shaka in the 1820s.

African representations of Shaka in the 1820s

A number of commentators on the reworkings of the Shaka story ascribe the focus on Shaka's cruelties to white distortions and inventions, deriving from the legacy of the early whites' need "to deflect their involvement in the murder of the king with a campaign of vilification against him . . . and with false statements about the popular acclaim at Dingane's accession."[99] Cobbing, for example, claims that Stuart's informants resisted his "fishing for horror stories" and asserts that there is a noteworthy contrast between "the solicitude for Dingane and the hatred for Shaka that threads through white propaganda, and the Zulus' favorable memory of Shaka and their fear and hostility towards the 'bewhiskered one from Mgungundhlovu [Dingane]'."[100] Cobbing's blanket claims are simply wrong. "White propaganda," as we have already seen, and as will be shown for later periods in subsequent chapters, was not unanimous over time in support for Dingane and vilification of Shaka. Dingane's murder of Piet Retief was responsible for a major shift away from this interpretation in some (but, again, not all) "white" accounts of Zulu history. The "Zulu" memory of Shaka was likewise not unanimously favorable toward Shaka and opposed to Dingane.

The great well of bitterness toward Shaka that permeates the entire testimony of an informant such as the Qwabe woman Baleka kaMpitikazi (discussed in detail below) was no mere response to Stuart's promptings. The Qwabe chiefdom was in rebellion for much of the reign of Shaka and was subject to brutal repressive measures.[101] Baleka's own father, Mpitikazi, nearly lost his life at Shaka's hand. It is clear from a close reading of the recorded text, attention to its powerful and emotive language, and examination of its internal rhetorical structures and coherence, and the connections made by Baleka between the sufferings of the Qwabe and the cruelty of Shaka that much of the testimony owes its form to her father's experiences under Shaka and to the legacy of hatred left by Shaka's persecution of the Qwabe, and not to the interviewer Stuart's promptings.[102] This is not, of course, to suggest that Shaka was indeed a monster. Rather, it is to assert that the demonization of the Zulu monarch was not the sole preserve of white commentators.

Events inside the Zulu kingdom were responsible for sharp debates over Shaka, not merely between his supporters and detractors during his lifetime, but also subsequently, as different interests within and beyond the Zulu kingdom drew on different "Shakas" to support their actions in new circumstances. Any attempt to discover the kinds of views of Shaka that prevailed in 1824 in the Zulu kingdom must test the oral traditions for subversions or mutations that occurred subsequently. In particular, African versions of Shaka gained new content and relevance throughout the nineteenth century at times of succession disputes. The following discussion of the connection between succession disputes and changing productions of the image of Shaka offers a background against which the perceptions of Stuart's informants must be evaluated. To the extent that this background suggests where and how changes in the story of Shaka came about, it also defines the limits and possibilities of such changes. Hofmeyr has pointed out that any oral interview suggests three primary fields of investigation: the dynamics of the interview situation; the events recalled; and "an intervening period during which both the informant and the meaning of the events recalled have changed."[103] The following analysis attempts to capture something of this third factor, to look particularly at the impact of major political events[104] on the constitution of historical memories.

"Succession disputes cause slanders": periodizing oral traditions about Shaka

The observation by one of Stuart's informants, Mayinga kaMbhekuzana, that "succession disputes cause slanders"[105] offers a guide as to how the impact of a long period of time on an oral tradition can be assessed in conjunction with a focus on the subjectivity of its transmitters. In the almost one hundred years under consideration—from Shaka's lifetime to the period when James Stuart did his interviewing—there were at least five major succession disputes in which versions of the life story of Shaka were contested.

Dingane's accession, following the death of Shaka, was the first major occasion when Shaka's image was subject to alteration and refurbishment. In the face of Dingane's ruthless suppression of anyone who expressed regret at the murder of Shaka, numbers of Shaka's closest supporters chose to leave the Zulu kingdom rather than challenge the usurpation: Nqeto, a previously compliant Qwabe chief, was a case in point. The controversy escalated when rumors arose that Shaka had a son by a lover, and that the boy was being concealed by Shakan loyalists.[106] Nzwakele, chief of the Dube people, was killed by Dingane for claiming that a son of Shaka was living at his mother's home.[107]

Forced to underpin his coercive onslaught with an ideological initiative, Dingane joined in the battle over the image of Shaka. His campaign entailed maligning in the popular "media" of the time (songs, praises, etc.) his predecessor as an illegitimate tyrant, and the justification of his role in the death of Shaka. In Dingane's praises recorded by a contemporary, J.T. Arbousset, the following lines occur:

> Death-defilement antidotes were eaten, within;
> They were eaten by Mmama and Mnkabayi.[108]

Mnkabayi (sister of the father of Shaka and Dingane) was widely credited with having been the one who confirmed Dingane as the successor of Shaka, and who exonerated him from having had a direct hand in the death of his brother, an act that otherwise would have eliminated him from the succession. This crucial gesture of legitimization was thus recorded in his praises of the time. According to Baleka,

Dingane called himself "Malamulela" (the Intervener) "because he had intervened between the people and the madness of Tshaka," a point supported in the analysis of this praise, and related eulogies, by D. Rycroft and A. Ngcobo.[109] Dingane appropriated for himself one of Shaka's most powerful and threatening praises, "The bird which devours all others," and killed off one of Shaka's chief propagandists, the royal *imbongi* (praise singer), Mxhamama.[110]

The corollary of this was that dissatisfaction about Dingane's reign took the form of appeals to Shaka's spirit. When, in June 1830, Dingane dispatched an army on a winter campaign against the recalcitrant Bhaca, his disaffected generals began to claim that the spirit of Shaka was appearing to them in dreams, urging them to retreat. Such was the impact of this claim that Dingane was obliged to back down and withdraw his forces.[111]

A further succession dispute developed in 1839, when another of Shaka's brothers, Mpande, allied himself with the Boers and led a large secessionist movement from the south of the Zulu kingdom into Natal. Known as "the breaking of the rope" (*ukudabuka kwegoda* or *ukugqabuka*), this was the first major split in the Zulu kingdom. In January 1840, at the battle at amaQongqo hills, south of present-day Magudu, Dingane was defeated, and was subsequently killed. Mpande was then installed by the Boers.

Mpande faced a difficult task in justifying his alliance with the Boers. The term "the breaking of the rope" captures the enormity of this action. The "rope" was the grass cord that united all Zulus, that "runs through Zulu national life from generation to generation."[112] It was thus a perfidy of epic proportions, and it demanded extensive retrospective legitimization, particularly in the face of Boer seizure of large tracts of Zulu territory following the defeat of Dingane, which left Mpande with a considerably reduced kingdom. Moreover, after the defeat of Dingane, the Boers had taken it upon themselves to proclaim Mpande king. To all intents and purposes, it appeared that he owed his accession to the Boers.[113]

Mpande was forced to move quickly to shore up his position. Dingane had killed off all the remaining sons of Senzangakhona, with the exception of Mpande and Gqugqu.[114] Mpande took over the Zulu kingship, dispatched Gqugqu and was then able to claim to be the legitimate successor of Shaka, and to present his actions as the defeat of Shaka's usurper and assassin, Dingane.[115] Thenceforth the crucial lines about the legitimization of Dingane by Mnkabayi were dropped from Dingane's praises. During the reign of Mpande, whenever the royal eulogies were declaimed by the leading *imbongi*, Magolwana, a prologue criticizing Dingane for "thrusting an evil spear into Zululand" was inserted before his praises.[116] Rycroft and Ngcobo note a difference between the eulogies of Dingane recorded during his reign and those recorded subsequently. In the latter Dingane is held responsible for the murder of another of his brothers, Mhlangana.[117] Dingane was thus invested with the tyrant's mantle, a move that accorded well with the image of Dingane propagated by Mpande's Boer allies following the massacre by Dingane of one of their leaders, Piet Retief. Shortly after the murder of Gqugqu, his adherents followed a sister of Senzangakhona, Mawa, in flight from Mpande, into Natal.[118] Mawa's base in Natal became a point of refuge for those opposed to Mpande.[119]

Mpande, as was to be expected, proclaimed Shaka's legitimacy in the strongest terms, and basked in his reflected glory. He was praised with the actions of Shaka, even where such actions were not incorporated into Shaka's own praises, and claimed proudly that he had served in a high position during Shaka's reign.[120] Adulphe Delegorgue, a visitor to Mpande's emigrant court in Natal at the time of his recognition by the Boers in September 1839, (erroneously) understood him to be a full brother of Shaka and a half-brother of Dingane. He reported hearing from Zulu sources that "Panda had . . . incontestable claims to royalty."[121] In a pattern that continues into the present, the image of the first Zulu king began to rise and wane in response to that of the second.

Mpande had, moreover, fathered a child for Shaka with Monase, a woman reputedly given to him for this purpose by Shaka. The evidence as to the biological paternity of this child, Mbuyazi, is debated in the sources. Some state that when Monase fell pregnant by Shaka, he installed her in Mpande's household.[122] Other sources indicate that the child was conceived after the death of Shaka.[123] There is no evidence that *lobolo* (bride wealth) was ever paid for Monase, but it had been paid for Ngqumbazi, who was supposed to give Mpande his heir. A dispute then arose between the rival claims of Mbuyazi—possibly a biological son of Shaka—and Cetshwayo—the son of Ngqumbazi—which erupted into the Zulu civil war of 1856. Once again, the status of Shaka was relevant. Cetshwayo implicitly challenged the claim that Mbuyazi was a son of Shaka by asserting that both he and Mbuyazi were the second sons in the houses of their mothers, the first son in each case having been killed by Shaka.[124] The implication here was that Shaka would not have fathered a second son in the house of a woman by then married to his brother. With the death of Mbuyazi in the battle of Ndondakusuka, Cetshwayo was able to follow Mpande in emphasizing the close connection between his branch of the family and that of Shaka, and Dingane continued to be vilified.[125] According to a missionary at Ulundi, Cetshwayo's capital, it was "Tshaka's song" that was the Zulu "National Anthem" in the 1860s.[126]

The next period when the status of Shaka as a son of Senzangakhona was of heightened relevance occurred after the Anglo-Zulu War of 1879. The defeated Zulu king, Cetshwayo, was imprisoned in Cape Town, and the British authorities proceeded to divide up the Zulu kingdom into thirteen chiefdoms. The rationale for this division was that, with their victory in 1879, the British had succeeded in liberating the Zulu people from the tyranny of the house of Shaka. The post-war settlement was thus described as a return to the pre-Shakan distribution of peoples.[127] The settlement effectively terminated the rule of the dynasty of Shaka, as most of the chiefs who gained office by it were not members of the Zulu royal house. The only two members of the royal family to be included in the settlement were Hamu, son of Nzibe, and Zibhebhu, son of Maphitha, and both were to dominate the other appointed chiefs, and to lead them in a campaign to break the last vestiges of power of the legitimists seeking the return from exile of Cetshwayo.

Both Hamu and Zibhebhu were genealogically distant from the Zulu succession. Hamu's father, Nzibe, was a half-brother of Shaka and a full brother of Mpande. He died during Shaka's Balule campaign in 1828. Mpande subsequently "fathered" Hamu for Nzibe, by means of the leviratic-like institution of *ngena,* and placed Hamu in the Mfemfe homestead of Nzibe. Although biologically the son of Mpande, Hamu was thus genealogically the son of Nzibe and, as such, was not of the line of Shaka. Zibhebhu's royal connection was more tenuous still. Zibhebhu was head of the Mandlakazi section of the Zulu royal family. The founding member of this section was reputedly Ngwabi, a boy captive reared in the Zulu chiefly household as an orphan grafted onto the royal family. Foundlings in Zulu society typically assumed the *isibongo* (clan name) of their adopted families. Ngwabi grew up and married, but died before begetting an heir. His widow was then impregnated in terms of the *ngena* custom by one of his adoptive brothers, Mhlaba, son of Jama, and brother of Shaka's father, Senzangakhona. The child of this union, Sojiyisa, was considered to be Ngwabi's heir. Nonetheless, Sojiyisa, and later his son, Maphitha (the father of Zibhebhu), were raised as members of the ruling family, and under Shaka and his successors were accorded all the privileges due to princes of royal blood.[128] The genealogical distance of both Hamu and Zibhebhu from the line of royal descent traced through Shaka meant that neither had a strong claim to the Zulu throne.

Nonetheless, with the deposition of Cetshwayo and the backing of British authorities, both Hamu and Zibhebhu sought to enhance their prestige and power. Their ultimate goal would in all probability have been recognition by the British of one of them as the new Zulu king. In 1879, however, the installation of a new king was not an immediate possibility. British policy at the time was to keep Zululand divided under separate chiefs. Nevertheless, a struggle for ideological preeminence began within royal circles. One form that this took was the casting of doubt on Shaka's legitimacy. By suggesting either that Shaka was not begotten by Senzangakhona or, if he was, that he was not recognized by Senzangakhona as a son, and that his later accession was illegitimate, Hamu and Zibhebhu began to pave the way for the accession to power of another branch of the Zulu royal family, one that did not trace its descent from Shaka, but rather from his father or grandfather.

This period saw a contest between two versions of the origins of Sojiyisa: the one claiming that he was the biological son of a Zulu chief, and the other emphasizing that Ngwabi was an outsider and suggesting that Ngwabi's wife was already pregnant when he died, a claim designed to deny any consanguinity between the Mandlakazi and the royal Zulu.[129] The parentage of Hamu was equally contested. The chief argument advanced against his ambitions was that he was an *emsizini*, that is, a child born out of intercourse between a king and a woman of the *isigodlo* (king's establishment of women) and therefore of inferior rank in the family.[130]

This review of some of the most significant moments in the nineteenth century when the image of Shaka was the subject of controversy, and of significant re-working, indicates that simplistic notions of a single, unchanged "Zulu voice" are as untenable for the rest of the nineteenth century as they are for the period of Shaka's reign itself. At the same time, the review posits a number of very specific contexts and forms for such changes. The range of such occasions discussed here is by no means exhaustive, but provides a starting place for the consideration of changes of this kind.

All these succession disputes occasioned debate over Shaka's legitimacy, both in terms of the circumstances of his birth and accession and in terms of his own actions (the merit argument), and entailed a corresponding refurbishment of the relevant oral traditions. To ascertain which, if any, of these moments had a bearing on a particular tradition, it is necessary to look closely at the informants concerned and their participation in these events and in such argumentation.

Oral accounts of the story of Shaka from the 1820s

The three productions of Shaka have been chosen for discussion here because they purport to date back to the time of his reign; they differ in significant ways from one another; and there exists sufficient background material to reconstruct something of their context of production and transmission. In particular, the discussion focuses on the way in which each of these versions treats the circumstances of Shaka's birth, his accession, and his reputation as tyrant or hero. Interestingly, there are no differences of any significance in accounts of his assassination. One feature of the death of Shaka that should be noted, however, is that a host of traditions refer to a death-bed prophecy by Shaka to the effect that the land would eventually be taken over by whites.[131]

The first account was recorded in 1902 by Stuart from Ndlovu kaThimuni. The main elements of Ndlovu's version of Shaka's birth were that Shaka was illegitimate (born "*esihlahleni*"—literally, in the bushes; in other words, outside the normal social setting for a birth); that Senzangakhona acknowledged having a liaison with Shaka's mother, Nandi; that Nandi and Senzangakhona were never married; that Senzangakhona subsequently attempted to pay *lobolo* for Nandi, but her parents pretended she was dead; that Shaka's birth was not widely known about at the time, and (specifically) that it was hidden from Senzangakhona.[132] Dealing with the equally sensitive question of the circumstances of Shaka's accession, Ndlovu asserted that Shaka was treated by Dingiswayo, which gave him a "magical" ascendancy over his father and caused the latter to sicken and die. Ndlovu claimed that Senzangakhona died after Shaka's return to the Zulu chiefdom, and he considered Shaka to have been responsible for the murder of four of Senzangakhona's leading councilors, including Ndlovu's own grandfather, Mudli. Finally, in Ndlovu's account, Shaka emerges as a leader of great ability, an innovator, and a hero in battle.[133] In response to a query from Stuart regarding Shaka's alleged atrocities, Ndlovu commented: "People were concocting stories about him."[134] Ndlovu dealt with specific instances apparently illustrative of Shaka's cruelty by offering glosses that placed the accounts in contexts which explained the actions or militated against wholesale condemnation of the king.

Ndlovu owed his knowledge of Shaka to one Sipika, a man of Senzangakhona's Mnkangala *ibutho,* and to Ndlovu's own father, Thimuni. Sipika was actively involved in events leading up to the death of Senzangakhona and the accession of Shaka, while Thimuni, a member of the left-hand (*ikohlo*) side of the Zulu royal family, was himself the son of one of the main protagonists in Shaka's accession, Mudli, chief adviser to Senzangakhona.[135] Before the content of this account can be used as a source for ideas about Shaka that might have prevailed during his reign, the question must be addressed as to what extent Stuart's informant, Ndlovu, altered, either consciously or unwittingly, the stories he heard from Sipika and Thimuni.

One measure of Ndlovu's editorial intervention is given by the fortuitous recording by Stuart of an account of Shaka's life provided by another son of Thimuni, Mhuyi. Comparison of the two testimonies reveals that they diverge to a degree and in a form beyond what might be attributed solely to poor memory or faulty transmission in a chain of testimony. The essential difference in their accounts concerns the question of Shaka's status as a son of Senzangakhona: Ndlovu states that Shaka was illegitimate, while Mhuyi says that he was not, and each account contains narrative details supporting its claim.

Stuart interviewed Ndlovu first, in 1902, and again in early 1903. A few days after the latter discussion, he interviewed Mhuyi, and subsequently held joint discussions with both brothers, at which another of Stuart's informants, Ndukwana, was also present. On this occasion the discrepancies between the accounts were discussed explicitly. Neither Mhuyi nor Ndlovu was adamant in adhering to the less significant details of their versions. On the central question of the legitimacy of Shaka's accession, Mhuyi was prepared to concede that Ndlovu was correct.[136] Ndlovu, by way of contrast, persisted more firmly in his conviction that the circumstances of Shaka's birth showed him to have been illegitimate.[137] There are two possible circumstances, not mutually exclusive, that could have underlain the development of the debate in this form: either Mhuyi was less interested in the account than Ndlovu, and less well informed, in other words simply a poorer source; or Ndlovu could have had a particularly strong motivation for promoting his version of events.

Comparison of the two testimonies shows that Ndlovu's much longer account was also far richer in historical detail. Stuart himself observed that Ndlovu demonstrated an especially strong interest in and knowledge of historical matters.[138] He had nothing comparable to say about Mhuyi, whose testimony lacked the detailed knowledge of that of his brother. For instance, in sharp contrast to the specific knowledge of obscure residences displayed by Ndlovu, Mhuyi could not recall the names of Senzangakhona's imizi beyond those of the very famous Nobamba and Siklebeni,[139] and Mhuyi admitted that he did not have much opportunity to hear about past matters. In fact, Mhuyi never lived in the Zulu kingdom, whereas Ndlovu was chief of a section of the royal house, based in the Maphumulo division.[140] Finally, Mhuyi only heard his account from Thimuni, who was an infant at the time of Shaka's accession, whereas Sipika, Ndlovu's additional informant, was an eyewitness to the events debated.[141] The texts, and the circumstances of the two informants, suggest that the first proposition, that Ndlovu was better informed than Mhuyi, holds up. It is also likely that Ndlovu's greater knowledge was a product of his interaction with Sipika, a source not shared by Mhuyi.

The possibility, on the other hand, that Ndlovu was especially motivated in promoting the view that Shaka was illegitimate is not fully substantiated. Ndlovu was a supporter of Mkhungo, the only surviving son of the house of Mbuyazi, the house connected directly to Shaka (see above, p. 57).[142] This alignment would presumably have placed pressure on him to affirm Shaka's legitimacy in whatever form was most appropriate. This he did by claiming that, while Shaka was born "esihlahleni", there was no doubt that he was fathered by Senzangakhona. Another factor can be found in the circumstances of the death of Ndlovu's grandfather, Mudli, at Shaka's hands. If Ndlovu's branch of the royal house, angered by the murder, had harbored a grudge against Shaka and wanted to malign him, they would have done well to suppress other details of Ndlovu's story, details that explain crucial lacunae in Shaka's personal history. The suppression of these details would have allowed them to suggest that Shaka was not Senzangakhona's son, but an impostor of other origins. Either the wholesale blackening of Shaka went beyond the limits of historical credibility, or it was not precisely their aim.

Thimuni and his brother Sigwebana were, moreover, obliged to leave the Zulu kingdom during the reign of Dingane when the king sought to kill them, under circumstances unfortunately not further elaborated by Ndlovu.[143] This turn of events presumably set them against Dingane. In practice, enmity toward Dingane tended to mean support for the house of Shaka, at least in retrospect. If Thimuni's branch of the royal family opposed Shaka during his lifetime as a result of his murder of their kinsman Mudli, events in the 1830s seem to have turned them back into the "Shakan" fold. Indeed, as the house of Thimuni and Mudli was the *ikohlo* branch of the Zulu royal family, they, unlike other branches such as those of Hamu or Zibhebhu whose connections to royalty predated Shaka, were precluded from laying claim to the Zulu kingship through a denial of Shaka. The *ikohlo* house conventionally could never accede to the chiefship.

It is significant that within a few years of giving his testimony to Stuart, Ndlovu led an uprising in the Maphumulo district, a sequel to the major rebellion headed by Bambatha in 1906 against the Natal colonial government. Marks suggests that chiefs such as Ndlovu acted out of feelings of "national pride and a stirring precolonial tradition," that they were, in effect, early Zulu nationalists.[144] Although the role of Dinuzulu, then Zulu king, in the events of 1906–8 is extremely difficult to specify, and although Ndlovu formally denied acting on the Zulu king's instructions, there is no doubt that he saw his actions as supportive of Dinuzulu, and himself as a bearer of the tradition of Shaka and, after him, the royalist uSuthu, who supported the claims of the house of Cetshwayo against those of Hamu and Zibhebhu.[145]

A further possible explanation for the ambiguities in Ndlovu's attitude toward Shaka lies in the claim by another of Stuart's informants, Jantshi of the Mabaso people, that Ndlovu's father, Thimuni, derived his information from Jantshi's father Nongila, and not from the family of Mudli. Indeed, the accounts by Ndlovu and Jantshi are remarkably similar. Nongila, as will be elucidated later, was a staunch Shaka man, in a way that Thimuni's immediate family may not have been.[146]

The foregoing discussion suggests that a variety of conflicting pressures were brought to bear on Thimuni and subsequently Ndlovu, in terms of the image of Shaka to which they ascribed. Before a final assessment of Ndlovu's testimony can be attempted, however, it is necessary to examine Nongila's view of Shaka, as presented by Jantshi.

Nongila was an eyewitness to the birth and accession of Shaka.[147] His story was recounted to Stuart by his son Jantshi about a month after Ndlovu's interview, at Ndlovu's instigation.[148] Jantshi's account was similar to that of Ndlovu. He asserted that Shaka was illegitimate; that no *lobolo* was ever paid; and that Nandi and Senzangakhona never married. However, he claimed that the birth of Shaka was *not* concealed.[149] Jantshi concurred with the story of Dingiswayo treating Shaka and the connection between this and the death of Senzangakhona. But Jantshi claimed that Senzangakhona died before Shaka's return to the Zulu chiefdom, and that no one was ousted when he took over. He stressed that Sigujana, Senzangakhona's heir, although touched by Shaka on precisely the spot where he was later to receive a fatal injury, died away from Shaka's presence in battle. He remarked: "It is probable that Tshaka was *offered* the position of the king" (my emphasis).[150] Jantshi's view of Shaka was one of a successful conqueror, and not of a ruthless killer. "As a matter of fact," he commented, "Tshaka did not put to death the kings and kinglets he defeated, if, when he proceeded against them, they ran away and did not show fight. He made them *izinduna* [officers]."[151] Nevertheless, Jantshi did note that Shaka frequently caused people to be put to death. He related how Shaka fed people to the vultures, but linked such acts to the maintenance of authority and discipline in the Zulu kingdom more directly than did Ndlovu. According to Jantshi, Shaka would cut off a man's ears if he did not listen—that is, obey—and he would pick out anyone wounded in the back in battle and kill him for being a coward, for running away. In Jantshi's account, Dingane was unfavorably compared with Shaka as being more venomous, treacherous, and tyrannical, and less accomplished.[152]

Nongila, Jantshi's father and informant, belonged to the inTontela *ibutho*, originally one of Senzangakhona's *amabutho* and later taken over by Shaka. It was made up of men born between about 1785 and 1790.[153] Although he "was looked on as a hereditary member of the [Zulu] tribe," Nongila's *isibongo* was Mabaso.[154] He was, moreover, a spy, highly trusted by the Zulu kings. This was a task generally reserved for members of the Zulu proper. After Shaka's assassination, Nongila remained at his post under Dingane, but later narrowly escaped death at the hands of the new king. In 1839 he crossed into Natal with Mpande, and played a key role in Mpande's campaign against Dingane. He returned with Mpande and continued in the service of the Zulu royalty until 1856 when he again fled the Zulu kingdom, just before the battle of Ndondakusuka between supporters of Mbuyazi and Cetshwayo. He was, presumably, an Mbuyazi supporter, for it seems that the family did not return to the Zulu country. These involvements all align Nongila with factions that promoted Shaka, rather than with his detractors, and indeed Jantshi recorded his father's admiration for Shaka. For Nongila, there was only one king, and that was Shaka.[155]

For his part, Jantshi, who was born around 1848, lived in the Zulu kingdom until the age of puberty, and seems to have identified closely with the Zulu proper. We know little about his subsequent experiences and his political allegiances. It is, however, significant that in his adult life he lived in Natal, and did not participate in any of the events surrounding the succession disputes. Finally, it should be noted that his testimony is marked by careful distinctions which he drew between what he was told by his father, what his father was witness to and what he heard from others, and what was gleaned from generalized hearsay. Moreover, Jantshi distinguished between his own opinions and what derived from those authorities, and freely acknowledged where his information was incomplete. Although Ndlovu observed that Jantshi was an *imbongi* of note, it is unlikely that he was a composer of praises, in the sense of an ideologue seeking to present a particular worldview. Rather, he seems to have been an *imbongi* who praised using eulogies created by others, a relayer of ideas, rather than a maker of them. He evinced a romantic attachment to "things Zulu," discernible in his testimony and demonstrated by his pilgrimage back to the old lands of the Mabaso.[156]

In summary, then, Jantshi's testimony was probably derived largely from his father. Any alterations for which he was responsible seem likely to have been accidental or random, rather than directed by the wider context in which he moved. Nongila's account, on the other hand, was probably shaped by his personal experiences. On the whole, they would have tended to influence him to present an advantageous picture of Shaka, one that was probably not far removed from the view of Shaka that he held, as a supporter of Shaka, during the king's lifetime. In so far as Nongila's knowledge and opinion of Shaka shaped that of Thimuni and, through him, that of Ndlovu, it would likewise have been in a manner sympathetic to Shaka.

The final account of Shaka's birth and accession that can be dated with some certainty to the reign of Shaka is that of Mpitikazi, recounted by his daughter Baleka to Stuart in 1919, already discussed above.[157] In Baleka's much shorter account of the birth of Shaka she asserted that Shaka was illegitimate but that Nandi was married to Senzangakhona, and that Senzangakhona did know of Shaka's existence. Baleka professed ignorance on the *lobolo* question. On the other hand, she further claimed that Shaka was not reared in the Zulu chiefdom, but by his maternal grandmother. Here, the detail in Baleka's account is significantly richer than that of the other texts, presumably because her father grew up in the same family as Shaka. On the question of Shaka's accession, Baleka merely commented that "When he [Shaka] arrived among his people his father died." Her remark does not strive for the same niceness on this point as that achieved by Ndlovu and Jantshi. Baleka narrated this story to Stuart during their second meeting, and her tone and attitude toward Shaka was markedly more restrained than in subsequent interviews. It is nonetheless significant that in what is otherwise a powerful indictment of Shaka, she did not suggest that he was a usurper, responsible for the death of his father. Indeed, when Stuart read Ndlovu's account to Baleka, she responded by saying that her father had never put forward such a version.[158]

Mpitikazi, Baleka's father and informant, was raised among the Langeni people, at the home of his mother. In fact, his mother was a close relation of Shaka's mother, Nandi. Mpitikazi was a member of Shaka's Fasimba *ibutho,* made up of youths born around 1795–8, and was thus in his late teens at the time of Shaka's accession. Mpitikazi had a somewhat checkered existence under Shaka. His career began under a cloud, as he was responsible for warning the Langeni people of his mother's house to flee when Shaka attacked them after the king's accession. Baleka describes the hopelessness of her father's plight as he sought refuge from Shaka without success. Finally, Mpitikazi turned himself in and was saved from certain death by the intercession of his maternal relative Nandi, who begged her son Shaka not to kill him. Mpitikazi went on to fight in a number of Shaka's campaigns, including the ill-fated Balule expedition to the north. With the death of Nandi in October 1827, however, Mpitikazi lost an important bulwark between himself and the Zulu king. He was, moreover, a Qwabe by birth, closely linked to Qwabe affairs. Baleka noted, for example, that her father was a skilled *imbongi* of the Qwabe chiefs. In the reign of Shaka, identification as Qwabe could be dangerous. The Qwabe chiefdom was in rebellion for much of the time and subject to brutal repressive measures.[159]

Mpitikazi died in 1888 and Baleka provides no information about his career after the death of Shaka. A few details gleaned from the text, such as Mpitikazi's marriage to a woman of Mpande's Ngcosho *ibutho,* suggest that Mpitikazi remained in the Zulu country for some time and then fled into Natal. Baleka got her name (from *ukubaleka*—to run away) as a result of her birth at the time of the battle of Ndondakusuka, when many people were in flight. She does not state which side of the conflict her family was on. The name "Baleka" would lead one to think that it was that of Mbuyazi, as his followers crossed into Natal after the defeat by Cetshwayo. This is supported by the fact that Baleka was born in the Majozi chiefdom, just inside Natal, and must have remained there for quite a while, for she remembered seeing the Majozi chief, Ngoza, in whose territory she grew up.[160] If Mpitikazi was an Mbuyazi-ite he would most probably have been exposed to strong pro-Shaka sentiments later in life.

The circumstances detailed above suggest that much of this testimony owed its form to Mpitikazi's experiences under Shaka and to the legacy of hatred left by Shaka's persecution of the Qwabe, possibly ameliorated by Mpitikazi's subsequent support for Mbuyazi. It is in these terms that Mpitikazi's version of the birth, accession, and reputation of Shaka, as relayed by Baleka, must be interpreted. Baleka noted the details of Shaka's persecution of the Qwabe, and recounted a host of gruesome tales told to her by her father about Shaka's inhumanity and wanton cruelty, including stories of the Zulu king cutting open a pregnant woman, and feeding human corpses to the vultures.[161] Her judgment of Shaka was harsh: "That man used to play around with people. A man would be killed though he had done nothing, though he had neither practised witchcraft, committed adultery nor stole."[162] For Mpitikazi and Baleka, Shaka was best summed up by this one of his praises: "The violently unrestrained one who is like the ear of an elephant."[163] Finally, they regarded Shaka, who refused to father children, and whom they credited with having killed his own mother for concealing a child of his, as an animal: "A person like Tshaka is like a wild beast, a creature which does not live with its own young, its male offspring."[164]

The three accounts considered above—that of Mudli's family in so far as it is contained in Ndlovu's account (together with that of Sipika, a member of Senzangakhona's entourage), Nongila's as given by Jantshi, and possibly relayed by Ndlovu as well, and Mpitikazi's as related by his daughter Baleka—offer us three views of Shaka: a complex, even ambiguous, view from a related section of the royal house, a positive view through the eyes of a loyal servitor, and a negative view from a foe. In all three accounts there is a discernible core content that relates back to the reign of Shaka as well as identifiable signs of later accretions and modifications. The core is open to structural analyses such as that of Golan which identifies in the Shaka stories a set of clichés composed of epic motifs. However, there are also historically contested elements of the story of Shaka which demand attention.

The most significant feature of all three accounts, despite the different allegiances of their narrators, is that they all claim that Shaka was a son of Senzangakhona. In other words, whereas Golan considers the tension in Shaka narratives to lie in the existence of two different notions of legitimacy—an old pre-state (and pre-Shakan) notion of blood inheritance and a new state notion of the right to rule on a merit basis—in these accounts the focus can be seen to fall on the kinds of argumentation that were possible within a paradigm that asserted birthright as crucial. The key difference between the accounts lies in the degree of explanation they offered for the irregular circumstances surrounding Shaka's birth and his precise status as a son of Senzangakhona. Ndlovu and Jantshi grounded the issue in the argument that Shaka was born before Senzangakhona was of marriageable age.[165] Ndlovu recalled his father Thimuni saying: "A Zulu chief does not father children."[166] This was given as the reason why the birth of Shaka was concealed. In conversation with Ndlovu, another informant, Munyana, drew an analogy between this practice and the custom of a leopard: ". . . when say three young are born, one of them a male, the male is taken away and hidden by its mother and suckled where hidden, for fear lest the father should kill it."[167] Ndlovu agreed that Zulu kings (and lions) followed this practice.

The claim that Shaka was born before Senzangakhona was of marriageable age was essential to the rest of their story of Shaka's birth, for it formed the rationale for the separation of father and son. Both Ndlovu and Jantshi claimed that Senzangakhona's chief adviser, Mudli, arranged for the child to be born in the Langeni chiefdom.[168] Although the details vary, in their accounts it was Mudli's actions that lay at the root of the estrangement between Shaka and his father. This emphasis clearly owes its existence in part to the informants' privileged access to the testimony of Mudli's own son, Thimuni. The story that Senzangakhona was not yet of marriageable age and, more particularly, the details of Mudli's intervention thus provided a specific explanation for the unusual circumstances of Shaka's childhood and his status, an explanation that was entirely absent in Baleka's more bald account of events. The claims of Ndlovu and Jantshi that Shaka was the son of Senzangakhona are thus much stronger than that of Baleka, which is contradictory and unsatisfactory on this score. Moreover, the contrast between Baleka's failure to offer detailed comment on Shaka's birth and her comprehensive account of his childhood away from the Zulu chiefdom was open to interpretation as evidence that Shaka may not have been of Zulu origin. Interestingly, none of the accounts attempts to argue the case for the legitimacy of Shaka's accession in terms of the house position of his mother within Senzangakhona's household, which would have been the case if a marriage between Senzangakhona and Nandi had been widely recognized.

It is significant that while the testimonies of both Ndlovu and Jantshi emanated from sources generally well disposed toward Shaka, neither informant tried to claim that Shaka was legitimate, nor did they attempt to hide the unusual circumstances of his upbringing. Indeed, obfuscations of that nature would have been impossible in Shaka's time, for it seems that Shaka was not known at the Zulu court before his accession. He did not speak the same dialect as the rest of the royal family, while his half-siblings were known to have been born of a Qwabe father, and all these facts were widely advertised by factions opposed to his accession. Instead of trying to deny these points, the accounts by Sipika, Thimuni, and Nongila relayed through Ndlovu and Jantshi sought to account for the anomalies in the Shaka story. The fact that they did this is a function of the limits of credibility within which they were constrained to operate in the early nineteenth century, whereas accounts that date from later periods, such as that of Mhuyi (which cannot be traced back to Shakan times), are not similarly confined.

The versions of the Shaka story relayed by Ndlovu and Jantshi offered a similarly sophisticated response to the allegations that Shaka killed his father and his father's rightful heir. By stressing that Shaka was indirectly behind their deaths, these versions contrived to invest Shaka with magical powers, at the same time neutralizing the worst of the allegation. This was achieved by at once admitting *some* involvement, but also by clearly establishing a satisfactory distance between Shaka personally and the deaths. As with the circumstances of his birth, this suggests that an outright denial of Shaka's involvement in Senzangakhona's death would not have washed with his new subjects. Similarly, neither of these versions of the story of Shaka sought to *deny* the so-called atrocity incidents. Rather, they again attempted to neutralize them by accounting for them.

As was noted above, however, the component elements of the productions of Shaka by Ndlovu and Jantshi were not identical. Jantshi, more readily than Ndlovu, found explanations for the atrocities. Jantshi's claims that Shaka was not hidden from Senzangakhona, and that Shaka was not yet in the Zulu chiefdom when Senzangakhona died, were also much less ambiguous than Ndlovu's remarks that Shaka's birth was concealed from Senzangakhona and that he was already present in the Zulu chiefdom when his father died. These differences presumably relate to the operation of the Mudli factor in Ndlovu's account, giving that account origins in a bias less favorable to Shaka. Ndlovu's version can thus be seen as containing a residue of the factionalism within the royal house dating back to the reign of Shaka, overlain by the *ikohlo* branch's subsequent alignment with factions that promoted a positive image of Shaka. Under these circumstances it is possible that the Mudli factor, which could be interpreted as evidence of Mudli having conspired against Shaka, was given a slightly different emphasis in narration by Ndlovu and used to provide additional interior evidence for the story of Shaka as having been hidden from Senzangakhona.

Baleka's account, on the other hand, lends itself to being read as derived from a production of Shaka by his enemies during his lifetime. Mpitikazi's alignment with Mbuyazi after Shaka's death might be expected to have caused him to tone down his criticisms of Shaka. The only area of the testimony in which this is discernible is that of the circumstances of Shaka's birth and accession. Any claims that Shaka was not the son of Senzangakhona, or that he was responsible for the death of his father, would have undermined Mbuyazi. While Baleka's testimony otherwise indicted Shaka in the most severe terms, it was ambiguous on these two crucial questions.

Finally, we need to consider to what extent Ndlovu, Jantshi, and Baleka, as well as Thimuni, Sipika, Nongila, and Mpitikazi, used the story of Shaka metaphorically. Whereas Golan suggests that oral versions of the Shaka story are metaphors for changes in the succession practices from a birth to a merit basis, this discussion indicates rather that in these stories Shaka was a metaphor for discussion of the relationship between order and chaos. In all the versions, Shaka is always the embodiment of both: at once "the violently unrestrained one" who fathered no children, and the highly accomplished leader who imposed rigorous discipline. The versions differ in the way the Shaka story was used metaphorically as a means of discussing the complex relationship between social order and chaos. Tied to the relationship between order and chaos is the equally important issue of the role of a ruler in society. Each tradition offers a view of the nature of rulership and sovereignty. The equation of Shaka's "monstrous" features with transcendent political authority was a shared characteristic of all the traditions. We see in these traditions the origins of a metaphorical reading of the story of Shaka that was, as we shall see in later chapters, subsequently adopted and reworked in certain central, colonial appropriations of Shaka.

Before we move on to a discussion of the appropriation of Shaka in colonial texts and in written form, we should note that African oral productions of Shaka in the 1820s were not confined to the Zulu kingdom.

Indigenous perceptions of Shaka in the frontier region, 1827–1828[169]

As early as May 1825, the colonial administration at the Cape was beginning to wrestle with the "Fetcanie problem"—"tribe[s] of savages . . . advancing on the frontier of the colony."[170] The first recorded mention of the involvement of Shaka in the disturbances immediately north of the border occurred on July 25, 1827, when the landdrost in Somerset, W.M. Mackay, interviewed a "Fetcanie" refugee. The informant claimed that his people, the "Masutu" and "Manquana," under "Maheta" and "Mathiana," were defeated by Shaka, who had then taken their cattle. This, the informant claimed, led his people, the "Fetcanie," to attack others for their cattle.[171] The report of this interview was subsequently discussed at the highest level in Cape Town, and the agency of Shaka duly noted.[172] Three weeks later, Lieutenant-Colonel Henry Somerset, commandant of the frontier, recorded a conversation he had had with the "Tambookie" chief, "Powana," who said that he could not return to his country as long as Shaka continued his wars against the "Fetcanie." Powana continued: "Chaka is driving these people on and as long as he does I cannot remain . . . I heard it [the fact that Shaka was advancing] from the Fetcanie."[173]

George Thompson's *Travels and Adventures in Southern Africa* was published in 1827, and by August that year was being read by colonial officials.[174] James King's description of Shaka as "a cruel and despotic monster" which appeared in the *South African Commercial Advertiser* was reproduced in Thompson's *Travels*, and although the report contained no mention of Zulu campaigns anywhere near the colony, it is possible that it intersected with and reinforced the news from African communities on the Cape frontier of Shaka as the cause of the disturbances.[175] Nonetheless, it is notable that, although in this period the administration's frontier policy was determined by this identification of Shaka as the force behind the frontier disturbances, the officials did not set any store by King's report, nor did they adopt anything of King's hysterical rhetoric.[176] In other words, the colonial administration's understanding of Shaka as the agency behind the disturbances was not, as Cobbing claims, the result of the Natal traders' propaganda.[177] Rather, the association of the name of Shaka with the upheaval on the frontier was reported as coming straight out of the mouths of the inhabitants of the frontier region.

Cobbing's work suggests that these reports by local chiefs attributing the upheavals on the frontier to Shaka were colonial fabrications. His argument that the colonial officials invented the idea of Shaka's attacks to cover up the fact that the frontier was in turmoil as a result of colonial procurement policies is both far-fetched and reliant on the existence of an unlikely web of conspiracy.[178] Furthermore, it takes no account of the crucial fact of the administration's skeptical approach to King's attempts to present Shaka as a similar kind of threat. On balance, the reported conversations with local leaders suggest that the African communities on the frontier viewed the advent of Shaka with considerable fear and trepidation.

History as alibi; alibi as ideology

This chapter has shown that the image of Shaka-the-monster and the idea of "Zulu tyranny" only became typical of the representations of the early traders after Shaka's death. Even then the negative depiction of Shaka was no mere invention of the traders, but was drawn from a repertoire of ideas held by the Africans among whom the traders lived and traveled. In the 1820s they were well entrenched in the oral traditions of both Shaka's supporters and his enemies, although in different forms. In 1829, however, following his death, these images became for the first time dominant in both Cape Town and the Zulu kingdom.

Of course, after the 1820s, African versions of the life of Shaka continued to be generated in diverse forms. The range of testimonies about Shaka in the *James Stuart Archive* testifies to this diversity and continued interest in Shaka, as do the many versions of Shaka's *izibongo* brilliantly discussed in Malaba's doctoral dissertation.[179] The traditions and the praise poems emphasize the disruptions of Shaka's reign, with an accumulation of detail upon detail, frequently in powerful poetic forms, which convey a strong sense of their authenticity and integrity as African productions, rather than the distortions of their recorders. While these traditions and the praise poems are extremely difficult to provenance—each requires the kind of analysis done on the three traditions discussed above—the cumulative weight of their insistence on Shaka imaged as chaos and order, and, as Malaba has shown, the reinforcement of these points of content in choice of literary devices, together with the expressive play of the language used, make a strong argument for the location of the roots of this image in African contexts. We need to be cautious about the assumption that it was a convenient, racist European invention.

Cobbing and the many other scholars of history—including the current Zulu king[180]—who favor the latter course argue a familiar case: that in South Africa history is distorted to cover up past misdeeds and to legitimize conditions in the present. In that form, history becomes a component of the dominant ideology. The implication of this is that it happens in a mechanical and reductionist fashion, that ideologues "invented" the version of the past which best served white interests, and that this "invention" was then incorporated wholesale into a dominant ideology.

The argument presented here is that, like alibis, histories and ideologies that are successful resonate in a body of information known to both their promoters and those whom they seek to persuade. Moreover, although any one version of the past may be the best-known one, or any one ideology the dominant one, neither exists independently of other versions or views. Rather, the struggle between dominant and subordinate ideologies and versions of the past is part of each one's *raison d'être*.

New versions of the past, no less than the ideologies they seek to underpin, must articulate different perspectives on the past in such a way that their potential antagonisms are neutralized, and the argument is convincing. The various elements that make up a version of history which serves well any particular ideology must incorporate and neutralize the arguments of the opposition. Since any ideology is always in a state of being struggled over—that is, is always "in process"—so, too, is the historical account constantly shifting to take cognizance of the changing terrain of the struggle, and the subtle elaborations and shifts in the argument of the opposition.

The men who would be Shaka:
Shaka as a model for the
Natal native administration

> **"** *. . . and in any place where they fight, a man who knows how to drill men can always be king. We shall go to those parts and say to any king we find—'D'you want to vanquish your foes?' and we will show him how to drill men for that we know better than anything else. Then we will subvert that King and seize his Throne and establish a Dynasty.* **"**

(Rudyard Kipling, "The Man Who Would Be King"[1])

Following Shaka's assassination in 1828 the character of the first Zulu king was viciously maligned by the selfsame traders who for so much of the 1820s had sought to persuade Cape mercantile interests of the excellence of his disposition. The reasons for this reversal have already been discussed. In 1836, Isaacs' two-volume *Travels and Adventures in Eastern Africa* was published, and it established a definitive portrait of Shaka as a duplicitous, savage despot. This view, sometimes tinged with faint hints of admiration, prevailed in colonial society for much of the nineteenth century, and was the basis of almost the entire corpus of fiction about Shaka by white writers that followed.[2] But, as this chapter will show, important dimensions of the meaning of the image of Shaka were added by developments within native administration in the second half of the nineteenth century.

When the Zulu king Mpande died in 1872, his son Cetshwayo was installed as the new ruler of the independent Zulu state. Deep in heart of the kingdom the installation ceremony was presided over by Theophilus Shepstone, secretary for native affairs (SNA) in the neighboring British colony of Natal. While it is remarkable in itself that a colonial administrator officiated at the installation of the monarch of an independent state, of even greater interest is the fact that both

Shepstone and the Zulu councilors who invited him to participate in the ceremony understood that he did so in the persona of the "monstrous tyrant," Shaka. In a message to the Natal authorities, the Zulu leaders claimed "that by Zulu law Mr. Shepstone represents Chaka, and is therefore in the place of Cetywayo's father; that he was the witness before whom Cetywayo was proclaimed as heir by Panda more than ten years ago, and that he represents the British Government."[3] Shepstone described his participation in similar terms: "I came as Chaka . . . I was commissioned by the Zulus, and by the Government that was superior to the Zulus, and I had my own special rank besides; no-one could contest that right with me and no one had ventured to contest it."[4]

The first part of this chapter focuses on Shepstone's assumption of the mantle of Shaka. It reviews his role in events leading up to and during the installation, and goes on to establish the rationales of both Shepstone and the Zulu leaders in casting the Natal secretary for native affairs in the role of Shaka. Here the focus is on the way in which a dramatic script about authority and sovereignty was authored by Shepstone and also—but not always in harmony with his view—by Cetshwayo and his senior councilors. The central argument put forward is that Shepstone drew on existing African conceptions of rulership articulated in the image of Shaka to establish a model for colonial domination and native administration, and as a legitimization of colonialism. Shepstone's Shaka differed thus from the highly negative image nurtured by many of his fellow colonists, but was not wholly irreconcilable with their ideas.

The chapter goes on to look at the way in which Shepstone's reading of Shaka was overwhelmed in the run-up to the Anglo-Zulu War of 1879, as the authorities sought to use Zulu despotism as an excuse to go to war with Cetshwayo. In the aftermath of the war, the imprisonment of Cetshwayo and the Zulu civil conflict that followed, the situation again reversed itself as the authorities, notably Shepstone, argued once again that the successful administration of Zululand depended on the Zulu monarchy and the patrimony of Shaka.

The mantle of Shaka

The appropriation and manipulation of symbols and signs that lay at the core of the colonial encounter have been the subject of a number of influential studies stimulated by the work of Terence Ranger on "the invention of tradition," and most recently extended in exciting new directions by historical anthropologists.[5] These studies suggest that events and actions such as the installation were not neutral, nor did they have inherent meanings. Rather, such acts acquired meaning and significance according to the political and cultural premises of those involved in their representation and interpretation.

The creative activity entailed in the acquisition of meaning or the "invention of tradition" in these events has been a major focus of such studies. Less investigated are the constraints that operated to limit the scope of the imaginative acts of colonial power. This chapter seeks to extend the work on "the invention of tradition" to encompass analysis of the limitations on "invention" in a particular context. The explication of a symbolic act such as the installation demands historical inquiry, not only into the events of the past, but also into the logic that underlay interpretations of the event. This approach allows us to examine the installation, and more particularly the role accorded in it to Shaka, in terms of the cultural logic of the Natal colonial officials on the one side, and the African population of the Zulu kingdom on the other. These logics themselves are understood to be the products of particular historical processes which set limits on the extent of their possible manipulation.

The two logics were invoked by Shepstone, and to various degrees and in different combinations in a range of settings they became enmeshed with each other in the representation of Shaka. Investigation of the historical process of their intertwining allows us to identify the conditions of and limitations on the representations of Shaka in Natal and the Zulu kingdom in the mid- and later nineteenth century, and also their connection to the development of what was known as "native policy" in this period. The genealogy of the image of Shaka is thus shown to have gained its "powers" not simply through reiteration or manipulation in historical and fictional texts (both oral and written), but through its inscription in the discourses of power and domination of both the Zulu imperium and the Natal native administration.

Jean and John Comaroff have argued that in relation to the colonized the final objective of "generations of colonizers . . . whether it be in the name of a 'benign', civilizing imperialism or in cynical pursuit of their labor power . . . had been to colonize their consciousness with the axioms and aesthetics of an alien culture."[6] This chapter reveals other—even opposite—processes at work. It highlights the way Shepstone sought, in his terms, to shield the African population of Natal from precisely such alien influences, and tries, through a focus on the image of Shaka, to tease out the context, nature, and significance of his "conservatory" efforts. To emphasize Shepstone's appropriation of the "axioms and aesthetics" of the indigenous culture is not to suggest that he facilitated the preservation of such features intact. In fact, Shepstone intervened quite extensively in African "custom." The argument here is that he did so in a way that was informed, but also constrained, by what he understood to be the cultural logic of the society concerned.

The Comaroffs preface their study of the colonization of consciousness, *Of Rev-*

elation and Revolution, with an evocative account of the London Missionary Society's gift to their mission at Dithakong of a clock whose hours were struck by carved wooden soldiers. The authors draw out the way in which this proclaimed the value of time and symbolized the imposition of "order" and "civilization," subjecting the local Tswana community to the bondage of its rhythms. By way of contrast, this chapter shows how Shepstone and his system of African administration sought in indigenous systems of thought a model of order and control—a model represented by Shaka. It also explores the way that the Shepstone system appropriated to itself and its project of domination indigenous rhythms of time, in which cause and effect were not chronologically determined, but rather in which prophecy and preordination, recounted retrospectively, functioned to explain and justify. Here we begin to look at the way in which prophecy—a central motif in many African oral historical narratives[7]—reverses the idea of re-inventing the past by predetermining the future. The focus on the appropriation of indigenous concepts by the colonizers offers us a fresh perspective on the processes of the "colonization of consciousness."

Shepstone "as Chaka"

In 1873, following the completion of the rituals prior to the public acknowledgement of Mpande's death, Zulu leaders sent a delegation of three envoys together with Cetshwayo's white adviser, John Dunn,[8] to Theophilus Shepstone—or "Somtsewu" as he was known in *isiZulu*—the Natal secretary for native affairs. The delegation requested him, as "Father to the King's children," to participate in the installation of the heir, Cetshwayo, or as they put it, "to establish what is wanting among the Zulu people."[9] In a subsequent message, the Zulu leaders stressed that the invitation to Shepstone was based on Shepstone's witnessing of the nomination of Cetshwayo as Mpande's heir at a ceremony twelve years earlier, in terms of which "by Zulu law Mr. Shepstone represents Chaka."[10]

Two months later this request took Shepstone to Cetshwayo's residence in the Zulu kingdom, accompanied by a large retinue consisting of the Royal Durban Artillery, two field pieces, a military band, a substantial Volunteer Corps, and a party of "three hundred Natives under their several headmen,"[11] as well as a large marquee, a crown, and a cloak of scarlet and gold—the trappings with which he would conduct the "coronation" ceremony.

Shepstone's installation of Cetshwayo has largely been ignored by historians, who tend to dismiss the event as an empty imperial gesture.[12] Jeff Guy describes Shepstone's official report of the proceedings as a "typically long, obfuscating and vainglorious despatch."[13] It is indeed self-inflated, but in so far as it reveals

Shepstone's understanding of the possibilities of exploiting notions of sovereignty prevalent in the Zulu kingdom within the terms of indigenous cultural logic, the document is a complex and important text. Shepstone's narrative of the installation events reveals aspects both of his rationale for participating in the ceremony and of his understanding of the dramatics of power.

Shepstone planned to enter the Zulu kingdom, taking a route past Cetshwayo's residence, and there, in Shepstone's words, "take possession of him, and present him to the assembled nation and then proceed to install him as King."[14] This attempt to assert a form of complete British suzerainty was preempted when part of the ceremony was carried out while the British expedition was still *en route* to the designated site. In the days immediately preceding the ceremony over which Shepstone was to preside, Mpande's principal officer, Masiphula kaMamba of the emGazini people, proclaimed Cetshwayo king in a ceremony held in the ritually significant *emakhosini* area, alongside the graves of the early kings and the site where Shaka had been installed.[15] This earlier ceremony, and the events surrounding it, have also received little attention from scholars.

On the day of installation presided over by Masiphula, all the rituals of investiture were completed, including the manufacture of new national symbols (such as the *inkatha,* a coil of grass and bodily substances representing the unity of the nation), the fortifying of the new king, and the rendering of the royal *bayete* salute. Then the majority of assembled people dispersed back to their homes.[16]

When Shepstone arrived at Mthonjaneni, overlooking the *emakhosini,* he found it "ominously" deserted. In his report Shepstone confessed that the "situation was embarrassing," and he demanded a full explanation and some appeasement from the Zulu authorities before he would proceed.[17] Shepstone noted in his report, without any further explanation, that at this point he received news of the death of Masiphula, the chief officiant at the preemptive ceremony. Further messages were exchanged with Zulu envoys, who assured Shepstone that the earlier ceremony was no slight on him, nor a substitute for any portion of the forthcoming "coronation." Shepstone reported the messengers as saying that no one could carry out the actual installation but himself, for "I came as Chaka."[18]

At this point Cetshwayo and his advisers proposed a change of venue for the ceremony over which Shepstone was to preside, to a place removed from the ritually significant *emakhosini*—"the place of kings" and the site of many royal graves—to a venue close to one of Cetshwayo's major military establishments, emLambongwenya. The recording in Shepstone's text of these maneuvers by the Zulu leaders allows us to begin to discern something of the thinking behind the installation from the Zulu side. The change of venue to a less significant site effectively downgraded Shepstone's role in the proceedings. Shepstone's account reveals that a strategy of containment was implemented by the Zulu rulers in a number of other ways as well.

The secretary for native affairs, fully cognizant of the ritual significance of the *emakhosini,* initially refused to accede to the proposed change of venue. Shepstone suggested that his reluctance was connected to doubts about Cetshwayo's intentions toward his expedition. In response to such allegations, Cetshwayo, according to Shepstone, commented: "Let my father come . . . and let me act the parricide they wished to paint me; by killing him I should have done nothing towards vanquishing the English. Chaka was master of all the black people, but even he said the English were his superiors."[19] Thus he explained his own actions in terms of a prediction made forty-five years earlier by Shaka. This prediction was given as the guarantee of Shepstone's safety in 1873 and as an affirmation of his paternal status. Shepstone's reference to the prediction through the words of Cetshwayo was itself an invocation of the past in a manner resonant with nineteenth-century indigenous historical narratives.[20] Reassured, the expedition finally moved on to the new site proposed for the installation, thus conceding the first round. But the struggle over the precise role Shepstone was to play in the ceremony was not yet over.

The next wrangle occurred over which party would be the first to pay its respects to the other. Shepstone called on Cetshwayo to come up to his camp. The Zulu king responded by pleading that he was indisposed because of a swollen leg. Finally Cetshwayo moved up to his nearby establishment of emLambongwenya. Shepstone then urged him to come the whole way to his encampment. Here Shepstone's and Cetshwayo's accounts differ, with each claiming it was the other who gave way first.[21] Shepstone sought to precipitate matters by sending a carriage to fetch Cetshwayo, thus circumventing the latter's excuse regarding his indisposition. When Cetshwayo finally did pay a visit to Shepstone—and it is not at all clear whether this was the first visit of the series or not—he did so by walking behind the carriage, thus refusing to be taken up by the conveyance but also, through the act of walking, revealing that his leg was in fine shape. When Shepstone began to show annoyance at the possibility that he was being made a fool of, Cetshwayo hastened, or at least Shepstone claimed that he did, to demonstrate in private that the injury was real. Cetshwayo seemed to be treading a careful line between showing public independence of Shepstone and privately endeavoring to mollify him sufficiently for the ceremony to continue.

Once Cetshwayo had visited his encampment, Shepstone agreed to go to emLambongwenya to hammer out an agreement concerning British support for the Zulu in the latter's border disputes with the Transvaal Republic. At this point, the initiative seems to have passed into Shepstone's hands. A magnificent firework display the night before the installation was his opening salvo, and he continued in a style of high panoply. On the following day, September 1, 1873, in the presence of some ten thousand warriors (considerably fewer people than were present at the ceremony presided over by Masiphula), Shepstone caused a large marquee—housing the many presents for the king—to be erected in the cattle byre of em-Lambongwenya. At the expedition's nearby encampment a procession was formed, with Shepstone at the head, followed by the brass band, the two field pieces, and the column of mounted Volunteers. The procession entered emLambongwenya and took up positions at the top end, near the marquee. Shepstone, speaking in fluent *isiZulu,* and pausing throughout to obtain vocal assent for all his propositions from the councilors and nobles around him, read out a series of "laws," specifying conditions for the passing of death sentences and prohibiting the indiscriminate shedding of blood in the Zulu kingdom.

Then, followed by the most important European officials present, Shepstone led Cetshwayo, accompanied only by his *inceku* (a special personal attendant), into the marquee. The flaps of the tent were drawn and guarded by two sentries of the Royal Durban Artillery. "Cetywayo had not in any way interfered with, or suggested any portion of the program," commented Shepstone,

> but he was anxious that, in accordance with the theory upon which we had hitherto acted, I should at some part of the ceremony take possession of him, and so transform him that his own people would not know him; it must not be done in public; the Zulus had given him over to me; I must take him from their sight a minor and present him to them a man; I must take him as a Prince, and restore him to them their King.[22]

Inside the marquee, Cetshwayo was then "transformed" by Shepstone's placing the scarlet-and-gold mantle (borrowed from the wardrobe of an amateur dramatic group in Pietermaritzburg)[23] on his shoulders and putting the crown—a design derived from a Zulu warrior's headdress, "improved upon by the master tailor of the 75th Regiment, and signify[ing] the Zulu trappings of war subdued to a peaceful purpose"—on his head. Meanwhile a carpet had been spread outside the tent in a conspicuous spot facing the people, and on this stood the "Chair of State," with another of a less pretentious nature placed alongside it for Shepstone.[24]

At a word of command the marquee was opened, the sentries stood to attention, and Shepstone led forth Cetshwayo, duly seating him on his throne. After a pause lasting a few minutes he rose and presented the king to his brothers, his councilors, and his nobles, pointing out to them that "he, who a few moments before had been but a minor and a Prince, had now become a man and a King."[25]

The band struck up, heralds went among the people proclaiming Cetshwayo as king, the military escort stood to attention, and the Durban Artillery fired a salute of seventeen guns. Shepstone then handed over to Cetshwayo the tent, the chair, and the carpet. With a final gesture designed to ensure the sanction of Shaka for the proceedings, the official party went to pay a visit to "a little kraal named Shaka's saddle, to interview Shaka's sister,"[26] the only surviving member of the first Zulu king's immediate family.

The final dispute of the ceremony was about whose heralds would go out to inform the people about the new laws. Shepstone wanted the laws widely proclaimed in his presence, to prevent their being stifled by the nobles. Cetshwayo agreed, but wanted it done by Shepstone's people, not his own. In the end, it was settled that heralds from both parties would go, Cetshwayo's to make the actual proclamation, Shepstone's "to correct and supply the omissions."[27]

Shepstone's account reveals that the meaning and significance of the series of events leading up to the installation, and the drama of the ceremony itself, were thus in part contested, and in part agreed upon. In interpreting his actions as "taking possession" of Cetshwayo and "transforming" him, Shepstone was claiming to have accomplished the quintessential colonial gesture. He subsequently asserted that his "crowning" of Cetshwayo was implicitly recognized by the king as a mark of British suzerainty over the Zulu kingdom. Shepstone's own report, however, suggests that Cetshwayo had maneuvered to avoid precisely this construction, while Cetshwayo's accounts of the installation and other subsequent statements confirm this. Cetshwayo specifically stated that Shepstone had acknowledged that he, Cetshwayo, was recognized as king of the Zulu people *first* by the Zulu. Cetshwayo reported Shepstone as saying: "Here is your king, you have recognized him as such, and now I do also, in the name of the Queen of England. Your kings have often met violent deaths by the hand of your own people, and if you kill this one, we shall require his blood at your hands."[28] This statement makes it clear that, while Cetshwayo resisted some of the interpretations, like Shepstone he accepted others, notably those that conferred British support and protection.

The last act of the installation expedition took place the next day, when Shepstone paid his farewell visit to the king. "A remarkable incident occurred during this conversation," recorded Shepstone.

Uhamu, who has always been looked upon as the King's brother, and for some time before the installation, as his rival, said he wished to take advantage of my presence to explain publicly what his real position in Zululand was, for though it was well-known to the Zulus it was not known to the white inhabitants of Natal and of the Transvaal Republic. In both these countries he had been frequently accused of designing to usurp Cetywayo's place; and if it were not that Cetywayo and the Zulus well knew that such a thing was impossible, these accusations would long ago have cost him his life. He then went on to explain that, although he was really Panda's son, he was legally the son of Panda's deceased brother, and that he already possessed all the rank and property, namely that which belonged to Unziba, which he could claim, that he had no right to claim anything that belonged to Panda's family; and that, before any such right could accrue to him, every male member of that family in Zululand and Natal, and even he who is in the Transvaal, must die and leave no son behind. All present listened attentively to this statement, and earnestly assented to it; Cetywayo said he wished to assure me that it was strictly true, and he was anxious that it should be known.[29]

Shepstone offered no further explanation for this declaration by Hamu. He returned to Natal, and when his report of the installation was completed in 1875 he sent a copy to Cetshwayo.[30]

The "coronation" drama seems at first glance to be a classic example of the accoutrements of "civilization" being brought to bear as the opening gambit in the colonization of the consciousness of the people of the Zulu kingdom, in the manner elegantly explicated in other contexts by the Comaroffs. However, the maneuverings by Cetshwayo as revealed in Shepstone's own text point to another, rather different, reading of these events. The first step in clarifying that reading is to establish the Zulu leaders' reasons for soliciting Shepstone's presence at the installation. The second step is to draw out Shepstone's rationale for participating in the ceremony. Finally, we shall examine the Zulu leaders' motivation for conferring on Shepstone the mantle of Shaka, as well as Shepstone's reasons for accepting it.

The Zulu leaders' reasons for inviting Shepstone to the ceremony[31]

The Zulu rulers calculated that the invitation to Shepstone to install Cetshwayo would draw the British into a longstanding border dispute between the Zulu kingdom and the Transvaal over the Ncome River area. Cetshwayo (and, indeed, Hamu, whose territories abutted the disputed area) hoped that the establishment of a special relationship between the Zulu kingdom and Natal would contain Boer encroachments on the northwestern flank. The Zulu envoys who bore the original invitation noted that "Chaka many years ago sent an embassy to the Cape, and thereby decided which way the Zulus should look, and they have determined to look only as their Chief Chaka directed them"[32]—in other words, toward the Cape and British power. Indeed, this claim to a connection dating back to Shaka was repeatedly invoked by the Zulu leaders in the course of the next decade as they sought British support against the Boers.[33] We observe here the use by the envoys of the notion of Shaka's vision as determining events in the future to support their argument. When Shepstone cited Cetshwayo as explaining his actions in terms of Shaka's foresight, he was, it seems, using a trope rooted in indigenous historical narratives.

Cetshwayo perceived correctly that the idea of a "special relationship," which the Zulu rulers needed, would appear desirable to Shepstone for other reasons, and that it would prove an irresistible bait to lure the British into involvement in the border dispute. Had Shepstone declined, it seems likely that Cetshwayo would have reversed his policy of using the British against the Boers. On Mpande's death the Zulu leaders had also sent cattle to the Boers and had reputedly invited them to install Cetshwayo.[34] When questioned on the matter by the British, the Zulu leaders denied that this other message was a "coronation" invitation.[35] It is difficult to know what to make of this exchange, but it does lend itself to the interpretation that the Zulu leaders were hedging their bets, and speaks to the imperative in Zulu foreign policy at this time of gaining the support of a powerful neighbor.

The involvement of Shepstone (or, possibly, the Boers) in Cetshwayo's installation served the further purpose of making it difficult for Natal (or the Transvaal in the alternative scenario) subsequently to promote the claims of another candidate living with the Zulu kingdom's neighbors. As it turned out, it was Shepstone and the British who became embroiled in this strategy, but it would have had a similar outcome if it had been the Boers, although Boer participation would probably have proved especially costly to the northwestern border royal, Hamu.

The Natal government had long been associated with attempts to intervene in the Zulu succession. At the time of the announcement of Mpande's death, rumors abounded that Mbuyazi, one of Cetshwayo's brothers, who was thought to have been killed in the 1856 battle at Ndondakusuka, was still alive and being kept by the British to be promoted as a rival nominee.[36] Shepstone's was seen as the guiding hand behind these plans. Indeed, Mtshayankomo, the son of Mpande's *imbongi*, narrated a story in which an omen appeared to Mpande before his death, in the form of a buck: "It was said that the buck had been sent by Somsewu to hold back (godhla) the people of Mpande. It was said that Mbuyazi was still alive. It was said that this strange event had been caused by Somsewu, and that he had caused it on behalf of Mbuyazi."[37] Again we note the device of prediction—the omen—being used in Mtshayankomo's retrospective account (given in 1922) to explain subsequent events in his narrative, namely the accusation that Shepstone was involved in the promotion of rival candidates.

Mbuyazi was not the only rival whom Cetshwayo's supporters feared on the eve of his installation. Five other sons of Mpande were sheltering in Natal, while Hamu kaNzibe was another powerful possible candidate who had already clashed with Cetshwayo.[38] As discussed in an earlier chapter, Hamu's genealogical father was Nzibe, a half-brother of Shaka and a full brother of Mpande, but his biological father was Mpande.[39] During his reign, Mpande had caused marks of special respect to be shown to his late full brother Nzibe, Hamu's father. Nzibe was praised on occasions when the Zulu kings were praised, and it was claimed that Nzibe had enjoyed a special status as the "senior" son of Senzangakhona. Hamu guarded jealously his status as a "great" prince. He was viewed as a power that rivaled Cetshwayo. "Cetshwayo never went to KwaMfemfe [Nzibe's and, later, Hamu's residence]," noted a contemporary. "He never set foot there, for it was clear that Hamu was another king." Even in Mpande's time, Hamu enjoyed special privileges that acknowledged his status. Hamu carried out his own *umkhosi*, had his own *isigodlo*, and called up his own forces, all the marks of kingship.[40]

Shepstone's account of the installation reveals a struggle between Cetshwayo and certain of his senior councilors. This struggle also underlay the final act of the installation—the speech by Hamu—and in order to be able to make sense of his speech it is necessary to go back to reconsider the issue of the earlier "preemptive" ceremony carried out by Masiphula.

One possible reading of this earlier ceremony is that the Zulu rulers never really intended to involve Shepstone in the ritual heart of the installation, but merely offered the British a subsidiary but public role, sanctioning what had already taken place. Indeed, this is close to the way in which Cetshwayo represented Shepstone's involvement when, in later years, the Zulu king discussed his installation during an appeal to be restored to his kingdom. However, Cetshwayo did acknowledge that Shepstone was greeted with the royal *bayete* salute in 1873.[41] In response to a question put to him by the Cape Commission on Native Laws and Customs of 1881, as to whether he in "anyway acknowledge[d] the authority of Shepstone" over him, Cetshwayo was translated as answering that "when his father died, he sent messages with a large ox to Shepstone, to report it to him, and to say that he wished Shepstone to see about the country being settled under him because the Zulu nation was a relation of the English."[42] It may well have suited Cetshwayo, constructing as he was his arguments after the collapse of the Zulu power, to acknowledge a British role in the installation that he might have been less ready to admit in 1873. Even allowing for such pressures, Cetshwayo's testimony seems to accord Shepstone an important role in the proceedings. Indeed, it is unlikely that Shepstone would have agreed to participate in the ceremony if he thought he would not play the central role, and it seems further unlikely that, given Shepstone's famous intelligence network, he would not have heard of advance preparations for a preemptive ceremony, had such a ceremony been on the royal agenda from the start.

While it is probable that the Zulu leaders planned to contain the extent and significance of Shepstone's participation, and that Shepstone hoped to expand on it as much as possible, elements of evidence available from the testimony of Mtshayankomo kaMagolwana, a member of the inGobamakhosi *ibutho* which was present for the ceremonials, suggest that the decision to carry out an earlier ceremony was prompted by a possible challenge to the succession by another claimant, one who was thought to have been preferred, or at least condoned, by Shepstone.

Mtshayankomo's testimony provides evidence both of a conflict between Shepstone and Masiphula and of a struggle among the Zulu leaders themselves.[43] According to Mtshayankomo, when the forces of the British and the Zulu converged on emLambongwenya, a mutual show of strength ensued. Shepstone's men fired off blank cartridges, causing the Zulu forces to take fright. Then the Zulu units sounded the *ingomane,* a thunderous beating of raised shields, which in turn caused the horses of the Natal contingent to bolt. This so rattled Shepstone that he turned on Masiphula (still living, in this account) and accused him of trying to stir up trouble.[44] While Masiphula had wanted this display of strength to be made, other leading men of Cetshwayo's, such as Mnyamana kaNgqengelele of the Buthelezi, Mavumengwana kaNdhlela, chief of a section of the Ntuli, and Hamu kaNzibe, had not.

Mtshayankomo expressly depicted the three chiefs as opposed to Masiphula, and indeed represented Cetshwayo as cognizant of Shepstone's interventionist role in the politics of the Zulu kingdom. He recorded Mnyamana as describing Shepstone as "a good man, one who pisses with his legs apart; he plants one leg on the other side of the Thukela, and the other in the Zulu country!"[45] He described Masiphula, supported by Ntshingwayo kaMahole of the Khoza, as being opposed to Shepstone. It was Masiphula who had interpreted the buck omen (see above, p. 81) that appeared to Mpande prior to his death as meaning that Shepstone was maneuvering on behalf of Mbuyazi. On that occasion Masiphula was reputed to have prophesied that Shepstone "will destroy the land."[46]

Masiphula's interpretation was opposed by others among Mpande's councilors and by Mpande's diviners. In turn, Mpande was reported to have predicted Masiphula's death: "You too will die, Masipula; you will die the day that I die. They [the sons of Mpande] will kill you."[47] Whether Mpande was truly prescient when he prophesied that Masiphula would be killed by the royal claimants, or if, as it seems, the prediction motif was merely a rhetorical strategy typical of this kind of historical narrative (which is used to account retrospectively for developments that occurred after the occasion of the prophecy), the story of the buck itself speaks of a succession conflict that raged on the eve of the installation. The rival claimant was not, however, the long-dead Mbuyazi—who featured in Mpande's vision—but rather Hamu, the son of Nzibe, fathered by Mpande. The prophecy also stressed the involvement of Shepstone in these disputes.

After the show of strength at emLambongwenya between Shepstone and Masiphula, Mtshayankomo claimed that an open quarrel broke out between the two sides. "We went to sleep," he noted, "in the knowledge that the *izinduna* [officers] were quarrelling."[48] At some point in these proceedings Hamu reputedly accosted Cetshwayo, declaring, "You shall never rule the country . . . So you are destroying the Kingdom? You will never rule it."[49] Cetshwayo then went to the home of "his father," Masiphula, where he consulted *izinyanga* (diviners) who divined—in yet another form of preordination—that he was being plotted against by Mnyamana and Hamu. Nothing was done about it because the two chiefs were too powerful. Following this, Mtshayankomo ascribed Masiphula's death, by poisoning, to the rival faction led by Hamu. "That," said Mtshayan-komo, "was when the split occurred between Hamu and Cetshwayo," with Hamu claiming that Cetshwayo would never hold the *umkhosi* ceremony, scheduled for some months after the installation, at which Cetshwayo would have been finally recognized as the new king.[50]

While the chronology of Mtshayankomo's narrative presents difficulties, its overall thrust is clear, and it discusses a set of events that has been lost from historical view only because they were unsuccessful, rather than because they lack significance. The testimony, together with the holding of the early preemptive ceremony, suggests that in late July 1873 Mnyamana and Mavumengwana may have hoped to install Hamu in Cetshwayo's stead.[51] Before the end of the year, however, both had pledged themselves to Cetshwayo's service.

Hamu on the eve of the installation looked very powerful and was a strong rival candidate. It would seem that Masiphula moved to preempt a challenge from Hamu by conducting the ceremony earlier than expected and, according to Mtshayankomo, was as a result poisoned by his opponents.[52] It is possible that once it became clear that Hamu had been outmaneuvered and Cetshwayo's installation was guaranteed, the two powerful councilors, Mnyamana and Mavumengwana, moved swiftly to remove their rival, Masiphula, and shore up their positions as senior royal advisers. That there was no investigation over the remarkable timing of Masiphula's death is testimony to the delicate balance of forces that prevailed in the few days around the two ceremonies.[53] Precisely what Shepstone's role in all this was, and what options he toyed with, are unknown, but it seems likely that Mnyamana assumed that Shepstone would readily install Hamu (or Mbuyazi, had he been alive) in Cetshwayo's place.[54] Indeed, the promotion of "own" candidates rather than recognized heirs was a feature of the way Shepstone controlled chieftaincy in Natal, and doubtless he would not have hesitated to play the same game with one leg across the Thukela. Annexation of the Zulu kingdom by the British was not a possibility at this time, but, as will be shown below, the establishment of British influence in the Zulu kingdom would have benefited Shepstone significantly. So anxious were the Zulu leaders about Shepstone's intentions that, according to one informant, all the objects used at the "coronation" were burned "as it was thought they might in some way have come in contact with Mbuyazi and so contaminated."[55]

In summary, Cetshwayo's position both within the Zulu kingdom and in relation to his powerful neighbors made it imperative for him to secure the backing of a powerful external party for his candidacy. In addition, Shepstone's involvement in the installation served to inhibit any plans that the Transvaal Boers might have had of elevating their protégé, another son of Mpande, Mthonga, to the kingship.

Shepstone's rationale

Shepstone's participation in the installation had no direct benefits for Natal, beyond the intangible but powerful assertion of Natal's involvement in the definition of Zulu sovereignty. At this time, the Zulu kingdom was important to Natal because of the promise it held out. One possibility it offered was as a source of land for the growing African population of Natal, and land was a question that preoccupied all Natal's inhabitants, Shepstone in particular. By 1860 the African population of Natal had begun to spill out of the areas designated for their habitation, and settler disaffection was growing, exacerbated by Shepstone's opposition to increases in the hut tax, which would have forced increasing numbers of Natal Africans into wage labor. When the project for a southern reserve, and a subsequent plan to annex Moshoeshoe's Sotho kingdom, both proved stillborn, Shepstone began to cast glances north of the border to alleviate the pressures on Natal's landed resources.

This was part of the context of his involvement in the affairs of the Zulu kingdom long before the installation. Another component was the growing importance to Natal of conditions inside the Zulu kingdom, especially those that were viewed as being behind the tide of refugees from the Zulu kingdom who were moving into Natal. The settlers' perception of instability in the neighboring kingdom made it of interest to Shepstone to try to influence developments north of the Thukela to Natal's advantage.

The "coronation" invitation thus came at a time when Shepstone was facing problems within Natal that encompassed settler anxieties over land and labor shortages, as well as fears about a Zulu invasion of Natal. Shepstone calculated that settler demands and worries would be assuaged by the demonstration of imperial leverage in Zulu affairs. He maintained that it was vital for the British government to be seen to be influential in what were known as "native affairs" both in and beyond Natal. Discussing the invitation he argued that

> a calm consideration of the circumstances never admitted of a doubt that, if the Government of Natal declined this opportunity, it must fall from its high position over the Natives and become the sport of all the alarms and uncertain panics which are so serious and evil to Governments no longer capable of sufficiently influencing the politics of their neighbours.[56]

Shepstone saw the installation as a means of acquiring "a good deal of additional influence and real power, not only over the Zulus, but over all the other native powers of South Eastern Africa," for, as he put it, "the power to control the Zulus includes that of controlling all the rest."[57] Such influence meant the possibility of ensuring the conditions necessary for the safe passage of migrant workers from further north, a point of pressing importance in the labor-hungry colony. At the same time it would provide an opportunity to persuade the Zulu leaders to allow Natal to annex a strip of land that at once would contain the Transvaal, preventing it from obtaining an outlet to the sea, and would offer an extension of the land available for the occupation of the Natal African population.[58]

Demonstration of a capacity to exert influence over Zulu affairs was designed not only to calm settler fears, but also to make contumacious subjects in Natal wary of rebellion, as well as closing off their opportunities to look north for external Zulu support. Terror of a general uprising permeated settler consciousness in Natal, and Shepstone himself feared the consequences of forcing the large numbers of Africans spilling out of the locations back onto reserved land. By April 1873, it was clear to the Natal administration that developments among the Hlubi people under Chief Langalibalele in northern Natal were heading for a showdown. When Langalibalele failed to ensure that all guns in his area were registered, and refused on three occasions to appear in Pietermaritzburg before the supreme chief (the governor of Natal), all the worst fears seemed to be coming true. Langalibalele's next move was to open discussions with a range of other African leaders within Natal and beyond the borders, including the Zulu rulers, and it was widely believed that this issue could spark off more widespread resistance.[59] Shepstone's approach was to put off dealing with Langalibalele until after the installation. Shepstone had always feared the possibility of the African populations of Natal combining against the numerically smaller colonial establishment, and sought to put a stop to the contagion of revolt. Demonstration of influence north of the border was one way of asserting imperial hegemony.

The members of the Harding Commission of 1852–3 into the condition of the African population of Natal had made it clear that the colonists saw a direct link between what they understood to be native bloodthirstiness and cruelty, an aversion to labor, and Zulu power. It was autocracy, chieftainship, militancy, and discipline, they implied, that kept people out of wage labor. The Zulu power north of the Thukela stood as a symbol of all this. A weaker Zulu kingdom, it was argued, would result in more labor for Natal, and this translated into the representation of the Zulu power as inclement and capricious—as warranting intervention. The same ruthless power was represented as holding women in an untenable position of subordination, causing their labor power to be held captive in the homesteads. Cumulatively, this amounted to a moral outcry emanating from Natal concerning repression and directed at its powerful Zulu neighbor, an outcry that was translated at the time of the installation into a call from Natal colonists for the extension of what might be termed "civil liberties" north of the Thukela.

Shepstone was able to deploy the necessary influence by making his participation in the installation contingent on Cetshwayo's agreeing to the extension of these "civil liberties." He began by making his embarkation on the expedition dependent on an undertaking from the Zulu authorities that there would be no "indiscriminate shedding of blood." This thrust was further developed in the set of laws he put forward at the installation which embraced the principles of open trials for anyone facing a possible death penalty, no execution without a right of appeal and the consent of the king, and the imposition of milder sentences for less serious crimes.[60] As Shepstone had no power to enforce the laws, they were clearly designed with an eye to public opinion in Natal. In part, the regulations offered the possibility of halting an indiscriminate flow of people into Natal. At the installation Cetshwayo agreed to permit Tsonga workers to migrate through Zulu territory into the labor-hungry Natal colony. The right to tax these migrants brought Cetshwayo an important new source of revenue.[61] The laws were also put forward in response to missionary pressures, and as such have generally been interpreted as an attempt by the Natal administration to ameliorate the despotism of the Zulu king.

In a subtle analysis of the "coronation oaths," Richard Cope has suggested that the view of the laws as being directed against the Zulu king is the product of the way they were interpreted by the British high commissioner, Sir Bartle Frere, on the eve of the Anglo-Zulu War. To read the "coronation laws" as prefiguring subsequent imperial designs on the Zulu territory is, however, to allow later events and subsequent reinterpretations of the installation to obscure the contemporary rationales for the ceremony. The "coronation laws" should be seen as a strategy to reduce the power of senior Zulu chiefs.[62] Cope marshals a wide body of evidence to demonstrate that relations between Cetshwayo and his senior councilors had been strained for some time and that "the despotism to be ameliorated was that of the chiefs rather than the king."[63] Thus while Shepstone sought to placate the Natal settlers with the "coronation oaths," he effectively bolstered the principle of centralized power in the Zulu kingdom.

Cope's analysis of the oaths as directed against the powerful chiefs raises the question why it was that Shepstone allowed his participation in the installation to shore up the power of the Zulu monarchy. The answer to this puzzle lies in Shepstone's conception of native administration.

Shepstone and the Natal native administration

In 1846, after an already impressive career in the Cape civil service, Shepstone was appointed diplomatic agent to the African population and justice of the peace in the new colony of Natal. A key feature of Natal in this period was the steady growth in its African population, as refugees from earlier upheavals sought to return to historical lands. Shortly after his arrival, Shepstone joined the Commission for Locating the Natives, the decisions of which were to set the course of Natal native policy for much of the nineteenth century in the mold of what became known as the "Shepstone system." The first principle of the system was that Africans should be taxed to cover the costs of their administration: this led to the introduction of the hut tax in Natal. Secondly, despite widespread settler opposition, Natal Africans were recognized as the original inhabitants of the land and over two million acres were set apart for African occupation. Shepstone insisted, moreover, that the land so designated be arable and capable of supporting the communities located on it. He believed that African societies should be maintained separately from colonial Natal and, in the early 1850s, he devised a scheme to remove as many Africans as possible to an area between the Mzimkhulu and Mzimvubu rivers, south of Natal. Lieutenant-Governor Pine, who opposed many of Shepstone's attempts to secure lands for Africans, approved this scheme, but higher authorities vetoed it.[64]

Shepstone also believed that "native law and custom" should be preserved as far as possible, "to save the soul of the people."[65] In particular, he upheld the institutions of chiefship, polygamy, and *lobolo*. He viewed the maintenance and manipulation of chiefship and other existing forms of social organization and control as essential to successful administration in the face of strict fiscal constraints. Shepstone recognized that polygamy and *lobolo* arrangements were fundamental to homestead production, for they were the bases of labor power within the homestead and they regulated relations between homesteads. Moreover, Shepstone was supported by powerful *rentier* interests who wished to keep Africans tenants on the land and productive enough to meet rents.[66]

When the charter of 1856 established representative government in Natal, the Native Affairs Department was exempted from control of the legislature. Since Africans contributed the greater part of the colony's revenue, £5,000 a year was set aside by the charter for "native purposes," effectively making the secretary for native affairs independent of the legislature and solely responsible for the African population of Natal. Missionaries disapproved of this policy, which put Africans under the direct control of the SNA, and of the existence of a separate code of "native law," because adherence to "native law" sanctioned institutions such as polygamy to which they were implacably opposed. Many colonists also objected to the amount of land made available under the system to Africans, and they complained incessantly about a lack of labor.

As secretary for native affairs under the system he had put in place, Shepstone, assisted on a day-to-day level by a network of "native magistrates"—that is, white magistrates with jurisdiction over Africans—who dispensed justice by using their "knowledge of the customs of the natives,"[67] became the primary interlocutor between the African and European communities for much of the nineteenth century.[68] Not only did he play Shaka at the installation to establish Natal's influence in the Zulu kingdom, and develop connections with the Swazi kingdom by accepting the bride sent to him by the Swazi rulers (though he gave her away in marriage to his head *induna*), but he was also called upon constantly to explain to the European inhabitants of Natal the significance of any new developments in the African communities around them. Although he kept out of the public eye, Shepstone was perceived by the Natal settlers as their bulwark against being overwhelmed by Africans. It was Shepstone who provided the analyses that assuaged the worst settler fears. This is not to say, however, that he was beyond their criticism.[69] The acts of interlocution were a primary premise of the Shepstone system, and depended on knowledge of African ways of thinking and acting: the system thus placed a high premium on "the native expert," and Shepstone himself was widely recognized as the most "expert" of all.

Ultimately Shepstone envisaged that by using their knowledge, he and his local magistrates would come to replace the chiefs as the rulers of African communities. Thus, when settler fears that the "native magistrates" would represent African interests in opposition to settler interests forced the replacement of "native magistrates" by resident magistrates (magistrates with jurisdiction over blacks and whites within a given area), Shepstone argued that this undermined the essence of his system.[70] Shepstone's conception of "native magistrates" and the possibility of their taking over from chiefs demanded a form of acceptance of indigenous culture and custom that was the opposite of that advocated by the missionaries and settlers, for it involved a limited number of white colonial officials crossing, as it were, into an African world, and ruling through the use of the cultural logic of that world, modified where necessary "to suit the circumstances of the Colony and the character of civilized Government."[71] A familiarity with African society was thus fundamental to his system, and was to be demonstrated and enacted in endless displays of knowledge and ceremonials of power, of which the installation was but the most elevated.

Shepstone believed that the success of the colonial project depended on the maintenance of the fabric and institutions of native life. Such maintenance demanded in turn that their fundamental nature be closely analyzed and well understood. Shepstone recognized further that his own system of administration, in building on indigenous forms, demanded an articulation between the colonial administrators and their local equivalents, most notably with respect to continued control over the productive and reproductive labor of women. The key concepts in Shepstone's understanding of native administration were patriarchal command and a strong centralized government. Furthermore, Shepstone found in the Zulu monarchy a model for his own administration. This underlay his willingness to assume the mantle of Shaka.

Shepstone and the researching of the Shakan past

When Shepstone became the secretary for native affairs, "Shaka" was the name of one among many African chiefs who were little known outside southern Africa. It was only with the Anglo-Zulu War that the Zulu achieved a special recognition in the eyes of the British public. What was known about the first Zulu king in the mid-nineteenth century was ambiguous: the image of Shaka that prevailed in settler and missionary literature was of a Zulu king who had been a cruel tyrant among his own people, but also the one Zulu monarch who had been good to early white visitors to his kingdom. In general, Shaka was at once favorably compared with his successor Dingane, who had been responsible for the death of the Boers at the battle of Ncome River (known to the settlers as the battle of Blood River), and caricatured as a monster.

In September 1863, at the behest of the lieutenant-governor of Natal, John Scott, Shepstone embarked on a project to collect information on the historical grounds for African land claims in Natal. In an excellent discussion of Shepstone's research and his methods, John Wright concludes that, while Shepstone consulted earlier written sources, "Shepstone's histories were the product mostly of the testimony given him by his own informants."[72] Wright establishes that Shepstone conducted historical interviews with about fourteen informants, and used the data gleaned as the bases for two documents which he drafted in 1863–4.[73] Although Shepstone was not conducting research on the reign of Shaka, the two documents provide a clear image of how Shepstone viewed the figure of Shaka in the mid-1860s.

Shepstone's first document was a history of the Natal "tribes," the other an account of the rise of the Zulu power. The first comprised short histories of ninety-three groups resident in Natal before the reign of Shaka. Most of the groups discussed were described as having been attacked and dispersed by Shaka, or by another power itself displaced by Shaka. As such, Shepstone's investigations gave him a picture somewhat different from the settler stereotype which ascribed all devastations to Shaka. As Wright, who is concerned to trace the origins of the *mfecane* stereotype, puts it:

> Shepstone's researches indicated to him that the established notion of the tribes of Natal as virtually all having been dispersed or annihilated by Shaka's Zulu armies needed a certain degree of modification. The testi-mony which he collected from some of his informants suggested that many of the tribes had been broken up, or at the very least disturbed, not by the Zulu but by one of at least four non-Zulu groups of "refugees" from north of the Thukela, and one from the Natal midlands.[74]

Thus, in Shepstone's document the extermination that occurred was ascribed as much to the actions of "other tribes"[75] as to the Zulu. The "driven-by-Shaka" motif was nonetheless very strong in his informants' accounts,[76] but, significantly for the purposes of the present discussion, they were relatively bare of the atrocity stories that occur in many contemporary settler accounts. Shaka was presented as an irresistible invading force rather than a monstrous savage. Natal was shown to have been devastated and to have become, in contrast to the Zulu kingdom, an uncultivated wilderness where cannibalism was rife[77] and "universal anarchy" reigned.[78] The set of oppositions with which Shepstone built up his narrative were not those of "the West"/"civilization" and "the Other"/"barbarism," but of the Zulu kingdom/order and the rest (specifically Natal)/chaos. These particular oppositions occur frequently in African oral texts of the late nineteenth century.[79]

The second document, "Historic Sketch of the Tribes Anciently Inhabiting the Colony of Natal, as at Present Bounded, and Zululand," was based on the evidence presented in the first document and gave an account of the rise of the Zulu power which focused on Shaka. Shaka's rule was described as autocratic and "uncompromising,"[80] but, on the whole, the narrative was concerned with Shaka's military successes and the expansion of the Zulu kingdom. While it is true that these two documents were the main sources of the *mfecane* "devastation hypothesis," it is worth noting that they were generally free of the sensationalism that marked the accounts of earlier writers such as Isaacs and Robert Godlonton.[81] Instances of despotism were represented not as wanton savagery, but as linked to processes of rule:

> The large tribes who had been the first to disturb the Aboriginal inhabitants of Natal, in their endeavours to pass through the country now known by that name, to escape from Chaka, having been overtaken and dispersed by Chaka's armies in their new residences, and their Chiefs mostly killed, now found further flight useless, and the great body of their population returned and became subjects to the Zulu King, who distributed them among his head men and chief officers, and incorporated the young men into his army as soldiers. . . .[82]

Thus, for Shepstone, the *mfecane* did not, as the Comaroffs have argued for colonizers generally, "confirm the savagery of Africa"[83] so much as offer a discourse for the discussion of questions about the nature of effective domination in an African setting. The "Historic Sketch" was overwhelmingly a narrative about the establishment of Zulu sovereignty and the extension of Zulu control over new territories and peoples.

While peoples were "overtaken and dispersed" and chiefs "mostly killed," Shepstone's accounts are remarkable for the extent to which they were *not* faithful to the stereotype of Shaka present in much contemporary missionary and settler literature. The two accounts certainly were Shepstone's constructions, but the unusual concern that they manifest with questions of sovereignty does not have a precedent in previous settler histories. As a "native administrator" Shepstone certainly had more reason to be interested in questions of sovereignty than most of his fellow white Natalians. But, as contemporary African narratives about Shaka from other sources make clear, he was not simply seeing in the accounts collected a possible reading that could be twisted to suit his own purposes. African accounts of Shaka were themselves fundamentally concerned with matters of sovereignty and the nature of power and domination.[84]

The "Historic Sketch" opened, not with a chronicle of historical events, but with a distinctly anthropological discussion of the nature of African sovereignty and government before Shaka. The account went on to focus on the political and military changes brought about first by Dingiswayo and, later, Shaka, culminating in a short review of the reign of Dingane. Throughout, the central theme was a concern with how power was wielded in the Shakan kingdom. This was the framework for all allusions to Shaka's aggressiveness and autocracy.

With the production of Shepstone's two documents in 1863–4, the first glimmerings of a whole new way of discussing Shaka began to enter colonial productions of Zulu history. Although Shepstone's two documents were only published in the 1880s, they were influential in shaping colonial thinking at the time of their preparation, and they foreshadowed a more expansive exploration and enactment of the connections between Shaka and the notion of sovereignty that Shepstone was to engage in during the installation of Cetshwayo.

The new politics and worldview pioneered in the British campaign against slavery placed colonial governments under pressure to find new systems of administration free of direct coercion but also capable of executing the colonial project. The institution of wage labor was one option, and a number of studies have examined this choice and its impact on colonized societies. Shepstone sought to resolve the dilemma posed in a different way—by recourse to an African model of domination. Essentially, Shepstone found in Shaka a model of ruling the African population of Natal that allowed him to circumvent the liberal principles of government increasingly entrenched in Britain but prohibitively expensive to implement in the cash-strapped Natal colony. In a way that was fundamentally at odds with metropolitan notions of individual rights, but justifiable as an indigenous system, Shepstone sought to make all members of a chiefdom responsible for actions of individuals, including the chief, and vice versa.[85] Shepstone understood punishment of the innocent along with the guilty to be a feature of cheap administration. Likewise, the system of forced public labor, or *isibhalo,* which was introduced into Natal in 1848, was problematic in times of anti-slavery. Shepstone was able to justify all these aspects of his administration as features of Shakan times and as appropriate to the government of ex-subjects of Shaka.[86]

Despotism of the kind being investigated by Shepstone was the opposite of British constitutional government and was regarded as an aspect of the English past. But, by the middle of the nineteenth century, Thomas Carlyle's notion of the heroic governor as an alternative to Victorian democracy appealed to many who hoped that a heroic British leader might prove to be a bulwark against social disintegration.[87] A colonial administration based on Shakan principles might thus be likely to receive support from some quarters in London.

The terms in which Shepstone described Shaka's administrative problems mirrored almost exactly Shepstone's own position: "The policy of Chaka saw his peculiar position as despotic ruler of a people composed almost wholly of conquered tribes, compelled him to mass them as much as possible around him, to intermingle them as much as possible, and so rule them as to destroy their old associations and hence he would not permit the occupation of the entire country he conquered."[88]

This reading of Shepstone's treatment of Shaka is very different from that of

Golan, who talks about Shepstone's "de-emphasis of Shaka," and his fight "to break the political dominance of Shaka's heirs, the royal family of Zululand."[89] Shepstone did, at a much later point, work with the colonial authorities in trying to rein in Zulu royal power but, in principle, he held an opposite position to theirs, namely, that a strong central power modeled on the Shakan regime was essential to the control of the Zulu kingdom and the African population of Natal. This underlay an almost obsessive interest on Shepstone's part in the reign of Shaka.[90] It also explains his support of Cetshwayo against his most powerful councilors, through the "coronation oaths."

When Shepstone was offered the opportunity "as Chaka" to install Cetshwayo, he understood it in terms very different from that of playing the part of a "savage monster." Rather, he perceived that the invitation offered him the chance of intervening directly in matters of Zulu sovereignty. It was, Shepstone recognized, an opportunity loaded with possibilities. To recognize the potential and to explore it required a grasp of the cultural logic of the African population of Natal and the Zulu kingdom, and the role of Shaka. This, it seems, Shepstone had achieved in substantial measure by 1873.

Shepstone: "Father to the King's children"

We have already discussed why it was that Cetshwayo wished Shepstone to be present at the installation. We turn now to an analysis of the reasons why Cetshwayo and his advisers wanted Shepstone to be present *as Shaka*. We noted that Cetshwayo feared the promotion of rival candidates by neighboring powers such as the Boers and British. The invitation to the British to participate in Cetshwayo's installation was a device to secure British recognition of Cetshwayo. There was a danger that, if invited across the Thukela, Shepstone would use the opportunity to install an alternative candidate. As we have seen, Cetshwayo's greatest rival was Hamu. As the genealogical son of Nzibe, Hamu was not of the direct line of accession through Shaka as traced through Dingane and Mpande. Significantly, if a son of Nzibe were to gain the kingship, it would belie the legitimacy of Shaka's own accession. By designating Shepstone "as Chaka," the invitation specifically made it difficult for him to install Hamu, whose very candidacy was framed in terms opposed to the house of Shaka. This interpretation is supported by evidence that Cetshwayo sought in a number of other ways to stress his connections to Shaka, including the act of reviving the homesteads of Shaka which had died out.[91]

In describing Shepstone as Shaka, the Zulu envoys also referred to the role Shepstone had earlier played in 1861 at Nodwengu as witness to the nomination of Cetshwayo as Mpande's heir. It is to a discussion of the events of 1861 that we now turn to grasp the significance of Shepstone's assuming the mantle of Shaka for the installation.

In a memorandum prepared in 1873, prior to his departure on the installation expedition, Shepstone explained his designation "as Chaka" in the Zulu invitation as the consequence of a series of events that had occurred twelve years earlier. Since the battle of Ndondakusuka in 1856 (a battle that claimed the lives of Mbuyazi and five other sons of Mpande) Cetshwayo had emerged as a powerful and increasingly restless contender for the succession. In 1861, in a bid, as Shepstone put it, to "tranquillize" the situation in the Zulu kingdom, he had put pressure on Mpande to recognize the prince as his heir, and traveled to Nodwengu to be present at the ceremony of nomination. On his way to the nomination, Shepstone was asked to wait about ten miles outside Mpande's residence.

> In the discussion that took place it was admitted that in deference to the position of Supremacy occupied by the British Government towards the Zulus, as laid down by Chaka when he sent his Embassy to the Cape some thirty years before, and in consideration of the position I held in Natal, the highest salute should be used but the difficulty presented itself, that this was the Zulu royal salute, and had never been used in Zululand except to the Sovereign: to overcome this difficulty it was decreed that I should be looked upon as Chaka, that is, that I should personate and take that Chief's rank, and thus become, according to their view, entitled to receive the salute they were anxious to give.
>
> Accordingly when I reached Panda's residence I found a regiment drawn up, and although evidently against the grain—for the country had just emerged from fierce revolution—the regiment saluted me as it would have saluted the King.[92]

Shepstone argued that his presence at the nomination in 1861 was designed by Mpande to "afford pressure enough to carry such an unheard of measure [the nomination] with the Nobles."[93]

Norman Etherington has dismissed Shepstone's claims that he had received the *bayete* salute as one who stood in Shaka's place, and that it was this that caused him to be invited back to crown Cetshwayo in 1873, as "mostly nonsense."[94] In some senses he is right. Shepstone almost certainly embellished his accounts of his visit to Nodwengu; and the invitation to Shepstone to participate in the subsequent installation was the result of important contemporary political developments both in the Zulu kingdom and in Natal, rather than a consequence of events in 1861. To dismiss Shepstone's claims is, however, to lose sight of the intricate and developing logic of the various appeals to the past made by a range of actors involved in these events, their connections to contested issues of sovereignty, and the complex emergence of Zulu historiography at this time.

Indeed, while the only account of the 1861 encounter that directly corroborates Shepstone's version of his designation "as Chaka" is the messengers' request of 1873,[95] there is a host of narratives discussing the logic and meaning of Shepstone's presence at the earlier nomination, and debating his status as a participant in the act of naming Cetshwayo as the heir. These texts themselves require close reading and detailed reconstruction of the context of their genesis. This task has been undertaken elsewhere, and a summary of the main points is presented here.[96] Five accounts in particular, other than Shepstone's memorandum and the Zulu messengers' statements, open themselves to closer examination.[97]

All the accounts, representing a range of perspectives supportive of and opposed to Shepstone, accord the secretary for native affairs a significant role in the nomination and explore issues of sovereignty. On the question of Shepstone's involvement in the nomination, all the accounts, regardless of whether they are derived from retrospective analyses of the events of 1861 or from contemporary accounts, concur that the central matter at issue was that of sovereignty. They view the nomination as a struggle over the issue of transcendent political authority and identify Shepstone as a central witness to the nomination—this being the case in the accounts that sought to deny the occasion as a moment of British sovereignty, as well as those that wanted to advance it as that.

A significant number of the versions identified ongoing tension between Mpande and his heir, and the existence of a threat posed by Cetshwayo both to Mpande and to the overall stability of the kingdom.[98] This suggests it is likely that Shepstone's involvement in the nomination was actively solicited by Mpande. Shepstone's presence was of further interest to the Zulu ruling house because Natal had long been viewed as a supporter of rival claimants. In addition to those already discussed, another son of Mpande, Mkhungo, who was at this time sheltering with Bishop Colenso in Natal, was referred to by the bishop as "the future king (most probably)."[99] When, in 1859, Colenso made his first exploratory trip to the Zulu kingdom in the company of Shepstone, it was widely viewed as the preliminary to a challenge to Cetshwayo's right of succession.[100] There are thus reasons for thinking that Shepstone's presence at the nomination, and his designation as Shaka, would certainly have served a number of purposes for Mpande, and possibly even for Cetshwayo, despite the latter's disputes with Shepstone regarding the meaning of his presence.

The designation of Shepstone "as Chaka" had the further significance of speaking to an important aspect of the late Mbuyazi's claim to the succession, the debate over his biological paternity. Mbuyazi was Mpande's son born of Monase, a woman given to him by Shaka. Claims were made that Monase was a member of Shaka's household who became pregnant by Shaka, and was then passed on to Mpande.[101] In other words, supporters of Mbuyazi claimed that he was the biological son of Shaka. Indeed, Mpande was quoted as saying: "Is not Mbuyazi the son of Tshaka, the king of the earth?"[102] The investiture of Shepstone with the mantle of Shaka for the 1861 nomination of Cetshwayo, whether made in 1861, or only retrospectively in 1873, by implication allowed the claim to a Shakan connection or sanction, which Mbuyazi had previously enjoyed, to accrue to Cetshwayo. Likewise, it was impossible for Shepstone "as Chaka" to install Hamu, for his candidacy would have had to be predicated on the illegitimacy of Shaka's own succession. In wishing to see Shepstone journey north "as Chaka," Cetshwayo had thus sufficiently strong motivations to outweigh the possible capital Shepstone could make out of his investiture with the mantle of historical authority.

Shepstone, for his part, was equally keen to play the part of Shaka. He was alert to the possibilities of stretching the significance and meaning of Shaka in connection with the issue of sovereignty, notably the idea that Shaka had recognized British sovereignty over the Zulu. In his explanation of his designation "as Chaka," Shepstone added the gloss that the *bayete* salute was to be given to him in 1861 at least in part "in deference to the position of supremacy occupied by the British Government towards the Zulus, as laid down by Chaka when he sent his Embassy to the Cape some thirty years before."[103] He went on to note: "It will be seen hereafter that the Zulus still consider this declaration of the Chief, whose memory they most respect, to be sacredly binding upon them."[104] Likewise, in his report of the "coronation," Shepstone carefully constructed British claims to a form of sovereignty over the Zulu through reference to Shaka. He prefaced his report of the installation expedition with a short sketch of the founding of the Zulu power by Shaka and preceding installations and successions. Shepstone's Shaka, whose "home rule had been relieved by acts of generosity and statesmanship," was not the villain that Dingane—"who lacked most of his predecessor's genius, all of his generosity, but none of his cruelty"—was. Shepstone went on to describe Mpande as "faithful and true to the declaration before described, as made by his great predecessor, Chaka."[105]

The precise nature of this sovereignty was left vague, but was cast in broadly paternal terms that accorded with the messengers' salutation of Shepstone as "Father to the King's children," with Mpande's and Cetshwayo's descriptions of themselves as children of the Natal government,[106] and with Shepstone's own understanding of his position in Natal African society. Indeed, Shepstone characterized his role in the installation as the fulfilling of a "parental duty."[107] An African contemporary of the secretary for native affairs, Lazarus Xaba, recalled that Shepstone invariably conducted himself as a grand patriarch, addressing everyone in isiZulu as "my child."[108] Anne McClintock has pointed to the extent to which Shepstone emphasized his paternal relationship to the indigenous inhabitants of Natal and even the independent Zulu kingdom.[109] But even that discourse was not without resonance in indigenous ideas. Shepstone surrounded himself with the trappings of Zulu kingship, including a praise singer and a snuff-box bearer, presided over Zulu dances, and gave African women in marriage to his loyal African henchmen.[110] Shepstone was, by this time, already adept at identifying and appropriating to British rule key African institutions and symbols. The annual first fruits ceremony, for example, was made the prerogative of the supreme chief in Natal.[111] Assuming the mantle of Shaka was but another enactment of Zulu conceptions of sovereignty in a panoply with which Shepstone was increasingly at home. As Shaka at the installation, Shepstone gave dramatic definition to himself as the transcendent political authority. In the manner in which he represented his part in the ceremony, Shepstone was also constructing himself in the eyes of the distant colonial authorities in terms of his ability to read the situation and to understand the native mind; in short, he was establishing his status as the expert who was almost part African. His Zulu name—Somtsewu (Father of the white man)[112]—by which he was known even among the colonists, symbolized his position.

Paternalism was a characteristic of colonialism generally, and has been the subject of a number of analyses which look at the way colonial subjects were "infantilized." Shepstone's paternalism took its particular forms of expressionfrom an indigenous African model and was, as has been shown above, conferred on, as much as asserted by, Shepstone, as a result of very particular political developments culminating in the installation.[113] Moreover, it was a form of paternalism in which responsibilities, as much as rights, were actively insisted on. Thus, Cetshwayo wanted Shepstone as "father" in order to enmesh him in paternal *responsibilities*.

Whether the installation of Hamu rather than Cetshwayo would have altered Shepstone's analysis of the connections between Shaka and sovereignty is impossible to say. But whichever way he played it, for or against Shaka, Shepstone's reading of the necessity of talking about sovereignty in terms that referred to Shaka prevailed and, indeed, took hold more widely in Natal colonial discourse. When in later years the British authorities removed Cetshwayo and sought to promote other chiefs, they were obliged to do so by arguing against the selfsame notion of sovereignty that the figure of Shaka stood for.

Guy has asserted that Shepstone failed to recognize the ways in which the Zulu rulers sought to manipulate him.[114] My reading suggests, on the contrary, that he grasped many of the complex logics on all sides, the significance of the questions of sovereignty, the possibilities of their public enactment, and the power of prophecy in conceptualizing the relationship between the past and present, and adroitly set all these points to work in his own interests. Likewise, Cetshwayo recognized that the invitation to Shepstone to crown him "as Chaka" would prove irresistible to Shepstone's Great White Chief mentality. Cetshwayo himself used the prophecy of Shaka and the matter of his foresight in sending an embassy to the Cape, as the justification for arguing for a special relationship between the British and the Zulu kingdom. The tussles that ensued were highly contested and the moves sophisticated, with each side demonstrating remarkable cognizance of the cultural logic and political imperatives of the other.

In contrast to the charge that imperial agents "sought, *methodically,* to 'make history' for people who they thought lacked it; to induct those people into an *order* of activities and values; to impart *form* to an Africa that was seen as formless; to reduce the chaos of savage life to the *rational* structures and techniques that, for the Europeans, were both the vehicle and the proof of their own civilization,"[115] Shepstone adopted the history of the people whom he sought to dominate, molding his arguments to carefully selected aspects of its form and logic. The Shepstone system annoyed the colonists precisely because it inhibited the imposition of a work ethic, monogamy, a need for clothing, commodities, and civilization. Shepstone distinguished between the chaos of disrupted Natal represented as "cannibalism" and other forms of savagery, and the order and rationality of the Zulu kingdom. So much form did he discern in the Zulu kingdom and in Zulu history that he sought to adapt it to his own purposes. Whereas the Comaroffs depict the missionary encounter with the Tswana as "the meeting of two worlds, one imperial and expansive, the other local and defensive,"[116] a review of events around the installation reveals Shepstone to have been embroiled in a situation of the meeting of two imperiums which gave its own special shape to the encounter of colonizer and colonized in the Zulu kingdom–Natal region.

The opposition between the Zulu kingdom, represented as the seat of order and culture, and its peripheries, regarded as the disordered wilderness of cannibals and of nature, was paralleled by another opposition, that between the highly ordered male militarized world, of both colonial and local Zulu-appointed administrators and soldiers, and the uncontrolled world of colonial and colonized women. Shepstone's exercise effected an alliance across racial barriers between male administrative classes in Natal and what became Zululand, allowing colonial authorities to use the indigenous system for the extraction of women's productive labor.[117]

Shepstone's understanding of "native administration" was thus founded on the capacity to enter effectively the African world he sought to control. Fundamental to this intention was the acquisition of knowledge of the world to be penetrated. Welsh has described Shepstone as showing "considerable anthropological insight"[118] in his assessment of African institutions. The Shepstone system placed a heavy premium on information gathering about colonized peoples and the development of "expert" knowledge of African societies. Whereas many previous studies stress the distortions in colonial knowledge of Africa, the focus on Shepstone highlights the premium placed by his system of administration on an understanding of local African societies in their own terms. To stress this emphasis, and to seek to trace its effects, is not, however, to suggest that the forms of knowledge of indigenous societies that were developed were objective, neutral, or accurate. Rather, it is to draw attention to the conditions of their making.

Through his historical researches, and his attempts to use Zulu history to provide a model for colonialism, Shepstone was responsible for the introduction into colonial productions of Zulu history—whether favorable to or denigratory of Shaka—of a new way of representing Shaka. While many analysts of imperial practice have focused on the way imperialist discourse remade African culture, the events and interpretations discussed in this chapter call our attention to the way African cultural logic shaped imperialist discourse. Colonial rulers brought to bear on the African societies of the region discourses of domination redolent with colonial stereotypes, the central tenets of which developed in the metropoles and within local settler society. These attached themselves powerfully to compatible indigenous ideas.

In the foregoing analysis we see Shepstone in a number of personae. We see him as the colonial bureaucrat preparing reports and justifying his actions in correspondence as well as suppressing rebellion and making law within Natal; at the same time we see him straddling the worlds of the white colony and the African populations of Natal and the Zulu kingdom. In this persona Shepstone repeatedly represented the one world to the other, in each instance offering his perspective as an "expert" view into the heart of things. Finally we see him as "Shaka" in the Zulu kingdom and as the great *induna* of the supreme chief in Natal. In each of these personae, Shepstone drew on the cultural logics of both worlds in different combinations, sometimes imperfectly and sometimes with great adroitness, combinations in some ways constrained and in other ways highly flexible.

The "Shepstone system" of native administration disposed Shepstone to recognize, and subsequently try to appropriate, a key convention in the representation of Shaka in African texts concerned with Zulu history and the Zulu power. The installation was an occasion of shared communicative praxis between Natal officials and the Zulu leaders, the source of which was African texts on sovereignty. Shepstone's readiness to be Shaka, and to use Shakan rule as a model for his administration, was a position at odds with the ideas prevalent at the time of seeing Africans as less than human, as bestial, and Africa as feminized—"seductively helpless."[119] Shepstone represented the Shakan kingdom as active, aggressively male, and ultimately as something to be emulated—not as a utopia inhabited by noble savages, but as a sensible, pragmatic system. The Africans with whom Shepstone was dealing were not part of nature, they were part of culture, and it was a culture that Shepstone sought to grasp in its fullest complexity.

These concerns ensured that Shepstone was at odds with the larger settler population of Natal, but he had devoted followers within his administration, including the compiler of the major historical record of the time, Natal magistrate John Bird.[120] Bird concurred fully with Shepstone's emphasis on the importance of knowing more about the African population and, like Shepstone, recognized their right to be in Natal.[121] Shepstone also had a close friend and ally at this time among the Natal missionaries, in John William Colenso, bishop of Natal. Colenso shared Shepstone's concern with the protection and preservation of African institutions and made it part of his life's work to protect the Zulu kings and to come to know as much as possible about Zulu politics. Indeed, he published widely on Zulu affairs. In 1859 he recorded a conversation between Cetshwayo and a missionary named Oftebro, in which the latter suggested that a possible reason for an outbreak of disease in the Zulu kingdom was divine punishment for Cetshwayo's having killed so many people. Cetshwayo replied: "But that is our custom, and how should a great chief maintain his power except by putting offenders to death or eating them up?"—to which comment Colenso added the following relativist gloss: "Are there sins committed among Christian people because it is the *custom,* or because it is necessary to maintain one's place in *society?* Are Ketchwayo's sins really more guilty in God's sight than these?"[122] Indeed, in this, Colenso demonstrated that he both shared Shepstone's view of the nature of political authority in the Zulu kingdom, and accepted it in a Zulu context.[123] Like Shepstone, Colenso was receptive to the power of the logics of the African communities around him, even attributing his controversial biblical criticism to the logic of an African convert. Likewise, although Colenso disapproved of polygamy in principle, he attempted to show that his interpretation of the Bible revealed no scriptural basis for condemning it among the Zulu.

A core of other officials and scholars believed that fluency in the local languages and intensive research into local history and indigenous institutions were essential to effective governance. They included, among others, the philologist Wilhelm Bleek and his patron, the Cape governor Sir George Grey.[124] Together Bleek and Grey asserted powerfully the need for in-depth local research within colonial administration. Their researches had massive implications, not least in that they defined new peoples. The work reflected the attitudes of the recorders and was drawn into the service of the colonial project. At the same it was also the conduit by means of which the ideas of the colonized were filtered into colonial practices.

"An aggressive exhibition of bloodletting and plunder"

On his return from the installation, one of the first things that Shepstone had to deal with was the simmering resistance of Langalibalele and the Hlubi in northern Natal.[125] In October 1873 Shepstone sent an ultimatum to Langalibalele to appear in Pietermaritzburg within fourteen days. In the face of the ultimatum, the Hlubi chose flight, but Shepstone was determined to make an example of what he regarded as Langalibalele's contumacy. The Shepstone system of native administration was fundamentally autocratic and demanded instant and complete obedience, and Shepstone's power within the system depended on his ability to impose his will on its subjects arbitrarily and immediately.

The Natal authorities marshaled a large force, considerably in excess of what was needed, with the objective of making an example of the Hlubi. Fresh from his performance "as Chaka" in the Zulu kingdom, Shepstone was not loath to deploy, as he viewed it, African forms of despotic justice—of the kind conventionally associated with Shaka—to serve as a deterrent to the rest of the African population of Natal. As John Wright and Andrew Manson reveal, the outcome of this showdown, namely the dismemberment of the Hlubi community, was decided on by Shepstone before the campaign commenced, and long before the trial that found Langalibalele guilty of treason.[126]

The campaign that ensued was initially a disaster for the marshaled colonial forces. One detachment suffered severe reverses at the hands of the Hlubi and, for the first time in the history of the colony, whites were killed in a war with blacks. The campaign took a new and increasingly vicious turn when the government forces devastated the Hlubi location, smoking refugees out of the caves where they were sheltering, and killing and plundering at will. The survivors were placed in forced labor and Hlubi cattle were confiscated. Eventually Langalibalele and his forces surrendered in Basutoland. The authorities then dismantled the Hlubi chiefdom, both as a vivid lesson to other African chiefs, and also to allow settlers access to the much-coveted territory the defeated chiefdom had occupied, and to make available the labor of the now dispossessed Hlubi. In short, the chiefdom was destroyed. The neighboring Ngwe, who had sheltered Hlubi cattle, were equally hard hit. It was, as Guy put it, "an aggressive exhibition of bloodletting and plunder."[127]

In this way, in late 1873, Shepstone wielded power in a manner that was every bit as "Shakan" as the system of Zulu rule he had described in the "Historic Sketch" compiled in 1863–4. In January 1874, Langalibalele was tried, in a trial that was a "mockery of justice";[128] the governor, Sir Benjamin Pine in his role as supreme chief, pronounced that the trial itself was a mercy, for under "native law" the accused would already have been killed.[129]

At this time the friendship between Shepstone and Bishop Colenso ruptured. Colenso, for a long time Shepstone's supporter in matters of native policy, was outraged by the atrocities committed in the course of the Langalibalele campaign, the harsh retributive moves of the administration, the authoritarianism of the secretary for native affairs, and the arbitrariness of the legal proceedings. Wyn Rees, editor of Frances Colenso's *Letters from Natal,* argued that all his life Bishop Colenso resisted tyranny.[130] Thus he opposed Shepstone "as Shaka." Colenso may have accepted "Shakan" forms of government as appropriate north of the Thukela, but he did not accept them in colonial Natal. Specifically, he objected to the concentration of judicial, legislative, and administrative powers in the hands of the secretary for native affairs. In short, Colenso protested at the demonstration of despotic rule by Shepstone.

As Colenso's protests grew more strident, the Colonial Office in London became uneasy about the obvious travesties of British notions of justice being committed by the Natal authorities.[131] The Shepstone system had, over the years, refined despotic rule in a form described as being based on African custom and Shakan precedent—forced labor through the *amabutho,* arbitrary justice, the holding of a whole community responsible for the actions of individuals, and so on. In the course of the Langalibalele affair all these features revealed themselves fully in the public gaze, as being painfully at odds with notions of governance current in Britain.

The prevailing liberal view required that courts be neutral—which Langalibalele's was not—and that the accused have access to legal representation—something Shepstone tried to avoid. Indeed, the Langalibalele affair called into question the whole system of native administration with regard to both its legitimacy and its practicalities in the eyes of the imperialists and the colonized.[132] By the 1870s the colonial authorities were talking about the necessity of extending the colony's coercive capacity, and were looking to the expansion of Natal's police and military. A fundamental contradiction had emerged into the open between the (admittedly adapted) African worldview that underlay the Shepstone system (notably the importance of displays of power and the manipulation of a politics of fear) and the colonial world wrought by the politics of empire and invested with notions of "civilization." The core of the contradiction focused on issues that were at the heart of each system, their respective notions of sovereignty and governance. Whereas the British system, its inequalities and coercive aspects notwithstanding, saw itself as based on equality, individual liberties, and civil rights, the Zulu system, as epitomized by Shaka, was presented in official accounts as highly organized and explicitly authoritarian, militarized, and despotically controlled.[133]

In 1875 recognition of the problem at the heart of Natal's native administration led to the recall of the governor, Sir Benjamin Pine, and his replacement by the colonial troubleshooter, Sir Garnet Wolseley, fresh from his latest triumph of crushing the Asante in West Africa. The crisis would also have had repercussions for the secretary for native affairs but for the fact that it was at precisely this moment that Shepstone was swept up in the latest plans of the secretary of state for colonies, Lord Carnarvon. Carnarvon viewed Shepstone as the ideal agent to carry out a proposed confederation of South Africa. Thus, for the moment, the Shepstone system remained in place while plans for the annexation of the Transvaal took precedence in the affairs of southern Africa.[134] Confederation nonetheless presented the likelihood of the British annexation of the Zulu kingdom and, in this context, even Shepstone's version of Zulu rulership raised concerns about monarchical tyranny.[135]

"Spilling the water on the ground"

In 1877 Carnarvon pushed toward a federation of South Africa by ordering Shepstone to annex the Transvaal. When Shepstone instructed Rider Haggard, then a member of his staff, to raise the British flag over the Transvaal, Shepstone's relations with the house of Shaka shifted decisively in a new direction.

As we have seen, the Zulu rulers had been prepared to pay the heavy price of Shepstone's participation in the installation in order to secure British support in their dealings with the Transvaal. The British had, for much of the 1870s, failed to meet their undertaking to act on Zulu appeals for mediation in their border conflict with the Transvaal Boers. In 1878 a Zulu deputation met Shepstone to discuss the border dispute, and found him reluctant to support their claims. In his narrative of these events as set down in 1881, Cetshwayo complained to the government about this lack of support, and noted a revocation of Shepstone's paternal status:

Then Usicwelecwele [Sigcwelegcwele, one of Cetshwayo's senior *izinduna*] stood up and said, "Is it so then, Mr. Shepstone, that after two men have been friends, and then one of them dies, and leaves his son fatherless, that the reviving [sic] man ought to be harsh with the son of the deceased? This

Cetewayo whom you have come to trouble and not to help is Mpande's son, and Mpande was your friend."

According to Cetshwayo, Shepstone responded, saying: "I have only come to talk about the boundary of the country, but the English nation will come and put matters right for you. Go and tell my child these words, because I know that he will understand me." Cetshwayo continued:

> Umbedjana . . . stood up and said, "Mr. Shepstone, we do not understand you." Mr. Shepstone then got in a rage and said, "Who is that calls me by my name, and does not address me by saying 'King'?" Then the other chiefs said, "No king in our country; although a man may be king, we chiefs call him by his name."[136]

For Cetshwayo, Shepstone was "no more a father, but a firebrand."[137] The interview concluded when a shot, by an unnamed party, was fired at Shepstone, leaving a bullet hole in his hat.

With annexation, the Transvaal Boers became *de jure* British subjects. In the changed circumstances of the confederation scenario, an independent and militarized Zulu kingdom, under a powerful leader, constituted a new kind of problem, and threatened regional unity. Or, to put it another way, it was precisely the Shakan system—which Shepstone had recognized as fundamental to order in the Zulu kingdom, which he had sought to help Cetshwayo uphold when the oaths were originally proclaimed, which he had in part emulated in his own administration, and whose legitimacy he had sought to harness to his own purposes—that was now deemed to be anachronistic and the chief threat to a new regional vision. In particular, the British authorities were anxious about the specifically Shakan legacies of a powerful centralized leadership with a "drilled" and obedient army.[138]

Shepstone was thus obliged to reject the Zulu delegation's land claims, and he presented them with a sudden ultimatum. Cetshwayo was ordered to make reparations for border infringements against the Transvaal and to accept revolutionary modifications in the social and political institutions of the Zulu kingdom. As a partial justification of the ultimatum to the Zulu people the British high commissioner, Sir Bartle Frere, cited Shepstone's "coronation" of Cetshwayo. He accused Cetshwayo of breaking the "laws" proclaimed by Shepstone at the installation. The demand in the ultimatum for adherence to the "coronation laws," as well as a call for the lifting of restrictions on marriage and the disbanding of the standing army—generally considered to be the two chief Shakan innovations—struck at the heart of the Shakan system, and thus at Zulu power. The Colonial Office in London was, however, reluctant to take on a war with the Zulu at this stage, and required further persuasion of the appropriateness of this timing from the officials on the spot in Natal.

At this point the representation in colonial discourse of Zulu history, and of Shaka specifically, shifted dramatically. Whereas in 1873 Shepstone had seen fit to install Cetshwayo "as Chaka," on the eve of the Anglo-Zulu War Sir Bartle Frere prepared a long analysis of the violent course of Zulu history set in motion by Shaka and sustained by Cetshwayo. He presented Cetshwayo as "anxious to emulate the sanguinary fame of his uncle Chaka,"[139] whose "history is written in characters of blood,"[140] and criticized him for trying to break "loose from all restraint and re-establish the regime of Chaka's unmitigated barbarism."[141] He accused Cetshwayo of trying to achieve this through the maintenance of regulations "directed to forming every young man in Zululand into a celibate Man-destroying gladiator."[142] The analysis underpinning the tirade was unmistakably Shepstone's.[143] But if the outburst was informed by his understanding of the nature of Zulu power, and if, in some respects, Frere and Shepstone employed similar language in discussing the reign of Shaka, Frere's version of the Zulu past, as well as the evaluation it contained, was in a very different register to that of Shepstone. For Frere, Shaka's reign was chaotic and dangerous; for Shepstone, it was, above all, a reign of order and restraint. Nonetheless, the secretary for native affairs could well see how that order itself might now be a threat to the proposed confederation. He could also see how the lack of it would disrupt native administration. Shepstone was caught on the horns of a dilemma.

The excessively short deadline attached to the ultimatum ensured that war between the Zulu kingdom and the British empire broke out early in 1879. When, at Isandlwana, the Zulu forces got the better of their aggressors, Britain—initially chary of the war—threw its efforts into breaking the Zulu power, and placed its faith in its favorite soldier, Sir Garnet Wolseley.

One of Wolseley's first moves was to announce that the British were not at war with the Zulu people, but with their brutal and tyrannical king. Once the war was won, Wolseley moved to depose the king, and, as he expressed it, to give the Zulu their freedom.[144] Wolseley depicted Cetshwayo as "influenced at times by drink and almost always by the crafty cruelty and craving for power he inherited from his fiendish ancestor, Chaka."[145]

The British victors did not annex Zulu territory, but dismantled the unitary kingdom created by Shaka, replacing it with thirteen chiefdoms ruled by British appointees, including prominent members of the Zulu royalty who were attached to clans collateral to the royal clan, notably Hamu kaNzibe and Zibhebhu kaMaphitha. Members of the house of Shaka were largely stripped of power and influence. In a rushed but symbolic cavalcade, the British paraded the captured Zulu king across Zululand *en route* to exile in the Cape and incarceration in Cape Town Castle.[146]

The authorities depicted the settlement as a return to the pre-Shakan status quo, although the thirteen new chiefdoms bore little relation to pre-Shakan political divisions. Within one of them, in the Mthethwa region, a separate initiative to assert a pre-Shakan legitimacy developed around one Sitimela, who claimed to be a descendant of Dingiswayo, the Mthethwa chief under whose paramountcy Shaka rose to power. The colonial authorities were not disposed to tolerate this challenge to the settlement, and suppressed Sitimela's initiative.[147]

The thirteen appointed chiefs struggled to exercise their new authority, and when Hamu and Zibhebhu attempted to do so, they were fiercely resisted by groups within their new chiefdoms who had been closely associated with the deposed royal house. At the end of 1881 civil war broke out in Zululand between a revived uSuthu royalist party, led by the closest relatives of the exiled king and the king's son Dinuzulu, and a faction headed by the Mandlakazi leader, Zibhebhu. The result was chaos and bloodshed across the country.

The British resident, Melmoth Osborn (known—like Shepstone—by a Zulu name, "Malimati"), did not technically have the authority to intercede in the conflict, although he increasingly overstepped his powers to assist Zibhebhu against the house of Shaka. His position symbolized the absence of a central authority under the new settlement, and he gradually sought to arrogate to himself such powers. For much of the 1880s, Osborn—as the man on the spot, the local Zulu expert—was to be the main interlocutor between the Zulu and the British officials.[148] As Frances Colenso wrote in 1888, Osborn was himself "creeping up into the place of tyrant, absolute and supreme."[149]

Shepstone—whose own reputation as an expert in African affairs continued unchallenged, except by Colenso—attacked the 1879 settlement. Although he now asserted that Zulu society consisted of a number of "tribes" yearning "for their ancient and separate existence, relieved of the terrible incubus of the Zulu royal family,"[150] Shepstone claimed that the settlement, which had replaced one tyrant with many, would lead to "anarchy of a dangerous kind."[151] He sympathized with the difficulties Osborn faced and advocated instead the implementation of his original system, rooted as it was in notions of the vesting of power in a single supreme chief. He wanted Natal and Zululand to be treated together and placed under the control of a British resident, with white magistrates in every district assisting local chiefs. In other words, Shepstone, ever the pragmatist, recognized that British interests were in conflict with the present royal house and, as at Nodwengu in 1861 and emLambongwenya in 1873, had no objections to seeing it supplanted by another branch of the family more amenable to imperial designs, or even by a white supreme chief. What he did object to, and considered foolhardy, was the authorities' failure to adhere to the *principles* of the Shakan system.

Shepstone's advice was not taken in 1879, and although he effectively retired from public life after 1880, he continued to work behind the scenes to promote his vision of native policy. He achieved this through what the Colensos called the "Shepstone clique." Guy identifies the members of the clique as Osborn, the special commissioners to Zululand—successively in the 1880s, Sir George Pomeroy Colley, Sir Henry Bulwer, and Sir Arthur Havelock—as well as Shepstone's brother John and his son Henrique.[152]

In the face of the ongoing upheaval north of the Thukela, Shepstone began to lobby for the reinstallation of Cetshwayo. He argued that authority in Zulu society had to be clearly defined and located in a single source. Indeed, Shepstone had not been part of Frere's vilification campaign against Shaka, although he had been severely critical of Cetshwayo. He remained alert to the enormous symbolic importance of the figure of Shaka in the African communities concerned. In 1879, for example, he was telling Wolseley that "Dingaan was a far greater monster than Chaka: that whilst the nation generally look back with pride to the memory of the latter as being a great king and organizer, noone even refers to Dingaan except with horror."[153] He also stressed the considerable power of the Shakan legacy within the Zulu kingdom.[154] Shepstone was careful to link the reinstallation to the excision from Cetshwayo's authority of a strip of southern Zululand, which would be open to settlement by Natal Africans, another cause for which Shepstone had long lobbied.

In 1883, when the British authorities agreed to Cetshwayo's return, Shepstone momentarily emerged from retirement to sally forth across the Thukela to Mthonjaneni once again, to supervise the restoration. This time, however, the arrangements were not conducted by the British in the name of Shaka. Rather, the authorities specifically continued to discredit the legacy of Shaka. Likewise, those chiefs who had gained positions and territory with the 1879 settlement resisted the reinstallation of the king through the assertion of pre-Shakan allegiances. Ntshingwayo kaMahole, the Khoza chief, one of the thirteen appointees in terms of the 1879 settlement, said he would have nothing to do with the house of Shaka.[155] Resistance to the attempt to excise a section of the kingdom was, in turn, stated in terms of the inviolability of the Shakan inheritance. As Batakati kaMnyamana put it, when asked to indicate to the authorities the extent of his domain, "How can I divide the land, when it is all the land of Tshaka?"[156]

In 1883 Cetshwayo landed on the Zululand coast and was met by Shepstone. The whole enterprise was greeted with extreme suspicion, with most people, as Shepstone put it, expecting "that we should present some counterfeit instead of Cetywayo himself." Once again, Cetshwayo refused the offer of a carriage to convey him to the first camp on the way to Mthonjaneni. In the walk to the camp, Cetshwayo began to challenge Shepstone's version of the restoration, passing out the message to his supporters who saw him *en route* that the proposed partition should be disregarded. This challenge continued, much to Shepstone's annoyance, for the rest of the trip.[157] When the first senior member of the Zulu royal family, Dabulamanzi, came to meet Cetshwayo, the occasion was marked by what Shepstone describes as the "dancing of Chaka's war dance."[158] Finally, the restoration party arrived at Mthonjaneni, the high spot overlooking the *emakhosini* where Shepstone had camped in 1873. Whereas on the previous occasion Shepstone was eager for the ceremony to take place in the *emakhosini* and was steered away from the Zulu heartland by Cetshwayo, this time Cetshwayo, anxious about the small show of support at the various stops on the journey up from the coast, wanted the proceedings to take place in the *emakhosini*. Shepstone, pleading heat, advocated the high ground of Mthonjaneni.[159]

In contrast to the high pomp with which Shepstone had enacted the "coronation," the British role in the restoration was subdued, or, as Frances Colenso bitingly remarked, "every effort was made by Sir T. Shepstone (and sons and parasites) to take the gloss off the affair. . . ."[160] Nonetheless, the struggle over the meanings and significance of the various ceremonies and their locations that ensued echoed the earlier ceremony. Once again the *emakhosini* rituals of kingship were conducted secretly and independently of the authorities, and prior to Shepstone's formal reinstallation of the king,[161] and a story was told that Shaka's spirit, in the form of a snake, was seen crossing the Thukela, on a journey up from Shaka's grave south of the Thukela, signifying the return of the king's *idhlozi* (spirit) to the Zulu kingdom.[162] This time, Shepstone waited eleven days at Mthonjaneni (as opposed to the seven-day delay in 1873) before issuing an ultimatum that he would leave if the leading uSuthu (the supporters of the royal house) did not present themselves for the restoration ceremony.

The notables finally arrived and a short ceremony took place, in the course of which Shepstone again read out a set of rules demanding observance of prohibitions on controlling the timing of marriage, on execution without "fair and impartial trial," and on the practices of witchcraft and "smellings out," as well as a ban on the calling up of *amabutho*. These rules, in contrast to the coronation oaths which were directed at the assertive Zulu notables, struck at the heart of the power of the Zulu monarchy. They were described as a return to the "good and ancient customs . . . known and followed in the days preceding the establishment by Shaka of the system known as the military system."[163] The controls over marriage and over the *amabutho* were the basis of royal power as constituted by Shaka.[164] Shepstone did his duty, playing the role that only he could play, and reinstalled the Zulu king. But he did so caught in a double bind. Having

Cetshwayo back in place was fundamental to his policy, but as the decade proceeded, and as the settlement eroded royal power, his vision of the administration of Zululand through a strong central king was becoming increasingly difficult to implement.

At the restoration ceremony Shepstone also announced the boundaries of the curtailed area that was to be under Cetshwayo's jurisdiction, as well as the limits of the reserved territory over which he was to have no say. Zibhebhu remained independent of Cetshwayo, and received compensation in the form of new territories in exchange for land which he was obliged to give up in terms of the revised settlement. Henry Francis Fynn was appointed British resident with Cetshwayo. Shepstone, ever conscious of the role of performance in the political discourse of the Zulu kingdom, then enacted his own withdrawal from Zulu affairs. He reputedly began by saying in *isiZulu,* "You see that I have been coming here to the Zulu country for a long time with government laws. You will not see me again because I am now weary of the government's work."[165] He went on to liken himself to an ox that has pulled a wagon for a long time and then is released and put out to graze. He ended: "It will not be inspanned again." And indeed, that was the last time Shepstone would play a part in the drama of colonialism.

Two months later, in March 1883, Zibhebhu defeated the uSuthu in a bloody battle and shortly afterwards attacked the royal homestead. The king went into hiding and a number of the highest Zulu officials were killed. Cetshwayo died in 1884, and Zibhebhu and Hamu continued to devastate the northern areas of the country. By this time, Carnarvon's dream of confederation had ended in humiliation for the British when the colonial forces were routed by Boer commandos. The contending parties in Zululand took advantage of the divisions. The uSuthu enlisted the aid of Boer fire-power in exchange for the land north of the Mhlathuze, and were finally able to counter Zibhebhu. At this point the British stepped in, and opened negotiations with the Transvaal Republic; the two powers partitioned Zululand between them, with the British formally annexing their section in 1887.

On annexation, the authorities tried to institute a form of the Shepstone system in Zululand, but without the strong central figure that was its linchpin. Resistance to the newly appointed magistrates continued to disrupt the territory. The authorities were most concerned about the recalcitrance of Cetshwayo's heir, Dinuzulu, and the regent, Ndabuko, in the Ndwandwe district, where the magistrate reported they were defying his authority. In November 1887 the governor travelled to Zululand to reprimand Dinuzulu and Ndabuko for continued intransigence and to fine them for activities since annexation. He declared: "Dinuzulu must know and all the Zulus must know that the rule of the House of Shaka is a thing of the past. It is dead. It is like water spilt on the ground. The Queen now rules Zulu-land and noone else."[166] Continued violence finally led to British troops entering the territory and the removal of the uSuthu leaders. The British authorities ac-cused Dinuzulu of being in revolt against them, tried him, and sentenced him to ten years' imprisonment on the island of St. Helena.

In the years before the attempted confederation, Shepstone had operated un-der tight fiscal constraints. He relied on imagination, pageantry, and symbolic acts of sovereign power to assert his influence north of the Thukela, and to bolster his authority in colonial Natal. He effectively harnessed the image of Shaka to his pro-ject. With confederation and the Anglo-Zulu War, sheer coercive weight replaced the dramaturgical and emic approach to domination. In the course of the war, the British authorities resolved to break the power of the Zulu royal house and sought to justify their intervention in the independent Zulu kingdom. To do this, they embarked on a campaign to discredit and annul the symbolic power of the image of the first Zulu king. This campaign, of which Shepstone was critical, and which he believed to be unworkable, was a corollary of confederation, which he sup-ported. In the face of this contradiction Shepstone restored Cetshwayo on terms fundamentally at odds with the system of native administration that he advocated.

The authorities' plan to discredit Shaka was foiled in two ways: firstly, the im-age of Shaka enjoyed a widespread appeal beyond that which they, with the excep-tion of Shepstone, recognized, and was not easily banished from the conscious-ness of the inhabitants of the former Zulu kingdom. Secondly, the "pre-Shakan" settlement they sought to impose on the territory lacked a central authority, and this led to widespread instability across the territory. Ultimately the British were forced by the conflicts that resulted to annex Zululand and, eventually, to restore Cetshwayo. As Shepstone had recognized, the prospect of government without a central figure posed problems beyond the capacities of the local administration to deal with. Indeed, European powers generally did not have the power to conquer, rule, and exploit their colonies without tapping into existing centers of power and making symbolic use of indigenous conceptions of power. Moreover, those in-digenous ideas were in themselves too potent and too resilient to be excised in the way that the British hoped they could be.

Whereas Shepstone had looked to the Zulu past and found in Shaka a model for the Natal native administration, in the course of events leading up to and fol-lowing the Anglo-Zulu War Shaka and Shakan times were transformed into a metaphor for contemporary politics. As I have argued, the metaphor did not sim-ply involve an image of Shaka as a tyrant, but rather had compressed into it a much richer complexity of meanings incorporating Shepstone's positive evalua-tions and Frere's negative ones, as well as echoes of the pragmatism which under-lay the restoration.

Zulu: "a household word"

The Anglo-Zulu War altered fundamentally Europe's appreciation and understanding of the Zulu people and the Zulu kings. With the war "the Zulu" achieved a distinct and recognizable identity in the eyes of the British. It was an identity that, on the eve of the new era of mass circulation, the popular press was—for the first time—key in giving shape to.[167] Illustrated weeklies sent their artists off to Zululand, some of the first photographs date from this period, and publishers commissioned heroic portraits. As Fred Fynney put it in a lecture given in about 1880, "'Zulu' has become almost a household word."[168] Indeed, it was as though the act of being written about established the existence of a distinct people, "the Zulu." On the whole, the press tended to follow Frere's line, that the Zulu people had to be freed from the cruelty and despotism of Cetshwayo and the legacy of the tyrant Shaka. This theme was pursued in a host of books, articles, pamphlets, lectures, and other ephemera that followed the war. Colonists, officials, and military personnel who served in the war all had their say.[169]

Yet at the same time as the tyranny and despotic savagery of the Zulu rulers was emphasized, the defeat of the British at Isandlwana also led British writers to explore themes of the exceptional abilities of the Zulu, especially their remarkable military system, their display of discipline, unity, and courage, which commanded respect and admiration. Queen Victoria herself described the Zulu as "the finest and bravest race in South Africa."[170] This emphasis on the exceptional qualities of the Zulu was echoed elsewhere in the empire where defeated but challenging enemies—worthy foes such as the Asante, the Gurkhas, or the "Fuzzy-Wuzzies" who broke the British square—came to be admired. In so far as this admiration focused on the military system, it followed closely Shepstone's own analysis of Zulu power. But the post-war regard was also based on grounds more limited than the admiration Shepstone accorded the Zulu system. Where Shepstone favored the despotism of the Zulu kings, the post-war admiration was solely for the drilling and the discipline of the Zulu army.

There were, of course, some opposition views, notably those voiced by clerics such as Colenso. Colenso's understanding of the Zulu kingdom was qualitatively different from that expressed in the official pronouncements of the Anglo-Zulu War. With the support of the Aborigines' Protection Society (APS), and through the medium of his own printing-press at Bishopstowe, letters to the London papers, and APS pamphlets,[171] Colenso took issue with Frere's account of Zulu history, which had depicted Cetshwayo's rule as a reversion to the Shakan model and as a reaction to the mildness of Mpande's reign. He argued that Frere had been unceasing in his efforts to blacken Cetshwayo's character and to make him appear odious in the eyes of Englishmen, who would never have endured, as they have done hitherto—very reluctantly, it is true, and with grave misgivings— that such things should have been done in their name in these parts, if they had not been led to suppose that the Zulu King was really the loathsome monster which Sir B.Frere has persistently represented him to be.[172]

Colenso's approach was to expose Frere's tactics and to defend Cetshwayo, and not to enter into debate about the earlier kings.

Bishop Colenso died on June 20, 1883, and from then on his arguments were developed and carried forward by his family. Frances Colenso, in her account of the Zulu War, written together with Anthony Durnford, argued that Cetshwayo had made great advances since the times and practices of his predecessors, Shaka and Dingane, and, like Bishop Colenso, she gave scant attention to historical background, according the most space to events leading up to the war. She rejected Frere's argument that the origins of the war lay in Shaka's legacy.[173] In a lecture on Zululand, Harriette Colenso covered Shaka's reign only briefly, noting however that the first Europeans soon began "to dissipate the idea of his celestial character."[174]

Interest in the Zulu kingdom waned after their defeat at Ulundi, and then, in 1882, experienced a recrudescence when Cetshwayo visited London to plead for his restoration. Henry Rider Haggard's book *Cetywayo and his White Neighbours* was timed to coincide with the visit, and inaugurated Haggard's career as one of the foremost and most prolific representers of "the Zulu" outside Zululand. By this time, Haggard had already published three reports founded on his experiences in South Africa, and begun to establish himself as a knowledgeable commentator on the country. His first article, "The Transvaal," had been published in *Macmillan's Magazine* in May 1877. In it Haggard gave a brief account of the territory's history and made the case for annexation. His second article was a description of "A Zulu War Dance" published in the *Gentleman's Magazine*. Haggard based this account on his direct experience of a dance he had attended as a member of Sir Henry Bulwer's staff at the homestead of Chief Pakati. In September of the same year, a third article appeared in the *Gentleman's Magazine,* an account of the visit he undertook as a member of Shepstone's staff to the Pedi chief, Sekhukhune.[175]

Haggard then moved back to England and wrote *Cetywayo and his White Neighbours.* The book was a carefully researched presentation of recent political developments in southeast Africa. Haggard criticized the division of the Zulu kingdom into thirteen chieftaincies, advocating instead a return to the Shepstone system. He argued that the "laws" proclaimed at the "coronation" were in no way binding on the independent Zulu king.[176]

In this work, Haggard was critical of aspects of colonial policy toward the Zulu kingdom, but he defended the secretary for native affairs and the Shepstonian system:

It is very clear that things cannot remain in their present condition. If they do, it is probable that the Resident will sooner or later be assassinated; not from any personal motives, but as a political necessity, and some second Chaka will rise up and found a new Zulu dynasty, sweeping away our artificial chiefs and divisions like cobwebs.[177]

The book opens with a discussion of the possibility of Cetshwayo's restoration. "To understand the position of Cetywayo," Haggard writes, "both with reference to his subjects and the English Government, it will be necessary to touch, though briefly, on the history of Zululand since it became a nation, and also on the principal events of the ex-king's reign." Naturally, Haggard begins with Shaka, the "African Attila" whose "invincible armies . . . had slaughtered more than a million human beings." If Haggard's Shaka was "the presiding genius of a saturnalia of slaughter," his methods of government and warfare were nonetheless "most effective." Detailing the first Zulu king's achievements, Haggard concluded that "the result was, that though Chaka's armies were occasionally annihilated, they were rarely defeated and never ran away." For Haggard, the Zulu military system "was the universal-service system of Germany brought to absolute perfection."[178]

Haggard's study acknowledged the pressures of this system on Cetshwayo, notably the link between killing and the maintenance of authority, but Haggard refused to countenance the Colensos' argument that this constituted a defense of Cetshwayo:

To admit that the Zulu king has the right to kill as many of his subjects as he chooses, so long as they will tolerate being killed is one thing, but it is certainly surprising to find educated Europeans adopting a line of defence of these proceedings on his behalf that amounts to a virtual expression of approval, or at least of easy toleration.

In these respects Haggard's rhetoric echoed that of the war-mongering officials seeking to "liberate" the country from the tyranny of the Zulu kings. But Haggard's criticism of Colenso was contradictory, for elsewhere he makes practically the same judgment as Colenso.[179] Haggard also disputed another claim about Cetshwayo, Sir Garnet Wolseley's assertion that Cetshwayo's rule was built up "without any of the ordinary and lawful foundations of authority, and by the mere vigour and vitality of an individual character."[180] Haggard believed that Cetshwayo's authority was based on a combination of the legacy of Shaka and the present king's own abilities—the relevance of ability being itself a Shakan legacy—as well as a perception within the Zulu kingdom of the need for a strong central authority. Haggard further acknowledged that vast numbers would rally to the side of Cetshwayo's legal heir.[181] For Haggard, writing in 1882, the choice was either that the British government would have to step in as a clearly defined political authority or Cetshwayo would have to be restored and "allowed to rule in his own fashion or not at all."[182] Thus he reproduced Shepstone's analysis of the nature of political authority in the Zulu kingdom, and acknowledged its potential powers.

In 1888 a second edition of *Cetywayo and his White Neighbours* appeared, with a new introduction. In the introduction Haggard, discussing the annexation of Zululand to the British crown in 1887, invoked the Shepstonian conception of the peculiar nature of Zulu political authority: "In the Zulu people the Queen will, I am convinced, find subjects as loyal and as devoted as any she owns . . . and for so long as it [the Zulu country] is ruled as Zulus expect to be ruled, with firmness and without vacillation, there is little fear of serious disturbance."[183]

Like Shepstone, Haggard viewed the dispossession of African lands by white farmers as "little short of wicked,"[184] and he manifested the same relativism with regard to the identification of savagery and civilization. Again, like Shepstone, this was cast in the typically evolutionist language of the day.

> I could never discern a superiority so great in ourselves as to authorise us, by right divine as it were, to destroy the coloured man and take his lands. It is difficult to see why a Zulu, for instance, has not as much right to live in his own way as a Boer or an Englishman. Of course, there is another extreme. Nothing is more ridiculous than the length to which the black brother theory is sometimes driven by enthusiasts. A savage is one thing, and a civilised man is another; and though civilised men may and do become savages, I personally doubt if the converse is even possible. But whether the civilised man, with his gin, his greed, and his dynamite, is really so very superior to the savage is another question, and one which would bear argument, although this is not the place to argue it . . . Savagery is only a question of degree.[185]

In the new introduction to *Cetywayo and his White Neighbours,* Haggard condemned the war against the Zulu as "unjust" but indicted Cetshwayo for offenses against his own people, "whom he ruled with considerable cruelty." For Haggard, by 1888, Cetshwayo was "a man of some virtues and many faults, who inherited much of his great-uncle Chaka's ferocity without his genius."[186]

Later in the year that *Cetywayo and his White Neighbours* was published Haggard wrote two essays for *The South African,* on "The Restoration of Cetywayo" and "Some Aspects of the Native Question in the Transvaal,"[187] which made many of the same arguments as the book. Effectively, the Anglo-Zulu War had created an interest in the Zulu; Haggard fed that interest, but he fed it not with Frere's version of Zulu history and of Shaka, but with that of his "old friend and chief," Shepstone, overlain, perhaps, with some of the post-war sentiments of the Zulu as worthy foes. This was the view Haggard relayed to a readership hungry for tales of Africa.

While *Cetywayo and his White Neighbours* was influential, it was in the realm of popular romance that Haggard really succeeded in entrenching Shepstone's Shaka. In 1884, Haggard published *The Witch's Head,* which rehearses in fictional form a number of his arguments in support of Shepstone. The book features Shepstone, whom Haggard described as "the white t'Chaka" and "father of the Zulus,"[188] as well as the battle of Isandlwana; the model for another of the characters, Mr. Alston, was Melmoth Osborn, and the book includes sections of Haggard's real-life conversations with Osborn.[189] The book was well received, selling thousands of copies, and appearing in numerous editions.[190]

In September 1885 Haggard published his most famous romance, *King Solomon's Mines.*[191] Haggard wrote the book in six weeks in response to Robert Louis Stevenson's *Treasure Island.* It was soon heralded as "The Most Amazing Story Ever Written."[192] Stevenson himself commented on Haggard's remarkable "command of the savage way of speaking,"[193] the young Winston Churchill was "absorbed" by the tale, while the former prime minister William Gladstone was another of its fans.[194] In 1887 Haggard published *She,* the story of a quest that leads three British travelers to the land of the cannibalistic Amahagger ruled by Ayesha, She-who-must-be-obeyed, an immortal and beautiful white queen reigning in the interior of Africa. This book, too, was an instant bestseller.[195]

While none of Haggard's earliest novels was set in the Zulu kingdom, Zulus figure prominently in them, either as fine and special individuals, as acknowledged models for the fictional communities in the novels, or even as the pole that defined their opposite: people of the sky/heavens (Zulu) as opposed to the people of the rock (Amahagger), or the orderly, well-trained Zulu as opposed to the cannibalistic Amahagger.[196] In this we detect a direct echo of Shepstone's use of the Natal/cannibalism and Zulu kingdom/social order oppositions. In 1887 Haggard introduced his first fully developed Zulu character—Umslopogaas, "the bravest Zulu of them all"[197]—into his latest novel, *Allan Quatermain.*

"The novelist of indirect rule"—Shepstone style

In an analysis of *King Solomon's Mines* and *She,* the literary scholar David Bunn argues that Haggard "invents an African landscape so as to explore a model of colonial development."[198] While Bunn is primarily concerned with the significance of this for the ideological conflation in colonial fiction of the image of women and the image of Africa, his proposition has implications for the understanding of Shaka as presented in Haggard's novels. Bunn argues that *King Solomon's Mines* and the other novel he looks at briefly, *Allan Quatermain,* chart the development of British indirect rule in Africa. "As such," he concludes, "they are an historically specific account of the structures and strategies that put imperialist ideology into practice."[199]

Norman Etherington, who also considers the connections between the image of women and Africa in Haggard's work, describes Haggard as "the novelist of indirect rule." Etherington argues that the "Shepstonian ideal of good imperial government was never absent from Haggard's mind when he wrote about relations between captive nations and their conquerors," and suggests this sophisticated perspective as the resolution to the contradictions that many critics have identified in Haggard between his overtly imperialist politics and the anti-colonialist stances of many of his novels.[200]

Bunn and Etherington correctly point to the discussion of themes of imperialism in Haggard's novels, but fail to explore how Shepstone's version of colonial rule differed from that of indirect rule elsewhere. They are not alert to the extent to which colonial discourse drew on early African discourses, notably the connection between Shaka and questions of sovereignty. Specifically, they neglect the impact on Haggard's novels of African narratives as transmitted and translated through Shepstone. They fail to explore the significance in Haggard's works of the entry of Europeans deep into African society beyond the easy identification of their journeys as "penetration," and they miss the intertwining of indigenous and colonial logics that is reflected in the novels.

In *She,* for example, the novelist explores the nature of rule by an outsider—the immortal white Ayesha—over a local African society. Political authority in Ayesha's case is based on the awe she inspires. Like Shepstone, who lacked the coercive and financial means to establish a real basis for his power, Ayesha has no standing army. She asks of her British visitors, "How thinkest thou that I rule these people? I have but a regiment of guards to do my bidding, therefore it is not by force. It is by terror. My empire is of the imagination."[201]

In *King Solomon's Mines,* the Englishmen—Allan Quatermain, Sir Henry Curtis, and Captain Good—penetrate deep into Kukuanaland, involving themselves in local politics and ultimately becoming an important force in the overthrow of

King Twala. They install in his place a member of their own party, Umbopa, the long-absent rightful heir. Like Shepstone at Nodwengu, the three Europeans are treated like "kings" from the time of their arrival. They are greeted with the royal salute, and gain the power over life and death. Finally Haggard has the newly installed Umbopa rehearse Cetshwayo's restoration oaths. In so far as the restoration oaths curtail the indigenous monarch's right of access to the labor of women, they cut into the heart of his power.[202]

In 1892 Haggard published *Nada the Lily*. The idea for this book originated with Haggard's friend and critic, and one time co-author, Andrew Lang, who wrote in the *Scots Observer* at much the same time as he was urging Haggard to write this piece, "how delicious a novel *all* Zulu, without a white face in it, would be!"[203] *Nada the Lily* is an "all Zulu" book about the reign of Shaka told "in a popular shape." "An attempt has been made in these pages," writes Haggard in the preface, "to set out the true character of this colossal genius and most evil man,—a Napoleon and a Tiberius in one. . . ." The novel tells the story of the origins of one of Haggard's most popular characters (already encountered in the novel *Allan Quatermain*), Umslopogaas. In *Nada the Lily* Shaka is portrayed as both a bloodthirsty tyrant and as a noble and able leader, one who would "always save the life of a brave man." Haggard narrates how Baleka, a paramour of Shaka, conceives the king's child and pleads with his mother, Nandi, to help her save the child from the death that is the fate of all the king's progeny.[204]

One of Shaka's senior councilors, Baleka's brother Mopo, is drawn into the plan to save the child. When his wife gives birth to twins, Mopo exchanges the body of his own stillborn son for that of the king's son, whom he has been ordered by Shaka to kill. Shaka's son, the child "Umslopogaas," is then reared as Mopo's son and brother to the other twin, Mopo's daughter, the wondrously beautiful Nada, after whom the book takes its title.

In this way, Haggard invents a real heir for Shaka, and uses his descent from the Zulu king to invest him with exceptional abilities, which make him able to achieve astonishing things in the course of the novel. In this story, Haggard explores the notion of traditional leadership: both the charismatic leadership of Shaka and its transformation into inherited leadership as invested in Umslopogaas. Shaka's power is, on the one hand, ordained. Haggard—employing the technique of prophecy with origins in biblical texts, but also in African oral traditions—has the young child Shaka foretell his own greatness early in the book. His status is also represented as a consequence of his own bold deeds and his capacity to provide decisive leadership. Likewise, Umslopogaas, whose royalty is inherited, demonstrates the same abilities and daring, a point Haggard has Shaka recognize in the book, saying, "Why this calf is such another one as was dropped long ago in the kraal of Senzangacona . . . As I was, so is this boy."[205]

Over time, the Zulu king's power and authority came to be invested with a new legitimacy: after Shaka's death, Haggard has Mopo note that there were "many in the land who loved the memory of Chaka . . . For now that Chaka was dead, people forgot how evilly he had dealt with them, and remembered only that he was a great man, who had made the Zulu people out of nothing, as a smith fashions a bright spear from a lump of iron."[206] Mopo, like Shepstone, is a kingmaker, who advises Shaka on how to trick his witchdoctors, who hides the rightful heir, kills Shaka, and plays Mpande off against Dingane, to bring down the latter. Haggard, like Shepstone, suggests that Zulu terrain can be appropriately searched for concepts of sovereignty that might be useful for colonial rule. The reading of power in *Nada the Lily* is strongly Shepstonian. Unlike the despotism of Ayesha in *She,* Shaka, while cruel, is also benevolent and capable. The novel explores the way the Shepstone system sought to reach into a Zulu world to discover the principles by which it might best establish its authority. As in Shepstone's texts, the oppositions in Haggard's novels are not simply those typical of much late-Victorian literature.

When completed, *Nada the Lily* was serialized in the *Illustrated London News*[207] as well as the *New York Herald,*[208] and the book appeared in May 1892. Haggard dedicated the book to Shepstone. Investing him with yet another paternity,[209] and addressing Shepstone by his Zulu name, as "Sompseu, my father," Rider Haggard invoked the tale of how Shepstone "first . . . mastered this people of the Zulu" by outsitting the Zulu at the nomination of Cetshwayo: "Thus, Sompseu, your name became great among the people of the Zulu, as already it was great among many another tribe, and their nobles did you homage, and they gave you the Bayete, the royal salute, declaring by the mouth of their Council that in you dwelt the spirit of Chaka."[210] In this way Haggard established Shepstone's expertise on "the Zulu" and on questions of sovereignty, and, through it, his own authority to write about Shaka and the Zulu. Haggard sent a copy to Shepstone, who wrote back:

> I need not say how gratifying to me that gift was; nor how deeply touching to me the kind words of the Dedication were. Indeed, you give far more credit than I am entitled to. Your kindly expressions, however, vividly brought to mind a whole chapter of the pleasant past between us, the exact counterpart of which will, I suppose, never occur to any other two.[211]

It was to be the last communication between the friends, for on June 23, 1893, Shepstone died.

The dedication to Shepstone of *Nada the Lily* makes explicit its Shepstonian legacy: the connections between the novel and issues of administration, sovereignty, and Shaka. The novel was at once a recognition of the power of the image of Shaka and an imaginative exploration of its possibilities in distinctly Shepstonian terms. Thus the novel entrenched the legacy of Shaka. As Mopo said in the novel:

> Many of the great chiefs who are friends to me hate Dingaan and fear him, and did they know that a son of Chaka lived . . . he may well climb to the throne upon their shoulders. Also the soldiers love the name of Chaka, though he dealt cruelly with them, because at least he was brave and generous. But they do not love Dingaan, for his burdens are the burdens of Chaka but his gifts are the gifts of Dingaan; therefore they would welcome Chaka's son if once they knew him for certain.[212]

Umslopogaas' various adventures cause him to lose a taste for power—though had he wished for it, he would have achieved it. Instead, he ended up fighting on the side of Mbuyazi against Cetshwayo at the battle of Ndondakusuka. Through his support of Mbuyazi Umslopogaas, as Shaka's real heir, lends the sanction of the direct line of Shaka to Mbuyazi's claim to the kingship. In the novel the machinations of Mopo, the statesman, on behalf of Umslopogaas, the son of Shaka, ended at the battle of Ndondakusuka, the point at which began, in real life, the machinations of Shepstone, the statesman, regarding the Zulu succession. The novel is filled with imperial longing for a real alternative to the existing house of Shaka, as well as a typically Shepstonian acknowledgment of its symbolic power. Indeed, the telling of the story that Haggard records in *Nada the Lily* takes place on the grave of Shaka, where the elderly Mopo has retired.[213]

In placing the narrator, Mopo, on the grave of Shaka, Haggard demonstrates an understanding of the significance of Shaka which the colonial authorities at the time of Anglo-Zulu War lacked, but which Shepstone grasped in full measure. Yet *Nada* was not just a novel shaped by the concerns of early Natal native policy. The story of *Nada the Lily* also rehearsed later views of Zulu politics: Shaka was portrayed as a tyrant "who slaughtered more than a million human beings." Haggard's imagery constantly invokes upheaval and wanton butchery. In Shaka's domain, even the sun sank "redly, flooding the land with blood." It was as though, Haggard continued, "all the blood that Chaka had shed flowed about the land Chaka ruled." Indeed, the story was so gory it caused an outcry at the time of its publication.[214] The representation of Shaka as a bloodthirsty tyrant thus justified his murder in the book by Mopo. The echo in the novel of imperial arguments to justify intervention in the Zulu kingdom on the eve of the Anglo-Zulu War is unmistakable. But Haggard's Shaka was also a gifted leader of ability, a king who succeeded, in Kipling's terms, in "drilling" men. He had a "military organisation, perhaps the most wonderful the world has seen."[215] Through his novels, Haggard entrenched in the popular mind the image of the Zulus as natural fighters. As it was put in *King Solomon's Mines,* "There are two things in the world as I have found it which cannot be prevented: you cannot keep a Zulu from fighting or a sailor from falling in love upon the slightest provocation." Shaka's perfectly trained regiments were depicted by Haggard as the source of his power and his kingship, and his own daring, confidence, and abilities were part of the legitimacy of his kingship. This depiction was partly the legacy of the post-war fascination with "the Zulu," but it also had origins in Shepstone's understanding of the first Zulu king and his system of administration.

The image of Shaka that Haggard promoted was not his invention. It was, obviously, powerfully governed by the prevailing conventions of popular romance in English literature. But it was also shaped in the course of three developments. The first was Shepstone's enactment of Shaka in the development of a model for Natal native policy; the second, the invocation of Shaka-the-tyrant as the reason for British involvement north of the Thukela; and the third, a return to the emphasis on Shaka as a source of order and discipline, in strong echo of Shepstone's original view of the first Zulu king.

Haggard's *Nada* demonstrates a recognition that the questions of power and sovereignty were harnessed inextricably to Shaka and, as such, captured not just the dilemmas of indirect rule, but the peculiar problems posed by Shepstone's unique apprehension of the logic of Shaka and its ideological power. The novel develops the implication of Shepstone's views of Shaka and establishes the Zulu king—"one of the greatest geniuses and most wicked men who ever lived"[216]—as a fully ambiguous figure in relation to power and sovereignty.

The burden of the argument here is that the ambiguity which characterizes many accounts of Shaka, and which has been variously ascribed to the contributions of twentieth-century authors such as Thomas Mofolo, Ernst Ritter, or Mazisi Kunene, derived originally from African oral texts and indigenous political developments. This ambiguity was taken up and given a particular shape by Shepstone. His appropriation of Shaka as the basis of Natal native policy in the middle decades of the nineteenth century, the rejection of Shaka in the period leading up to the Anglo-Zulu War, and the post-war admiration of the Zulu were all part of the fashioning of that image. All these processes made Haggard's Shaka deeply ambiguous.

The work of scholars such as Anne McClintock reveals other themes in Haggard's writing that can be related to the Shaka image, and, while not central to the argument being advanced here, have much to add to this analysis. McClintock shows, for instance, that Haggard's representation of women was not simply a pathological form of imperial patriarchy. She offers a nuanced reading of the narrative disciplining of female reproductive power in *King Solomon's Mines* in terms of an imperial concern with the regeneration of the Family of Man and of Victorian patriarchy. In the course of her argument McClintock observes that it is female interference in the succession of male inheritance that plunges Kukuanaland into chaos. Noting that certain details of the story (such as beliefs about the dangers of twins) are derived from Zulu ethnography and served Haggard's interests by figuring a perilous threat to patriarchal continuity, she does not explore the way in which the Kukuana succession fracas is modeled directly on the story of Shaka's own succession, the twin detail excepted. Indeed, the idea of female interference in the succession of male inheritance and its capacity to plunge the land into chaos is an element of the indigenous nineteenth-century African narratives that Haggard drew on directly[217]—stories about Shaka's paternal aunt, Mnkabayi, constituting a case in point.

Haggard's writings were profoundly influenced by his visit to South Africa, and his close friendship with Shepstone and the other "native experts" who were part of the annexation party that made the trip to Pretoria with Shepstone in 1877. He acknowledged them repeatedly as the sources of many of his tales: Osborn's eyewitness account of the battle of Ndondakusuka, for example, was used in a later novel.[218] Haggard admired Osborn's fluency in *isiZulu* and credited him with an intimate knowledge of the "Zulu" mode of thought. From the colonial administrator Fred Fynney, Haggard heard tell of a great witchfinding which he used as the basis for the witchhunt scene in *King Solomon's Mines*. For Fynney, Shaka, "the Lion of the Zulu Nation," had "great ability as a general"[219] and he expressed his view of Shaka's establishment of his political authority in admiring terms:

> After destroying the head of a tribe, Tyaka showed great consideration for the people, supplying them liberally with cattle, and, whilst dreaded, he was said to have a liberal hand, and to be a benefactor to those with small kraals, so that each day found him adding numbers of subjects to his already large following, and thus increasing his power. It may be a matter of wonder that such a man could gain esteem; but he did, and was literally worshipped. He did all he could to re-assure those whom he conquered.[220]
>
> Tyaka's character appears to have been one which was an enigma even to the Zulus themselves, for as one of his old indunas once explained to me, it was impossible even to say with him what the next move would be. He said, ". . . He was a strange man, nay, a *silwana* (a wild animal), but we Zulus loved him for all that." He never allowed a brave man to go unrewarded, or a coward to go unpunished. . . .[221]

Furthermore, Fynney saw Shakan atrocities, such as the killings that followed the death of Nandi, as clever strategies employed by Shaka.[222] Fynney was thanked by name in the preface to *Nada the Lily,* and Haggard consulted his writings, as well as David Leslie's *Among the Zulus and Amatongas,* Bird's *Annals of Natal,* and relevant official documents.[223] Indeed, Haggard wrote of *King Solomon's Mines* in 1894: "It would be impossible for me to define where fact ends and fiction begins in the work, as the two are very much mixed up together,"[224] and he noted that many readers took books such as *King Solomon's Mines* to be true accounts.[225]

The ambiguity of Shaka as portrayed in *Nada the Lily* raises another theme that Haggard's books explore: the relation between savagery and civilization. Etherington has argued that the consistent identification of the European past with the African present which pervades the earlier novels, such as *King Solomon's Mines* and *She,* is played out in parallel between the "all Zulu" novel, *Nada,* and the book Haggard wrote immediately before it, *Eric Brighteyes,* in which all the characters were white, and the plot very similar to *Nada the Lily.* Etherington argues that the similarities were a consequence not just of Haggard's use of a formula, but of his preoccupation with the theme of common humanity.

Etherington further suggests that Haggard's popularity as a novelist was the result of his ability to give

> unique expression to a powerful mythology which sprang up after Darwin and which still grips the imaginations of large numbers of people in all walks of life. The basic ideas that people harbor within themselves vestiges of mankind's wild primitive past, and that the discovery of those hidden facets of the personality is akin to a journey from civilized Europe into darkest Africa, can be expressed in complex "serious" literature as variously as it can in "trashy" best-sellers or movies.[226]

In other words, the interior core of European man is equated with the African savage. With this argument, Etherington is developing Margaret Atwood's view of Haggard's work as a journey into the unknown region of self, the unconscious, and a confrontation with what lurks there. For Freudians or Jungians, Haggard is understood to have dredged up eternal truths from within his own psyche. Thus Etherington attributes the potency of Haggard's romances penned between 1885 and 1892 to their unique metaphorical expression of late-Victorian concepts of evolution, psychology, and anthropology. For those writers, Haggard's treks into Africa were forays into the unconscious unknown self. Etherington's arguments are compelling. However, this chapter suggests that Haggard's internal explorations operated within limits and constraints which were located outside the unconscious, and which were historically established. Thus Haggard's specific dualities must be seen as a reflection or legacy of Shepstone's views and as a replaying of Shepstone's dilemmas. The argument here is that, as much as the novels were inventions of "an other" in order to know the self, so too were their form and content the product of a particular historical process. To make this point is not to exclude Etherington's argument, but to suggest that it needs to be considered in the light of a historicized image of Shaka.

Inquiry into the origins of Haggard's ideas, as well as close analysis of their content, is a crucial exercise because the impact of Haggard's writings was enormous. More than any other writer, then or now, Haggard was responsible for establishing the popular images of Shaka and the Zulu people. *Cetywayo and his White Neighbours* was widely read, and informed a host of important opinion makers, men such as Lord Carnarvon, Lord Randolph Churchill, and Haggard's old associate from the annexation days, Marshall Clarke. The reprinted section alone sold over 30,000 copies. The critics were unanimous in their praise of *King Solomon's Mines,* and *The Spectator* devoted an editorial to the book, nominating it as the most exciting book ever published in a modern language. It was the first African story to find a wide readership. Within three months of publication, the publishers, Cassells, had to reprint it four times, and it sold 12,000 copies in the first twelve months. In Haggard's lifetime more than 650,000 copies were printed, and to this day it has never been out of print. In 1887 Haggard was almost certainly the country's best-paid novelist, and his works were widely read and extraordinarily popular. They were also prescribed for school use. *King Solomon's Mines* inspired over a dozen film versions, and other stories of his were produced in a host of editions, as well as made into films, stage productions, radio serials, an opera, and even a ballet, not to mention the various comic-book versions. A line from *Nada* inspired Rudyard Kipling's *Jungle Books,* and even Stevenson noted how much he liked Haggard's depiction of Shaka. Among the more than a hundred translations of Haggard's works, *Nada the Lily* was eventually translated into Zulu in 1954, and *King Solomon's Mines* into Afrikaans.[227]

In addition to his writings, Haggard was for a time chairman of the Anglo-African Writers' Club, and co-director and editor of a weekly newspaper called *The African.* He was offered the job as *The Times* war correspondent to South Africa in 1900. This he declined, but accepted an offer from the *Daily Express* to write a series of articles on "The New South Africa" after the war was concluded. The series never materialized, for the publishers agreed with Haggard's conclusion, after his visits to South Africa in 1901 and 1902, that it was too depressing. Haggard enjoyed thus a reputation as both an expert on the affairs of southern Africa and one of the premier writers of romance.[228]

With their "phenomenal print-runs" and acclaimed illustrated editions, Haggard's writings influenced generations of later readers and writers as well. Their ranks included Edgar Rice Burroughs, Edgar Wallace, C.S. Lewis, J.R.R. Tolkien, Laurens van der Post, D.H. Lawrence, Henry Miller, Stuart Cloete, and Graham Greene, as well as a later coterie of science fiction writers. King Edward VII, for example, preferred Haggard to Hardy.[229] As Morton Cohen comments, "Haggard's impact upon his time was probably greater than has been estimated. Almost every tale of wild adventure in strange lands that appeared after *King Solomon's Mines*—and they appeared by the hundreds—showed the Haggard stamp."[230] Haggard also influenced subsequent fictional renditions of Zulu history such as Sol. T. Plaatje's *Mhudi*, E.A. Ritter's *Shaka Zulu*, Peter Becker's *Rule of Fear, Chaka the Terrible* by Geoffrey Bond, and P.J. Schoeman's *Phampatha: The Beloved of King Shaka*.[231]

More difficult to evaluate is Haggard's influence on the writings of the academy. Three points can be made in this connection. Firstly, there are clear indications that books such as Ritter's *Shaka Zulu* which were themselves influenced by Haggard have, in turn, been drawn on by historians. Indeed, until recently, Ritter's text was cited in the *Encyclopaedia Britannica*. Secondly, many early scholars, and not a few contemporary ones, read Haggard's adventure stories in their youth. In 1895 Haggard was elected to the Athenaeum Club for distinguished scientific and literary authors, between a quarter and a third of whose members at the time were also members of the Royal Anthropological Institute. Finally, Haggard, who became a member of the Royal Colonial Institute in 1916, influenced directly the colonial officials on whose reports and records much academic history is based.[232] Coming chapters look in detail at the influence of Haggard on one particular official, James Stuart. Stuart is an especially significant indicator of the influence of Haggard, for he both read and enjoyed Haggard's novels, and also established a friendship with him. Moreover, Stuart, in his turn, influenced significantly both writers of texts that are much cited by historians—the work of the Rev. A.T. Bryant being a case in point—and, increasingly, through the *James Stuart Archive*, professional historians.

Graham Greene captured the power of Haggard's writing very nicely when he commented: "Far more than Scott, Haggard gave us a sense of History."[233] His visions of Africa and of "the Zulu" became the bases of those of thousands of readers. Morton Cohen summed it up: "Zulus could not be otherwise than Haggard pictures them."[234] One of the chief architects of a vision of Africa and of its introduction to a British public, Haggard was responsible for entrenching in popular form what was essentially Shepstone's view of the Zulu people, Zulu history, Zulu sovereignty, and the figure of Shaka.

Conclusion

In engineering the Zulu War, against the express wishes of the Colonial Office in London and in the face of the strenuous opposition of the Colensos and the Aborigines' Protection Society, officials on the spot in Natal found themselves under considerable pressure to provide strong vindication for their aggressive actions. The line of justification they opted for was the representation of Cetshwayo as an oppressive and cruel tyrant, and the designation of the war as a campaign against the king for the freedom of the Zulu people. When direct evidence of Cetshwayo's despotism proved hard to come by, the officials invoked instead a generalized notion of the tyranny of the institutions of the Zulu monarchy as established by Shaka and the military system on which its power rested. This led to the creation of an elaborate literature of vilification—unmatched since the vitriolic writings of Isaacs in the 1830s—on the subject of Shaka, his descendant Cetshwayo, and the Zulu system. Drawing on Shepstone's own analyses, the authorities identified the Shakan military system, represented as intact and ready for activation by Cetshwayo, as the root of the problem. The aim of the propaganda campaign, and the war, was not merely the removal of Cetshwayo, but also the disabling of the chief institutions of Zulu power. The campaign was both ideological and coercive.

The image of the Shakan legacy which officials such as Frere promoted did not go unchallenged and, while widespread during the war and in its immediate aftermath, was soon reshaped by ongoing developments. The major direct challenges came from the Colensos and their associates, who did not offer a different representation of Shaka so much as accuse Frere of gross misrepresentations, defend Cetshwayo against specific allegations, and expose the real reasons behind the war.

The first modification of the official campaign of vilification resulted from the battle of Isandlwana where the defeat of the British by the Zulu, and the manifest bravery and discipline of the Zulu forces throughout the war, earned the admiration of commentators and captured the imagination of the British public. The official image was thus tempered by a notion of the Zulu as a noble and worthy enemy, exceptional among the African peoples of southern Africa. "A remarkable people the Zulu," said Disraeli: "they defeat our generals; they convert our bishops; they have settled the fate of a great European dynasty" (the last being a reference to the death of the Prince Imperial of France in the Anglo-Zulu War). The same discipline that evoked this admiration was increasingly mobilized as a reason for annexation, for the Zulu were represented as ideal subjects, accustomed to firm control. In this way, an attempt was made to reharness the Shakan legacy, which Shepstone had earlier promoted as part of Natal native policy, to the post-conquest ideological project of the implementation of colonial rule.

"Prophecy," wrote Haggard in 1888 in the new introduction to *Cetywayo and his White Neighbours,* "is a dangerous thing."[235] Haggard went on to note that, while some of the predictions of that book had been shown over time to be misplaced, a central prediction was correct—his concluding remarks to the chapter on Zulu history—where he wrote: "On the whole, I am of the opinion that the Government that replaces Cetywayo on the throne of his fathers will undertake a very grave responsibility, and must be prepared to deal with many resulting complications."[236]

Shepstone's adoption of certain African conventions in the representation of Shaka did more than simply bring Shaka into the imperial repertoire. It brought a host of associated symbols, meanings, and narrative devices peculiar to African oral tradition and the renditions in those forms of the story of Shaka. Haggard followed Shepstone in bringing into western fiction narrative devices from Zulu texts. Appropriating the device of prophecy into the heart of his stories, Haggard entrenched in a mutated form one of the core explanatory devices of African oral histories. *Nada the Lily* opens with a prophecy from the child Shaka: "I am little to-day, and my people are a small people. But I shall grow big, so big that my head will be lost in the clouds; you will look up and you shall not see it. My face will blind you; it will be bright like the sun; and my people will grow great with me; they shall eat up the whole world."[237] And the narrator, Mopo, remarks that the last words he ever heard Shaka utter were also words of prophecy: "The whites will come and take away your royalty."[238] Likewise, Mopo's own mother foretells through a dream the killing of Shaka. These prophecies, like the one Shepstone uttered dramatically at the 1861 nomination, drew directly on a narrative trope from African oral tradition. Indeed, Mopo constantly prophesies in the novel and offers visions of doom and judgment.[239] Haggard further depicts Mopo as playing a key role in the setting of Shaka's trap for the false diviners—themselves credited with the ability to foresee—ironically only to be "smelt out" himself. Haggard's readers readily accepted the many prophecies that drove his narratives forward, for these resonated with the biblical narratives with which they were already familiar.

In 1911 Rudyard Kipling read his story "The Man Who Would Be King" to his close friend Rider Haggard.[240] This tragicomical story, like many other of Kipling's works, brings together "separate worlds and dimensions into confrontation and to set up a creative tension between them."[241] While the quotation from Kipling that heads this chapter introduces the plan for such a confrontation—in which the western world will try to overcome the eastern one—this chapter shows that this simple imperial agenda was, in a sense, confounded by Shaka, who had already drilled his men. Shaka had no sons. Unlike Dravot, the man in Kipling's story who would be king, Shaka tolerated no heirs. Dravot refused to abide by his original contract with his partner, Peachey Carnehan, not to get involved with women, even when Peachey reminded him that the "Bible says that Kings ain't to waste their strength on women, specially when they've got a raw new Kingdom to work over."[242] The central issue for both Kipling and Haggard—and, before and behind them, Shepstone—was the nature of imperial power in such a confrontation. Having taken up Zulu despotic rule, Shepstone tried to be the "White t'Chaka," but the problem remained of the appropriate heir for Shaka. Shepstone crowned Cetshwayo, but might easily have accepted a usurper. Effectively, Shepstone saw *himself* as Shaka's figurative heir. Haggard, in turn, invented Umslopogaas, only to have him eschew power. Under different conditions and much later in time, separate development and apartheid nominated, in their turn, their own paramount chiefs.

In his study of moments of cultural contact between natives and outsiders in the Marquesas, Dening notes that "model and metaphor are transpositions, readings of experience, products of consciousness. Their distinction," he continues, "lies in the fact that metaphors are understood and models are imposed."[243] Initially Shepstone entered into the experience of the Zulu kingdom, and sought to share in the metaphors of power that prevailed there. Over time, he translated those metaphors into a model for despotic authority that became the basis of the Shepstone system. Whereas the metaphor of Shaka was originally open-ended—an instrument for the daily understanding of issues of power and authority, capable of accommodating paradoxes and contradictions—as a model it became closed, static, structured, and simple. Shepstone imposed his model—much as Shaka imposed his rule—and Shaka became thus a means to power. Developments around the Anglo-Zulu War and the subsequent Zulu civil war brought about the transformation once more—although in changed form—of Shaka into a new kind of political metaphor, in other words a way of talking about power, in the new context of direct colonial domination backed by increased military power.

The latest work on the historical anthropology of cultural confrontation focuses on the question why some European cultural forms were incorporated into the everyday world of the colonized while others were contested or rejected. This chapter, however, looks at the opposite process, the incorporation of certain African cultural forms into the world of the colonizers. This incorporation was not the consequence of African resistance, but rather a result of the recognition by the colonial bureaucracy of the strength and suitability of African ideas. It reminds us that the colonization of consciousness involved much more than the imposition of some or many European capitalist cultural forms. It may be that these incorporations were very specific to the Zululand–Natal area and that they begin to explain the resilience there of precolonial identity and forms of consciousness.

In sum, the process of cultural confrontation was by no means as one-sided in terms of cultural transfer as is often thought, and an anthropology of the colonial encounter is incomplete without investigation of the cultural forms adopted by the agents of imperial domination. This chapter reveals the appropriation of a key symbol of the African precapitalist world, and its incorporation into the heart of early indirect rule.[244]

An influential engraving of Shaka, after a drawing by James King, which appeared in Nathaniel Isaacs' *Travels and Adventures in Eastern Africa* (1836)

10.5.14. (Sunday)

"Baleni ka Silwana ka Nohlovu ka Kuba ka Mnukwa ka Mpungose. I am of Mpungose tribe. (Accompanied by Menggqayi ka Mhangwa [wa kwa Mpungose]) I am of Dhloko regiment. I was born after Dingana had begun to fight with Boers; I was born in Dingana's reign. I was born at White Umfolozi in Mahlabatini valley. My father was of Sixebe regt. ie of those who cited Ndwandwe. He died *[towards end of 1839]* npombango ka Dingana no Mpande He was killed in battle & Magongo. I was a small boy when he died. I knew him. I do not know Nohlovu, my grandfather, exceptiways mpofu I grew up near Mfule river, Entonjaneni.

I to xega'd kwa Ndabakawombe — of one of Mpande's kraals. This kraal was at Mehlehat & on the Mfolozi ie on north bank. Ndabakawombe kraal was lower down White Mfolozi than Nodwengu & nearer Mlambongwenya.

I heard most of my history from Sigongo wa kwa Kanyile. Sigongo was of Sikezi regiment.

My mother was iNenyane class, la kwa Nobamba, nga pakat' ekaya.

My father had many children. The chief one"

Opposite, above: Henry Francis Fynn
Opposite, below: Sir Theophilus Shepstone
Above: Page from James Stuart's notebooks recording evidence by Baleni about Shaka (KCM 24188)
Right: James Stuart
(Killie Campbell Africana Library)

Above: Gathering at Cetshwayo's installation *Below left*: Cetshwayo enthroned
Below right: The crown made by the 75th Regiment's tailor (KCAL)

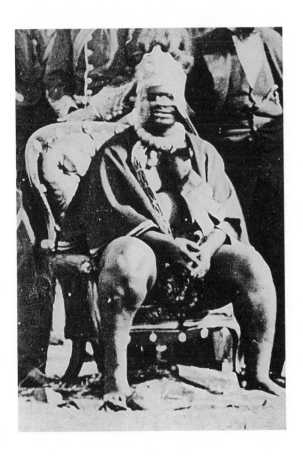

Kists on sale at the Mai-Mai Market, Johannesburg, with insets depicting
Shaka and other Zulu kings

Above: Spear-making at Shakaland, with the cultural adviser on the left
Below: The "boma" where guests dine (Photos courtesy of Eleanor Preston-
    Whyte)

Above: The culutral adviser greeting the homestead head (partly obscured) at
the entrance to the Great Kraal
Below: Shakaland's *isivivane* and model homestead

Henry Cele as Shaka in the television mini-series *Shaka Zulu*

"The establishment of a living source of tradition": James Stuart and the genius of Shakan despotism

The origins of an idea

Sir Theophilus Shepstone died just one year after the publication of the novel Haggard dedicated to him, *Nada the Lily*. The funeral was held in Pietermaritzburg on Sunday, June 25, 1893. Among the large crowd of mourners was a young man whose life's work was to become a campaign for the implementation of Shepstone's vision of native policy, James Stuart (1867–1942).

Stuart, a fluent Zulu linguist, had been employed since 1888 in the fledgling Zululand administration, based in Eshowe.[1] In a rather poignant letter written to his mother describing Shepstone's funeral, he observed that

> hundreds of natives from the surrounding country made a point of being present at their "Father's" funeral—it seemed almost as if they felt his death more than the Europeans did, and knowing their feelings I felt very sorry that no room was made for them in the procession—at any rate to the bigger men—and that no opportunity was given them for expressing the genuine sorrow they felt.[2]

Stuart later made a contribution to the Shepstone memorial which was erected in Pietermaritzburg, and mourned the death of "Natal's 'Grand Old Man',"[3] and the passing of an era.

A few weeks later, on July 4, 1893, Natal achieved responsible government. Until his death Shepstone, and indeed for a long time the Colonial Office in London, had resisted the push for responsible government because they feared that settler concerns would dominate local government and would direct native policy in a way that would serve their narrow sectoral interests to the detriment of the colony as a whole. In particular, they recognized that the settlers would limit African access to land in an effort to force increasing numbers of people onto the labor market.

In the year before his death Shepstone, having for his entire career withstood settler demands for the release of African labor from the homesteads, fired his final salvoes. In 1892 the *Natal Mercury* published his last treatises on "The Native Question," later reprinted in booklet form.[4] Arguing that "Short cuts which ignore the great gulf that separates the social and political ideas of the two races must sooner or later bring disaster," Shepstone lobbied hard against new developments in Natal native policy and what he saw as pressure from Natal colonists for the dismantling of the "tribal system." Shepstone first reminded Natalians that the African inhabitants of the territory were aboriginal, and further argued that recent changes in native law were confusing, inconsistent, and inappropriate. The central thrust of his argument concerned the preservation of indigenous institutions. Stressing the importance of greater "knowledge of native manners, customs and laws," Shepstone ended with a strong warning: "One thing is beyond doubt that to suppress native management by their own laws in Natal would be to release every native in it from all the special personal control that he fully understands, that he so much needs, and that he has all his life looked up to."[5] It was a warning that Stuart was to take to heart. Stuart had Shepstone sign his copy of the booklet, a symbolic statement of his respect for Shepstone and, as we shall see, of the continuity Stuart perceived between his own understanding of native affairs and that of Shepstone.

With the establishment of responsible government, Frederick Robert Moor was appointed as the new secretary for native affairs (SNA). The *Natal Witness* and the *Times of Natal,* reacting to Moor's appointment, pointed out that he was "not especially knowledgeable" about Africans.[6] S.O. Samuelson, who was considered knowledgeable, was appointed under-secretary. Before his appointment, Moor had been considered an outspoken opponent of the Shepstonian system.[7] Nevertheless, in the first ministry under responsible government, Moor, supported by Samuelson, continued to uphold the principle of African administration through "the tribal system."[8] The major issue that was to preoccupy Moor was the question of the exemption of educated Christian Africans from customary law. While few Africans had petitioned for exemption under the previous SNA, many did so during Moor's administration, encouraged by the American Board Zulu Mission, which was actively opposed to the subjection of Christian Africans to customary law. Moor was uncertain how to treat the exempted natives: were they entitled to the same rights as the white colonists, or were there to be forms of discrimination, such as their being subjected to liquor and vagrancy laws? Exempted Africans were bitterly disillusioned by his hesitancy. Heated debates concerning the position of exempted Africans raged in the American Board Mission's publication, *Inkanyiso.*

In 1893 a new resident commissioner was appointed in Zululand, Sir Marshall

Clarke, who, along with Osborn, Fynney, Haggard, and the real "Umslopogaas," Shepstone's head attendant, had been a member of Shepstone's annexation party. The change marked the beginning of what Marks has called "a brief spell of new thinking about Zulu problems."[9] Clarke, instead of trying to divide and rule and undermine the power of hereditary chiefs, wanted to grant considerable power to them and to certain of the loyalists. He set plans in motion for the return of Cetshwayo's exiled successor, Dinuzulu. Clarke's proposals, which were quite close to suggestions previously made by Harriette Colenso, rejected attempts to confine or curtail the Zulu leader, and sought to harness his authority to the administration.[10] In fact his ideas were a partial return to the original principles of the Shepstonian system.

When the Natal government got wind of the proposals to restore Dinuzulu, they presented the governor with an ultimatum demanding that Zululand be incorporated into Natal before Dinuzulu was returned. Marks offers a number of reasons for this demand, which include the prospect of Natal's gaining access to a variety of Zululand resources from land to coal and labor, and the possibility of sending the surplus Natal African population north of the Thukela. To these motives she adds the question of prestige in a context where rival powers and centers were expanding. Natal's desire for territorial aggrandizement was complemented by claims that the potential for disturbances if Dinuzulu returned was so great that Natal would need to be in a position to control it. After many delays, the king's return to Zululand was made conditional on incorporation, and in 1898 Dinuzulu was returned to Zululand, but as "government induna" rather than as king. This period also saw the transfer of Sir Marshall Clarke to Southern Rhodesia and the appointment of C.R. Saunders in his place as civil commissioner and chief magistrate.[11] Saunders had worked under Osborn at Eshowe, yet was in some respects more influenced by the policies of Clarke and more sympathetic to African concerns than Osborn was. Despite this, Clarke's ideas were largely ignored as Saunders came under pressure from nervous settlers and officials, particularly during the Anglo-Boer War, to try to minimize Dinuzulu's influence over the Zulu people.

James Stuart, by this time acting British consul in Swaziland, was developing a curiosity about African institutions and a critical stance on their interpretation by European administrators. He started to take detailed notes of conversations and interviews conducted with informants identified as knowledgeable on African custom. In particular, Stuart began to share Shepstone's misgivings about the existing code of native law.[12] When, in about September 1900, Stuart was posted to Ladysmith as acting magistrate, his anxieties meshed with certain concerns of contemporary African opinion in Natal.[13]

This period saw the growth of African protests against the policies of the Natal native administration, notably in the pages of *Inkanyiso*, "The First Native Journal in Natal." The protests were led by the *amakholwa*—Christian, educated Africans who sought exemption from "tribal authorities" and "tribal law." In 1901 Samuelson drew up a report on policy and matters relating to Africans, in which he deprecated the existence of a class of Africans who were free of "tribal control." A month later, Moor recommended the repeal of the exemption law of 1865.[14] The Hime ministry, then in power, decided against the repeal, but imposed new restrictions on exempted Africans. Massive dissatisfaction among the *amakholwa* resulted in increased political activity.

In June 1900 the Natal Native Congress (NNC) was formed with the aim of extending the activities of an earlier body, the Funamalungelo Society of exempted Africans, which had led the way in fighting for representation and rights for exempted Africans in the 1880s. The inaugural meeting of the NNC drew fifty-seven delegates and undertook to promote African rights and liberties. The members were largely *amakholwa*, although an attempt, initially unsuccessful, was made to include chiefs. The congress was not campaigning for full political rights for Africans; merely for the right to be represented in parliament by sympathetic whites. As Mark Radebe put it at the inaugural congress, "the natives must not rely too much on themselves, but where possible, must endeavour to enlist the sympathy of English gentlemen."[15] One such English gentleman who was present at the June meeting was an old associate of Stuart from the time of his Swaziland sojourn, George Hulett.[16] Hulett spoke good *isiZulu* and was well acquainted with African affairs. Hulett was accused by the Natal prime minister, Hime, of being instrumental in initiating and organizing the Natal Native Congress, and in refusing to allow the under-secretary for native affairs to attend. Hulett and the activities of the NNC were soon the object of a police investigation.[17]

Evidence directly indicative of Stuart's attitude to the NNC is elusive. There are, however, several significant pieces of evidence which show that at this time he shared certain of the concerns of the congress. As acting magistrate in Ladysmith, Stuart was frustrated by the trivial nature of his daily tasks, but found opportunities to pursue a growing interest in African law and the position of Natal Africans. One of the signs of a degree of sympathy between Stuart and sections of the NNC was that fairly soon after his arrival he was approached by local Africans who inquired whether he would be available for nomination to represent them in parliament, a request that obviously delighted Stuart.[18]

In a further indication of the nature of his concern with NNC-related matters, Stuart and his assistant, Ndukwana kaMbengwana,[19] began to have lengthy discussions—many of them held in Stuart's room, no. 12, at the Royal Hotel in

Ladysmith where he was staying—with local Africans, including prominent leaders of the local *kholwa* community,[20] regarding their problems. Topics covered included disaffection with the government, discussions of the current and earlier systems of native administration, land grievances, the breakdown of chiefly authority, the alleged looseness of African women, and the loss of control of fathers over their daughters.[21] This was a period of increasingly desperate struggle by Africans in Zululand and Natal to retain access to land, and to meet the requirements of taxation and maintain the integrity of homesteads. The 1891 Code of Natal Native Law laid down procedures for the regulation of virtually every aspect of African life. This codification of customary law was of enormous concern both to Stuart, imbued as he was with a deep sense of the more flexible Shepstonian system, and to the *amakholwa,* who were expressing increasing opposition to their exemption from it.

Of his conversation with John Khumalo, headman of the Roosboom *kholwa* community, Stuart noted down that Khumalo was averse to the abolition of the "tribal system" and was disaffected with the administration, charging that most officials did not know what they were doing. "John does not place great reliance in the young Englishmen of today," noted Stuart; "they do not go as thoroughly into matters as Somsewu [Sir Theophilus Shepstone], Mr. J. Bird, etc., and yet they fancy they know more than their elders."[22] Stuart's conversations with John Khumalo reveal Stuart, however, to be made in the mold of Shepstone and Bird: his notes of the conversation are testimony to careful, sustained discussion over a number of days—matters gone into most thoroughly—as well as to a genuine concern to elicit African opinion. The picture they paint of Stuart in nightly consultation in his hotel room with well-informed Africans suggests a scenario hitherto little seen in Ladysmith. John Khumalo himself commented on the unusualness of the arrangements, laughingly calling Stuart's room "*KwaSogekle, kwaTulwana,* for it is there that elderly men meet."[23] *KwaSogekle* literally means "the place of the maze," the maze of spittle drawn on a hut floor by men engaged in communally smoking hemp. The Thulwana was one of Mpande's *ibutho,* made up of men born around 1834.[24]

The discussion in room 12 was by no means shaped by Stuart's agendas alone. His companions were only too well aware of his official position and the possible significance of his information-gathering activities, and were active in lobbying administrators and law makers in a host of other forums.

It is difficult to establish both the degree to which Stuart determined the topics for discussion, and the extent to which his agendas may have been subverted by unexpected turns in the conversation. Likewise, it is impossible to know how much his notes reflected the fullness of the conversation. Only closer comparative textual analysis of individual accounts would enable one to suggest how and to what extent Stuart's interviewees tailored their accounts both for Stuart and also to what they understood to be the exigencies of recording in written form.

In response to the complaints ventured in these conversations Stuart suggested that what was needed was a man responsible for native affairs who must be "a good and reliable Zulu scholar, be entirely independent of the Natal Government, hold office for five years at a time and be allowed to be re-elected, or let him go on indefinitely during pleasure, and be in direct touch with natives in every part of Zululand and Natal. Let all native cases," he continued, "civil and criminal, all executive work, be dealt with by the present Secretary for Native Affairs etc., and let the officer's duties be purely diplomatic." Khumalo and Ndukwana, Stuart noted, "thought such proposal would give great satisfaction." "I think," Stuart continued, "that such an appointment, of a man who has native interests at heart, would safeguard and promote native interests better than having representatives in the House."[25] In effect, Stuart was restating Shepstone's long-held position. While Shepstone had, in his own way, been both "a good and reliable Zulu scholar," and independent of the Natal government, in 1900 the Native Affairs Department could claim neither qualification.[26]

Like Stuart, the *amakholwa* were also protesting at the lack of knowledge of African matters and the silencing of themselves.

> We Natives are not admitted to the franchise, consequently we are unrepresented in any political matters, thus we are forced into the state of dumb beasts, which can never express the pains of their bodies, nor advise as to the best way of managing them in order to get good service from them. . . . I am afraid the Government's knowledge of us is entirely derived from Magistrates, Administrators of Native Law, the Secretary for Native Affairs, and farmers.[27]

Stuart, perhaps more than any other Natal colonial official of his time, was precisely one such interlocutor. His inquiries would, in all likelihood, have been resented precisely because they perpetuated the system of second-hand knowledge, but because of his insistence on thorough inquiry he would also have constituted an important conduit for the relaying of information. This was a dilemma that resonated with *kholwa* politics at this time, and would have left its imprint on the interviews in room 12. But if Stuart was not directly supportive of the NNC, he was certainly preoccupied with similar concerns. André Odendaal has described the Natal Native Congress as intending "to cultivate political awareness," and as a "forum for ventilating grievances."[28] It is difficult to view room 12 at the Royal Hotel in this period in different terms. It was these shared concerns that led Stuart to a vision of native administration and of his own future that underpinned what was to become a truly monumental research effort into the history and customs of the Zulu and neighboring peoples.

In another conversation with John Khumalo, in December 1900, Stuart and Ndukwana discussed the notion of Christianity as *ukukhanya* (literally, to light up). The thrust of the conversation was critical. Ndukwana "strenuously maintained that the *Zulu life and civilization* was *ukukhanya*,"[29] a point that Stuart and the others present seemed to agree upon. Stuart sketched the scenario of a girl who is adopted by a European family, and who is treated as one of the family until a certain age, when the parents send her to eat her meals apart in the kitchen "thereby letting it be understand [sic] that there is an impassable barrier between the two." "What kind of enlightenment is that," railed Stuart, "which allows its clergy to shake hands with their native parishioners at the mission station, and when they meet them in the street in towns will pass them by practically as strangers?"[30] Stuart's comments as recorded in this conversation were, for the time, extraordinarily radical, significantly in excess of the remarks made by the identified "agitator," George Hulett. Whereas Hulett at the inaugural congress of the NNC comfortably asserted the superiority of whites over blacks, Stuart's comments reveal him to be markedly less confident of white advantage, and significantly less arrogant.[31]

The possibility that Stuart's interest in the NNC and the Ladysmith conversations were forms of intelligence gathering needs to be considered. Stuart's evident sympathy for the situation of his informants, his active engagement in suggesting solutions, together with the absence, as far as I have been able to ascertain, of any official reports of the conversations, argue against this. Furthermore, there are indications that at about this time he received a severe reprimand from his superiors. It is difficult to establish the exact reason for it, but one possibility is that his concern with African grievances was not looked on favorably.[32] This suggestion is supported by the fact that Stuart was subsequently upbraided for allowing Africans to discuss new taxes and to voice their opposition.[33]

Stuart addressed an extraordinary letter to his mother just a few months after his posting to Ladysmith, in which he revealed himself to be possessed of a powerful life motivation. The letter is so strangely and strongly worded that it is worth quoting at length.

It will interest you to know that I am making slow sure progress finding nothing to retract but everything to confirm and establish. My ideas of things broaden day by day thanks to my perpetual heavy reading and systematic inquiry. I am in reality directing the whole of my intelligence to storming a fort of vast magnitude. The chances to every ordinary mortal are of course dead against my ever succeeding but I don't care a rap what anyone thinks. I just go plodding along in my own way. Nearly four years of this perpetual haggling and nagging at generalities and universals in numberless aspects has opened my eyes more and more to the meaning of what I am at . . . I am moving along slowly and I think, surely, and the day will come, I can't say when, when my work, carefully and methodically prepared, will be able to bear the public gaze and stand criticism. The more I think of it the more I feel that this great subject depends for its exposition not so much on talent as on intention. A great object had to be attained, to show that this Idea is true, well, it doesn't really matter how this is done so long as it is done . . . I hope you will keep in mind that not the manner but the substance is the important point. I am still, as I have always been, master of my Idea. The whole thing takes its orders from me. Is it no triumph to be master of such Idea so vast if not vaster than that of Christianity? And so, day by day, I will proceed, tramping this way and that way through this vast jungle and forest trying to find the day. I am humble and, I hope, cautious and persevering. And so another year is coming to a close leaving me I think the richer in light than I was at its beginning.[34]

Nowhere in this letter does Stuart explicate directly what his "Idea" is, but, as the coming pages show, it is difficult to resist the conclusion that Stuart was talking here about his work in collecting African testimony and information, and his conception of himself as the ideal interlocutor between African and white colonial societies.[35] Precisely how he understood his task, and what constituted his "Idea," are among the questions that the rest of this chapter explores.

Stuart was at this time also taking down detailed notes of conversations on topics such as the *sisaing* of cattle, "Zulu festivals," controls over women's marriages, symbols of office, diviners, marriage, burials, circumcision, clan names, land and land tenure, as well as historical matters such as details of Shaka's life and death, origins of the Zulu, and many other subjects besides.

The intense and often frank discussions that Stuart held in this period with Khumalo and Ndukwana were central in shaping his conceptions of native policy. Khumalo was an educated Christian who, according to Stuart's notes, perceived the value of conserving old forms and whose ideas on the role of traditions in securing social stability accorded with Stuart's. Khumalo's concern with indigenous forms is not entirely characteristic of the identity and ideology typically espoused by *amakholwa* at that time, and alerts us to the profoundly ambiguous position of the *amakholwa* and the complexity of this engagement with Stuart. Stuart's own position as imposer of colonialism and, increasingly, as self-appointed advocate of the colonized was becoming equally ambiguous. His support of the preservation of "traditional tribal institutions" was a resultant paradox. He was to insist on "going into matters in a thorough fashion," and believed that Africans needed a good (white) man on whom they could rely to mediate between them and the government. The interviews with Ndukwana imbued Stuart with an abiding sense of the necessity of gaining a depth of knowledge about African "customs" before the real nature of key institutions could be properly understood. The Ladysmith conversations thus, on the one hand, exposed Stuart to the extent and nature of African grievances and the richness and meaning of African cultural practices and, on the other, led him to make a vital connection between the two. Thenceforward Stuart was to argue that the key to native policy lay in greater knowledge and understanding of indigenous institutions and practices.

Stuart's early years in native administration laid in place his "Idea" for the collection of materials on African history and "custom," and forged his understanding of the position of Africans in Natal and Zululand. Over the next twenty-six years Stuart was to record the testimonies of nearly 200 informants on a range of topics concerning the history of the Zulu and their neighbors. For much of that time he occupied senior positions in the administration and was indeed master of his ideas, accustomed to giving orders, to ruling, and to collecting information from within a context of domination. Yet, as the rest of this chapter will show, the particular concerns that he understood as relevant to the exercise of assembling the necessary knowledge with which to rule guaranteed the capacity, then and now, of his researches to "bear the public gaze."

In April 1901 Stuart took up the position of assistant magistrate in Durban.[36] The move inaugurated a new period in his life, as he now entered directly the world of white colonial politics, coming closer to the seat of native policy making, and under the spotlight of the Durban press. While in Durban, he continued to advocate the importance of appointing a knowledgeable expert in African customs to high office in the native administration, but his writings and public pronouncements were freer of the overt political concerns that dominated his stay in Ladysmith and governed his communication with men such as John Khumalo.

The dominant issue in native policy in Natal at the time of Stuart's Durban appointment was the failure of the Native Affairs Department to ensure a constant and adequate labor supply for the colony. With the completion, in 1895, of the Durban–Rand railway line, the Rand was increasingly able to attract Natal laborers to the Highveld on contracts. Natal settlers held strong notions of the inbred idleness and irresponsibility of Africans, and the necessity of teaching them the habits of industry and the value of labor. Labor was viewed as the first step toward civilization. The position of African women was the object of special settler attention, for women's labor was seen as the means that enabled African men to be idle and to avoid the colonial labor market.

The Native Affairs Department refused the colonists' demands that it prevent the migration of Natal labor to the Rand and increase the hut tax. While the colonists required the government in power to do everything it could to ensure a constant labor supply in the colony, the secretary for native affairs, Moor, also considered it his duty to see to the welfare of the African worker.[37] Moor was, nonetheless, under pressure from his white constituents and, as a member of the farming community himself, was not unsympathetic to their needs. He responded that Africans were active on the colonial labor market, but that demand exceeded supply. He had several plans to increase the supply. One plan, which was not successful, was to import labor from Portuguese East Africa. Another was to provide adequate accommodation in the towns for migrants from outlying areas. Moor wanted more than mere barracks, but the Durban town council, reluctant to spend the money, resisted his plans. It was in this period, on June 1, 1902, that the first passes were issued in Durban. Essentially, Moor was trying to maintain a delicate balance between white employers and African workers.

When Moor left office in August 1903, Natal had had ten years of responsible government, for eight of which he had controlled the Native Affairs Department. Moor had run the department in what was essentially the mold of Shepstone but with the added complication that he was an elected official and thus more susceptible to settler pressures than Shepstone had been. Like Shepstone, Moor believed that the "tribal system" was the only effective means of governing Africans. In his view the authority of the supreme chief, the secretary for native affairs, and the African chiefs had to be maintained. Following the Shepstone tradition, he discouraged exemption from customary law which had been provided to make it possible for Africans to turn their backs on traditionalism and "tribal" life. Likewise, Moor was opposed to granting the franchise to the Africans. He also resisted the idea of land being held in freehold, and this became a major issue on the mission reserves.[38] However, whereas Shepstone was highly critical of the existing Code of Native Law, Moor saw it as an effective instrument through which absolute control over the Africans could be achieved.

Stuart shared a number of his superior's views, notably his belief in the importance of maintaining the "tribal system." He was thus able to flourish—at least, to a degree—under the Moor administration. In some respects, however, he was critical of Natal native policy. In Stuart's view, one of the problems with Moor's approach was that he was following Shepstone's system without the necessary qualifications. Shepstone's system depended on an intimate knowledge of African society and on Shepstone's ability to play the role of chief.[39] As an editorial in the *Natal*

Witness of January 19, 1901 pointed out, Moor did not have that knowledge, nor was he able to build the kinds of relationships with African chiefs that Shepstone had enjoyed. Stuart's reservations about the existing native administration as a whole were focused on precisely this problem.

With his move to Durban in 1901 Stuart had to deal on a daily basis, as magistrate, with issues and problems raised by these defects in the administrative system. He protested against the implementation of the poll tax because it was, in his view, oppressive and a danger to the maintenance of the indigenous social system, and because it was widely regarded as oppressive. The labor problem also impinged on him directly. One of Stuart's greatest concerns at this time was the problem of *togt* (daily) labor. Since 1870 *togt* daily laborers had been required to obtain licenses to work. This enabled the authorities to control the influx of Africans into the towns. In 1902 the Togt Labour Amendment Act tightened still further the regulations controlling *togt* laborers, requiring them to live in designated premises.

In April 1902 Stuart, in his role as acting assistant magistrate in Durban, pondered the problem of the "precariousness of domicile of the Native."[40] Prefacing his discussion with a description of "the bloodsucking greed of invisible speculators" which resulted in widespread rent squatting and references to "our somewhat unsympathetic form of Government and civilization," Stuart argued "altruistic measures" were necessary "to combat baneful selfish grasping." The solution he proposed was the establishment of a "native township" in Durban, which was not a "location . . . the slovenly huddling together of 'blind mouths'," but

> the institution, on a large scale, of a school of practical training in the ways of civilisation in a way which does not interfere with their own modes of life, whilst steadily inculcating our own and which actively assists them in combating blazing economic influences on their homes, wives and children— tending to very destruction—which irresponsible speculating Companies and individuals in all parts of the Colony bring to bear on them.[41]

In advocating education as a source of security, Stuart was going further than Moor, who was strongly criticized by some administrators and liberal colonists for a failure to provide for African education in his period of office in the Native Affairs Department.[42] Despite the fact that Stuart's argument was radical for its time, it was filled with stereotypes such as the notion that African life was precarious, owing as much to "the perpetual motion of Africa" as to the indicted land companies, while on other occasions he advocated the discouragement of permanent urban residence for Africans.[43] Stuart echoed the settlers in talking about "the indolence natural to the native" and the need to inculcate a love of labor, and he shared their concern about urban Africans' disorderliness.[44]

While a prisoner of certain stereotypes, Stuart broke free of their bondage in other areas. This escape was a consequence of his close contacts with Africans in Natal. Over the next few months, Stuart had a series of discussions about native policy with a range of African acquaintances.[45] On one occasion he discussed the dubious benefits of European civilization, and suggested "a vigorous attack on European civilization. I called up Rousseau's *Contract Social* and his doctrine of "back to nature," and said those who could read between the lines would see in my published views something very akin to Rousseau, although in penning them I had not got Rousseau in mind." Stuart continued: "Europeans must somehow be universally educated in regard to Zulu affairs, for only in that way can they arrive at a firm, right, universal policy. The sufferings of the Zulu people lie too deep for words; they feel, but cannot tell what they feel."[46] Stuart felt that the Code of Native Law misunderstood fundamentally a number of the basic institutions and practices of African society. These ideas underlay his researches into "customs." The need for Europeans to learn more about African society, especially in order to make policy, was to be a constant refrain in Stuart's writing, and was a motivating force behind his collection of material on African history and society.[47]

In the course of his emergence as an "expert" on Zulu affairs, Stuart's "Idea" began to gain clearer shape, as evidenced by this long stream-of-consciousness sentence in his private notes:

> Begun without any definite aim, the work has at length, by its scope and fullness so impressed its character on me, as to give rise to an intention to convert the whole . . . into an instrument for bettering the future of the people, and this in two principal ways (a) by placing so much of their folklore, language, history, habits and customs, praises, proverbs etc. on record as to form perhaps the nucleus of a far more extensive and thoroughgoing undertaking, having for its object the establishment of a living Source of Tradition upon which subsequent generations must more and more depend, not from idle curiosity, but vital national necessity; for, to keep fresh and alive the traditions of a people otherwise losing them through the peculiar circumstances they are placed [in] as regards the white races, is to provide them with a fountain at which all must at all times drink in order that, mindful of a strenuous past, they may be men of character and backbone, not a mongrel set of waifs and strays, blind as to the past and, therefore blinder still as to their future, for 'tis ever the past that lights up the future.
>
> Now as to the second way in which the future of the Zulus can be bettered.
>
> Not only would a systematic record of Zulu life, character, and achievement serve to inspire others to improve it, it would help materially to

enlighten the white people among whom the Natives live as to what the latter really are. Europeans are eager to have this information, but it is not properly forthcoming. The gulf between the two races continues to yawn, with nothing to bridge it. And yet it is on this and this alone that mutual trust and sympathy are built up and depend.[48]

For Stuart, answers to "the native question" lay in historical knowledge of African society.[49] Not only did that research have to be done, and a thorough inquiry made, but it also had to be written down and preserved for the Africans concerned as much as for the administrators. A great deal has been written in recent years about the connections between colonial rule and the modes of generating the forms of knowledge necessary for the domination of the colonized. Stuart's project was precisely such an exercise in harnessing knowledge of the colonized to the project of colonial rule. Moreover, the promotion of indigenous institutions had the well-recognized effect of entrenching a separation of rural and urban societies, a division of the population into those considered "tribal" and those seen as "civilized," as well as of excluding Africans from full political participation under colonialism, and laying the foundations for what later emerged as the ideology of segregation. But if Stuart's concern with the preservation of "tribal life" was by no means exceptional, his research methods and his attention to historical detail were.

Stuart began systematically at the time to research the early history of the inhabitants of the Zululand–Natal area. One of the chief objects of his attention was the reign of Shaka. Like Shepstone, he saw in Shaka a model of African government. Stuart pursued this subject diligently and enthusiastically in a score of interviews with African informants between 1903 and 1905, accumulating hundreds of pages of closely written notes on the topic. While he interviewed informants over a much longer period, an in-depth focus on this period conveys a picture of the intensity and scope of his activity.

In the period July 1902–October 1903 he resumed with vigor the recording of Ndukwana that he had begun in Ladysmith, on custom and historical matters.[50] In early 1903 Stuart sent Ndukwana to fetch Jantshi kaNongila from Stanger.[51] In numerous conversations at which Ndukwana was present, Jantshi provided Stuart with an account of the life of Shaka as well as other matters.[52] Jantshi's testimony is particularly revealing of Stuart's interviewing techniques. Jantshi gave Stuart an account—his "evidence" (a word Stuart used throughout to describe the content of these conversations)—of the history of Shaka's times, and then Stuart, in his own words, "cross-examined him."[53] When the interview resumed the next day, Stuart headed the page, "Jantshi still under cross-examination."[54] In this way,

Stuart brought to his interviewing the legal language and approach that he used in his official capacity.[55]

Another informant who provided Stuart with a rich account of the life of Shaka was Ndlovu kaThimuni, a chief in the Maphumulo district, whom Stuart interviewed in 1902 and 1903.[56] In January 1903 Stuart interviewed another son of Thimuni, Mhuyi, on the topic of Shaka's early years and recorded both the *izibongo* of Shaka from Jantshi, who was present at the interview, and those of Shaka's uncle, Mudli, from Mhuyi.[57] In May he met with Tununu, who gave him an account of Shaka's birth, as well as material on the reign of Dingane.[58] He also interviewed Magidi kaNgomane of the Mthethwa, who maintained that Shaka had fathered a child.[59] In July he heard from Madikane kaMlomowetole, the Qadi chief, a rich account of Shaka's birth, early years, and accession to the chiefship of the Zulu.[60] In August the discussion with Madikane was resumed over a number of days.[61] In February the following year, in conversations over three days, Stuart obtained yet another version of the story of Shaka's life, from Mbovu kaMtshumayeli.[62] On two occasions in August, in October, and in November 1904, Stuart resumed conversation with Mbovu on the topic of Shaka.[63] Also in August 1904 Stuart discussed the reign of Shaka with Meseni kaMini,[64] and in September and October dealt with Shaka's relations with the Qwabe, with Mmemi kaNguluzane.[65] In February 1905 Shaka's dealings with the Cele were covered in an interview with Maquza kaGawushane.[66] In April 1905 Stuart met Mkehlengana and Mkotane, sons of Shaka's famous officer Zulu kaNogandaya, and recorded from them a host of stories about their father and about Shaka, as well as the *izibongo* of Zulu.[67] In April Stuart also interviewed Maziyana kaMahlabeni of the Ndelu,[68] Mcotoyi kaMnini,[69] and Melapi kaMagaye,[70] all of whom added material to his data on Shaka. In May Magidigidi kaNobebe provided information on relations between the Chunu and Shaka as well as material on Shaka's military system.[71] In May, June, and July, Stuart re-interviewed Madikane repeatedly, checking his story against the information he had since received from his other sources.[72] Stuart also interviewed Mayinga kaMbekuzana for information on Shaka in July 1905.[73] Shaka was not Stuart's sole interest, and in this period he also interviewed informants on a range of other topics.

At this time Stuart noted the existence of sharply conflicting versions of the life of Shaka. The account given by Ndlovu, he commented, was at variance with those of Ndukwana and Mkando. "Some of the men I have spoken to stoutly deny Tshaka was ever illegitimate," he noted, "whilst others with equally cogent reason, maintain, if not the exact opposite, then something near to it."[74] He compared the oral testimonies he collected with the written accounts by Fynn, Isaacs, and Shepstone, and noted further discrepancies. He seems to have given considerable credit to Ndlovu's version. "It has to be remembered," he noted, "that Ndhlovu takes a deep interest in these matters, and that he heard them from his father," who was, as Stuart observed, present at many of the events concerned.[75]

The research was not limited to the views of Africans. To his oral archive Stuart added the fruits of his researches among documentary sources. He began combing the writings of early travelers for information, which he cross-checked against his oral sources.[76] In September 1903, for example, Stuart acquired a copy of Nathaniel Isaacs' two-volume account of his sojourn in Natal, *Travels and Adventures in Eastern Africa*. Stuart's markings in the margins of his copy of Isaacs' *Travels and Adventures* show that he cross-referenced details in the text with the African oral testimony he had recorded,[77] as well as with a host of other written accounts, both published and unpublished.[78] Where Isaacs described Shaka as a "savage," Stuart penciled in the margin, "A mistake. He was a barbarian."[79] The distinction for Stuart was clear: barbarism was, following Edward Tylor,[80] the middle culture, an advance on savagery. The lifestyle of a savage was unpalatable; that of a barbarian different from his own, rougher perhaps, but fully comprehensible. Stuart likewise annotated his notes of oral interviews with references to published sources, highlighting discrepancies between them.

One of the written sources to which Stuart had access was the papers of the late Henry Francis Fynn. He had been consulting Fynn in Bird's *Annals of Natal* but around this time, Fynn's son gave Stuart his father's papers to prepare for publication.[81] In a letter to a London publisher regarding the editing, Stuart spelt out his method of dealing with the Fynn papers and specified the kinds of editorial interventions he was making.[82] The letter is significant, for Fynn's *Diary* (finally published in 1950) has been subject to considerable criticism—even labeled a forgery—because of the difficulties of distinguishing the hand of Stuart from that of Fynn. The letter, taken together with an understanding of Stuart's working methods more generally, provides a starting-point for close textual analysis of the *Diary*. Having the Fynn papers in hand was a great advantage for Stuart, and they probably influenced his syntheses of Zulu history in no small measure.

Many years later, after he settled in England in 1922, Stuart augmented his oral and published sources with archival material. He systematically combed newspaper sources such as the *South African Commercial Advertiser*, the *Cape Town Gazette and African Advertiser*, and the *Grahamstown Journal*, as well as missionary publications at the British Museum for items pertinent to the early history of Natal and Zululand.[83] He used these data both to flesh out Fynn's *Diary* and to augment his own writings. Throughout his researches, however, Stuart carefully provenanced every new detail of information, and rigorously distinguished between evidence from different sources.

By January 1904, having perceived the magnitude of the task involved in the implementation of his "Idea," Stuart was advocating the establishment of "a Department for studying natives, for listening to their grievances and suggestions as to their own government as well as guiding and advising them on the one hand, and the Natal Government on the other."[84] Stuart envisaged that one of the department's first tasks would be the production of a monograph on the state of native affairs. "The whole should be presented *from the Native point of view,* indeed, the work's chief value would be the fact that it represented the problem from the Native standpoint."[85] Stuart's desire to see his "Idea" translated into a formal project was not motivated by practical concerns alone. Linked to his developing perception of the importance of greater knowledge of indigenous institutions was a desire to invest his researches with a coherent methodology, and to win the support of the scientific community.

In December 1905 Stuart prepared a memorandum for the British Association of Science, a delegation from which visited South Africa that year. In the memorandum[86] Stuart advocated the establishment of a department of anthropological science in each colony, with a carefully selected person heading each division. Describing anthropology as "the Queen of the Sciences," Stuart argued that it had hitherto been despised because it failed "to combine interest in human nature of the past with that of the present" and was not yet "a guide and adviser in the world's affairs." Stuart observed that anthropology had the potential to study fruitfully the process of contact between Africans and Europeans. Noting that, because of "deeply rooted prejudices," European colonists, evidencing "repulsion in every feature of social and industrial life," denied Africans an equal share in their "advantages," Stuart argued that their prejudices and the consequent injustices were the result of "ignorance." The appeal to the scientific community was an attempt to gain support for his view of native affairs in the face of settler ignorance. Indeed, Stuart suggested that anthropology offered the means for overcoming these prejudices. He also argued that while the move toward the rapid Christianization and civilization of Africans looked, on the face of things, progressive, it was a notion based on an ethnocentric judgment informed by an inadequate understanding of African society. "What South Africa needs, as far as the Natives are concerned, is something which is radical and immediately radical and it is absurd to suppose that can be obtained otherwise than under the agis [sic] of Science and by men competent to deal with and interpret facts brought before them."[87]

Stuart's vision accorded perfectly with the aims of the association. Its president, the anthropologist A.C. Haddon, was at this time a persistent advocate of the establishment of an imperial bureau of ethnology. Haddon urged colonial officials to attend to the practices of subject peoples. If "officials unwittingly violated traditional customs their subjects would revolt; and officials seeking to improve the lives of colonized peoples required their subjects' cooperation—which could be secured only if officials' proposals appealed to local values."[88] In his presidential address to the anthropology section of the British Association meeting in South Africa, Haddon spoke of Bantu social organization as lending itself to discipline and giving African people the capacity for great achievements when they were led by those of their own who possessed great ability—men like Shaka.[89] Haddon's and Stuart's positions were almost identical.

In an effort to promote greater understanding of African institutions, Stuart conducted scores of public lectures on various aspects of Zulu history, law, and customs. In these lectures he drew on his growing knowledge of African customs and history to provide background material for analyses of matters of current concern in the colony. Some five years after beginning to collect historical materials systematically, Stuart was offering detailed accounts of the precolonial history of the region. While he was interested in a range of other topics on the early history of the Natal–Zululand region, the reign of Shaka and the various institutions on which the Shakan system was based were his chief concern. In February 1903 Stuart produced his first draft of the life of Shaka.[90] Other drafts followed, and in August 1905 a revised version entitled "Tshaka: His Life and Reign" was delivered in a lecture in Pietermaritzburg.[91] In the lectures (and in the drafts) Stuart tended to go beyond a focus on the Zulu king, to look at society more generally, and to reveal the workings of the system on which Zulu power was based. Commenting on Shaka, Stuart remarked: "We see him as through a veil, the dark veil of savage and terrific majesty."[92] Stuart's project was to lift away that veil.

Stuart's various texts lend themselves to a detailed analysis of their differences. By registering those differences against the accumulation of his interviews on Shaka one can attempt to establish how Stuart's own understanding changed as he gathered new information. Likewise, a close analysis of differences in texts produced for various audiences would be useful in adding to our understanding of Stuart's authorial activities. Such a task is a project in its own right and will not be attempted in this study. The major point to be made here is, rather, that there is a very clear distinction between Stuart's synthesized accounts of the reign of Shaka—even where they draw heavily on information from African oral sources—and his notes of conversations with informants on the same topics.

The synthesized versions are marked by Stuart's methodological sophistication in using the oral materials. He was alert to the fact that "Much that belongs to anterior days is often attributed to a later Sovereign, especially if remarkable and successful." Stuart was also keenly aware of the problem of information passing out of oral accounts where there was not a clear-cut memory "hook" for it. For oral data to survive historically, he noted, "they must possess qualities likely to endure and to pass into succeeding generations whilst their activity or genius should be such as to leave a mark in regions in which they dealt."[93]

Stuart's synthesized accounts were organized chronologically, in sharp contrast to the notes of interviews. Moreover, they were based on a comparative examination of the "recognized [written] authorities" as well as "independently enquiring of the natives themselves for such facts as tend to bring about more exact knowledge." While in his notes he was rigorous in keeping information from different sources precisely provenanced, he explicitly billed his lectures as syntheses. His own synthetic Shaka, not unexpectedly, was very different from that of Ndlovu, or Jantshi, or Ndukwana, and, for that matter, from that of the early traders Isaacs and Fynn. He was a powerfully constructive figure:

> Almost synchronizing with that of Napoleon, in Europe, the career of Tshaka in South Africa, instead of being fraught with failure, met with success and that in a truly remarkable manner. Beginning with a small and little known tribe he by degrees lifted it together with many surrounding tribes within a five hundred mile radius into becoming a great nation.[94]

Stuart's Shaka did "not destroy merely for destruction's sake. He destroyed in order to construct, and herein lies the supreme merit and genius of his truly terrible reign."[95] Thus Stuart's representation of Shaka echoed Shepstone's. His researches, however, went much deeper.

Stuart's text rehearsed some details that would have been familiar to his Durban audience but also, as we have noted, introduced them to materials he had recorded from his informants.[96] In drafts dating from 1903 Stuart tried to move his audiences beyond the question of Shaka's goodness or badness:

> The exploits of one whose match you may in vain turn over the pages of world history to find, may for a moment amuse you; the revolting cruelty of a man whose deeds outdid Nero himself may, for a moment appal you; the achievements of a general whose numerous rough and ready campaigns surpassed even those of Napoleon in dash and daring, of Genghis Khan in energy and irresistibility and Marlborough in completeness and inevitability of success may, for a moment, astonish, but these things, surprizing though they be, will cause you to take a deep and lasting interest in the people themselves, I am afraid I must take leave to deny.

He insisted on a deeper, more probing knowledge of Zulu affairs. He continued:

> What is the good of knowing anything about a Kaffir? Vote something for education, give missionaries facilities for Christianizing and teaching, stop polygamy, break down chieftainship, pulverize the tribe, taboo ancient customs and

habits, compel labour et cetera and we have done all that can in reason be expected of us to do. How we, who know so little, can be ready to do so much, so much that is amazingly drastic, is to me a profound mystery.[97]

Decrying the lack of knowledge was a passionate refrain of Stuart's in this period. He returned again and again to the point that an in-depth understanding of African affairs was an essential prerequisite for the making of "native policy." That understanding was to be gained only through systematic inquiry. It was precisely such an inquiry that Stuart perceived to be his life's work.

In his lectures Stuart discussed the various institutions Shaka introduced, or made use of, "to govern his country by means of an army, and to make that army as perfect as possible."[98] For Stuart the collapse of the Shakan system had had terrible effects on the social fabric of Zululand.

> What goes on now-a-days, both in Natal and Zululand, is not in any way a picture of what used formerly to take place. The necessary royal sanctions having been removed, the moral standards having been undermined by foreign ideas, the people now, one and all, pursue their own inclinations, not unlike the savage waters of a sea which has overthrown the dyke that formerly held it back. The removal of that great restraint, which the awe-inspiring name of a despotic monarch imposed on a whole people, has resulted, under British rule, in a widespread dissolution; and it is already, not without difficulty, that we can collect together the several parts of a political system rapidly becoming effete.[99]

This, then, was Stuart's response to the political anxieties of the disaffected Africans with whom he had been consulting intensely over the previous four years, and the anxious and fearful white settlers in his Durban magisterial district. Whereas the Natal Native Congress was advocating the opening up of colonial society as a means to redress the problems experienced by educated and Christianized Africans, Stuart, developing an analysis out of his historical researches, and influenced by his contacts with anthropologists such as Haddon, advocated what was in a sense the opposite solution, the recognition of the strength of indigenous institutions, and in particular the importance of strong central leaders such as Shaka.

Stuart's researches revealed that it was Shaka who was responsible for the development of "the endless and enormous power of discipline" in "Native life,"[100] manifest in the *amabutho* system and achieved through the maintenance of strict controls over marriage. "If, as has been pointed out," commented Stuart, "the individual sometimes suffered, the community at large derived very great advantages from such strict and universal discipline, although the custom itself was not altogether a popular one."[101] The scarcity of women under the system "caused [men] to redouble their energies"[102] in earning the right to marry. In Shaka's day this occurred on the battlefield. In twentieth-century Natal, Stuart argued, this would occur through labor. "And yet, if Tshaka succeeded in building up the strongest native army in modern times, why may not we, accepting our responsibilities to the full, with a becoming patience, and guided by a similar, though not so cruel or barbarous, policy, direct steadily the energies of this fine people into other channels, and teach them not how to fight, but how to work."[103] Thus for Stuart the answer to the problems of native policy were to be found in the exertion of greater controls, and the most satisfactory means of doing this, in his view, was through the system that was most familiar to the African population, the Shakan system of government. To use that valuable resource, however, required that it be properly understood.

The language of Stuart's lectures, publications, and official communications was carefully modulated to meet the expectations of his various audiences. In public he tended to be moderate and diplomatic. As we have seen, in his private notes—and occasionally in public—he railed fiercely against the injustices experienced by Africans under colonial rule. The strong imagery and harsh tone of some of his remarks suggest an angry young man.

> If we are to know the Zulu or any other people on this earth, we must first *want* to know them. There must be the preliminary wish, the desire, the enthusiasm to know. *That* is the spark which in some way or another must be kindled in our bosoms. Until that real desire for truth arise, the Native Question and all that belongs to it will be not a "living" but a "dead" question. Native *Question.* Who asks the question? Can we take no more interest in the Natives than in our cats and dogs? A question is an inquiry made by one who *wants* to know, *really* wants to know and asked of those believed to be able to answer it. True answers are vital to our present and future welfare. Cannot the Zulus tell you something about the Native Question? Why then, I pray, don't you ask them? Why do you invite me to lecture on subjects I know nothing about, except what I myself have picked up by asking?[104]

This statement, marked "omit" in the margin and perhaps never actually delivered in the lecture, summed up the fundamentals of Stuart's approach, and his awareness of what he could say in public and what he needed to suppress.

Some time in 1903 Stuart began to plan a book—possibly stimulated by the suggestion made by a correspondent, Major Lewis, that the lectures should be published in book form.[105] Stuart was, however, wary of the finality of publication. His notes show that he understood research of the kind he was undertaking to be by definition constantly changing and far from a final truth. "For this purpose some method must be established which is always *continuous* and *accumulative*. I write today what I know, tomorrow I or 1000 others may add to it. And so it is an open book I desire to start which shall become the central authority."[106]

Stuart worried specifically about authors having "a way of rounding off what they are not competent to complete and what ought never to be closed down until it is complete."[107] The open-endedness of method conveyed in this expression of anxiety is the hallmark of Stuart's work. Effectively his archive is such an "open book," to which Stuart constantly added new material, meticulously provenancing each addition, cross-referencing but never merging, never synthesizing or ironing out contradictions, and never rounding off what ought not to be completed. It is precisely this open-endedness that makes the Stuart archive a "central authority" rather than a "tainted well."[108]

Stuart's commitment to a continuous and accumulative method was one of the reasons why he never published his own synthesized reconstruction of Shakan times. In 1904 he noted that he envisioned the quarterly production of "accessions" to the body of knowledge, to be published at a low cost. These did come out, in the form of the published lectures and reports.

It is likely that the Rev. A.T. Bryant—whose published account of Zulu history, *Olden Times in Zululand and Natal,* more than any other single account, has influenced historians writing about Shakan times—was in the audience for some of these lectures, or at least that he read the published lectures and reports. In 1904 Stuart and Bryant were in active correspondence with one another, exchanging historical as well as lexical and orthographic information.[109] At this time Stuart was also corresponding with Harriette Colenso on similar matters, as well as with John Shepstone. S.O. Samuelson was another contemporary who enjoyed a lecture by Stuart on Shaka and was left pondering the future of "our natives."[110] In sum, while Stuart published relatively little, his views were communicated to his contemporaries and were likely to have influenced their thinking and their publications in no small measure.

The work of research and preservation that Stuart deemed imperative demanded fluency in *isiZulu*. But his language concerns went deeper. Stuart, Bryant, and Colenso also exchanged word lists. In search of translations they inquired deeply into the nature of indigenous institutions and concepts. Orthography was, of course, an important issue at the base of these lexical endeavors. Mutual concern for the correct orthography to be employed led to the establishment of a

Committee on Zulu Orthography and, on September 6–9, 1905, to a General Orthography Conference, held in Durban and chaired by Stuart. The conference was attended by delegates from a number of local missionary societies, Chief Dinuzulu, at least three Zulu speakers who were especially interested in the topic—such as John Dube, the editor of the *isiZulu* publication *Ilanga lase Natal*—and a number of "experts" such as Harriette Colenso and Bryant.[111]

Orthography proper was not the only concern of the conference. Attention was drawn to the need for a formal translation from English into *isiZulu* of a vocabulary of power, authority, and sovereignty. The conference tussled with the distinction between "The Governor" (for which one delegate proposed "*umbusi*") and "Government" (for which he suggested "*urulumeni*"). "Parliament," it was agreed, would be translated as "*umpakati*."[112] In formalizing these translations, the committee was giving specific meaning and content to the concepts concerned.

Debates over the merits of conjunctive and disjunctive orthographies characterized two further orthographic conferences held in 1906 and 1907. Proponents of the conjunctive system argued that "whatever in the Zulu language is united in one vocal effort under one penultimate accent is that which in the Zulu mind forms one word or complete independent speech and should, therefore, be written together as one united whole. . . ."[113] Stuart favored the disjunctive system because it would encourage use of the language by non-Zulu speakers. This accorded fully with his demand that the colonists learn more about the African people among whom they lived. To speak to them, as Stuart insisted they must, language access was an essential prerequisite. From a translator's point of view, the disjunctive method itself brought written *isiZulu* a step closer to English. And Stuart was, in every sense, a translator, or interpreter, of the African world to the European one, and vice versa. Thus while Stuart was committed to the fullest understanding and precise documentation of African ideas, and was uncompromising in the need for recording them with the fullest integrity, in their translation and in making them generally known—as in his synthesized lectures—he also took on the role of rendering them accessible. So, too, in orthographic matters, Stuart sought the "exact" meaning of words, but preferred the most accessible format. In the movement from the aural to the graphic that is entailed in the writing down of the spoken word, Stuart insisted on fidelity of content, and forwent what was already lost, an attempt to maintain consistency of form across media. Even when he made notes in *isiZulu*, his orthographic choices constituted a specific kind of intervention with consequences for the overall understanding and interpretation of the text.[114]

This raises a crucial issue in relation to the use of the Stuart collection as a historical source. As we have seen, Stuart was motivated by a complex and powerful drive to accumulate as much knowledge as possible about African society and history. He took down accounts of indigenous history in a particularly meticulous fashion. He sought, as faithfully as possible, to record the original content of the testimonies he was given. Of course, within such constraints, Stuart himself affected what was recorded in all sorts of ways. He did not reproduce that content exactly. Indeed, he could not have done so, no matter what techniques he employed. The full content of an oral text is always, inevitably, lost in recording.[115] While all recording techniques are, in the nature of things, unable to be faithful to the original, Stuart's specific recording techniques remain highly relevant. His meticulous documentation of dates and background information of other kinds, for example, can be seen as adding valuable content to the interviews.

Stuart's notes cannot be regarded as "pure" reflections of the oral histories related in contemporary African society. Rather, they are accounts of information elicited from a huge range of informants, the content of which he sought to record in a form as close to the original words as he could. The topics discussed were often, though not exclusively, dictated by his own concerns. The form of the interviews was shaped by his training as a magistrate with the use of cross-examination to establish "the facts," a preference for eyewitness accounts and the establishment of the original sources of information repeated as hearsay, a concern for genealogical and other background information, an emphasis on lines of inheritance, and other issues related to questions of native administration. In all likelihood Stuart stripped out from his notes unsolicited references to myth in favor of past events. His respondents were themselves able to negotiate the interview situations with skill, alert to the need to insert information they wanted recorded, and quick to contest his assumptions. Yet Stuart himself exerted the final authority over what he chose to note down, how he did it, and what he excluded as irrelevant. One of the biggest interventions that Stuart made in recording a mass of oral material was to bring about a massive change in form, transforming spoken text into writing.

With the recording of the oral testimonies of large numbers of informants and their transformation into written words, Stuart established a corpus of material that was less changeable than its oral precursors. At the same time as it gained permanence and became visible as words, it also acquired new authority. The written word claims the right of being a reliable record of what a person said. For Stuart, knowledge of African society demanded research that involved asking and listening, but it also entailed writing down, preserving, and fixing, and, in so doing, conferring authority on the written word. The public impact of his recording exercise was, at the time, limited because Stuart published little, with the exception of a series of Zulu readers produced in isiZulu in the 1920s, but it is of increasing importance with the publication since 1976 of his notes.

Much current discussion about orality and literacy challenges the idea that "oral" and "literate" peoples think differently and deploy different systems of logic, with the oral being privileged as somehow the more authentic and pristine version.[116] The previous chapter makes it clear that the oral and written accounts of Shaka were subject to much the same kinds of adulteration and modification. Likewise, much of this chapter focuses on the interdigitation of oral and written forms of Zulu history. To refuse to privilege oral texts as more authentic than their written counterparts and to decline to see the oral and the written as binary opposites is not, however, to deny that written and oral texts may, by virtue of their form, tend to prefer certain styles of narration and types of structure. Again, to make this observation is not to suggest that these preferences are not then transposed to the other medium. They are transferred precisely because they seem typically "oral," or in some cases "written," and therefore are able to lend authority to the other medium.

There is a marked distinction between Stuart's notes (written "transcriptions" of spoken texts) and his synthesized accounts (often speeches given from written texts). The oral accounts recorded by Stuart seem to have been fluid and loose narrative compositions, and it is possible to detect different features in the texts that Stuart regarded as transcriptions of oral texts and the syntheses he created. The latter are more uniform and more sequential (or linear) than the transcripts. The logic of the arguments presented in the two kinds of texts is different. In the transcripts time is typically mixed up and not linear. The temporal pattern between the beginning and the end of the story is often anarchic, dependent on the psychodynamics of the incident described and the narrative occasion. Prophecy is often a feature of these accounts. It causes the event to be understood as inevitable or ordained, and eliminates the need for chronologically organized explanation in terms of cause and effect. By previewing a story, prophecy offers a map of the coming narrative, which was probably useful in a situation where the text cannot be pored over.[117] Accounts of historical events are interspersed with material on other topics, and digressions abound. The very nature of explanation seems to differ in the transcripts from that in the syntheses, with the imperative for the story to explain stronger in the syntheses. In the transcripts illumination, rather, is the dominant mode. While he controlled the topics discussed, there are countless signs that Stuart tended to record the accounts in the form in which they were given, using many of the narrators' codes and conventions, and their acts of memory and narrative webs.

Stuart's own syntheses, whether spoken or written, were chronologically ordered into tightly organized historical narratives, favoring explanation over elucidation. While the notes manifest a preference for structuring historical knowledge in terms of stories and personification, Stuart's syntheses approach historical knowledge in terms of systems and concepts. Thus whereas Stuart's informants focus on episodes in the life of Shaka, and on his personality, in his syntheses Stuart examined key institutions such as the licensing of marriages and their effects, and the innovations ascribed to Shaka. While the notes contain many features typical of contemporary oral accounts, and the syntheses many characteristics of contemporary written accounts, both the notes and the syntheses combine both oral and literate features.

Stuart believed that the transcription of African oral texts into written form—making them, thereby, into permanent, unchanging texts—would open them up to scientific inquiry—in other words, open African history up to objective and critical investigation; render it, in his terms, truly analyzable; and ultimately, make it authoritative. Writing, in his view, allowed for the accumulation of knowledge, and this had, of course, implications for the corollary of increasing information—control. Indeed, Stuart overtly linked his recording activities to the building of a more effective bureaucracy.

At the same time as Stuart was interviewing well-informed Africans, lecturing to his fellow colonists, and establishing a standardized orthography he was also lobbying hard for a particular conceptualization of native policy. Stuart pursued his crusade for increased knowledge of the African inhabitants of southern Africa in his evidence to the South African Native Affairs Commission of 1903–5. The commission was established with the aim of gathering "accurate information on affairs relating to the Natives and Native administration" for the purposes of common understanding on native policy.[118] Stuart was, on the face of it, precisely the kind of native expert whose testimony the commissioners considered they needed, for it offered the possibility of informing them of the opinions of the "stolid gentlemen of the 'Tribes' who are implicitly antagonistic to their 'educated' brethren."[119]

The thrust of Stuart's evidence was that Africans should be consulted about their future government and the form it would take. To this end, Stuart proposed the establishment of a native council (or councils, if country-wide). He went on: "As this Council is for the purpose of dealing with purely native matters and would concern itself entirely with native welfare, so it must necessarily consist of natives or those enjoying the very fullest knowledge of native affairs and at the same time sympathizing with the people and possessing their confidence."[120] Membership of the council was to be permanent, thus avoiding the problem faced by elected officials such as Moor who were responsible to a white electorate whose interests often clashed with those of the African population. Stuart envisaged that the council would be set up by the governor of the colony in his capacity as supreme chief (with the advice, Stuart added, of "a man like Mr. John Shepstone"), and be under the presidency of "an European officer who may be known as the Secretary to the Supreme Chief." The council would meet twice a year and, in between, the secretary with a small staff would be responsible for the conduct of its business. Stuart did not confine his view of its work to comment on native policy. Rather, he envisaged a dramatically proactive role for the secretary.

> The work referred to will be to collect all information he can regarding native habits and customs; he will prepare a history of native policy in Natal as well as in South Africa; he will acquire from all available sources the history of the various tribes; and he will make a systematic study of all such grievances of natives, especially those of major importance. . . .[121]

Stuart declined on principle to offer comments on the questions posed by the commission, arguing that these were matters for African comment and, where discussed by Europeans, demanded access to African views and vastly extended research. "I am of the opinion," he commented,

> that no man has any right to lay down the law on matters he knows next to nothing about. The European has no actual experience of communal land tenure, of living under a tribal system, of being polygamist, consequently his impressions are slight and faulty and his deductions therefore must necessarily be narrow because not giving sufficient weight to all the factors as, for instance, they would come before the mind of an intelligent native living under such a system, if only he could sufficiently express himself.

In his submission, and in his subsequent cross-examination by the commission, Stuart warned of the consequences of failure to hear and understand African grievances, and to act on them. Thus in certain respects Stuart refused precisely the role he was considered most fitted for, that of speaking for the "native."[122]

During the examination by the commission, the heart of Stuart's argument was starkly revealed. The commission cross-questioned him closely on the subject of Shakan rule:

"Was that not practically a despotism?"

"Yes, it was," admitted Stuart.

"A despotism of martial law which proved a success?"

"Yes," responded Stuart.

"Directly that was withdrawn?" inquired the commission.

"The controlling influence being withdrawn, the people tended to disintegrate."

"Therefore," the Commission enquired, clearly puzzled, "you believe in despotism?"

"I do," responded Stuart, "that is despotism for this race of people we are dealing with in South Africa."[123]

The commission went on to explore the question of "repugnant" practices associated with the despotic government of Shaka. To this Stuart responded:

I think the European people are apt to misconstrue the way in which these people governed their own people. Things that they did which appear to us arbitrary and cruel, were not necessarily so. It was a system which they fully understood and many of these practices which we mark down as being contrary to civilised usages, were just in themselves; it was justice.[124]

For Stuart—like Shepstone—the key was viewing the whole as a system. What was indefensible under a Christian government was, in his view, defensible "under a native system."[125] While he admitted, when pressed by the commissioners, that the Shakan system in its entirety could not be reestablished in modern times, he considered a modified form a feasible goal. "The whole genius of native life is to live under a patriarchal system,"[126] of which, for Stuart, the Shakan system was but the most developed form. He argued further that under this system hereditary chiefs had obligations toward their followers which ensured that they represented more than their own narrow sectoral interests.[127] In particular he considered that, contrary to current practices in Natal native administration, "tribes" should be kept intact and not broken up, that hereditary rather than appointed chiefs were desirable. Finally, Stuart argued that the native system of rule contained within it a concept of guardianship that was vested in the king. "Owing to our having conquered the country, it is now vested in ourselves, and it confers on us very extensive rights. . . ."[128]

Shepstone's legacy is obvious. The Shakan system was the ideal solution to the problems of native administration in Natal. It was closely tied to imperial domination but—and this was Stuart's central thesis—neither opportunistically nor superficially so. While Shepstone was anxious to know the natives so as better to rule them, Stuart was further concerned with the importance of knowledge of the past for Africans. He recognized that history and "custom" were crucial components of the identities of Natal's colonial African subjects.[129]

Stuart and the lessons of the "Bambatha rebellion"

At the end of 1905 the authorities introduced a new £1 poll tax on top of an already onerous tax burden. The new tax was aimed at the African peasantry, to oblige young men to enter wage labor so as to satisfy European labor needs. The poll tax caused widespread dissatisfaction in Natal. Rumors of a general uprising abounded, small incidents of recalcitrance sparked off a panic, and martial law was declared. In April the Zondi chief, Bambatha, who had been summarily deposed by the Natal authorities, went into open rebellion, soon to be joined by a number of other prominent chiefs. The rebels were rapidly defeated by the colonial forces, but a host of small incidents continued throughout 1907, until the Zulu king, Dinuzulu, who was thought to be behind the continuing ferment, was arrested, and charged with high treason.[130] Stuart, holding the rank of captain in the Natal Field Artillery, was an intelligence officer with the colonial forces, and was credited with bringing in Dinuzulu.

Stuart's involvement in quelling the uprising and his motives in subsequently publishing a comprehensive account of the disturbances merit a study of their own.[131] For the purposes of this work it is sufficient to note that Stuart was opposed to actions that dislodged the African peasantry from the land, and had long expressed opposition to a poll tax. He was, moreover, personally acquainted with some of the rebels, men such as Ndlovu kaThimuni, whom we have already had occasion to mention, and was sympathetic and understanding toward their grievances. On the other hand, he was also a member of the colonial service, and he believed that native administration depended on strong governance in the Shakan mold. Thus, when Bambatha challenged the government, Stuart, while against the poll tax, found himself in agreement with the authorities that firm action had to be taken. To deepen further the ambiguities of his position, it was precisely his status as a "native expert" that earned him the post of intelligence officer, and obliged him to use that knowledge in the suppression of the community from which it emanated.

After the disturbances were over, the government of Natal invited Stuart to compile a history of the rebellion. By the time the manuscript was completed, about five years later—Stuart being a slow and meticulous accumulator of data—the new Union government of South Africa declined to meet the expenses. This is not surprising, for the criticisms leveled in the book at the Natal native administration in 1906 applied equally to native affairs in 1912 under the new Union government in which Stuart by then held the post of assistant secretary for native affairs.

The book, which Stuart eventually published privately in 1913, was a powerful critique of the errors in native administration that led to the disturbance.

But although government of the Natives mainly in accordance with their own laws and customs has been the outstanding feature of Natal's policy, changes being introduced with care and deliberation as they appeared to be necessary, there have not been wanting occasions on which instead of being sympathetic, Her administration has been cold and artificial; instead of being content with advance in harmony with nature's slow processes she has imposed laws involving sudden and widespread change; instead of being occasional and simple to understand, the laws have been frequent and to some extent unintelligible, having in view rather the benefit of the higher than of the lower race. Instances of such inconsistency will be given later; for these indeed, are the stuff out of which the bonfire of the Rebellion was built up. Had Natal been true to herself, had she but steadily adhered to the general principles above outlined, it is not too much to say, there would have been no Rebellion.[132]

It was also a statement of the need under all circumstances for firm responses and strong governance.[133]

The details of the struggles in the Native Affairs Department in the years preceding and following Union await detailed investigation. Suffice it to say that Stuart found himself in opposition to the policies of the Union Native Affairs Department on three counts. Firstly, he felt that entrenched separate development was central to the maintenance of the fabric of African society.

Natives must be granted special areas within which they can live unaffected or rather affected as little as possible by European ideas and manner of living—this may be described as a policy of segregation, but is really a policy of recognition of rights and privileges to which natives are due, not merely as individuals but as communities.[134]

Secondly, he argued it was imperative that Africans had a say in, and control over, their own affairs; and finally, he regarded as imperative the appointment of an interlocutor between the African communities and the government—in effect, a Shepstone figure.

Within these areas should be appointed Europeans who are sympathetic towards native life and character. These may be Commission[ers]—who, in their turn must all be subject entirely to the Native Affairs Department. This complete subjection to the N.A. Dept, will cause them to take special interest and pride in their work, there will be esprit de corps among them. The scheme will resemble the giving of a charter to the N.A. Dept. as suggested by the Natal N.A. Commission.[135]

The ideal man to head up this corps was, of course, none other than Stuart himself. In the last section of his book, on "Native policy," Stuart argued that the core of the problem was "the inadequacy of the organic connection between Europeans and Natives." As he put it, "the want of an organic connection between their race and that of the white man takes the form of a request for the appointment of a *person* to act as intermediary, one to whom they can go with their troubles, and one who would lay these before the Government for favourable consideration."[136]

Stuart criticized Union policy as an attempt to impose "Western Civilization" on Africans, and he depicted the Bambatha affair as standing for a deep-seated rejection of precisely that:

> Bambata, as many natives believe, in spite of every proof to the contrary, is still living. For them his spirit, i.e. dissatisfaction with European rule, or, to put the same thing positively, a desire to control their own affairs, not on European lines, but on those sanctioned by the collective wisdom of their own race, is certainly alive, though he may be dead.[137]

One of the major effects of his proposals that Stuart foresaw was that it would remove "the existing conditions under which a continuous impulse is given to living in accordance with European ideas and customs" and "the spirit of native custom and creed will prevail."[138] In 1913 Stuart was advocating a form of native policy that was very much a successor to Shepstone's ideas.

While the thrust of the argument in this chapter is that Stuart regarded his views as being in the best interest of Africans, and had devoted considerable energy and time to ascertaining African opinion on the question, it is also argued that effective colonial governance was one of Stuart's motivating concerns, as it was of a host of other contemporary "native experts." As Adam Ashforth has observed, the "'Native Question' was the intellectual domain in which the knowledge, strategies, policies, and justifications necessary to the maintenance of domination were fashioned."[139] Stuart's interventions were no exception:

> Thus, in a certain sense, there would be a restriction of liberty as well as of individualism. People by self choice, would tend more and more to submit themselves to a form of social and political life to which they are accustomed and which, so to speak, runs in their veins. They would therefore, elect to be under a form of control, provided this were exercised by themselves, in the same way that we find Ethiopians [independent African Christian churches] desirous of controlling themselves apart from all European interference.[140]

In terms of the new Union constitution, the head of the government was also the supreme chief of all the African inhabitants of South Africa. In Stuart's eyes this was a perversion of the Shepstone system and destined to fail. This supreme chief was distant and unknown, and, in turn, did not have the necessary knowledge of the African communities under him to rule in the Shepstone—or Shakan—manner.

In order to draw attention to the differences between this distorted version of the Shepstone system and "Somtsewu's" original conceptualization, Arthur Shepstone, in consultation with Stuart, wrote in 1911 to Rider Haggard, requesting him to undertake the task of writing a biography of Sir Theophilus.[141] Haggard, who had accompanied Shepstone on his journey to annex the Transvaal in 1877, and who had been charged with the responsibility of running up the Union Jack over Pretoria, had been a personal favorite of Sir Theophilus.[142] He had championed Shepstone and his system of native administration in his book *Cetywayo and his White Neighbours,* and considered him always "my beloved chief and friend."[143] The motivation for the biography, Arthur Shepstone stressed, would be its capacity to speak to "the native question . . . an evergreen and vital matter out here."[144] Indeed, it seems that Arthur Shepstone and James Stuart were keen to have Rider Haggard deploy his popular writing style to lobby public opinion, for it was their plan that Stuart would do all the research, and that Rider Haggard would not even have to come out to South Africa.[145]

As we have seen, following the publication of *Cetywayo,* Haggard began to be considered something of an expert on South Africa, a reputation that was only enhanced by his enormous popularity as the writer of fiction set in Africa. As Arthur Shepstone put it: "I know of noone else in whose Judgement, savoir-faire and literary ability such entire confidence could be reposed as in yourself."[146] But Haggard was unable to oblige. In his reply to Arthur Shepstone he pleaded overwork, but offered to help Stuart in any other way. His recommendation to Stuart to fill up the biography with Zulu accounts, "taken down in their own manner of speaking—not in the white manner and rendered into the appropriate English idiom,"[147] struck an immediate chord with Stuart, ensuring that the two would continue to correspond. Indeed, in his notes made in preparation for the biography, Stuart did precisely as Haggard suggested, notably with regard to his treatment of the matter of "Sir Theophilus Shepstone having been regarded by the Zulu nation as representing Shaka."[148] Stuart made a start on the biography, drawing up a chronology of Theophilus' life and asking John Shepstone questions, as well as interviewing Africans, as suggested by Haggard.[149] The research into Shepstone's life and practice surely touched chords for Stuart, their life works being in many respects akin, and their differences from the broader settler populations being so similar. Like so many of Stuart's projects, however, it was hampered by his policy of not rounding off what could not be completed, and was never finished.

In 1912 Rider Haggard sent the proofs for the second book of what was to become a trilogy on Zulu history to his new acquaintance for correction.[150] Stuart approved his labors and proclaimed them to be animated "by the true Zulu spirit."[151] Coming from Stuart, the acknowledged Zulu expert of the time, this was high praise indeed, and Haggard went on to dedicate the book, *Child of Storm*—in which Rudyard Kipling had a hand[152]—to Stuart, noting the endorsement in the dedication.

In 1914 Rider Haggard traveled to South Africa, and arranged to go with Stuart on a trip to Zululand. Accompanied by the knowledgeable Socwatsha whom Stuart had invited along specially, and Masuku, Haggard's old retainer from his previous trip, Stuart and Haggard then toured Zululand together with the resident magistrate, J. Gibson.[153] Socwatsha provided Haggard with a great deal of material which was subsequently used in Haggard's next book, *Finished,* the last of the trilogy on Zulu history.[154] Although Haggard had declined to write a biography of Shepstone, Shepstone appears as a character in *Finished,* in which Haggard describes him as the "African Talleyrand."[155]

In 1914 Stuart, in his turn, went to England as an adviser on "Zulu habits and customs" for a stage version of *Child of Storm,* produced by Oscar Ashe. Stuart purchased the costumes, supervised the Zulu dances, and otherwise attended to details of authenticity.[156] Stuart and Haggard thus entered into each other's worlds: Haggard interviewed Stuart's informant Socwatsha while Stuart helped craft fiction. The relationship was mutually influential.

Throughout the 1910s Stuart continued to interview knowledgeable Africans on topics of historical interest. Then, in 1916, he finally married, and shortly thereafter, at the request of the government, accompanied the Native Labour Corps to France. He returned to South Africa in December 1917. In the period 1918–22 Stuart resumed interviewing, as well as work on the Fynn papers. He lectured on Zulu history and ethnography. Arguing that the Zulu did not want "the sublime and airy types of liberty civilisation has to offer," Stuart criticized the British government for failing to fulfill its responsibilities in ruling Zululand, for taxing its subjects mercilessly, and otherwise being "neglectful of the welfare of the black people." "Bad government," he continued, "signifies to them that European civilisation itself is to that extent bad or defective."[157]

Stuart continued working on drafts of his history of the reign of Shaka, and persistently lobbied for the appointment of a special native commissioner, as well as advocating the establishment of university chairs in subjects such as anthropology and colonial history.[158] Finally, in 1922, he and his family set sail for England.

Stuart, very much "the Zulu expert" in London, made contact with the African-language specialist at the School of Oriental Studies in the University of London, Alice Werner. Stuart and Werner exchanged books such as Fuze's *Abantu*

Abamnyama and Maine's *Ancient Law,* and Werner invited Stuart to lecture in London.[159] As had been the case in Natal, Stuart's expertise in London was communicated in spoken presentation far more than in written form. He lectured very widely on a range of subjects—with the reign of Shaka ever a favorite topic—representing "the Zulu" in the metropole. Stuart took charge of the Zulu section of an Aldershot pageant and the 1924 Wembley exhibition, and when the praise poet who was part of the pageant was stricken with stage fright, Stuart, with arms, face, and legs blackened, played the part most successfully, undiscovered in his disguise.[160]

Then, on May 28, 1925, fourteen days after the death of their mutual friend, Rider Haggard, Stuart met Rudyard Kipling in Downing Street.[161] Kipling used the occasion to urge Stuart to publish in English. At this time Stuart finally had three of a series of five books published by Longmans, in *isiZulu*.[162] In a review of the first reader, *Tulasizwe*, the Natal superintendent for native education, D.M. Malcolm, noted that the books would be prescribed in schools, and urged teachers to acquire copies as soon as possible.[163] Each of the four readers contained a mixture of historical narratives, discussions of what might be termed "customs"— topics such as the forging of metal in early times, cattle, the manufacture of knobkieries and knobsticks, the carving of headrests and spoons, and so on—and praise poems. Of the historical accounts, about one-sixth are concerned with the reign of Shaka, while the *izibongo* of Shaka are given in installments in four of the readers.

Remarkably, Stuart's Zulu readers have been ignored in most reviews of Zulu historiography, with the exception of the work of Rycroft and Ngcobo, Malaba, and Gunner.[164] These studies deal only with the *izibongo* published in the readers. Rycroft and Ngcobo argue that the readers were "very influential in presenting a wide range of Zulu cultural and historical material which made its mark on future Zulu writers."[165] They note that the readers were withdrawn from school use in the mid-1930s when changes in the official orthography made earlier (disjunctive) publications unacceptable. However, it should be said that they were reissued in the new conjunctive orthography and probably continued to be influential for an even longer period.[166] In comments that pertain largely to the praise poems, Rycroft and Ngcobo point out that Stuart's readers were the bases for the novels of R.R.R. Dhlomo and C.L.S. Nyembezi's publications. La Hausse, by way of contrast, points to the influences on African writers of contemporary Zulu historians, men such as Petros Lamula who, in sharp contrast to Stuart, were fiercely antisegregationist and opposed to the forms of paternalism so favored by Stuart.[167] It seems likely that Stuart was finally prompted into publication to challenge the versions of Shakan history being produced at this time by the Zulu-speaking intelligentsia.

Rycroft and Ngcobo show in relation to the praises of Dingane that the Stuart readers presented a version of the Zulu king's praises that was cobbled together, by Stuart, from a range of sources, and that Stuart's intervention in the creation of these texts was quite substantial. This is not surprising: many *izimbongi* patched together lines in a similar fashion, and Stuart was himself, after all, an *imbongi* of some note. Rycroft and Ngcobo's findings concerning Stuart's methods in putting together the published version of Dingane's praises are broadly borne out by Malaba's analysis of the praises of Shaka, also published serially in the readers.[168]

Gunner argues that Stuart was responsible for fixing praise poems in a particular form and for losing sight of the creative work of individual *izimbongi*, while Golan builds on this criticism to argue that Stuart "created the impression that *izibongo* were fixed texts of which he had obtained the real or official versions."[169] This reading of Stuart is, in my view, misplaced. While the effective consequence of the writing down of *izibongo* was, inevitably, their fixing in written form, Stuart cannot be blamed for this. Their further freezing in a particular version was also a consequence of their publication. At the same time, it must be recognized that Stuart was enormously sensitive to the existence of many versions of the praises of Shaka, and the impact of the circumstances of delivery and composition on those versions. Moreover, in an essay on praising in one of the readers, Stuart expressly asserted that praises were "unfixed" texts. In sharp contrast to Golan's assertion that Stuart claimed to have recorded the true or official versions of the *izibongo*, and that he was "responsible for the common belief that the time and place in which the praise poems were sung, and the ability of the bard were of no importance," Stuart actually detailed in his essay a variety of circumstances of praising. He noted that *izibongo* incited people to bravery, that praises were always being composed and that anyone could praise—"Izibongo azi kete muntu munye, ukuti nang' o qam' izibongo."[170] He was, moreover, alert to the different abilities of various bards.[171]

There is a tendency in the literature to view Stuart's readers as sites for the promotion of his versions of Zulu history. This is implicit in Golan's evaluation of Stuart.[172] In contrast to the praises, which *were* Stuart's syntheses, the historical narratives in the readers were not. In the historical sections of the readers, Stuart expressly eschewed the idea of collating material from a number of sources. Instead, he preserved the stories largely as recorded in his original notes. Introducing the first book, Stuart noted that the contents of the reader "are original, having in every instance been collected by me." Review of the stories about the reign of Shaka bears out the validity of this claim. The stories about Shaka can be provenanced to one or another of Stuart's informants. Stuart used versions from a range of informants of very different political persuasions, whose accounts were both for and against Shaka. The individual narrative style of the original testimonies is largely preserved in the readers. The structure of the original narratives is likewise substantially retained.

Moreover, the contents of the readers reflect Stuart's collection process. The author resisted imposing a chronological order in the arrangement of the stories or the systematic pursuit of themes, while the eclectic mixture of historical material, information on "customs," and praises reflected the contents typical of any one of Stuart's interviews. The stories appear to have been selected for inclusion because of their interesting content, dramatic narration, and richness of detail. An ideological reason behind Stuart's selection of particular stories for inclusion is not readily apparent, although it is possible that as knowledge of the historical context of their production develops, such rationales may become evident.

To note that the stories that appeared in the readers were not Stuart's syntheses is not, however, to suggest that they were untouched by Stuart's authorship. Closer textual analysis is likely to focus in detail on small differences between the published stories and Stuart's notes. These may reflect a series of linguistic choices made by Stuart to enhance the sense of orality and authenticity in the published accounts. They may include minor changes designed to facilitate his readers' understanding. Such advances will increase substantially our view of colonial publishing exercises in general, and of Stuart's interventions in particular, thereby enhancing scholars' capacities to evaluate more closely the historical materials assembled by Stuart.

In summary, a brief survey of Stuart's only substantial publications reveals that they reflected relatively closely his notes of interviews. Minor differences between the two forms do exist which will merit closer study, as textual sensitivity in relation to Stuart advances. This chapter heralds what is likely to be a new interest in close analysis of Stuart's many texts, published and archived. These include the Fynn *Diary*. Stuart died on April 8, 1942, leaving the task of editing the Fynn papers still incomplete. The papers were brought back to South Africa and passed on to Malcolm, and ultimately published in 1950.[173]

Conclusion

The insistent presence of Stuart's collection of historical materials as the single richest source of evidence concerning the precolonial history of southeast Africa focuses a spotlight on the profoundly ambiguous figure of James Stuart himself and on colonial practices of historical investigation. This chapter on Stuart has argued that the private, unpublished Stuart stands in marked contrast to the public figure. Stuart employed a different language in his personal papers and correspondence from that of his public pronouncements. In the former Stuart was more tentative and more exploratory, frequently revealing himself to be morally outraged by the effects of colonialism on the African communities of Zululand and Natal. In the latter Stuart spoke as an authority on Zulu customs and history, at the same time stressing the importance of still further research. The public Stuart was a dynamic policy maker imbued with a powerfully paternalist vision regarding British rule over its colonial subjects. This chapter is not intended to suggest that there were two distinct faces to Stuart, one private, the other public. There were many features common to both visages. The first was never fully free of the imperial ideology and racial prejudice common at the time, nor was Stuart's sense of moral outrage ever wholly absent from the second. In both aspects, Stuart was concerned with the fundamental issue of the nature of African and European integration, and the problem of the differences between the "lower" and "higher" races. In both, Stuart was also concerned with "bettering the future of the [Zulu] people."[174] In a single document Stuart could assert the superiority of the European, and call for equality of opportunity for Africans.[175]

As an administrator Stuart was much preoccupied with the "native question." As Ashforth has observed, to speak of a social question as a "problem" is to name the people concerned as a subject of power, "the power presumed capable of 'solving' the problem they constitute."[176] Stuart, following Shepstone, helped establish a body of ideas about African society which was aimed at solving the problem and which became part of the terms of reference for later discourses of segregation and domination. He was especially active in the generation of forms of knowledge and expertise that underpinned those discourses. Yet, partly as a result of his immersion in Zulu affairs and his noted linguistic skill, he was no mere perpetuator of imperial hegemony, or representative of his "unpleasant generation." Rather, he was a highly self-conscious cross-cultural broker, mediating between the African and European colonial worlds in which he moved.[177] He sought not simply to implement imperial policies, but to reform and reshape them. He was highly critical of Natal native policy and very receptive to the articulation of African grievances. His approach was essentially tactical, and he was adept at choosing the right languages for all the many audiences, African and European, whom he had occasion to address, and whom he sought to sway. The great ambiguities of his position are perhaps best captured by the countless lists of proposed, but always ultimately rejected, book titles that survive in his papers. "The White Man's Tyranny in Africa" was one cry straight from Stuart's heart; "Civilisation of Lower Races: A Tyranny" was another mediated through the discourse of his time.[178]

There is no escaping the fact that Stuart's acts of cultural interlocution, his researches, and his orthographic disciplining of the languages spoken in Zululand and Natal were exertions of colonial power. John Dube recognized this when he attacked Stuart for these endeavors, and in particular for his pursuance of Shaka's rule as a model for colonial native administration. "Why now praise Zulu severity," Dube fumed, "when at the time it was enforced it was condemned at the muzzle of the rifle and the cannon?"[179]

That said, and fully acknowledged, the argument presented here goes on to suggest that crude caricatures of Stuart as the exploiter of African oral tradition for resources that would facilitate and legitimize white access to land, and the labor of Africans need to be modified by the mass of evidence pointing to his grand "Idea" and his complex understanding of the task he had set himself. Stuart, like Shepstone before him, sought to protect Britain's colonial subjects from the land and labor demands of the settlers. Again like Shepstone, Stuart sought in African tradition a vision of sovereignty on which to base native policy. The image on which he drew, like Shepstone, was that of Shaka.

Marks is quite correct to see in Stuart's recording efforts and his publication of the readers an effort to shore up what he saw as Zulu tradition.[180] But we also need to understand how Stuart viewed the relation between knowledge of African tradition and native policy and, secondly, the extent of his particular interventions in the material he collected and published. Stuart had an extremely serious commitment to getting to know a vast deal about the African inhabitants of Natal. He was irritated by more facile approaches, and he employed a methodology that kept synthesizing activities out of his notes and, ultimately, also out of the Zulu readers.

Stuart remarked that he often felt that the Zulus "deserve a Thomas Hardy of their own, someone able on a large canvas to portray their various manners and character, and set down their merits and achievements. . . ."[181] Stuart fancied himself to be precisely such an interlocutor, able to see, portray, and interpret the humanity and culture of "the native"; able, like Hardy, to appreciate the hero in the rustic yokel that his contemporaries denigrated.

Finally, and perhaps most importantly, a sharp distinction must be drawn by scholars using Stuart's materials between his notes and his own compositions. There are strong motivations for regarding his notes as being remarkably, though by no means completely, faithful to the spoken originals. The chief changes were a product of a change of *form* from oral to written text. His collection is a complex "archive" presented through a range of intellectual and political filters and indeed, as further research is likely to show, literary ones, which cannot be dismissed simply as a "contaminated well."

The rationale for the focus on Shaka, first by Shepstone, and later in a more developed, professionalized, and "scientific" form by Stuart, was a prudent, even strategic, regard for indigenous sentiments, and the need for a legitimization for colonialism. In the late nineteenth and early twentieth centuries, it was assumed that a king could not govern without the support of his people.[182] In other words, large states headed by kings were viewed as archetypal constitutional monarchies.

The compulsion inherent in such a system was understood to be necessary so that when confronted with an enemy, disciplined collective action was possible. This kind of thinking allowed administrators such as Shepstone and Stuart to reach out and appropriate to the colonial project the reign of Shaka, and thereby to legitimize that project, doing so in a way that took serious cognizance of indigenous sentiments.

Chapter Five

Shaka as metaphor, memory, and history in apartheid South Africa

The insistence, first by Shepstone and later by Stuart, that successful and effective native government through the utilization of indigenous institutions, practices, and knowledges depended on a deep interior knowledge and appreciation of the systems so appropriated was a battle lost by the time the policy of segregation was implemented in South Africa in the 1930s. A strong element of segregationist thinking had, of course, always underlain the two officials' manner of coupling historical knowledge and administration, just as it was also a thread in the political programs of early African nationalists such as Stuart's contemporary and critic, John Dube. Following Union, the new Native Affairs Department came under considerable pressure to implement policies that guaranteed industrialized South Africa sufficient labor at low wages, as well as ready access to land. As a consequence, in the early decades of the twentieth century native policy was increasingly freed from the constraints that Shepstone and Stuart had been so concerned to safeguard. The agenda of research into the history and customs of those governed was, however, never wholly uncoupled from administration. In the 1920s the first Bantu studies courses were established at South African universities with the specific aim of providing training for native administrators, while in the 1930s the government set up the Ethnological Survey under N.J. van Warmelo with a brief that effectively amounted to continuing Stuart's life project of recording a living source of tradition.

Whereas Shepstone and Stuart had seen in the Shakan system a blueprint for native administration, and understood that the knowledge required had to be appropriate to an exercise in modeling, the administrators who followed them increasingly regarded the indigenous systems as a resource from which to draw features of their own apparatuses of government. Acknowledging the widespread effects of social and political change, they adopted far more instrumentally only those aspects of indigenous government that they regarded as compatible with modern South Africa. As Anthony Costa has shown, in the disputed succession following the death of the Zulu king Solomon kaDinuzulu in 1933 (overseen by yet another administrator who prided himself on his knowledge of "native customs," the native commissioner at Nongoma, H.P. Braatvedt), customary law in codified form was treated as inflexible in ways that would not have happened in its original context, while at the same time the authorities invented precedents to resolve the matter satisfactorily.[1] Not only were officials in the Natal Native Affairs Department after Union less systematic in their researches into the past than Shepstone and Stuart had been, but they remained determined to bolster the power of the chiefs against that of the king, whom they saw as a threat to stability in the region.[2]

If Shaka was no longer a model for native administration, he was increasingly invoked as a historical metaphor. The popular appeal of segregationist and, later, apartheid ideologies among many white South Africans lay in part in a handful of associated ideas about the innate barbarism and violence of black South Africans, and in views about the inevitability of intertribal conflict. Examples of texts that make these points through reference to Shaka are legion and, as discussed in chapter 1, they have been widely studied, Wylie's work being both the latest and most skilled. Discussing a range of publications from the 1940s and 1950s, Wylie demonstrates how in this period the story of Shaka was used by white writers, mostly of fiction, to illustrate "the black man's total decline in South Africa"[3] and the tragedy of the failure of recognizing and maintaining racial boundaries. Wylie gives special attention to E.A. Ritter's 1955 book *Shaka Zulu* because, as he puts it, it "heralded a significant turning away from the monstrous image established by Isaacs, and effected [a] substantial reorientation of subsequent literature."[4] While Wylie sees the more admiring components of the Ritter text as an innovation of this period, this study provides them rather with a long historical lineage.

If images of a tyrannical Shaka and marauding Zulus, even where qualified with observations about Shakan achievement, were nonetheless the metaphorical bearers of many of the ideas that underpinned racial dominance, so too did the image of Shaka come to carry comparable metaphorical weight when invoked by those who sought to resist such ideas. The rise of Zulu nationalism in a regional form in the 1920s, manifest in the establishment of the early Inkatha in 1923, has been extensively documented elsewhere.[5] Building on Marks' earlier work, Nicholas Cope's study of the reign of Solomon kaDinuzulu, from 1913 to 1933, identifies the social forces that underpinned the emergence of a Zulu ethnic identity in this period. He shows how, rather than an innate form of Zulu political consciousness, it was a modern political force, constructed principally by Zulu social and political elites in the altered circumstances of industrializing South Africa.[6] Cope's study, together with that of La Hausse,[7] reveals the 1920s to be a period of intense cultural activity. This decade witnessed the development of a new historiography written in *isiZulu* by nationalists seeking to shore up their political position in the face of the push toward segregation by the Union government and the concomitant erosion of African political rights. In their resistance to segregation, the nationalists had recourse to Shaka and to associated notions of precolonial "civilisation."[8] Their aim was to have Solomon recognized as paramount chief of all the Zulu across the domain that historically was Shaka's.[9] It was at this time that the Zulu nationalists began to collect money for a special memorial to Shaka, erected at Dukuza in 1932; and R.R.R. Dhlomo's novel *uShaka* was published in 1937. Designed to provide a hero with whom his Zulu-speaking readers could identify, the novel immediately became a bestseller. This version of Shaka, like the earlier Zulu-language publications of nationalists such as Petros Lamula, was nonetheless heavily influenced by the Zulu histories produced by white writers such as Shepstone and Stuart.[10]

Appeals to the historical legacy of Shaka were not confined to Zulu nationalists. Similar invocations characterized a range of resistance texts over the following decades in forms as diverse as short profiles in *The African Communist* and that massive black nationalist tract, Mazisi Kunene's *Emperor Shaka the Great*.[11] Significantly, however, the texts of the advocates of racial domination as well as those of their opponents seldom presented Shaka as either wholly villain or hero. Even the latter-day Inkatha organization, reconstituted in 1975, offers a profoundly ambiguous Shaka, both succorer of visitors and unrelenting toward foes.[12]

The burden of my argument is that the image of Shaka was not, as many commentators have argued, a colonial invention. Nor was it uniformly negative until the interventions of the Zulu nationalists from the 1920s onward or alternatively, in other lineages, that of Ritter. Rather, it gained its complex mix of ingredients, negative and positive, in slightly different proportions according to various menus, at least in part as a consequence of the history of the image as it had evolved in the course of the nineteenth century. First-hand experiences and secondary knowledge of Shaka were highly varied during his lifetime, whether those of his allies, associates, or enemies, his neighbors or distant powers, both black and white. After his death in 1828 these images were subjected to vigorous reworkings. They resulted in the creation of a range of images of the Zulu king that defy categorization as being negative where propagated by whites or positive if produced by blacks. Preceding chapters have shown how these images were powerfully shaped, on the one hand, by the politics of succession within what was historically the Zulu kingdom and, on the other, by developments within the Natal colonial administration and the Union government that superseded it. A powerful connection was thus forged between the story of Shaka and the agenda of domination that lay at the heart of colonial and Union native policy. The discourses of history and of domination, mobilized by both the colonizers and colonized, or, more accurately, local white rulers and their Zulu-speaking subjects, were deeply intertwined, each taking extensive cognizance of the other. The strength of the coupling of history and administrative control, the complexity of the associated discussions of civilization and barbarism as they adhered to the image of Shaka, and the mix of responses to Shaka across racial lines—these all underlay the establishment of Shaka and Shakan rule as an important metaphor in South African politics.

If, as this study has suggested so far, Shaka cannot simply be reinvented to suit the latest current political purposes; if white writings about Shaka are profoundly affected by black productions and vice versa; and if the whole project of writing about Shaka is fundamentally implicated in grappling with the complexity of racial domination and race relations, how do we understand the concern with Shaka that was manifest in South Africa in the run-up to the first democratic election in 1994? In posing this question the focus is not so much on Inkatha's mobilization of Shaka, the political advantages of which were, and still are, largely self-evident, but rather on the responses to and concerns with Shaka outside Inkatha. To answer this question, posed as it is against the backdrop of the foregoing historical review, this chapter examines in depth two highly elaborated engagements with the figure of Shaka, particular to two slightly different historical periods, the late-apartheid television series *Shaka Zulu* and the transition-period holiday resort, Shakaland.

A positional gambit: *Shaka Zulu* and the conflict in South Africa

In late 1986 the South African Broadcasting Corporation (SABC) screened a new television mini-series, *Shaka Zulu*. Within a year it had been seen by a remarkable 100 million viewers in South Africa and abroad. Equally astonishing was the series' cost, a staggering $24 million. Hailed by some critics as a rare instance of African history from an African perspective, and slated by others as racist propaganda, the series remained in the public eye well beyond its screening times.

Shaka Zulu was a historical drama centered on the earliest encounter between blacks and whites in southeast Africa. In the film Lieutenant Francis Farewell (Edward Fox) is commissioned by the British government in London to journey to southeast Africa, and there to make contact with Shaka Zulu (acted by local soccer player Henry Cele), the head of a powerful and warlike kingdom. In the series Shaka is presented as poised for an attack on the British colony of the Cape some 300 miles to the south of his domain. Because the British government is unable to provide the forces necessary to defend the Cape, an alternative plan is devised to send out "A solitary Caucasian" (Farewell), armed with little more than "civilization, years of tried and tested double-talk" to overawe and divert the Zulu monarch from an attack on the colony.

At the Cape Farewell recruits a band of men, adventurous and true, to accompany him to Shaka's kingdom. Their numbers include a compassionate Irish doctor, Henry Francis Fynn. The party sets sail, and is wrecked off the coast of Natal, on the southern periphery of the Zulu kingdom. Shaka, a shrewd tactician, realizes the possible advantages and strengths of the new arrivals in his kingdom, and orders the party up to his capital, Bulawayo (literally, "The place of killing").

Once at Bulawayo, Farewell finds that his task is not as simple as it seemed in London. Shaka is an intelligent man, ruling a highly organized kingdom, a diplomat well versed in debate and easily Farewell's equal in double-talk. Both Farewell and Fynn are drawn to Shaka, and are fascinated by the society in which they find themselves. During their stay at the Zulu court, they learn the story of Shaka's rise to power and the way in which the mighty Zulu kingdom was built.

Fynn records all that he hears in his diary. The diary, its contents narrated by Fynn, is the vehicle for a series of flashbacks which tell the story of Shaka's conception and birth, his stormy adolescence as an outcast son of the Zulu chief, and his accession to power. Shaka's life-course is believed to be controlled by a prophecy, and he is shown to be destined from birth to rule. The prophecy's fulfillment is assisted by the timely interventions of the ancient "witchdoctor" Sitayi. By the time the Swallows—as the Europeans come to be called by the Zulus—arrive in Shaka's kingdom, it has expanded under his leadership from a small, insignificant chiefdom to the most powerful state in southern Africa.

Farewell and company win Shaka's trust by healing him after an attempted assassination at Bulawayo, and by assisting him in a campaign against his most powerful enemies, the Ndwandwe, under Zwide. Farewell is then required to escort a Zulu deputation to conclude a treaty with the British on Shaka's behalf. Farewell and a number of Shaka's most trusted advisers set sail for the Cape in a homemade barque. During their absence, Shaka's mother, to whom he is obsessively devoted, dies, and the Zulu kingdom is plunged by the grief-crazed monarch into an orgy of mourning. One feature of this mourning is a destructive campaign in the direction of the colony. Reports of ravaging Zulu hordes pressing on the borders of the Cape sabotage Shaka's diplomatic mission, already under strain as a result of the derisive and shoddy treatment of the party by the governor of the Cape and his aides. Farewell and the Zulu chiefs return to Shaka's court to find the kingdom in turmoil, suffering under harsh mourning prohibitions. Farewell confronts Shaka, who realizes that his power is crumbling, but he rejects Farewell's overtures. To the end a servant of his destiny, Shaka then walks alone to meet his killers, his brother Dingane and others from his inner circle. The series ends with the Zulu kingdom in flames. Chaos prevails.

Historical accuracy, dramatic license, and propaganda

Bill Faure, the director of the series, defined its positions within southern African historiography: "Shaka's life was originally recorded by white historians who imposed upon their accounts bigoted and sensationalist values—often labeling the Zulus as savage and barbaric. It is our intention with this series to change that view."[13] Faure's statement of intent featured prominently in the official *Shaka Zulu* souvenir brochure provided at the series' press launch and was widely quoted in a host of comments and articles at the time of its screening.[14] *Shaka Zulu* was billed as "one of the most important and dramatic stories in the history of Africa, a story which will soon take its place in world history,"[15] and was widely acclaimed as a revisionist production.[16]

In a number of American cities, however, protests were organized and the series was condemned as "fascist," "violent," "historically inaccurate," and "racist propaganda."[17] More pointed criticisms came from a few isolated sources in South Africa: the mainly black-readership *Drum* magazine and the *Weekly Mail*, a publication that described itself as "the paper for a changing South Africa." "Who's [sic] Shaka is this?" asked *Drum's* Kaiser Ngwenya. "Why is it written through the eyes of Henry Fynn, the white doctor? Why couldn't one of our most famous stories be told simply as a black story?"[18] Under the heading "Shaka through White Victorian Eyes," the *Weekly Mail* reviewer noted: "Apart from Cetshwayo's brief words to Queen Victoria, blacks hardly speak in the first episode . . . This is not a series made or told by Africans. Control is still in the hands of whites."[19]

The producers responded to these criticisms by claiming that the series was originally filmed and edited in chronological order, beginning with the birth of Shaka and tracing his rise to power. Only then were viewers to see the entry of the whites. They maintained that the script was restructured and the flashback device introduced only when "American movie moguls" demurred that unknown black faces and black history would not capture international audiences.[20] If this claim is correct, it is worthwhile to note that international market constraints ultimately triumphed over Faure's much-vaunted aim of moving away from the original records of "bigoted" white historians.

Fynn's narration in the series was no mere sop to the international market or simply a convenient dramatic device. The series actively positioned the audience to identify with his character. Fynn was presented as the figure with the most integrity. He was invited to accompany Farewell because of his concern for the black population of South Africa; he was critical of Farewell, and even more so of the British authorities; and he was shown to be enormously sensitive in his dealings with Shaka. Separate from, but privy to, the thoughts of both protagonists, his was advanced as an objective account of events. The audience was also positioned to be sympathetic to the other main European character, the able but wily

Farewell. Developed as a likable and humane figure, Farewell cared for the men under his command and established an affectionate relationship with Fynn. He was a loving, if absent, husband to his beautiful wife. Fynn and Farewell were made to stand in sharp contrast to Shaka, who was portrayed as a man without warmth. "Love, love?" Shaka rails against his mother. "We are incapable of that emotion, Mother. All we ever felt is vengeance and hate."

Faure's aim of producing a film that did justice to the African past was further undermined by the emphasis given to the white adventurers far beyond what was due to their actual historical roles. Indeed, the Swallows were depicted as playing a decisive part in Zulu history. After the assassination attempt, Shaka is badly wounded. The Swallows heal him and then literally get him on his feet and back on his throne in time to foil a coup d'état. The Swallows' finishing touch to the king's healthy appearance is the application of macassar oil to his head. The oil hides Shaka's grey hair and, he believes, has rejuvenated him. In this way, the Swallows are shown to have gained control over Shaka's body and to have saved his throne for him.

They are also depicted as becoming the key force in the military power of the kingdom. Shaka demands that they participate in the battle against his strongest and most persistent foe, Zwide of the Ndwandwe. During the battle the Swallows, using a single cannon and a few muskets, put the Ndwandwe to flight. They succeed in breaking Zwide's power where previously the full weight of the Zulu army had failed. This incident was designed to suggest the extent to which real power, from that time, was not Shaka's alone. It also served as a reminder that the numerically inferior party of whites controlled the means to wipe out entire African armies if they so wished. "Amazing, isn't it, sir," remarked one of Farewell's men, "what a little gun powder does to 'em." In fact, neither of these incidents actually happened. Fynn did tend Shaka, but he was not instrumental in saving his life or his throne. The visitors did participate in a Zulu campaign, against the small and recalcitrant Khumalo chief, but not against the Ndwandwe, whom the Zulu routed unassisted.

At the same time key episodes in Shaka's reign in which the white visitors played no role were omitted from the series. The decampment of one of Shaka's top generals, resistance to Shakan rule in the Qwabe country, the visits to the royal residences by traders from Delagoa Bay and by the Swazi monarch, Sobhuza, were all events that are represented in the corpus of Zulu oral tradition still extant, are powerfully and richly narrated, and lend themselves to dramatization. The reason why these events did not occur on screen, while others that did were manifestly inaccurate, was that, despite protestations to the contrary by its makers, *Shaka Zulu* was not about Zulu history, but about black–white interaction in the 1980s.

Not only was the Swallows' role built up far beyond their actual historical significance, but they themselves were ennobled and their quest romanticized. In real life Fynn was not a doctor, but a callow youth of twenty when he arrived in Shaka's country. When he and Farewell fell out soon after their arrival, Shaka was able adroitly to play off the factions among the whites against each other. Farewell had been in the British army during the Napoleonic wars, but had since resigned his commission and become involved in shady dealing in India. He was an unlikely character for a delicate diplomatic mission: he misrepresented himself to Shaka as an envoy of King George IV, and used his assumed status to secure a grant of land from the Zulu king, and as an incentive to persuade Shaka to help him to collect ivory. In fact, the Europeans were given a specific instruction from the Cape governor not to make any deals with the Zulu king. They were to restrict themselves to what was their only true motive for journeying into the Zulu kingdom—profit through commerce.

To a man, the European visitors were a rough band of fortune seekers and adventurers. Two of the most colorful members of the original party were left out of the series entirely: the seventeen-year-old Jewish orphan Nathaniel Isaacs, who jumped ship at St. Helena, made his way to Natal, had numerous exciting adventures in pursuit of ivory, and later became a slave trader; and "Hlambamanzi" (Jacob Nsimbithi), the Xhosa interpreter of the party. The historical records suggest that "Hlambamanzi" warned Shaka about some of the whites' less reputable intentions and behavior, finally becoming such a problem to the visitors that they killed him. The inclusion of either of these figures in the series would clearly have posed problems for writers seeking to present the white pioneers as romantic figures.[21]

Historical accuracy was not, in fact, high on Faure's list of priorities. Instead, he allowed the series to establish its authority as a legitimate interpretation of the past through close attention to authentic detail. Tons of genuine animal skins, feathers, horns, and oxtails were used to make the costumes. Real skulls were favored over papier-mâché replicas; grass huts constructed by "time-honoured means" were built by skilled "Zulu tribesmen"; iron spears and hide shields were manufactured for the thousands of "real Zulus" who swarmed across locations in KwaZulu, playing the role of "their ancestors."[22]

The search for authenticity enmeshed *Shaka Zulu* in a series of contradictions at the level of production. The construction of sets on actual historical sites, often the places of royal burials, raised serious questions about the film-makers' respect for the history they were re-creating; production of any sort in an apartheid homeland was connected to the issue of the exploitation of an overabundant supply of labor at excessively low wages; equally questionable was the necessary reliance on the cooperation of compliant homeland leaders, desperate for outside sources of income and reluctant to impose operating constraints on crews. Indeed, it was precisely this set of conditions that made South Africa an alluring location for foreign film-makers in the 1980s.[23]

"The rich and awkward commotion of production"[24]

Faure's intentions were doomed from the moment he and his white co-authors began work on the script. "Black history suffers because it is mainly written by whites . . . I am a South African, and I felt it was time to rewrite the black history books," Faure stated, apparently oblivious of the contradiction in his claims.[25] For a moment, early in the history of the script's production, there existed the possibility that Faure might have broken free of Fynn and the "bigoted" constructions of Shaka by "generations of white historians," to offer, if not a Zulu version of the past, a script largely based on one. In 1979 Faure had in hand Mazisi Kunene's just-published epic poem, *Emperor Shaka the Great*. Kunene's text constituted a powerful reappropriation of Shaka by a Zulu-speaking writer. Based on oral tradition, it offered a compelling evocation of Shaka as seen through African eyes. Kunene's text was, however, characterized by a cursory and harsh depiction of the white visitors to Shaka's court.

Faure initially toyed with the idea of basing his script on Kunene's text, but the involvement of the state-controlled SABC in his project in 1981 put paid to the idea. In the eyes of the SABC, no matter how magnificent Kunene's poetry, it could not outweigh the fact that he was previously an official ANC representative and an outspoken critic of the government. The SABC was also likely to have eschewed a script based on Kunene's text for financial as much as political reasons. The need to appeal to the American market by featuring white interlocutors ruled out the use of an Africanist text such as Kunene's.[26] In 1982 an American, Joshua Sinclair, was brought in to rewrite Faure's original script; he himself was subsequently dismissed. The script underwent yet another change of writers before it was completed. At least two significant changes in the script, which seem to have occurred after Sinclair was fired, were designed to present the Swallows in a better light and to eliminate ambiguities in the series' vision of potential interracial cooperation.[27]

These late changes to the script are useful indicators of some of the forces which operated on Faure in the course of making *Shaka Zulu,* and modified his original artistic and imaginative objectives. Faure began his career at the London Film School where, in 1974, he presented a dissertation entitled "Images of Violence." Faure's study addressed the problem of the ubiquity of violence on screen. The solution posited in the dissertation was not the elimination of violence, but the provision of tools for viewers to deal with it. Faure returned to South Africa and began to work for the newly established television service of the SABC. According to Faure, he conceived the idea of *Shaka Zulu* in the immediate aftermath of the 1976 Soweto uprising. "It was time we rectified the misconceptions of history," he said, "and we needed to give black history a greater status."[28] *Shaka Zulu* was to be Faure's artistic and emotional response to political turbulence. The series developed his thesis on violence, by graphically portraying violence and then showing it to be misplaced. With *Shaka Zulu* Faure hoped to extend and liberalize the boundaries of consensual discourse in South Africa. In 1977, working with these ideas as an SABC film director, Faure was significantly ahead of his time.

However, as Keyan Tomaselli has shown with regard to other historical productions made for the SABC in this period, the director's "selection of content and sources was governed by a sophisticated understanding (or gut reaction) of what would have been acceptable to the SABC and/or its target audience."[29] Indeed, during the period in which *Shaka Zulu* was made, the SABC was moving in a more "reformist" direction. Faure, in turn, was succumbing to the pressures exerted by his backers—restructuring his script and switching from a Zulu to an English text.[30]

In its final form the script was ultimately faithful to the diary of the "bigoted white historian," Fynn, who originally recorded Shaka's life, and whose view of Shaka Faure was so eager to contest. To flesh out the areas in which Fynn's text was thin, the script primarily used two other sources: the account of another of the Europeans present at Bulawayo, Nathaniel Isaacs; and E.A. Ritter's popular account of the life of Shaka, published in 1955.[31]

Fynn's "diary" was reconstructed from memory after Shaka's death, and, as we have seen, was later substantially edited, leading one historian to describe him as a "fiction writer" and the diary as a "forgery."[32] The preface to the published *Diary* describes its genesis and makes it clear that the text is not an original journal reflecting daily events. In many respects, however, the *Diary* offers a detailed picture of life and events in Shakan times, as Fynn remembered them, that is remarkable and valuable to modern historians, and certainly a rich resource for a scriptwriter. Isaacs' text was, for its part, based on the writer's memories and the journal of his deceased companion, James King. Isaacs' objective in publishing was to encourage investment in Natal. Like Fynn, Isaacs learned to speak *isiZulu* and his account also offers valuable historical data, for he was an intelligent and interested observer and was present at a number of the major events during Shaka's reign. His dramatization of events and his romantic streak are easily discernible to the careful reader.

Nevertheless, Fynn's and Isaacs' texts reflect their authors' biases as lower-middle-class Englishmen of the early nineteenth century seeking adventure and fortune in Africa. In the 1830s, as we have already seen, both sought actively to draw Britain into establishing a colony in Natal, and to that end they stressed social disorder and upheaval in the Zulu country.[33] It was certainly in the subsequent interests of these authors to emphasize the "savagery" of Shaka. While the texts remain two of the most valuable sources for historians of the period, they require a careful disentanglement of their facts from their fictions, as well as close attention to their specific biases and their silences. Perhaps the most significant of these is the way in which they position both researchers and casual readers to look at the Zulu kingdom through white eyes.

E.A. Ritter's text was rather different. It purported to be an account of Shaka "as the Zulus saw him." Ritter attributed his knowledge of Zulu history to his boyhood attentiveness to the tales of knowledgeable old Zulu informants, and he demonstrated an obvious respect for Zulu oral tradition. Nonetheless, his book, like those of Fynn and Isaacs, reflected his own particular concerns. (Like Stuart, he was part of the force that suppressed the 1906 Bambatha rebellion and he later joined the Native Affairs Department in Rhodesia.) The book was glaringly inaccurate in places, and characteristically romantic. For Ritter, Shaka was a "despot" and the reasons for his "excesses" were to be found in his disturbed childhood:

> Modern psychology has enabled us to understand the importance in after life, of a child's unhappiness. Perhaps we may trace Shaka's subsequent lust for power to the fact that his little crinkled ears and the marked stumpinesss of his genital organ were ever the source of persistent ridicule among Shaka's companions, and their usual taunts in this regard so rankled that he grew up harbouring a deadly hatred against all and everything E-Langeni [the clan name of his tormentors].[34]

Sexual insults are as common in Zulu society as they are in many others, but this explanation for Shaka's rise to power, which was echoed in the television series, occurred in none of the many oral testimonies recorded by James Stuart at much the same time.

Faure claimed that the script also drew on Zulu oral history, but there was little evidence of this, except in so far as the accounts of Fynn and Isaacs were themselves based on oral accounts. Where it seemed that the scriptwriters may have had recourse to Zulu "tradition" was in the rendition of Zulu ceremonies and ritual. Authentic funeral and wedding scenes were a point of pride for the filmmakers.[35] Great attention was paid to the peculiarities of Zulu corpse preparation, the binding of the body in a seated position wrapped in a skin hide, and the practice of burying alive the attendants of a dead king or queen.

Scenes involving the "witchdoctors" of the time were handled in a similarly sensationalist manner. Sitayi, the ancient *isangoma* who controlled Shaka's destiny, was depicted as a grotesque creature, hundreds of years old. Zulu oral tradition holds that, in fact, Shaka was less influenced by his *izangoma* than were his predecessors and, through a skillful trick, robbed them of influence at his court. *Izangoma* were ordinary people who lived and died under ordinary circumstances, although it was believed that they possessed rare and valued abilities. In contrast to the otherworldly Sitayi, they were an integral part of the community, unlikely to command packs of hyenas and maintain dens of dwarfs. In the representation of the *izangoma,* and in a host of other ways, the series presented Zulu ritual as disgusting and frightening. It is difficult to credit Faure's contention that

> Irrespective of the impressions and license taken in the execution of this project, always paramount was our intention to place in historic perspective seventeenth-century *[sic]* Africa with its witchcraft and superstition, and to correct the misconceptions of those who judged the beliefs and traditions of Africa—not in the context of Africa—but rather through their narrow Christian perspectives.[36]

The depiction of Zulu society was another area of significant misrepresentation of the past in the series. Granted, some of the series' greatest appeal lay in its representation of a world and culture that was strange and "other" to viewers, both black and white, inside and outside South Africa in the 1980s. Instead of exploring and revealing a historical culture to the viewer, murky filters and molten colors were used together with clouds of smoke from fog machines to smudge the picture of Zulu society, to make its inner workings dark, barbarous, and finally incomprehensible. Whether in dance or at war, all movement in the Zulu kingdom took place always within a cloud of dust, stirred by thundering barefoot warriors and maidens. These scenes, mostly of the Zulu court, were complemented by black night-time scenes, shattered periodically by thunder, rain, and lightning in steely shades of blue and white; these occurred with the representations of the "witchdoctors"—scary, monstrous, and even more incomprehensible.[37] In the Cape Colony, by way of contrast, the air was always shown to be crisp and clear; images were sharply defined against blue skies and white buildings. Horseback regiments on parade and carriages in the main streets raised no dust.

The series' focus on the whites' actions, the use of Fynn as narrator, the reliance on Fynn's *Diary* and other texts by "bigoted" white historians, and the sensational treatment of Zulu life point to a sharp contradiction between the series' actual content and the director's stated aims. In order to explore the significance of this contradiction, it is useful to look more closely at the financing of the series. "*Shaka Zulu* took longer to shoot, cost more money and employed more people than any other production yet made in this country. It was also surrounded by rumour, gossip and tales of sensationalism. Even now, the facts are hard to find."[38]

The biggest scandal was centered on the production's cost. It seems that Faure initially planned to make the series independently, but as work on the script and the preproduction planning proceeded, it became clear that it would be one of the largest and most costly series ever produced in South Africa. By 1981 the SABC had taken over production and financing. *Shaka Zulu* would require two years of preproduction planning and research, two years on location, and one year of post-production work before it was shown on South African television at the end of 1986.[39]

In late 1983, or early 1984, the production scale expanded still further. It was at this time that American distributors were drawn in. Throughout 1984 and 1985 the original budget of about $1.75 million was rumored to be escalating monthly, and the SABC continually refused to make public any figures. The final cost admitted to by the SABC was $24 million.[40] The sudden pouring of masses of money into the production—"as if into a bottomless pit," as one cynic commented—came at a time when recession in South Africa was biting, the local film industry was depressed, and the SABC was cutting expenditure on other productions and placing a freeze on new ones.[41] The SABC justified the outlay through reference to the anticipated return to be earned on the international market. The American-based associate producer of the series, Frank Agrama, noted, however, that the production was a "calculated gamble." *Shaka Zulu* was, in fact, the most expensive mini-series ever produced for television syndication in the United States without a precommitment to network time.[42]

At this point the vastly extended scale of the series and changed circumstances of production began to have an impact on the series' form and content. Tensions between Faure and his backers were running high, until finally the Americans suggested that he be replaced by an American director. This was firmly rejected by the SABC.[43] When *Shaka Zulu* finally went into production, the key technical expertise was provided by overseas specialists. To explain the appropriation of the series in this way, and why the SABC took the enormous risk and embarked on such an expensive project when it did, it is necessary to look at the wider political context that prevailed when the series was being made.

South African politics went through a traumatic period in 1984. The United Democratic Front (UDF), formed in 1983, called for a boycott of the tricameral parliamentary elections (the first step in the apartheid government's so-called reform strategy), and an explosive backlash against "reform" swept the country. In 1985 "necklace" killings were reported around the country, government buildings were burned down, and hundreds of schools were closed. Between September 1984 and December 1985 nearly a thousand people died as a result of township unrest. Strike action reached an all-time high, and a super-trade-union federation, the Congress of South African Trade Unions (Cosatu), was formed.[44] The state responded to this moment of crisis with the increased use of its coercive powers. Troops poured into the townships and thousands of people were detained.

The image of civil war that South Africa was projecting, with nightly scenes of violence entering the living-rooms of viewers all over the world, proved disastrous for South Africa's image abroad.[45] "The cameras have a way of only finding the violence and not the positive side," noted Faure.[46] Indeed, within months of the uprising foreign banks refused to roll over South African loans, and both foreign and domestic capital began to withdraw from South Africa.

One step that the South African government took to change its image was to impose restrictions on the news media.[47] The SABC, always the government's handmaiden, at first reported events with biased glosses, but increasingly it limited visual coverage, and restricted itself to relaying official "unrest" figures for each day.[48] In one striking reversal of this policy, used to justify the increased use of troops in the townships, the torching of an informer was screened in gruesome detail.

Television drama was one way in which the SABC could project another view of South Africa. John Cundill, writer of a historical drama on the 1922 mineworkers' strike screened just before *Shaka Zulu*, gave an indication of the kind of thinking in influential quarters within the SABC at this time: "television is a powerful medium of communication, and the idea of using TV dramas as reform tools has strong relevance," Cundill said. "The projection of blacks and whites interacting in situations portraying reality and highlighting their common humanity would go far to ease the tensions of mounting racial strife."[49]

Shaka Zulu offered the SABC an opportunity for presenting black and white viewers in South Africa with a drama advocating interracial collaboration and portraying the dangers of its failure. The Shaka theme as developed through the nineteenth century by people such as Ndlovu kaThimuni, Shepstone, and Stuart was itself redolent with meaning about the nature of black–white interaction. The series also presented an opportunity to give another view of South Africa to overseas audiences, one which could be seen to advocate peaceful coexistence and respect for the African heritage, and which provided, by way of analogy, a comment on the apartheid government's "reform" plans. *Shaka Zulu* was thus extensively promoted outside South Africa. In the United States, in a piece of sophisticated marketing, the series was shown on a network of independent television stations across the country, aimed at between 70 and 90 million viewers.[50] Faure and the show's two leading Zulu stars did a promotional tour of the United States that was timed to coincide with the screenings—and with Black History Month. On tour, Faure and actor Cele made the series' propaganda purposes explicit. "We believe that it is time to shed light on South Africa, correct misconceptions and change the system," they claimed.[51] They made it clear that they saw the series as an analogy with the present. Echoing the words of Farewell and Shaka in the series ("Nothing is impossible if two kingdoms truly want to live in harmony"), Faure remarked, "there is a large core of white and black people who want to come together in harmony. People are using our situation to further their own ends [presumably a reference to the work of agitators—a common refrain at the time in the parlance of South Africa's frustrated reformers]. They don't give a damn if our children are killed. But Henry [Cele] and I care," Faure continued, enacting yet again a moment of white interlocution, "and so do a lot of other South Africans."[52] Faure and Cele also used the opportunity provided by the interest in *Shaka Zulu* to speak out against the imposition of sanctions against South Africa.[53]

"The politics of the tightrope"[54]

In the turbulent political climate that prevailed when the series was screened, *Shaka Zulu* offered an easily recognizable analogy for modern South Africa. The series vividly conjured up the numbers ratio obsessively debated by white South Africans. Farewell's party consists of only eight men. The crowd scenes at Bulawayo show masses of thronging black humanity. "There's an awful lot of them, isn't there," comments one of Farewell's men on their first sight of the capital. Indeed, at times the series' dialogue made the analogy less than subtle.

The violence of African society was explored at length. It was *the* problem to which a solution had to be found. White society at the Cape was represented as being under threat of attack by Shaka. Farewell's mission was to deflect that onslaught. (In fact, this was a scriptwriter's embellishment, for, as we have seen, the Cape was not threatened at this time.) Farewell and his party were also presented as being in danger at Shaka's court. Death was always a possibility. Shaka was shown to be a ruthless leader, dominated by the imperatives of power and revenge. The Zulu were pictured as a highly militarized nation, an irresistible warrior tide. In the series, this militancy was not censured. Rather, the Swallows were shown as seeking to control it and divert it from attack on white society.

The representatives of British imperialism in London served as symbols for the far right-wing, and a clear distinction was drawn between them and the whites on the spot in southeast Africa. King George IV, who considered the Zulus to be nothing more than "a tribe of savages running around in their birthday suits," was made an object of ridicule. The Colonial Office's understanding of how to deal with the Zulus was shown to be way off the mark, as were its ready assumptions of the superiority of "civilization" and the potential efficacy of a "solitary Caucasian" in dealing with Shaka. "If we cannot soothe the savage beast," they were scripted as saying, "we can at least confuse him whilst we mount an effective military defensive." The series made it clear that Shaka caused confusion as much as he was confused. "Your Colonial Office has no idea of what it is up against," remarked Fynn to Farewell on their first introduction to the full panoply of the Shakan state. Fynn saw the Swallows' relationship with Shaka as a game of chess between two skilled players. The Swallows realized that their position in southeast Africa was precarious, and that only the most careful strategy would see them through.

The strong rejection of the Colonial Office's racist attitudes struck a recognizably reformist note. Farewell's plea to Shaka to refrain from attacking the Cape was perhaps the most direct call of the series. "That yearning which has brought about everything that has happened was as much your fault as it is mine, but hating my people is not the solution. We must search for another, together."

Part of the solution was seen to lie in greater mutual understanding and respect. Farewell, in shades of Stuart, made this point explicit to the governor of the Cape Colony when he escorted Shaka's diplomatic mission to the Cape:

In the course of the three years that we have been amongst the Zulu people, I have endeavoured to reconcile Zulu interests with those of the British government. Now there have been many difficulties, of course, most of them related to questions of custom, such as you have just witnessed with regard to the seating arrangements [the deputation had just elected to seat themselves on the floor of the governor's office] and basic misunderstandings which affect communication. But more recently I have had the good fortune to win the confidence and the trust of the Zulu king. The result of which is the king's strong desire to show his goodwill by proposing an alliance with Britain.

At this stage of the drama Farewell had discarded parts of his European garb, donning instead elements of the costume of a Zulu chief. Thus he no longer looked like an imperial officer. Nor was he shown to be acting only in the interests of the British king. He had become—like Shepstone—a product of Africa itself, ambiguously placed midway between the Colonial Office and Bulawayo. In the early 1980s this was the terrain on which the advocates of "reform" in South Africa situated themselves, somewhere between the conservative forces and "the place of killing."

Shaka was depicted as the one Zulu with the vision to understand the importance of the whites and their "magic" for the Zulu people. Despite the warnings of his advisers and his izangoma, Shaka was determined to appropriate the power of western knowledge. His complete control over his people meant that he could enforce a vision of interaction if he so chose. Shaka's commanders were depicted as being utterly subject to his authority. "We share a common life," remarked Ngomane, the Zulu "prime minister," to Shaka. "My own!"

In much the same way that Shaka was the model chosen by Shepstone for colonial despotism, so too was Shaka the type of black leader with whom the proponents of reform in South Africa in the 1980s would ideally have liked to negotiate. Enlightened and authoritarian, his closest contemporary parallel was the leader of Inkatha and the KwaZulu homeland, Buthelezi. Like the Shaka in the series, Buthelezi personified Zulu politics. During the 1980s, moreover, Buthelezi enjoyed a media prominence that exceeded that of any other active black leader in southern Africa. The analogy between Shaka and Buthelezi was, and still is, a common one in South African discourse. It was a comparison often drawn by Buthelezi himself, by journalists, and by ordinary South Africans.[55]

The South African government's reform strategy was centered around the idea of political confederation. Buthelezi's mobilization of Zulu ethnic nationalism was highly compatible with the reformist vision. In the face of widespread opposition to the government's constitutional proposals, the cooperation of Buthelezi in "reform" became essential. Echoing Fynn's metaphor of a chess game, Faure remarked: "When the game is set and all the parties come together, it's going to be parties like the Zulus calling the shots."[56] For both Inkatha and the South African state, the 1980s saw the increasing inevitability of their mutual alliance against mounting radical opposition. "For some," commented Maré and Hamilton in 1987, "Inkatha offers the last hope of a peaceful negotiated settlement. For the state it may be the most hopeful partner in the first tentative steps beyond or away from the bantustan policy based on 'power-sharing' between 'groups'—a plurality of minorities."[57] Inkatha, under threat from the growing UDF presence in Natal, in its turn began moving closer to the South African state.

It is not sufficient, however, to see Buthelezi and the SABC simply as acting in concert in *Shaka Zulu* to further the aim of presenting the leaders of KwaZulu as the authentic representatives of African people in the region.[58] By the time the series was first screened, the South African state was certainly more squarely behind Buthelezi than ever before. But the series was characterized by far greater ambiguities than this simple interpretation allows, ambiguities that developed as the script itself evolved between 1979 and 1986.

The closing scenes depicted chaos when interaction with the whites was shown to have been rejected by Shaka. It offered a strong warning to independent black politicians such as Buthelezi not to try to go it alone. This was not surprising, as Buthelezi had seized the constitutional initiative from the government through the establishment of the Buthelezi Commission in 1980. The commission rejected as a "sop" the state's attempt to cater for black political aspirations through the establishment of a Black Advisory Council to the President's Council, and set out to explore constitutional alternatives. In 1986 Buthelezi's most ambitious venture, the KwaZulu–Natal Indaba, began to prepare the way for a multi-racial, multicultural legislature for the region.[59] The state, which rejected all these initiatives, was alarmed at the support Buthelezi was garnering at the expense of its own more fraught "reform" plans. A warning note was sounded in the very first scene of the series. Queen Victoria listens closely to Cetshwayo's account of the life of his ancestor, Shaka, and then remarks: "We are a practical woman, your Highness. We will not make an alliance with a legend."

Shaka Zulu offered more than just a caution to Buthelezi and others of his ilk. It neatly twisted the veiled threats that Buthelezi directed at the South African state when it seemed intransigent. It suggested by way of analogy that the modern *mfecane*, which Buthelezi threatened might erupt if whites continued to ignore him, would be as threatening to the Zulu leadership as to the whites. In the series, Shaka's decision to launch an attack on the Cape Colony was the beginning of his undoing. The lesson was there for Buthelezi, and any other black leaders, that a successful outcome for either party was predicated on close cooperation with the other. The alternative portrayed in *Shaka Zulu* was that everything would go up in flames and chaos would prevail. "Out of ashes will come more poverty," commented Faure, "and children will be denied opportunities to be educated. It will pave the way for Marxism and set the country back."[60] The end of the series was, of course, open to a more subversive reading than Faure allowed—that Shaka's failure was the inevitable and only consequence of cooperation with Farewell. The final fires could have been seen as the cleansing flames of revolution out of which at least some of the opponents of Buthelezi and of the apartheid government hoped a new order would arise.

The monopoly of power by the Swallows and the way they controlled the telling of Zulu history, while reassuring to white viewers, was a source of enormous embarrassment to Buthelezi. At a Shaka Day rally a few weeks after the special preview screening, Buthelezi attacked white historians, and Fynn in particular, for the distortion of Zulu history, especially the depiction of Shaka as a bloodthirsty tyrant. He railed against the Europeans' indiscriminate scattering of their semen across Zululand.[61] Buthelezi's virulent attack, widely reported in the press, successfully obscured a central contradiction between the rhetoric surrounding *Shaka Zulu*—the present Zulu king described it as a production of Zulu history "as seen through my people's eyes"—and the fact that the series portrays Zulu history through the eyes of a white visitor and a white director.[62] Moreover, although the series did show Shaka to be a leader of caliber and talent, it also repeated older stereotypes of his psychological imbalances and bloodthirstiness. It incorporated a host of very "unZulu," untraditional features that had at least some critics wondering how it could have been approved by the Zulu royal house.[63]

In fact, Buthelezi could not have afforded to dissociate himself from the series, despite its flaws. *Shaka Zulu* was a powerful endorsement of the KwaZulu leadership, needed urgently by Buthelezi at the end of 1986 as the battle for popular support in Natal was joined by the UDF and Cosatu. *Shaka Zulu* also put Buthelezi on the spot in another respect. More than any of the other South African "ethnicities," the Zulu identity was founded on "traditionalism." Indeed, Inkatha drew heavily on the symbols and institutions of the Shakan past. The positions of its leadership continue to be justified through reference to traditional rank. Buthelezi, for example, traces his ancestry back to Shaka on the maternal line.[64] *Shaka Zulu* was virtually the only visual rendition of the Shakan period in existence, and with it the SABC had vividly and powerfully appropriated the linchpin of Inkatha ideology. Buthelezi could not have afforded to lose the opportunity of riding on the dramatic success of the series. Its screening provided a chance too valuable to miss, enabling Buthelezi to make connections between himself and his illustrious predecessor. The price was to concede the point about white narration and other objectionable features of the series. Indeed, this compromise reflects the essential compromise of Buthelezi's political vision. In this, and in the depiction in the series of Shaka as "both the master and the victim of his regime," the "ambiguities of Buthelezi's dependency," to use Marks' term, were starkly revealed.[65]

In spite of itself, however, the series showed that whites were dependent in a similarly ambiguous fashion. Their options were limited—as Farewell acknowledged, they had nowhere else to go. In the series, the whites could not shape the course of events in terms of their interests alone. Shaka fell short of the demands made on him by the presence of the Swallows, and Fynn and Farewell suffered in the process as much as Shaka's own subjects. The South African state in the 1980s was, in turn, itself equally dependent on the cooperation of Buthelezi in the "reform" scenario. As Marks noted, "[Buthelezi] constantly faces the state with his contradictory presence both as critic and as collaborator extraordinary . . . He is simultaneously needed and feared."[66]

It was a striking feature of the series, and of the analogy that it set up, that so much hinged on the abilities of key individuals. Shaka's rise to power, for example, was explained in terms of the prophecy. For those viewers who may have doubted the power of magic, an alternative explanation was offered through reference to Shaka's character. He was ambitious, able, and successful. All the action revolved around him. Clearly, the centrality of a single leader in the series was an important dramatic device. The "Great Man" theory, however, promoted the idea that history was made by leaders, not by ordinary men and women. It suggested that they, by virtue of their exceptional abilities, could best judge the way forward. This perspective denied the struggles of ordinary people and their capacity to shape their own lives. Moreover, as the series so vividly showed, it implied—echoing Shepstone—that whoever controlled the leader controlled the people. When the attempt was made on Shaka's life, Farewell commented, "We need Shaka alive. If we can control Shaka's soul, we can control the whole of southern Africa." In denying ordinary people access to power, the South African state and Buthelezi stood united against the radical and militant popular movements.

Tomaselli argued that *Shaka Zulu* "endorses apartheid discourse which holds that blacks are 'different' and should develop in their 'own areas', safely out of white civilisation."[67] In fact, *Shaka Zulu* was no mere "racist propaganda": on the contrary, it advocated interracial interaction and mutual dependency. But it was not a simple rendition of the most progressive or coherent "reform" line coming out of Pretoria in the mid-1980s. A close look at the production reveals both the promotion of the "reform" vision and its limitation, its confusions as well as its subversion, in numerous and varied ways.

The contradictions and ambiguities of the series reflected its production during a period when the political landscape of South Africa was altering rapidly and when the nature of domination itself was in ferment. Rather than a reflection of a dominant ideology, *Shaka Zulu* was actually about the process of struggle for a new hegemony in South Africa—one that, in the mid-1980s, was not fully worked out by any of the parties involved. When, however, Nelson Mandela was released in 1990, and the transfer of power to the majority began to be widely recognized as inevitable, the image of Shaka was harnessed to a project that squarely confronted political transformation.

Shakaland on the eve of the first democratic election

In the year following Mandela's release a new tourist resort in the KwaZulu–Natal region hosted 32,000 visitors[68] ranging from the Spanish and Zulu royal families, Johnny Clegg, and Knight Rider to local school parties, and black and white family groups: Shakaland.[69] Described as "the new living museum to Zulu culture"[70] by one travel writer, and a "definite must for every South African and tourist" by another,[71] Shakaland was situated on white farmland adjacent to the KwaZulu homeland. The core of this resort was originally built as one of the sets for *Shaka Zulu*. Two of the cultural specialists on the film subsequently bought up the land, turning the set first, in 1986, into a film camp, and later into a "bush camp" and educational center. In 1988 the prestigious Protea hotel chain invested in Shakaland, and oversaw its transformation from a small, marginally successful operation into a major tourist attraction. One among a number of commercial ventures in Zulu cultural tourism, Shakaland was, by 1991, clearly the most successful. Analysis of its product suggests that this achievement was a consequence of the resort's capacity at that time to ease political anxieties and to prepare visitors for political change. This was accomplished by means of the classic tourist gesture of removing the subjects from everyday life.

On approaching Shakaland guests first passed a sign in burnished orange, red, and brown that recalled the design of the title of the series *Shaka Zulu*. A gateway made up of dramatically elevated lookout posts topped with waving pennants marked the entrance, and visitors were greeted by a gatekeeper in full warrior regalia. A large board at the entrance offered a potted history of the rise of the Zulu nation under Shaka and asserted its significance as one of the most dramatic events in southern African history. In a final flourish the resort was introduced:

> The romance which surrounds the name of the Zulu nation has lingered on for a century or more since the days in the mid 18 hundreds when their exploits were blazoned in dramatic headlines across the world. The tales of their deeds during those warring years read like the legends of forgotten time. But the Zulu epic is no fantasy! Today below the hills where once stood KwaBulawayo, the great military kraal of King Shaka, lies SHAKALAND.

Guests were then directed down a long and winding path fenced on both sides by a dense reed screen, similar to the closed approach to a game hide and carrying the same promise of a rare sighting. The reed corridor then opened into Shakaland, and the visitor experienced a marked sensation of entering another world.

The resort was divided into a hotel area and the immediately adjacent film set. Dining took place in a thatched "boma" with an open campfire area and bar. The whole overlooked the Mhlathuze dam and the rolling Ntembeni hills. The setting was, in the words of one travel writer, "spectacular."[72] Both cheap dormitory accommodation—used mainly by school parties—and luxurious guest rooms were available. The dormitories were thatched "beehive" structures, with relatively few concessions to modern-day comforts, while the deluxe guest rooms were spacious bungalow structures topped by skillfully woven and thatched "beehive" roofs. The walls of the guest rooms were decorated with choice "Zulu" artifacts. The pieces—wooden neck-rests, beer-pot covers, and woven grass mats—were individually displayed, and carried labels giving each item's Zulu name and its use, as well as its provenance and the history of its collection. Guests commented on how aesthetically pleasing the rooms were, and how the artifacts conveyed a sense of having been carefully selected, of being "the real thing." Indeed, the feel of the rooms was reminiscent of an art gallery and the display technique stimulated in the guests a desire to know more about the objects exhibited. "It stirs the interest," commented a travel writer.[73] Unlike a typical art gallery, however, Shakaland held out the promise of further opportunities for the viewer to learn about the objects.

Large artifacts built specially for the two television series filmed at the site were carefully preserved in the hotel courtyard. The first was "The Forge. Used in the filming of *Shaka Zulu* for the making of Shaka's spear" and alongside it was "The Boat. Used in the filming of *John Ross*." (The series *John Ross*, also set in Shakan times, was filmed on the same set, shortly after *Shaka Zulu*.) The walls of both the bar and the reception area were festooned with framed press clippings and posters about the television shows. Among glossy portraits of the stars of *Shaka Zulu* were accounts dating back to 1984 of the building of the set as well as the "rustic accommodation" to house the film crews. A number of press reports and framed information sheets traced the genesis of the Shakaland resort out of these various components of the old location. Even the takeover of the resort by Protea hotels was documented.

The film-set section of the resort was a cross between an enlarged living diorama and a theme park. "No detail has been overlooked to ensure that visitors get an authentic, dramatic introduction to this mighty nation," noted one promotional leaflet.[74] The set was built as the homestead of Shaka's father, a considerably less important figure than Shaka himself. It was a relatively modest establishment of some sixteen huts, which nonetheless achieved a highly dramatic effect. The "Great Kraal," as the homestead was called, was a cross between an ordinary homestead built on traditional lines that might still have been found in the KwaZulu–Natal countryside and the large royal residences still in evidence in neighboring Swaziland in the early 1990s.

In many respects, Shakaland offered a holiday package similar to those of its competitors. The accommodation provided in the deluxe bungalows was certainly more luxurious (and more expensive)[75] than that available anywhere else, but it was only a small proportion of the total Shakaland clientele who availed themselves of its comforts. In contrast to similar Zulu-theme resorts such as Ophapheni and KwaBhekithunga, however, Shakaland did not purport to offer tourists "the real thing," but rather the real film set. Even the goat grazing in the Great Kraal was not represented as a "typical" feature of the Zulu countryside, but was introduced as "William C. Forager, the real goat—the one that was in a scene from the film *Shaka Zulu*," while the goat's name was a play on the name of the television series' director, William C. Faure. Likewise, the Shaka in Shakaland did not seek to be faithful to early descriptions of the Zulu king, or even to a contemporary sketch of the monarch. Rather, the only Shaka present in Shakaland took the form of pictures of Henry Cele, the actor who played Shaka in the television series. In drawing attention to its genesis as a film set, Shakaland emphasized its artifice.

Of course, close identification with the film series was a drawcard, prompting easy recognition by the general public of the nature of the enterprise.[76] One of the reasons that Shakaland was doing better than its competitors in 1991 was that it was able to capitalize on the success of the television series and the widespread interest in the historical figure of Shaka. The promotional leaflet appealed directly to this double interest: "Experience the power of Shaka Zulu. Take a step back into time and enter the world of Shaka, King of the Zulus at his Great Kraal overlooking the Umhlathuze Lake. Shakaland, originally created for the film set of the epic *Shaka Zulu,* is one of South Africa's most unique tourist attractions."[77] The positive identification of the resort with the series and with the figure of Shaka explains why some tourists were initially attracted to the resort, but it alone does not account for its widespread acclaim and marked success.

While a survey of what Shakaland offered does not assist in accounting for its greater appeal, analysis of how the resort worked, and how it was apprehended by visitors in 1991, is more illuminating.[78] The central feature of a visit to Shakaland was what was termed the "cultural experience," designed by one of the directors of Shakaland, Barry Leitch.[79] An anthropology graduate, Leitch devised a script for the cultural experience that offered more information, and more accurate and often not widely known data, than any of Shakaland's rivals. He carefully avoided the biases, racist representations, and stereotypes characteristic of many other similar resorts operating at the time, and explicitly affirmed the culture being experienced. As Leitch put it:

> In Shakaland you are paying homage to a culture that everything else Western has tended to negate and look down upon . . . We are recognizing that the Western perspective is just one way of looking at things and within the Zulu perspective one recognizes that you have a whole range of intelligences; within the range of natural abilities you have a whole world there: it is the recognition that a man's intelligence and self-esteem does not depend upon whether he's got a Standard Eight or a Standard Ten [Grades ten and twelve].[80]

The script was sensitive to a relatively sophisticated international tourist market, as well as local visitors, large numbers of whom were, by 1990, to some degree aware of the distortions of African history under apartheid. Indeed, Leitch further made a point of inviting members of a local university anthropology department to inspect the resort, and he incorporated material into the script from the research of Natal Museum archeologists and university historians. The Shakaland script thus aspired to satisfy what were at the time demanding new criteria of political sensitivity, and academic precision and respectability.

The program was taught to staff on a training course, and included a handout prepared by Leitch, covering all aspects of Zulu history and life as presented in

Shakaland. In addition, extra reading and research by the staff themselves were encouraged, guided by a source list provided by Leitch. The "cultural experience" took place under the supervision of a "cultural adviser" following Leitch's script. There were three cultural advisers, all of whom were native Zulu speakers with an excellent command of English. Two of them had been recruited in Durban, while the third came from the nearby town of Eshowe. They all had tertiary qualifications of one sort or another, previous work experience in business or education, and were familiar with the backgrounds of their various Zulu- and non-Zulu-speaking guests. These criteria were viewed by Leitch as fundamental to the task they performed. The right sort of person for the job, Leitch noted, was hard to find. "You run into them. You can't actually advertise for them. You don't find them if you advertise for them. They are very difficult to identify."[81]

Guests gathered in the "boma" to meet their adviser, and received a short lecture which consisted of an outline of Zulu history (similar to that sketched on the board at the entrance to the resort) and a summary of the development of Shakaland. The adviser then led the way to the film-set homestead, telling the visitors to each pick up a stone *en route*. Some distance before the main entrance, the guide paused in front of a cabbage tree, at the base of which was a cairn of stones, and inquired of his followers if they knew what they were looking at. While they may have seen such a cairn before, even his Zulu-speaking guests struggled to account for it. They had halted, the adviser explained, in front of an *isivivane,* in earlier times a marker of important routes of travel. On nearing the *isivivane,* he continued, travelers would pick up a stone, spit on it, and toss it onto the pile, thereby marking the stages of their journey while they paused to gain their bearings, and to apprise themselves of any threats abroad. The adviser then spat and threw his stone, urging the visitors to do likewise. "When you spit on a stone and place it there, you are placing yourself in that area, greeting the spirits of that area and asking for good luck." The cairn thus grew with the passage of every party, and all left behind a mark of their participation. "It's a kind of communality thing," remarked Leitch.[82]

Behind the *isivivane* was a model of a homestead which the guide used to explain the layout of what was described as a typical "traditional" Zulu homestead. He noted, for example, that each of the wives of the homestead head had her own hut. He indicated that this was just a model, and that in practice few homesteads adhered to the ideal form. He went on to say that in current times most Zulu homes were built on more modern and western lines, while retaining certain features derived from the earlier structure. Implicitly acknowledging the poverty of many Zulu homes in 1991, he pointed out that these days few men could afford to house their wives in separate structures, if indeed they were wealthy enough to have more than one wife at all.

Questions from the visitors were actively solicited and carefully answered. The guides presented themselves as skilled cultural translators and used examples familiar to their diverse audiences to illuminate particular practices or events. Overall, the advisers readily historicized Zulu tradition, avoided enshrining "custom," and conveyed an accessible, but complex, picture of the interweave of old and modern cultural forms used by present and past rural Zulu speakers. In contrast to neighboring resorts, and the KwaZulu authorities in nearby Ulundi, Shakaland did not seek to authorize a return to tradition, but promoted instead an appreciation of "Zuluness" in diverse forms.

Reception of this script was undoubtedly highly varied and was difficult to gauge in its full complexity.[83] One of the most striking responses was the extent to which visitors to Shakaland recognized as superior the quality of the information provided at the resort. They valued the elements presented that deviated from the tired texts of other resorts, and frequently commented on how informative the experience was. Many visitors were sufficiently discerning to appreciate the attempt not to idealize the past. They felt that they had acquired the knowledge necessary for them to reconstruct the social context of the items that they purchased from local craft markets such as Umgababa, or the artifacts they viewed at exhibitions. By placing such items in context, they were increasingly confident of their ability to discern good artifacts from bad, genuine from imitation, and their status as connoisseurs was enhanced and affirmed. The promise of the guest-room décor was fulfilled.

By extension, this knowledge was seen to apply also to the tourists' understanding of "the Zulu" themselves. "You can see a real difference between the old kind of Zulu, and these new ones," commented one visitor, motioning first in the direction of the Great Kraal, and then at the cultural adviser sitting a short distance away. This knowledge was viewed by many of the guests as filling an important gap created by apartheid. Such views voiced by Shakaland guests in 1991 echoed sentiments expressed in a market survey conducted by the Reader's Digest prior to its decision to publish the revisionist *Illustrated History of Southern Africa*. In the survey, both black and white respondents, like many visitors to Shakaland, indicated profound dissatisfaction with the lack of information about African history available in educational and popular forums, and expressed an active desire to become better informed on the topic. The respondents objected to the biases as well as the tone and style of treatment in the few texts available. The *Illustrated History* was specifically designed to meet these needs and objections, and within six months of its publication in 1989 over 85,000 copies had been bought by a South African public hungry for a new history.[84]

The public that bought the *Illustrated History* at the then very high price of R85.00 (about $30.00) was overwhelmingly middle class, as were the bulk of the visitors to Shakaland. But the impact of both the *Illustrated History* and Shakaland went beyond the immediate purchasers of the respective products. Knowledge from both was passed on through schoolteachers and other producers of history materials and came to inform a broader and more diverse public and, in the case of black schoolchildren, one that was vocal in its rejection of apartheid history.

Shakaland, to use Mike Wallace's comments about Disneyland, "taught more people more history, in a more memorable way, than they ever learned at school."[85] Shakaland offered to re-create and preserve treasures that the folly and ideology of the apartheid order had expunged. In some respects, in 1991 it presented itself as the bad conscience of South Africa, and part of its attractiveness was the debt that it paid to destroyed historic cultures. For black visitors Shakaland further sought to meet a basic need for temporal connectedness, the need to establish links with the past especially at a time of widespread community destabilization.[86] The resort offered special programs for school parties and provided take-home educational materials. Programs tailored to meet specialist needs, such as those of performing-arts students, were also available. Many students left Shakaland expressing a strong wish to learn to speak *isiZulu* and demonstrated new enthusiasms for, and understandings of, manifestations of African culture. One travel writer, for example, noted that on their return from Shakaland her children promptly began to teach their friends the niceties of the various kinds of dancing they had watched and participated in at the resort.[87] Shakaland taught its visitors new forms of discernment and inculcated new criteria which allowed visitors to reinterpret as highly sophisticated and civilized that which they might previously have rejected as barbarous.

In another context, Rosenzweig has noted that commercial forms of history tend to take over where academic historians and institutions abdicate the terrain of popular history.[88] In 1991 such abdication was clearly becoming manifest in South Africa as history curriculum writers and museum curators were increasingly immobilized by the political changes, and admitted to being in a state of deep crisis.[89] In this situation, entrepreneurs perceived that there was money to be made in the provision of history to the public.[90] In order to sell its product on an already crowded ethnic tourism market, Shakaland distinguished itself from other producers of "Zuluness" and other products by creating distinctions within the market, between, for example, what Leitch calls "moth-eaten, flea-bitten outfits . . . trotting out the same old dances" and the Shakaland dance team "in full cry . . . exerting power through the strength of the dance routine itself . . . able to hold its own against the best dance teams in South Africa."[91] The distinctions occurred both in the quantity and the quality of the material available, but these features were not the core of its difference.

Shakaland offered more than a compendium of knowledge, both arcane and relevant, that filled the gaps in the textbooks and satisfied the curiosity and the growing public appetite for a new history. It presented itself as providing a cross-cultural experience, an experience that was denied to many South Africans by apartheid. As the guest relations officer for Shakaland wrote to a Natal Rotary club: "The Rotary Club of Eshowe have approached us with regards [sic] to sharing our 'UNIQUE ZULU EXPERIENCE' with the youth of Natal. We feel, as they do, any Cross-Cultural Experience can only better the understanding between racial groups. What better place to start than with the youth of South Africa, for they are OUR future."[92] The concern with cross-cultural experience implicitly acknowledged what the other resorts ignored, the tremendous anxieties that all South Africans, on the eve of the political transition, had about cultural others, especially the concerns of non-Zulu speakers regarding "Zulu-ness," and addressed them by offering a site for first-hand knowledge of this feared "Other."

Leaving the model of the homestead behind them, and moving forward to the entrance of the Great Kraal, the visiting party shifted from hearing about "Zulu-ness" to confronting it, and coming into first-hand knowledge of it. Here, the way was blocked by a barrier pole. The adviser paused at the pole, and called out in isiZulu. Nothing happened. He then outlined to the group the appropriate Zulu etiquette for making one's presence as a visitor known at a homestead. This involved the loud calling out of the praise names of the homestead head. Knowledge of such praise names is an esoteric business, and most Zulu speakers know the praises associated with only a few surnames, if any at all. To know the correct ones, and to call them out specifically—rather than to resort to a general alternative—is an "insider" sort of thing, and the guide took time to teach the group the names appropriate to the homestead. Then all were encouraged to call out and announce themselves. At this point, the "homestead head" responded, appearing at the entrance of the cattle byre ahead. Appealing to the tourists' desire for insider knowledge and for "getting in with the natives," Shakaland drew the visitors into its script as active participants.

As befits the head of a family who sees a crowd of strangers at his door, the man collected his stick and shield and approached cautiously, ready for come-what-may. In many respects, the homestead head looked exactly like the men in the news photographs of Zulu izimpi at Inkatha rallies, which were appearing regularly in the press in 1991. In isiZulu, and following all the normal forms of polite address, the guide told the man, whom he referred to in English as "the chief," that he had brought a party of visitors to see his home. He explained that they wanted to learn about the "Zulu" way of doing things, and requested the homestead head to accommodate them. This the chief graciously assented to, the bar was drawn back, and the party admitted. All present were introduced to the chief. The entire exercise was handled in such a delicate fashion that were it to be the homestead of an acquaintance that the party was entering, rather than a commercially available experience, the visitors would be assured that their behavior was in the best possible taste. Exactly what was going on, and the politeness of the entry, were not made explicit to those members of the party who did not speak *isiZulu,* nor were the terms at any point directly translated. The effect was, however, unmistakable to the visiting party.

In this, as much as in the quality of the information imparted, Shakaland showed itself to be cognizant of the sensibilities of its black visitors and the widening of the horizons of a white clientele increasingly eager to be able to behave appropriately in African settings. Indeed, Shakaland prided itself on its attractiveness to black visitors, anticipating that this section of its market would expand as tourism among black South Africans developed further.[93]

The visitors then entered the Great Hut, which the cultural adviser preferred to name in *isiZulu,* the *indlu nkhulu.* The guide had previously explained that guests are not made welcome in a home until they have been offered beer to drink. Inside, the visitors, now the guests of the homestead head, were given *utshwala* (home-brewed sorghum beer), an act signaling their formal acceptance. The *utshwala* was drunk from a communal receptacle, with all the attendant rituals and etiquette, and it was a measure of the momentousness of this act in the Shakaland script that few visitors were sufficiently inhibited to forgo the experience.

In these actions the tourists participated actively in the fantasy, but because of their own authenticity at this moment as (literally) consumers, fantasy and reality blurred together in such a way that the guests often found themselves making real gestures in the theatrical setting. In this context, they temporarily became Zulu themselves, and in so doing the image of the Other that "Zulu-ness" embodied, that haunted many South Africans on the eve of political change, and figured importantly in the consciousness of foreign visitors as quintessential Africa, became self, and was thereby altered. The shared cup, symbolic of mutual acceptance and respect, began to create a new community among guide, chief, and visitors. The drinking of the *utshwala* was the consumption of the Shakaland promise of a new future. In the setting of the *indlu nkhulu*—the repository of the family's most ritually and historically significant items—it was also the enactment of a symbolic connection with the past.

A discussion of Zulu dress followed the drinking of the *utshwala,* with reference to the accoutrements of the homestead head and his wife, and to items laid out on display. Here, the homestead head took over and discoursed in *isiZulu* on all the items and their functions. His explanations were translated into English by the adviser for the benefit of those members of the audience who did not understand *isiZulu.* The mode of presentation was of an elder, well versed in matters traditional, instructing not only the guests, but also the younger, modern cultural adviser. The performance achieved thus a special authority, emphasized by the many ways, including body language, in which the adviser demonstrated his respect for the older, more knowledgeable—at least in these matters—homestead head. The audience was thus made to feel that they had the benefit of explanations from "a real expert." The cumbersome translations enhanced the feeling of authenticity.

The guides at Shakaland played a key role as cross-cultural brokers. The "experience" was structured in such a way that the visitors were obliged to rely on their guide, allowing him to speak for them and to translate back to them, trusting him to protect them from social embarrassment in an unfamiliar world. For white visitors, this was an especially marked reversal of the forms of knowledge transmission to which they were accustomed. Indeed, the guides at Shakaland, while always solicitous, readily reproved guests who erred in matters of etiquette, and insisted that the visitors make the effort to learn material from one stage of the visit before the next commenced, as in the requirement that guests call out the praises of the homestead head before gaining admittance, and in a tendency in the guides' expositions to use more and more Zulu terms as the experience advanced. While the homestead head stood for the most traditional, the guides—sophisticated, urban Zulu speakers—were positioned midway between the worlds of their modern visitors and those being toured, the Shakaland staff in their "Zulu" setting. Not only did the guides name and explain, and offer a form of knowledge which the patrons felt had been denied to them by apartheid, but, in their dual proficiency in isiZulu and English, in their relaxed, though not complete, familiarity with both urban and rural etiquette, they offered an ideal, but also realistic, prototype of the new South African.

In the Great Kraal the guests developed a relationship with the homestead head that was increasingly demanding of them. The visit was structured in such a way that their admittance was dependent on his graciousness: they were his guests, and their experience was a result of his extension of hospitality to them. The visitors were bound over to behave as guests, and not as tourists paying their way. The relationship between guests and host developed through eye contact, joking (often in translation through the guide), and an appearance by the homestead head of taking pride in making the experience available, in manifestations of his concern for the guests' education in his domain. The "experience" thus took on the form of a normal, proper social interaction—such as might occur when adult children bring home friends met in distant places to the remote villages of their birth, and, by introducing their parents to their friends, seek to make each of their worlds gain in knowledge of the other. Because normal social interactions of this nature across racial lines were still rare in South Africa in 1991, the Shakaland enactment provided an opportunity otherwise elusive for whites to enter what they regarded as a black world, for Sotho speakers to penetrate an apparently Zulu one, and so on. Shakaland was, as Leitch put it, "an oasis within what was essentially an apartheid society."[94] It was, on the eve of political change, a safe, controlled setting for the crossing of boundaries and barriers that elsewhere were seen to be too dangerous to breach.

The visit to the Great Kraal brought the first part of the "cultural experience" to a close. In the evening, dinner was taken in the "boma," followed by a tremendous display of Zulu music and dancing at the *indlu nkhulu*. The display was at once a mix of the old and the new, rural and township, with *masikanda* and *ngoma*[95] all contributing to the spectacle. One of the managers of the resort, a young white man who spoke fluent *isiZulu*, provided the commentary and explanations of the dances. As much as the cultural advisers stood for the coming new South Africa, so too did the young manager, with his demonstrable facility in the contexts of both the dancers and the various visitors. To see a young white person in the role of cultural authority introduced the idea, at least in the minds of some white visitors, of the possibility that their submission to the tutelage of their guides would allow them access to the same confidence and authority.

The following morning, overnight visitors returned to the Great Kraal, this time accessible (the barrier was removed) and familiar. They moved quickly and confidently through the necessary greetings, and entered to watch the making of spears,[96] and to participate in "traditional sports." A demonstration of spear-throwing and stick-fighting ensued, in which the importance of physical prowess, agility, and adherence to strict rules was emphasized. The audience were invited to try their hands at both "sports." Finally, the cultural adviser conducted the visitors to the establishment of a *sangoma* (translated by the adviser as a "healer" and "diviner"—no "witchdoctors" here!) and the significance of various tools of the trade was explained, again with the *sangoma* speaking in *isiZulu*, and the adviser translating. *Impepho* (a burning herb) was passed around for the visitors to inhale, as is common before a consultation. The *sangoma* rehearsed the various steps in a diagnosis, and discussed some of the possible remedies for common complaints.[97] Depending on the time of year, and the resort's refurbishment or provisioning needs, there were other opportunities to view day-to-day cultural activities, such as wood-carving, hut-building, or beer-brewing.

The richness and variety of cultural activities and experiences that were on offer at Shakaland were greater than those available in any other single setting, such as in the real-life homesteads of the adjacent Nkwalini valley. Not only did Shakaland offer a reproduction of reality that was more concentrated than the real thing, it was also more perfect. Its finish was more immaculate, its attention to detail more precise, even its construction was sounder. It was, to use a phrase of Umberto Eco, an exercise in hyper reality.[98] This excellence was one of the features that initially attracted visitors to Shakaland. Their search for knowledge of "Zulu-ness" was then broadened through the interaction in the Great Kraal into a rich experience of "Zulu-ness." Through this experience, "Zulu-ness" became familiar, was assimilated, and was made understandable. Then the visitors were ready to face the real thing.

The final thrilling experience was a visit to a genuine homestead. For this visit, smaller parties were taken by boat up the narrows of the Mhlathuze lake. The journey—more than an hour long—passed through areas increasingly remote and wild in appearance. The boat finally moored, and the guests ascended with difficulty a steep slope to a distant homestead. Employing all their newly acquired knowledge with some assistance from the Shakaland staff who accompanied them, the guests made a visit. Here they experienced the real thing: the homestead was small and ill fashioned in comparison to the film set. The poverty of the residents was evident. The visitors were given a warm welcome, reminiscent of the previous day, but it was a warmth tied to the opportunity the visit provided for the residents to sell a few crafts which were strategically displayed, and which were snapped up by the visitors.

The visitors inquired suspiciously if the family was employed by Shakaland, and were told that it was not. As Barry Leitch puts it, visitors who go "on safari" to homesteads in the area "will meet independents and not contracted workers."[99] This assurance was the guarantee of the authenticity of the experience. Lest the visitors fear they had imposed themselves on the family, the staff offered the comfortable assurance that a properly reciprocal relationship existed between the families visited and the resort, whereby the heavily laden, the ill, and the elderly were freely lifted to and fro on the boat. The combination of these features, Leitch noted, was part of

> Shakaland's special hallmark, setting it aside from commercialized concerns which feature "ethnic experiences" totally out of their natural environment which often depend on the re-enactment of worn-out charades. Likewise, our lectures and the dancing entertainment are not all period museum pieces . . . The visitor will come away with insights that are not only historic, but also applicable to everyday life.[100]

The "safari" confirmed the Shakaland message that even in its most "raw" form, "Zulu-ness" was not threatening, but was something that could be visited and assimilated.

The Shakaland script pushed visitors beyond the passive acts of viewing or buying, into doing and acting. They were required to embark on a journey marked by stages, the completion of which altered their status—a change first signaled by the removal of the barrier at the entrance to the Great Kraal, and finally and fully realized in the "safari."[101] The vast number of stones on the *isivivane* was the symbol of Shakaland's success in this endeavor.

Turner's ideas of liminality and communitas used in the analysis of certain kinds of tourism, notably in the work of MacCannell, and Fine and Speer, are suggestive as to why this experience was so satisfying and how one might grasp what distinguished it from other tourist enterprises.[102] Drawing a connection between certain kinds of tourism and pilgrimages, these writers view tourists as "liminoid beings who travel outside their normal routes, experiencing things outside of everyday routines. In this period of release from structure, the travellers reflect on the meaning of basic religious and cultural values, and may experience communitas: a quality of communion."[103] Turner sees societies as being in a dialectical process with successive stages of structure and communitas.[104] Thus, people starved of communitas in day-to-day activities may seek it in the liminality of ritual. In the turbulence of the South African political transition, such starvation was obvious, the need for communitas was as pressing as it was elusive, and the possibility of its achievement in Shakaland was especially alluring.

Staging reality and making identity

For some visitors Shakaland was simply a safari experience, a convenient way of viewing the "Other." For the majority, however, the "cultural experience" provided what was viewed as much-needed knowledge of a perceived "Other," and indeed suggested that in the new South Africa the distinctions between self and Other might not be immutable or a matter of fear.

Karp and Kratz set up an illuminating opposition between "exoticizing" and "assimilating" exhibition styles. While the 1986 television series *Shaka Zulu* exoticized "Zulu-ness," the 1991 Shakaland script sought to assimilate it, creating "familiarity and intimacy with representations and their subjects."[105] In challenging visitors to understand the past, and to use that understanding to inform their comprehension of the present, Shakaland encouraged visitors to imagine new and optimistic futures.[106]

Shakaland thus took on the role of an agent of redemption and healing, offering to compensate for the failure of normal institutions of social life. It was an opportunity for travelers to seek epiphany, an intuitive grasp of reality through its simple and striking setting. It created a situation where people felt that they were beginning the work of reconstituting themselves and forging a new citizenship. Through the enhancement of knowledge of the other, the process of a visit to Shakaland resocialized, establishing through shared enterprise a sense of social cohesion. A symbolic new community was created out of visitors, guides, and other participants, prefiguring an ideal new South African society, possibly even a new nation.[107] Through revelation and progress the visitors were transformed, and in the process came to feel that they had embarked on a new set of social relationships. The staged quality of the setting was, in that instance, reassuring and facilitating of the promise of further development.

Tourism is an arena that frequently involves the enactment of cultural difference. In the early 1990s the emphasis in Shakaland on differences was not an act of discrimination, as it was in many other contemporary tourist settings, but "a mode of exploration and understanding."[108] The main issues the visitors to Shakaland were primed to reimagine were questions of people's differences and similarities. What Karp says about museums in general was equally pertinent to Shakaland:

> They define relations with communities whether they intend to or not. This process of making meaning, negotiating, debating—localized in institutions such as museums—provides the unwritten, ever-changing constitution of civil society. The social ideas of civil society are articulated and experienced through striving for consensus and struggling against the imposition of identity. Museums are one of a number of settings for these conflicting but simultaneously operating processes, which make social ideas understandable, but not always legitimate.[109]

Recent literature on exhibition practice recognizes that displays are seldom, if ever, politically neutral. Frequently, exhibitions are the arenas in which particular definitions of identity and culture are asserted. As such they play an important role in the making of identities, or, as Karp puts it, they are "sites for the play of identity."[110] While Shakaland was not conceived of as a museum, it was an exhibit about identity situated in a wider context of intense conflict about identity in which all meanings of Zulu identity were highly charged.

Shakaland offered an exploration of Zulu culture for people of other cultures, for modern, urban Zulu speakers interested in the past, and for Zulu traditionalists. It thus worked to define a Zulu identity as well as identities that themselves gain in definition through the defining of "Zulu." The definitions enacted in Shakaland potentially assisted both Zulu speakers and non-Zulu speakers to legitimize themselves in a new way. Mutual definition of identity meant that the resort was able to ratify different things for different people. While Shakaland offered a unique setting for this process, it did so on its own terms. The illusion that enabled the Shakaland project was also a source of fraud, the script a form of closure and limitation.

Leitch's program expressly banished discussion of material on politics. Apartheid relations were eschewed.[111] Nonetheless, the script was designed by a white anthropologist, the hotel was run by a white manager, and the land on which it was built was just outside the KwaZulu homeland, in an area designated white. Leitch believed that one of the truly distinctive features of Shakaland was the "Zulu" relationship at the resort between the white owners and managers on the one hand, and the Zulu-speaking staff on the other. He described how the resort was run on a headman system, with dispute resolution between the staff and the management conducted through the two headmen. Relating proudly how in one instance, when the general manager erred in following procedure, he was subject to a fine imposed by the headmen, Leitch commented:

> The two patriarchs of Shakaland are myself and my partner, Kingsley Holgate. We are essentially White Zulus. We conduct ourselves very much in the Zulu fashion. We don't conduct ourselves in a white fashion . . . and the whole way that we run Shakaland is exactly the same way as the head of a kraal or the head of a family would run a family in the rural areas . . . We formed Shakaland with people who have evolved with us. A lot of the dancers are people I have been friends with since my childhood . . . or people that my partner Kingsley has gleaned, people that have tacked on to him along his journey through life, people that have then come together in a kind of nexus at Shakaland. That's where the whole thing is distilled. So our roots in many cases go back to our childhoods. It is a truly South African situation, minus the negativity and the violence.[112]

But violence was not absent in the resort's labor relations and the hard realities of "patriarchal" relations inadvertently revealed themselves in the domineering behavior of white hotel personnel at the resort toward black employees. In response to questions probing the day-to-day running of the resort, one member of staff described how the white manager threatened them saying, "You are all Inkatha, and I am ANC, so you had better watch out."[113]

Similar fissures and contradictions were revealed in the "cultural experience" itself. Because the script depended on the interaction of guides and guests, on the frankness of the guides, and on the first-hand testimony of the guides and those being toured, there was space for its subversion. Indeed, when asked questions to which they did not know the answers, the advisers readily referred them to "actors" being viewed—mostly local Zulu-speaking inhabitants with a rural background, people like the chief—and thereafter incorporated the replies into their repertoires. The education of the guides in this form gave the "actors" a voice that was not scripted. These voices were frequently nationalist, even chauvinist—"The Zulu are the most powerful people in all the country; only the Zulu are really kings"—in forms expressly avoided in the script.

On some occasions the performers, guides, and visitors failed to communicate in the manner envisaged by Leitch, and the cultural experience took unscripted forms. The visit to the Great Kraal, with its emphasis on the division of the homestead into separate male and female domains, was readily transformed through gender-based banter between guides and audience into crude stereotyping of the role of women in Zulu society.[114] The displays of spear-throwing and stick-fighting were likewise easily subverted by audiences brimming with popular images of Zulu ferocity into confirmations of the stereotype of innate Zulu militarism. Recalcitrant audiences, reluctant to submit themselves to the tutelage of their guides, sometimes remained observers rather than becoming participants, and for them Shakaland, like the neighboring Zulu resorts of Phezulu or Ophapheni, continued to be a celebration of difference, a site for the viewing of the exotic and the primitive.

In addition to attempting to broker between the many worlds of their audience, the guides often had to move beyond Leitch's prepared text, to reach into their own experience. The advisers consistently introduced into the discussion images and comparisons drawn directly out of an experience of a South Africa wider than Shakaland. In explicating the Zulu *amabutho* system, one adviser drew a comparison with the South African Defence Force and its division into battalions, referring by way of example to one of the army's most notorious divisions then stationed in Natal and accused of committing a range of atrocities. To many readers of the daily newspapers, the very naming of "32 Battalion" was chilling. Likewise, in attempting to explain rituals observed around death, and the significance of branches of the buffalo thorn tree in bringing home the spirit of a relative who has died in distant parts, one adviser began his example thus: "If you are working on the mines and get shot and die in Johannesburg," this in 1991, the year in which the terror of the train massacres and hostel clashes involving Zulu speakers besieged the consciousness of all South Africans. Violence was the very sweat of the resort and it seeped through its carefully overstitched seams.

These examples alert us to what was a massive silence in the resort's script: the absence, in Shakaland's exploration of identity, of ethnic violence and the furore in the press and other public domains concerning issues of Zulu militarism, cultural weapons, and nationalism. "We are a proud people with warrior blood in our veins," was a frequent refrain of the traditionalist leadership of KwaZulu at the time.[115] "[O]nly warriors," claimed the Zulu king, Goodwill Zwelithini, "could have put KwaZulu together under the direction of that great and illustrious founder, King Shaka."[116] Zulu-speaking hostel dwellers endorsed the king's description of innate Zulu militarism: "Zulus are born fighters who can respond spontaneously to any attack." Another elaborated on the origins of this militarism: "The Zulu Nation is born out of Shaka's spear. When you say 'Go and fight', it just happens."[117]

In 1991, in South Africa, claims about what "Zulu-ness" really was were made against the backdrop of a conflict which began in Natal in the mid-1980s, and which surged dramatically in the early 1990s across the Reef. The violence most frequently saw Zulu *izimpi* (armed groups of men)—often made up of hostel dwellers—pitted against neighboring communities of non-Zulu speakers and supporters of the ANC. Political negotiations ground to a standstill as the ANC demanded that the government ban the carrying of "cultural weapons" by its Zulu-speaking opponents. In response, the Zulu king accused the ANC of having insulted his manhood and "the manhood of every Zulu man" with its demand.[118]

Journalists besieged university anthropology departments, the imagined "experts" on the matter, with urgent questions: "What is a 'cultural weapon'?" "Is it real, this Zulu tradition 'thing'?" Finally, when asked to judge whether "fold-up spears . . . roughly 50cm long . . . [with] detachable blades that screw into rectangular metal bases, and . . . fit snugly into an easily-concealable sheath made of industrial tape" were bona fide "Zulu cultural weapons," some of us contemplated unplugging the telephones.

The controversy surrounding these definitions of "Zulu-ness" and concern over their authenticity involved questions ranging well beyond the identities of the people who described themselves, or who were designated by others, as "Zulu." The backdrop to these questions was the painful emergence of the so-called new South Africa, and the controversy included struggles over what ideally would constitute this new society, as well as over changing and sometimes contradictory meanings of what it was to be "black" or "white," "Zulu," "Sotho," "Afrikaner," and so on.

Shakaland offered a vision of identity and reality which was a response to these struggles, but which, paradoxically, had to deny their existence to be effective. In Shakaland as designed by Leitch, the "tyrant" of history, Shaka, was Henry Cele, an actor, and assegais and sticks were instruments of sport, not weapons of war. The script attempted to banish from the stage the conflict between the ANC and Inkatha.

Faith in fakes[119]

Shakaland was not so much about Shaka as an invocation of the metaphor of Shaka as open to negotiation with whites, an analogy that was drawn directly out of the historical narratives about his foresight in sending an embassy to the Cape and his vision of the coming of whites. As such, Shakaland did more than simply market Zulu history and culture. In the 1991 situation of massive social and political upheaval in South Africa, the Shakaland product was successful because it addressed an important need for a new post-apartheid knowledge of Africa. It did so in the form of an accessible and polished package that could conveniently be completed in one or two days. At one level, it was a praiseworthy didactic and celebratory endeavor, and its product was of sufficiently high quality to satisfy the new and more demanding connoisseurship of its customers. At the level of cross-cultural communication through the provision of information it also enjoyed significant success, so much so that it provided a crucial reassurance to its participants about a culturally heterogeneous future. But Shakaland did more than provide new knowledge; its real product was "experience."

Many of the visitors, but especially the white guests, came to value not so much their viewing of the film set and the acquisition of information about Zulu history and life as their engagement with "Zulus"—the "advisers" and the "actors"—in a shared experience. They were satisfied by the interaction rather than the setting and the lecture, although these were, of course, essential prerequisites for the former. In the course of the experience, Shakaland successfully made the "Other" familiar and comfortable for its patrons. "Coexistence," wrote one travel writer, "is what Shakaland is all about."[120]

While the conventional mode of knowledge of Africa, that of white mastery and manipulation, seemed exorcised, it was not. Patrons gained a new and more sophisticated authority over "Zulu-ness" through the acquisition of knowledge and experience. Close examination of the resort revealed that it was governed by a script created by a white author and shaped by weighty market constraints, notably the need for manifestly "authentic" reassurances. In South Africa in 1991, Shakaland shared the peace-of-mind market with security companies, gunshops, and prayer. It was part of a search for security and control in an increasingly volatile and unknown world. Violence was excised because it would have confounded the vision of smooth transformation and the ritual reassurance that was Shakaland's special product.

The methodology of the Shakaland experience was fundamentally depoliticizing. The script placed the guest in the position of an "I-witness" in the sense employed by Clifford Geertz.[121] By using his or her experience ("I was there, I saw it happen") to testify to the reality of the experience, the range of imaginings was limited to the alternatives posed by Shakaland. The Shakaland vision of reality was further entrenched and made difficult to challenge because the structure of the experience ensured that the visitor took responsibility for the act of imagining, and thereby made the visitor complicit in Shakaland's vision of the future. Shakaland set strict limits on what that future entailed. When, as sometimes happens, visitors resisted the Shakaland script and constructed their own exhibit out of the film set, they substituted viewing for experience, thereby symbolically denying their shared inhabitation of the same world as Zulu speakers. In 1991 the success of Shakaland lay, at least in part, in its capacity to meet and accommodate visions of both the new and the old South Africa. By 1997 the Shakaland product was obviously tired: the cultural brokers had been transformed into tour guides who fed the tourists, mostly foreigners, a standardized fare of commercialized culture, neatly packaged and suitably exoticized. The resort, conceived as a response to political transition, had lost its founding rationale and had succumbed to the weariness of perpetual rehearsal.

As a highly realistic representation of Shakan times, Shakaland continues to enjoy a powerful visual monopoly over representations of the period, and it has influenced museum curators, film-makers, and, indeed, historians in subsequent attempts to envision precolonial times. It has successfully constituted itself as a new repository of knowledge and functioned to blur the boundaries of public and institutional history, high and popular culture. It has thus become a powerful form of iconic knowledge. To understand the past one must have an image of it, of the period. Where there are no photographs and so few drawings or other contemporary visual materials, reconstructions dominate. The iconic knowledge offered through Shakaland becomes in this context absolute.

In 1991 Shakaland developed as a site for the production of both history and social ideas. Yet, because it promoted itself as fake, as a fantasy experience, the ideas that it advanced so successfully disguised their political potency and seeped unchallenged into popular consciousness. While the Shakaland reconstructions were executed with absolute fidelity to reality, at the same time openly admitting their artifice, the script covertly excluded and suppressed other more uncomfortable realities. The "real Zulu," like the "real goat," was defined by grand gestures of imposture. Visitors to Shakaland, whether experiencing or viewing the resort, thus placed their faith in a double fake.

Chapter Six

"The Government resembles Tshaka"

Exploration of the moment of initial contact between the Zulu kingdom and early British traders based at Port Natal reveals that the origins of the traders' representations of Shaka lay in their experiences in the Zulu kingdom and neighboring Natal in the 1820s, and in the ideas of the Africans among whom they lived and traveled. The drama of Theophilus Shepstone's assumption of the mantle of Shaka highlights his appropriation of indigenous understandings of Shaka and Shakan rule to provide a model for the Natal system of native administration. While Shepstone's particular gloss on Shaka as an effective ruler was, for a time, overwhelmed in the run-up to the Anglo-Zulu War of 1879—when the British authorities sought to use Shaka as an emblem of unacceptable Zulu despotism—aspects of Shepstonian thinking continued to underpin native policy making well into the twentieth century. The image of the Zulu, and of Shaka, that was promoted in the enormously popular fiction of Rider Haggard was essentially Shepstonian and, like his views, was infused with elements whose origins lay ultimately in African views.

Recognition that the roots of the images of Shaka lie in indigenous discourses, subject from the moment of their inception to complex histories of reworking, has important implications for historians seeking sources for Shakan times. In the case of Shaka (and possibly for precolonial southern Africa more widely), historians have access—not unmediated, but access nonetheless—to derived indigenous views and understandings of Shaka embedded in the texts of officials such as Shepstone. More significantly, the historian of Shakan times can use the extensive notes of conversations with Africans identified as historically knowledgeable that were made by another colonial official, James Stuart. In these texts the common mediation is that of Stuart himself. He drew directly on Shepstone's reading of Shaka, and made similar arguments about the need to model native administration on the Shakan system. Stuart, even more than Shepstone, believed that to be effective native policy had to be based on an accurate understanding and in-depth analysis of indigenous institutions and practices. This belief gives a particular character to the corpus of material now known as the *James Stuart Archive* of African historical testimony, and underpins its usefulness as a historical source. As much as Stuart's own concerns and imperatives require historians' consideration, so too we must recognize that the accounts that Stuart heard were themselves already heavily mediated, in equally complex and thickly layered ways.

While much recent scholarship has shown how colonial authorities imposed their own axioms and aesthetics on the colonized, or expediently reshaped existing institutions in terms of their own criteria, this book argues that indigenous institutions were, in certain instances, taken up with significant regard to their full cultural complexity, so as to give shape and form to colonialism. In providing aspects of colonial discourse with form and content, contemporary African discourses limited the colonial imagination, and constrained colonial practices. They were not the only limits: trading imperatives, the fiscal reticence of the Natal authorities, the political and financial underpinnings of enterprises such as *Shaka Zulu* and Shakaland—not to mention the history of the making of the image of Shaka itself—all circumscribe the activities of invention and imagination.

The issue of expertise is closely linked to an argument about limits. One of the central constraints was the need to use concepts in native administration that were recognized by the African population. The identification and interpretation of such concepts demanded of colonial officials such as Shepstone and Stuart an expertise in what was termed "native affairs." Shepstone demonstrated his expertise by acting out in public ceremony the role of Shaka. Stuart sought to attain for his researches and knowledge the status of scientific objectivity and professionalism. This underlay his concern with orthography, as well as his contacts with professional anthropologists and linguists, and prefigured the establishment of anthropology and Bantu studies departments in South African universities designed to service native—or by then, as it was known, Bantu—administration. *Shaka Zulu* and Shakaland were similarly grounded in complex statements about authenticity and the use of "cultural" experts and expertise. The designation of the historian Wright and the archeologist Mazel as "academic body servants" spoke to contemporary challenges to this kind of "expertise," and the capacity of "experts" to analyze Shakan times.

Historians and other "experts" remain animated by the question of what Shaka and Shakan times were really like. To this end, scholars such as Jan Vansina have identified the importance of well-grounded methodological approaches to previously neglected oral sources. Such advances are implicitly challenged by work on the discourses of the "Other" and the construction of the colonial subject.

Scholars would seem to have little hope of reconstructing Shakan times when all the texts available to them are reduced to the status of imperial fictions. The historical narratives, textual readings, and arguments presented in this study challenge the idea of the inescapability of a discourse that kept the colonizers from engaging with the actuality of the lands they sought to dominate, and that keeps historians from engaging with the past they seek to study. They also suggest that in order to use these sources, researchers need to come to grips with the full complexity of the nature of the interlocutions involved, and with the various ways in which, and the various sites where, history is produced.[1]

The significance of this point is not confined to professional historians. For a host of different reasons, there is in South Africa today an enormous demand for knowledge about precolonial times. One question for which an answer is sought in that past was initially framed on the eve of the first democratic election and concerned South Africans' dispositions toward democracy. In attempting to grapple with this issue, political commentators examined the recent history of political organizations such as the ANC to assess black South Africans' claim to liberal and democratic traditions. The existence of manipulative inner caucuses, and the discipline and autocracy that followed from operating in exile and from participating in guerrilla warfare, lent themselves to the conclusion that the "ANC exiles returned home with a well-developed set of authoritarian and bureaucratic reflexes." At home, the analysis showed, they encountered a different political culture, that of unions and civic organizations with a higher degree of representativeness, democracy, and accountability. Even here, however, politics was often partisan and intolerant.[2]

Discussion of the democratic inclinations of black South Africans continues today, framed by a perception of the African continent as racked by social upheaval and disposed toward despotism or one-party states. Debates around this question frequently have recourse to stereotypes about the precolonial past. In one way or another, the "barbarism" of precolonial Africa is offered by commentators outside Africa as an explanation for what is identified as a continent-wide anti-democratic tendency. Many black South Africans, by way of contrast, appeal to a precolonial idyll—the communalism of the past and the consultative practices of precolonial chiefs. In 1993 the ANC legal affairs expert Zola Skweyiya argued that "traditional" institutions such as chiefship needed to be "cleans[ed] . . . of all the undemocratic attributes that were imparted to it both by colonialism and apartheid."[3]

In the debate that erupted in 1993 between chiefs and women over the potential conflict in the constitutional Bill of Rights between the equality clause (entrenching every person's right to equality irrespective of gender) and the customary law provision (protecting customary law in terms of which chiefs argued for the permanent minority of women), chiefs stressed men's assumption of responsibility for the protection and guardianship of women, and defended the clause as crucial in preventing the erosion of the foundations of African culture.[4] The chiefs' arguments against democracy serve their interests directly, allowing them to retain power and influence which they might otherwise lose. At the same time, many of the very people whose interests are not directly served by such arguments—indeed, whose situations are compromised by them—support at least the principles behind these arguments, mostly from a position that seeks to Africanize or indigenize modern political and social institutions.

Much current and self-consciously progressive political wisdom rejects the notion that such ideas are pristine survivals from precolonial times, and tends to dismiss them as invented traditions which serve directly the interests of chiefs and men. The question persists: why then do people who do not benefit from these inventions accept traditions that must obviously be seen as constructions and manipulations? Why do they believe them to contain some kind of truth and to embody values? What determines the material selected for use in an invented tradition, and how did that process of adaptation actually take place? What materials were available, why were they available for adaptation, and what were the limitations on their use? Such questions are especially pertinent to the issue of Zulu identity and traditionalism.

Since the early 1980s the image of Shaka has been extensively deployed as the focus of Zulu-ist politics. But although he was the founding father of the Zulu kingdom, and is celebrated for his role in creating the Zulu nation, the choice of Shaka as central icon is not self-explanatory. Among the many Zulu speakers who have been connected historically to the Zulu kingdom, Shaka is by no means uniformly remembered in positive terms, either in the past or today.

While politicians such as the IFP leader, Buthelezi, make much of Shaka's accommodation of the Port Natal traders, who were the first Europeans to have a sustained engagement with the Zulu kingdom, they stress constantly the warrior heritage of Zulu speakers as established by Shaka.[5] This heritage invoked by Buthelezi and by other Zulu speakers, both IFP supporters and others, consists of a number of elements, above all those of discipline and social order. The central paradox explored in this study is the way in which precisely those elements of Shaka's rule that are designated "barbarism"—such as the harshness of his rule— have historically also been translated as a basis for social order, and hence are also labeled "civilization."

Order and chaos: "Zoolacraticism" and "cannibalism"

By the time of Shaka's death in 1828, the Zulu kingdom had come, in the area between Delagoa Bay and the Mzimkhulu River, to represent the forces of social order, albeit a harsh one. It was depicted by contemporary African commentators as a center of civilization and efficient administration and was opposed to the chaos and anarchy of surrounding areas over which Shakan rule was not established, and in which cannibalism was reputed to be rife.

The various institutions of the early Zulu state from which this reputation for efficient administration and security derived are now well known and do not warrant extended treatment here.[6] Suffice to say, the *amabutho* system lay at the heart of what enjoyed a widespread reputation as a well-established state apparatus, augmented by an efficient bureaucracy, and the strategic placement of Shakan loyalists in regional positions of authority. The state and social structure were hierarchically organized, and political power emanated from above. The government used organs of state power—the bureaucracy, the military, and secret services—to repress dissent and to promote its policies.

The primary element of this system, in the view of Stuart's informants, was the talented leadership of Shaka himself in which patronage and the maintenance of discipline were carefully balanced. The Shakan system of government was thus strongly authoritarian, with great emphasis placed on "law and order." Command, obedience, and order were deemed to be higher values than freedom, dissent, and opposition. Shaka's legitimacy was, and is, understood to be founded, not on his birthright, but on his success and his achievements, which in turn depended on his army and its character as highly disciplined and effective, able to guarantee law and order in violent times. Shaka's ability to offer protection is attested in his praises:

> He who was a pile of rocks at Nkandla,
> Which was a shelter for the elephants in bad weather,
> Which sheltered Phungashe of the Buthelezi clan,
> Which sheltered Zihlandlo of the Mkhize clan,
> And the elephants ran away from the place.[7]

The analyst of Shaka's praises, M.Z. Malaba, offers the following gloss on these lines: "And shelter, it seems, is found in the person of the ruler—only in subservience is there hope for a measure of security, as opposed to mere survival."[8] Emphases like these found in the oral texts were transferred into European written accounts of Zulu history in a variety of ways, but most decisively when the Natal native administration began to draw on Zulu history for a model of domination and control.

That these were indeed violent times is well attested.[9] In fact, it is the only point agreed upon by the many contenders in the debates around the concept of the *mfecane*.[10] The *mfecane* stereotype has conventionally attributed the violence and upheaval of the early nineteenth century to disruptions caused by the invasions of Zulu armies. In a study of the Natal region south of the Shakan kingdom, John Wright has shown how misplaced is the concept of the *mfecane* that portrays these upheavals as a product of the violent expansion of the Shakan state. The area south of the Thukela was not devastated by the Zulu, and they were never able to occupy more than a very small part of it. Wright argues that these notions of Zulu devastation were the product of Cape merchant interests and those of their associates, seeking to encourage British colonization of the area. The idea was subsequently taken up by missionaries who used it as a justification for the need to bring "civilization" to the widespread disorder, and by settlers seeking to justify their land appropriations. As Wright puts it, "The notion that the African societies no longer had any coherent existence was clearly convenient to their purpose."[11]

Wright is quite correct to assert that the *mfecane* stereotype inappropriately attributes the upheavals to the Zulu, and he marshals considerable evidence to support his argument. However, in claiming that it was in the interests of the merchants, missionaries, and settlers to support the idea of the Zulu devastations, he downplays the extent of the upheaval and dislocation which did indeed prevail, and which provided the real meat of missionary claims to be the bringers of "civilization." In the minds of contemporary African inhabitants of the region, Natal was an area of massive social dislocation, and was contrasted with the Zulu state. They saw Shaka's kingdom, not, as the *mfecane* stereotype would have it, as the cause of the devastation, but rather as a center of civilization and order. Once the missionaries' and settlers' own centers of "civilization" and social order were established, it is not surprising that Shaka and the Zulu kingdom on the colonial periphery began, in turn, to be constructed as the savage, "cannibal" Other.

Despotic Shakan rule was, it seems, the price for social order and security that many local inhabitants were prepared to concede, particularly in the face of the anarchy depicted as existing beyond the borders of the Zulu kingdom. This anarchy was vividly represented as "cannibalism" and was said to be a phenomenon contemporaneous with the rise of the Zulu kingdom.[12] In sharp contrast to his representation in the *mfecane* stereotype, Shaka enjoyed a reputation for acting against the "cannibals."[13] Shaka's appointee, Jobe of the Sithole, established a number of outposts charged with the special task of guarding against the "cannibals," while the most notorious of all the cannibals, Mahlapahlapha kaMnjoli, chief of the Ntuli section of Bhele who lived on the Ndaka (Sundays) River, was finally routed by Dingane.[14]

Accounts of cannibalism have, in recent years, been treated with growing skepticism, as scholars have become increasingly aware of how the preconceptions of early European travelers in Africa fed into and shaped their descriptions of the societies they encountered. But cannibalism was as much a feature of nineteenth-century African consciousness. The opposition between cultivation and chaos, ordered society and cannibalism, was, as Adam Kuper has shown, deeply rooted in a local cosmological vision, made up of precisely such systems of oppositions conveying meanings.[15] The indigenous idea of *buzimuzimu* is often translated as "cannibalism" but is described by African commentators as the opposite of civilized.[16] This does not imply that anthropophagy was common in early nineteenth-century Natal, but rather that the idea of *buzimuzimu* was current in southeast Africa, and that it was counterposed to the idea of social order.

"Cannibalism" was understood to prevail on the peripheries of the Zulu kingdom, particularly in the areas to the south and west.[17] Among those designated as "cannibals" were sections of the amaDunge[18] and the amaBele.[19] "Cannibalism" was the major trope for the representation of social disruption, a state of cattlelessness and extreme famine.[20] "Cannibals" did not live in settlements, but in the bush or in caves.[21] They were bandits who would kill people and eat them and the produce of their gardens.[22] For fear of these marauders, "noone used to travel alone," proclaimed Stuart's informant Jantshi.[23] Not all those who were dislocated were deemed to be cannibals; some were seen as their victims, as refugees who were also prey to wild animals.[24] People designated as cannibals were also consciously used as "hitmen." When the Hlubi chief Langalibalele was captured by "cannibals" it was reported that they had been put up to it by a rival claimant to the Hlubi succession. In this case the victim escaped and went on to rule the Hlubi. Stragglers from amongst the "cannibals" and other "orphans" then joined Chief Langalibalele.[25] Likewise, those who fled from Shaka, such as the Chunu chief Macingwane, "died from a wandering existence (from destitution)," reputedly eaten by cannibals.[26] To be with Shaka was to be secure within culture, within an ordered, albeit tyrannical, system. To be outside his ambit was to be in nature, uncontrolled and "cannibal."

We should note, however, that Shaka, viewed from the perspective of another contemporary center of social order, Moshoeshoe's Thaba Bosiu, became the cannibal "Other." In BaSotho texts Shaka was in turn depicted as the devourer. David Coplan describes Shaka as a symbolic foil for the efforts of the Basotho's own Bakoena aristocracy at state formation: "a darkness against which to appreciate Moshoeshoe's light."[27]

The concept of a strong central authority as a bulwark against chaos was thus an idea that characterized the reign of Shaka, and one that was not obliterated but rather reinforced by colonial practices in the nineteenth century. As Mbovu ka-Ndengezi remarked to Stuart in 1904, "The Government built the country with money. Without money we would have become cannibals . . . Government is expanding, every few years. The Government resembles Tshaka, for he never got tired. Its army is money."[28] In a distorted form these ideas were incorporated into the policies of segregation and apartheid. In the twentieth century, much Zulu-ist politics has sought to challenge such distortions through a claim to the "real" version of Shakan order, this time as a bulwark against the chaos and social upheaval wrought under apartheid. In the politics of the 1980s and 1990s Inkatha's invocation of these ideas as a powerful counter to the ANC's program for democracy—envisioned as chaos—was thus not simply a reclamation of precolonial ideas, nor an expedient, invented tradition.

Through a focus on a single case, that of the political heritage of the Shakan system—termed "Zoolacratical government" by the contemporary observer Nathaniel Isaacs, who felt no ordinary word in English would serve—this study has considered the extent to which that heritage is a source of certain political habits and expectations ingrained in the minds of a significant number of South Africans. The broad answer it offers is that appeals to the Shakan legacy are, above all else, expressions of a desire and need for social order, where social order is understood as an alternative to anarchy and violence. The study traces historically the appropriation of a specific set of ideas about social order derived from the precolonial Zulu state and their incorporation into Natal colonial discourse and practice, and specifically into the Natal native administration. It suggests that certain of these ideas, reshaped and refurbished, were in turn incorporated into aspects of apartheid thinking and practice, as well as into the ideologies of resistance to apartheid. It indicates that an understanding of the history of the values that underpin these ideas of social order offers an important perspective on contemporary popular conceptions of authority and of rights, as well as contributing to the discussion of historical predispositions toward different political outcomes. The argument presented suggests that one of the reasons that supporters of Zulu-ist politics have preferred the authoritarianism of the Shakan legacy to the freedoms of liberal democratic politics is that they perceive it to be a necessary and effective bulwark against recent conditions of violence and anarchy. The irony that the ability of the Shakan system to guarantee order was based on military despotism, which was as much the cause of upheaval as an answer to it, is echoed in the IFP's own mobilization of violent authoritarianism.[29]

As South Africans in post-apartheid times seek to modify political practices to take cognizance of popular beliefs and historical predispositions, and temper the hegemony of western institutions, the pressure to seek models and justifications in the precolonial past is likely to mount still further. In discussions about political culture appeals to the precolonial past will continue to abound, both as a source of authority or legitimization for proposals made today, and in the form of metaphors used to discuss contemporary conditions.[30] As I have argued, any attempt to reach back to find examples from the precolonial past must be qualified by a clear understanding of the many and varied processes by which such ideas have been transported into the present. The simplistic idea of a precolonial "democracy" that was distorted by colonialism misunderstands both precolonial political relations and the extent to which the colonial native administration modeled itself on precolonial ideas. It makes too radical a separation between the precolonial and the colonial.

The potency of the symbol of Shaka in South Africa today is neither the consequence of how great Shaka really was, as Kunene would have it, nor the result simply of clever political manipulations in the present by Zulu nationalists. It is a product of the historical association within it of indigenous conceptions of sovereignty and the practices of colonial domination. The vision of discipline that the journalist Barry Renfrew conjured up with his picture of "three thousand of them breathing together, sound[ing] like the purring of a giant cat" is an image with its roots in indigenous ideas, reinterpreted by Shepstone as the basis for native administration, reinforced by the Zulu victory at Isandlwana in 1879, popularized in the novels of Rider Haggard, rehearsed in the many texts of Stuart, nested at the heart of the ideologies of segregation and apartheid, activated in the service of Zulu nationalist politics, and explored again in different ways in Shaka Zulu and Shakaland. In the historically developed discourses on Shaka, the corollary of the image of discipline, in each of these instances, is violence and domination.

Thus while for Shepstone, Stuart, and indeed Haggard, Shaka could be drawn on as a model for the administration of the indigenous population, in the course of the twentieth century "Shaka" increasingly became a metaphor in South Africa: a way of asserting racist ideas, and of resisting them; a device for discussing barbarism and civilization; and a means of exploring issues of social order and violence. The extensive collusion of the apartheid government with the IFP in creating a climate of violence in the run-up to the first democratic election—increasingly revealed through the investigations of the Truth and Reconciliation Commission—was a product of this legacy, while, paradoxically, the idea of a shared Shakan heritage at the same time helped garner support because of its apparent capacity to ensure social order.

The death-bed prophecy of Shaka, usually interpreted as foretelling white dominance, is just as firmly entrenched as an element of contemporary "Zuluism" as the images of discipline and violence. It likewise demands historical explanation for its potency. The appropriation by Shepstone of the device of prophecy reveals that the incorporation of indigenous historical ideas was not simply an adoption of their content, but also involved an assumption of their form.

When, in a letter to the Johannesburg newspaper, *The Star,* a Dr. Ntlotleng claimed that Buthelezi will never rule, for "even Shaka Zulu said so before he died," he was not reproducing, in an unthinking fashion, the imperial fantasies of a nineteenth-century European traveler or administrator. His call on the Shakan past is an argument about the nature of history itself, and draws its form and content from the complex history of the image of Shaka.

Glossary

isiBhalo   enforced public labor service

ukuBonga   to declaim praises

imBongi (pl. *izimbongi*)   praise singer

isiBongo (pl. *iziBongo*)   1. clan name; 2. (pl. only) praises

ukuButha   to form young men or women into age grades

iButho (pl. *amaButho*)   age grade, with military and other functions (*liButfo:* variation, *siSwati*)

iDlozi (pl. *amaDlozi*)   spirit of a dead person

inDuna (pl. *iẓinDuna*)   civil or military official

isiGodlo (pl. *iẓiGodlo*)   1. king's or chief's private enclosure at the upper end of his homestead, where the huts of his household are situated; 2. women of the king's establishment; 3. women presented to the king as tribute or selected from the households of his subjects and, as his "daughters," disposable by him in marriage

ka   prefix indicating parentage, e.g. Ndlovu kaThimuni, Ndlovu, born of Thimuni

inKatha (pl. *iẓinKatha*)   woven grass coil containing potent body substances and symbolizing the unity of the nation

iKhanda (pl. *amaKhanda*)   major military establishment

iKohlo   the left-hand house of clan or family, which is excluded from producing the heir

iKholwa (pl. *amaKholwa*)   Christian; literally "a believer"

umKhosi (pl. *imiKhosi*)   the annual "first fruits" ceremony held at the Great Place of the king or the chief in the December–January period, a festival at which the king or chief is ritually strengthened, the ancestral spirits praised, and the allegiance of the people renewed

inKosi (pl. *amaKhosi*)   king; paramount chief

amaLala   collective appellation for the clans of the southern reaches of the Zulu kingdom, despised as outsiders *ukuLobola*   to formalize a marriage by the conveyance of cattle or other property from the man's family to the father or guardian of the woman

iLobolo (sing. only)   cattle or goods handed over in a marriage transaction by the man's family to the father or the guardian of the woman

iMpi (pl. *iziMpi*)   armed force

iNceku (pl. *iziNceku*)   attendant in the king's or chief's household responsible for the performance of certain domestic duties

ukuNgena   to impregnate the widow of a deceased brother

iNsila (pl. *iziNsila*)   body servant, charged with the task of disposing of the bodily wastes of the king

amaNtungwa   people of the up-country, collective appellation for the clans that constituted the elite core of the Zulu kingdom

iNyanga (pl. *iziNyanga*)   healer, herbalist, diviner

ukuSisa   to place livestock in the care of a dependant, who then has rights of usufruct

siSwati   the Swazi language

isiVivane (pl. *iziVivane*)   cairn of stones placed next to a path by travelers

umuZi (pl. *imiZi*)   1. homestead, collection of huts under one headman; 2. the people belonging to a homestead

isiZulu   the Zulu language

(Adapted from C. de B. Webb and J.B. Wright (eds.), *The James Stuart Archive of Recorded Oral Evidence Relating to the History of the Zulu and Neighbouring Peoples*, vol. 1, Pietermaritzburg and Durban, University of Natal Press and the Killie Campbell Africana Library, 1976, glossary)

Notes

Introduction

1. See G. Maré's discussion of the relationship between the Zulu king and Buthelezi, in *Brothers Born of Warrior Blood: Politics and Ethnicity in South Africa*, Johannesburg, Ravan, 1992, chap. 5, "The King and I"; and Mzala's discussion of Buthelezi's attempts to muzzle the Zulu king and to prevent him from allying himself with other significant political figures (*Gatsha Buthelezi: Chief with a Double Agenda*, London, Zed Books, 1988, esp. pp. 112–14).

2. For details of developments around the Shaka Day fracas see *The Citizen*, September 7, 1994; *New Nation*, September 9, 1994; *The Star*, September 8, 1994; *The Sowetan*, September 19, 1994; *The Star*, September 20, 1994; *New Nation*, September 23, 1994; *The Citizen*, September 26, 1994; *The Sowetan*, September 27, 1994; *The Star*, September 27, 1994.

3. *The Sowetan*, September 27, 1994.

4. See also *Sunday Independent*, March 17, 1996.

5. The focus on Shaka begins to illuminate the processes of establishment of other aspects of a contemporary Zulu identity which merit detailed consideration in their own right, notably the entrenchment in Zulu identity of particular notions of maleness, machismo, and patriarchal authority.

6. *Natal Witness Echo Supplement*, May 30, 1996.

7. M. Mamdani, *Citizen and Subject: Contemporary Africa and the Legacy of Late Colonialism*, David Philip and Princeton University Press, Cape Town and Princeton, 1996.

Chapter One

1. Interview with stallholders, Mai-Mai market, December 24, 1992.

2. *Vrye Weekblad*, October 2–15, 1992, p. 5.

3. Shaka Day speech, Ngoye, November 4, 1984.

4. M. Makhanya, "I'm a Zulu—and I'm proud of it," *Weekly Mail*, April 3–9, 1992. Also see K. Mkhize, "Viva Zulu positiveness," *Echo*, November 15, 1990; "The history of bloodlust that stains the conference table," *Financial Times* (London), January 9–10, 1993; see also *Weekly Mail*, October 1–7, 1993. Not all Zulu speakers, however, see Shaka as the ideal role model. See, for example, the letter to the editor from N. Gumede on Shaka as the cause of black disunity, *Injula*, 3, 1990.

5. L. du Buisson, *The White Man Cometh*, Johannesburg, Jonathan Ball, 1987. For Du Buisson's criticisms of the television series and debates with other experts on the period see *Style*, February 1987; *Leadership*, 5, 3, 1986 and 5, 6, 1986; *Sunday Times Magazine*, October 26, 1986.

6. C. Ballard, *The House of Shaka: The Zulu Monarchy Illustrated*, Durban, Emoyeni Books, 1988.

7. For a detailed discussion of the three texts see my published review article, "'An Appetite for the Past': The Re-creation of Shaka and the Crisis in Popular Historical Consciousness," *South African Historical Journal*, 22, 1990, pp. 141–57.

8. For a more detailed discussion of the literary and artistic representations of Shaka see my

Ph.D. dissertation, "Authoring Shaka: Models, Metaphors and Historiography," Johns Hopkins University, 1993, pp. 6–7.

9. *Natal Witness,* January 24, 1990. For accounts of white South Africans who don "traditional" Zulu garb and regard themselves as "white Zulus," see the *Guardian,* November 14, 1992; *Weekly Mail,* November 6–12, 1992; *Namibian,* September 6, 1991.

10. *New African,* October 1990, p. 46; Jean Boudin, pers. comm., April 21, 1991. For a South African example of the choice of the name of Shaka to connote super-powers—and there are many—see Soweto's super-student, Joseph "Shaka" Mphele, *Sunday Times,* January 10, 1993.

11. M. Gluckman, "The Individual in a Social Framework: The Rise of King Shaka of Zululand," *Journal of African Studies,* 1, 2, 1974, pp. 113–44. Gluckman also noted the existence of a Philadelphia gang called "the Zulu Nation."

12. Shaka Day speech, KwaMashu, September 27, 1992.

13. Shaka Day speech, King Zwelithini, Stanger, September 26, 1992.

14. *Weekly Mail,* November 6–12, 1992.

15. *Natal Mercury,* April 11, 1991. Also see *Natal Witness,* May 13, 1994, for a report on a *sangoma's* claim that the spirit of Shaka needed to be appeased if the violence were to be ended.

16. Speech, Ulundi, August 20, 1983.

17. *Weekly Mail,* May 10–16, 1991.

18. Quoted in "Percy's World," *The Star Tonight!* July 13, 1992. Also see Peregrine Worsthorne, "Could Fascism Solve South Africa's Race Problem," *Sunday Telegraph,* December 14, 1986.

19. See, for example, Peter Hawthorne's article in Time, October 12, 1992; Michael Massing, "The Chief," *New York Review of Books,* February 12, 1987.

20. *Independent on Sunday,* October 14, 1990, pp. 3–4.

21. *Independent on Sunday,* October 21, 1990.

22. *Natal Witness,* April 6, 1992.

23. *Injula,* 1, 1989, repr. in the *Natal Witness Echo* supplement, February 2, 1989.

24. *Injula,* 2, 1989, also see letter by Otto B. Kunene, *Echo,* February 16, 1989.

25. Letter from N. Gumede, *Injula,* 3, 1990.

26. *Echo,* September 13, 1990–April 4, 1991.

27. *Ilanga,* February 14–16, 1991.

28. C. de B. Webb and J.B. Wright (eds.), *The James Stuart Archive of Recorded Oral Evidence Relating to the History of the Zulu and Neighbouring Peoples,* Pietermaritzburg and Durban, University of Natal Press and Killie Campbell Africana Library, 1976–86, 4 vols., proceeding.

29. *Ilanga,* February 21–23, 1991.

30. Shaka Day speech, Stanger, September 21, 1991.

31. See Harries' discussion of Buthelezi's familiarity with the academic historiography and the pertinent sources, as well as his criticism of academic historians whose portrayal of Shaka differs from his own: P. Harries, "Imagery, Symbolism and Tradition in a South African Bantustan: Gatsha Buthelezi, Inkatha and Zulu History," unpublished paper, department of history, University of Cape Town, 1987, p. 4; see also D. Golan, "Inkatha and its Use of the Zulu Past," *History in Africa,* 18, 1991, pp. 113–26; and P. Forsyth, "The Past in Service of the Present: The Political Use of History by Chief A.N.M.G. Buthelezi, 1951–91," *South African Historical Journal,* 26, 1992, pp. 74–92. On the objections of Inkatha leaders and ideologues to historians whose view of Shaka they disagree with, see G.M. Buthelezi, "The Bias of Historical Analysis," opening address of the Anglo-Zulu War Centenary, University of Natal, Durban, February 7, 1979; Oscar Dhlomo, Shaka Day speech, Stanger, 1978; and S. Maphalala, "The Black Man's Interpretation of South African History," unpublished paper presented at the University of Stellenbosch, October 14, 1981, published as Series B, no. 36, University of Zululand, 1983.

32. *The Times Higher Education Supplement,* November 1, 1991; *Weekly Mail,* September 13–19, 1991; *Vrye Weekblad,* October 25–31, 1991; also see J. Omer-Cooper, "The Mfecane Defended," *Southern African Review of Books,* July–October 1991; N. Etherington, "Shrinking the Zulu," *Southern African Review of Books,* September–October 1992; *Guardian Weekly,* June 21, 1992, letter by Mike Nicol; *Guardian Weekly,* July 19, 1992, letter by Paul Johns; conference reports in *South African Historical Journal,* 25, 1991, pp. 154–76. The debate continued in the *Journal of African History:* see articles

by E. Eldredge, "Sources of Conflict in Southern Africa, c.1800–1830: The 'Mfecane' Reconsidered"; and C.A Hamilton, "'The Character and Objects of Chaka': A Reconsideration of the Making of Shaka as 'Mfecane' Motor," both in 33, 1992, pp. 1–36 and 37–63 respectively. Also see C.A. Hamilton (ed.), *The Mfecane Aftermath*, Johannesburg and Pietermaritzburg, Witwatersrand University Press and University of Natal Press, 1995.

33. John B. Wright, "The Dynamics of Power and Conflict in the Thukela–Mzimkhulu Region in the Late Eighteenth and Early Nineteenth Centuries: A Critical Reconstruction," unpublished Ph.D. thesis, University of the Witwatersrand, 1990, chaps. 4, 5, and 6. Also see his "Political Mythology and the Making of Natal's Mfecane," *Canadian Journal of African Studies*, 23, 1989, pp. 272–91.

34. J. Cobbing, "The Mfecane as Alibi: Thoughts on Dithakong and Mbolompo," *Journal of African History*, 29, 1988, pp. 487–519.

35. C. Saunders, "Pre-Cobbing Mfecane Historiography," in Hamilton (ed.), *The Mfecane Aftermath*. Also see Hamilton, "'The Character and Objects of Chaka'."

36. W. Worger, "Clothing Dry Bones: The Myth of Shaka," *Journal of African Studies*, 6, 3, 1979, pp. 144–58; J. Raum, "Historical Concepts and the Evolutionary Interpretation of the Emergence of States: The Case of the Zulu Reconsidered Yet Again," *Zeitschrift für Ethnologie*, 114, 1989, pp. 125–38; D. Wylie, "Who's Afraid of Shaka Zulu?" *Southern African Review of Books*, May–June 1991, pp. 8–9; M.Z. Malaba, "Shaka as Literary Theme," unpublished Ph.D. thesis, York University, 1986, pp. 358–67.

37. D. Golan, *Inventing Shaka: Using History in the Construction of Zulu Nationalism*, Boulder and London, Lynne Rienner, 1994.

38. The process of the professionalization of history in South Africa is a topic urgently in need of research. Christopher Saunders' study *The Making of the South African Past* (Cape Town, David Philip, 1988) offers some insight into the process, but the development of the discipline is not a central concern of the study. My understanding of the process is informed by analyses of the professionalization of the discipline in other contexts. See for example, J. Higham et al., *History: The Development of Historical Studies in the United States*, Princeton, Prentice-Hall, 1965; P. Novick, *That Noble Dream: The "Objectivity Question" and the American Historical Profession*, Cambridge, Cambridge University Press, 1988. The main works on South African historiography on which this section draws are Saunders, *The Making of the South African Past*; K. Smith, *The Changing Past: Trends in South African Historical Writing*, Johannesburg, Southern Book Publishers, 1988; S. Marks, "The Historiography of South Africa: Recent Developments," in B. Jewsiewicki and D. Newbury (eds.), *African Historiographies: What History for Which Africa?* London and New Delhi, Sage, 1986, pp. 165–76. Also H.M. Wright, *The Burden of the Present: Liberal–Radical Controversy over Southern African History*, Cape Town, David Philip, 1977; F.A. van Jaarsveld, *Omstrede Suid-Afrikaanse Verlede: Geskiedenisideologie en die Historiese Skuldvraagstuk*, Johannesburg and Cape Town, Struik, 1984; and his *The Afrikaner's Interpretation of South African History*, Cape Town, Simondium, 1964.

39. G.M. Theal, *History of South Africa from 1795–1828*, London, Allen & Unwin, 1903; *History of South Africa*, London, Allen & Unwin, 1900, 11 vols.; *The Republic of Natal*, Cape Town, Solomon, 1886; South Africa, London, Fischer & Unwin, 1894; G.E. Cory, *The Rise of South Africa*, London, Longmans, 1910–30, 5 vols.; E. Walker, *History of South Africa*, London, Longmans, 1928. A notable exception is G.W. Stow, *The Native Races of South Africa*, ed. for publ. by Theal after the author's death, first publ. London, Swann Sonneschein, 1905, repr. Cape Town, Struik, 1964. Saunders argues convincingly that the liberal historians W.M Macmillan (*Bantu, Boer and Briton*, London, Cambridge University Press, 1929) and his student C.W. de Kiewiet ("Government, Colonists, Missionaries, Natives on the North-Eastern Frontier and Beyond, 1832–46," unpublished M.A. thesis, University of the Witwatersrand, 1925; and *The Imperial Factor in South Africa: A Study in Politics and Economics*, London, Cambridge University Press, 1937) were rather different in their treatment of African societies and should be distinguished from the more racist settler historians (Saunders, *The Making of the South African Past*, part 2).

40. Saunders, "Pre-Cobbing Mfecane Historiography."

41. See for example R. Plant, *The Zulu in Three Tenses, Being a Forecast of the Zulu's Future in the Light of his Past and Present*, Pietermaritzburg, P. Davis & Sons, 1905; M.S. Evans, *Black and White in*

South Africa: A Study in Sociology, London, Longmans, Green & Co., 1911; and his *The Native Problem in Natal,* Durban, P. Davis & Sons, 1906.

42. N. Isaacs, *Travels and Adventures in Eastern Africa,* first publ. London, E. Churton, 1836, republ. Cape Town, Van Riebeeck Society for the Publication of South African Historical Documents, 1937, and Cape Town, Struik, 1970, ed. L. Herrman and P. Kirby; W.F.W. Owen, *Narrative of Voyages to Explore the Shores of Africa, Arabia and Madagascar,* London, Bentley, 1833, 2 vols.; G.F. Angas, *The Kafirs of Natal,* first publ. London, Hogarth, 1849, republ. Cape Town, A.A. Balkema, 1974; Rev. A. Gardiner, *Narrative of a Journey to the Zoolu Country,* first publ. London, W. Crofts, 1836, republ. Cape Town, Struik, 1966; F. Owen, *The Diary of the Rev. Francis Owen,* first publ. 1838, republ. Cape Town, Van Riebeeck Society, 1926; Rev. J. Shooter, *The Kafirs of Natal and the Zulu Country,* first publ. London, E. Stanford, 1857, repr. New York, Negro Universities Press, 1969; Rev. W.C. Holden, *The Past and Future of the Kaffir Races,* London, William Nichols, 1866, republ. Cape Town, Struik, 1963; Rev. J. Ayliff, "History of the Abambo," *Gazette,* Butterworth, 1912; J. Bird (ed.), *The Annals of Natal: 1495–1845,* vol. 1, Pietermaritzburg, P. Davis & Sons, 1888, repr. Cape Town, Struik, 1965; J.C. Chase (ed.), *The Natal Papers,* first publ. Grahamstown, Godlonton, 1883, republ. Cape Town, Struik, 1968. See also Saunders' discussion of Theal's use of African sources (Saunders, "Pre-Cobbing Mfecane Historiography").

43. For example, E.J. Krige, *The Social System of the Zulus,* first publ. London, Longmans, Green & Co., 1936, republ. Pietermaritzburg, Shuter & Shooter, 1950. It is interesting to note that a number of the first ethnographers came out of missionary backgrounds, notably H. Junod, author of *Life of a South African Tribe* (London, Macmillan, 1927, 2 vols.). Likewise, the Rev. A.T. Bryant, author of a number of highly influential works on Zulu history, began his investigations into Zulu history while a missionary in Natal, and later became one of the first researchers in the Bantu studies department at the University of the Witwatersrand.

44. A.T. Bryant, "A Sketch of the Origin and Early History of the Zulu People," in *A Zulu–English Dictionary,* Pietermaritzburg, P. Davis & Sons, 1905, preface; "The Origin of the Zulus," *Native Teachers' Journal,* 1, 1, 1919, pp. 9–16; a series of articles in *Izindaba Zabantu,* 1910–13, repr. in A.T. Bryant, *A History of the Zulu and Neighbouring Tribes,* Cape Town, Struik, 1964; *Olden Times in Zululand and Natal,* London, Longmans, 1929. For an excellent discussion of Bryant's contribution to Zulu historiography see J.B. Wright, "A.T. Bryant and the 'Wars of Shaka'," *History in Africa,* 18, 1991, pp. 409–25.

45. J.W. Fernandez, "The Shaka Complex," *Transition,* 29, 1967, pp. 11–14.

46. P. la Hausse, "Ethnicity and History in the Careers of Two Zulu Nationalists: Petros Lamula (c.1881–1948) and Lymon Maling (1889–c.1936)," PhD. thesis, University of the Witwatersrand, 1993.

47. Texts produced at this time include M.M. Fuze, *Abantu Abamnyama Lapa Bavela Ngakona,* Pietermaritzburg, 1922; P. Lamula, *UzulukaMalandela,* Durban, Native Church Press, 1924. Sifiso Ndlovu's current Ph.D. research into African constructions of Dingane Zulu, Shaka's successor, is beginning to shed further light on the history construction activities of black intellectuals at this time.

48. N.J. van Warmelo, *A History of Matiwane and the amaNgwane,* Ethnological Publications, Pretoria, Government Printer, 1938; see also his *Preliminary Survey of the Bantu Tribes of South Africa,* Ethnological Publications, Pretoria, Government Printer, 1935, pp. 70–71; "Shaka's Grave at Stanger," *African Studies,* 2, 1943, pp. 108–12. The African states that Omer-Cooper saw emerging from the mfecane were regarded by historians such as Van Jaarsveld as the precursors of the Bantustans (Saunders, *The Making of the South African Past,* p. 183). For Afrikaner historiography of African societies see F. van Jaarsveld, *From Van Riebeeck to Vorster, 1652–1974: An Introduction to the History of the Republic of South Africa,* Johannesburg, Perskor, 1975, chap. 7. Also see the discussion of the trajectory of this historiography in A.M. Grundlingh, "George Orwell's 'Nineteen Eighty-Four': Some Reflections on its Relevance to the Study of History in South Africa," *Kleio,* 16, 1984, pp. 20–33.

49. Gluckman, "The Individual in a Social Framework"; "The Kingdom of the Zulu in South Africa," in M. Fortes and E. Evans-Pritchard (eds.), *African Political Systems,* London, Oxford University Press, 1940, pp. 22–55; "Analysis of a Social System in Modern Zululand," part B, *Bantu Studies,*

14, 1940, pp. 147–74; M. Wilson, *Divine Kings and the "Breath of Men,"* Cambridge, Cambridge University Press, 1959, see esp. pp. 23–24; J.D. Omer-Cooper, *The Zulu Aftermath: A Nineteenth Century Revolution in Bantu Africa,* London, Longmans, Green & Co., 1966, repr. 1971.

50. E.V. Walters, *Terror and Resistance: A Study of Political Violence with Case Studies of Some Primitive African Communities,* New York, Oxford University Press, 1969.

51. M.G.B. Mothlabi, "The Theory and Practice of Black Resistance to Apartheid: A Social–Ethical Analysis of the Internal Struggle for Political and Social Change," unpublished Ph.D. thesis, Boston University, 1980, see esp. pp. 203–04; J. Ngubane, "Shaka's Social, Political and Military Ideas," in D. Burness (ed.), *Shaka, King of the Zulus in African Literature,* Washington, Three Continents Press, 1976, pp. 127–62. Although cast in the form of an epic poem, Mazisi Kunene's epic poem celebrating Shaka in precisely the same terms purports to be historically accurate (M. Kunene, *Emperor Shaka the Great: A Zulu Epic,* London, Heinemann, 1981).

52. For a detailed review of these explanations see Hamilton, "Authoring Shaka," pp. 36–38.

53. P.L. Bonner, *Kings, Commoners and Concessionaires: The Evolution and Dissolution of the Nineteenth-Century Swazi State,* Cambridge and Johannesburg, Cambridge University Press and Ravan, 1983, chap. 2. Also see E. A. Alpers, "State, Merchant Capital and Gender Relations in Southern Mozambique to the End of the Nineteenth Century: Some Tentative Hypotheses," *African Economic History,* 13, 1984, pp. 22–55; J.B. Wright and C.A. Hamilton, "Traditions and Transformations: The Phongolo–Mzimkhulu Region in the Late Eighteenth and Early Nineteenth Centuries," in A. Duminy and B. Guest (eds.), *Natal and Zululand: From Earliest Times to 1910: A New History,* Pietermaritzburg, University of Natal Press and Shuter & Shooter, 1989.

54. C.A. Hamilton, "Ideology, Oral Traditions and the Struggle for Power in the Early Zulu Kingdom," unpublished M.A. thesis, University of the Witwatersrand, 1986; C.A. Hamilton and J.B. Wright, "The Making of the *AmaLala:* Ethnicity, Ideology and Relations of Subordination in a Pre-colonial Context," *South African Historical Journal,* 22, 1990, pp. 3–23; J.B. Wright, "Politics, Ideology and the Invention of the 'Nguni'," in T. Lodge (ed.), *Resistance and Ideology in Settler Societies, Southern African Studies,* vol. 4, Johannesburg, Ravan, 1986, pp. 96–118; Wright, "A.T. Bryant and the 'Wars of Shaka'"; and his "The Dynamics of Power and Conflict," chaps. 2, 3.

55. Worger, "Dry Bones," pp. 144, 147. C.T. Msimang has also tackled the issue of the image of Shaka ("The Image of Shaka," in M. Macnamara (ed.), *World Views,* Pretoria, J.L. van Schaik, 1980, pp. 91–97). Like Worger, Msimang attributes the existence of contradictory images of Shaka to differences in the worldviews of the commentators, but does not repeat Worger's careful handling of the various texts. Msimang actually distinguishes three reasons why contradictory images exist: exaggeration (inadvertent or intentional); difference in attitude; and misjudgment of motives. Close reading of his argument reveals that differences in worldviews underlie exaggeration and misjudgment as much as attitude.

56. D. Golan's 1988 doctoral thesis was subsequently published under the title *Inventing Shaka: Using History in the Construction of Zulu Nationalism,* Boulder and London, Lynne Rienner, 1994.

57. A detailed list of literary treatments of Shaka is available in Hamilton, "Authoring Shaka," pp. 41–42, n. 112.

58. E.A. Ritter, *Shaka Zulu: The Rise of the Zulu Empire,* first publ. London, Longmans, 1955, re-publ. Harmondsworth, Penguin, 1978 and London, Viking, 1985; P. Becker, *Path of Blood,* London, Longmans, 1962; *Rule of Fear,* London, Longmans, 1964. Rider Haggard's accounts are discussed in detail in chapter 3; R. Campbell, "The Flaming Terrapin," in G. Butler (ed.), *A Book of South African Verse,* Cape Town, first publ. Oxford University Press, 1959, republ. 1963; F.T. Prince, "Chaka," in *Poems,* London, Faber & Faber, 1938, repr. in F.T. Prince, *The Doors of Stone: Poems 1938–1962,* London, Rupert Hart Davis, 1963; T. Mofolo, *Chaka,* Morija, Morija Sesuto Book Depot, 1925; J.L. Dube, *Insila kaTshaka,* Mariannhill, Mariannhill Missionary Press, 1932; H.I.E. Dhlomo, *Valley of a Thousand Hills,* Durban, Knox, 1941; R.R.R. Dhlomo, *UShaka,* Pietermaritzburg, Shuter & Shooter, 1936. Malaba describes as "pornographic" the accounts by Ritter, Fourie, McMenemy, and Schoeman ("Shaka as Literary Theme," p. 330).

59. See for example, H.I.E. Dhlomo's early deification of Shaka, *Valley of a Thousand Hills.* Note that Herbert Dhlomo also wrote a play, *Shaka,* the manuscript of which is lost. See also B.W. Vilakazi's poems "UShaka kaSenzangakhona" and "Phezu kwethuna LikaShaka" (Grave of Shaka), first publ. in

Inkondlo kaZulu, 1935; E. Zondi, *Ukufa kukaShaka,* Johannesburg, Witwatersrand University Press, 1960; Kunene, *Emperor Shaka;* O. Mtshali, "The Birth of Shaka," in *Sounds of a Cowhide Drum,* New York, Third Press, 1972. For a discussion of the reinvigoration of the Zulu past during the inter-war years, see S. Marks, *The Ambiguities of Dependence in South Africa,* Johannesburg and Baltimore, Ravan and Johns Hopkins University Press, 1986; and N. Cope, *To Bind the Nation: Solomon kaDinuzulu and Zulu Nationalism,* Pietermaritzburg, University of Natal Press, 1993.

60. A. Ridehalgh, "Some Recent Francophone Versions of the Shaka Story," *Research in African Literatures,* 22, 2, Summer 1991, pp. 135–52, quotes pp. 142, 149.

61. See, for example, D. Blair, "The Shaka Theme in Dramatic Literature in French in West Africa," *African Studies,* 33, 3, 1974, pp. 113–41; E. Modum, "Le Mythe de Chaka," *Ethiopiques,* 14, 1978, pp. 49–58; I. N'Diaye, "Théâtre et Société en Afrique Noire 'Francophone'," Ph.D. thesis, Université Cheikh Anta Diop, Dakar, 1979; D. Kunene, "Introduction," in T. Mofolo, *Chaka,* London, Ibadan, and Nairobi, Heinemann, 1987; A. Gérard, "Relire Chaka," *Politique Africaine,* 13, 1984, pp. 8–20; J.M. Spronk, "The Shaka Theme in the Francophone Theatre of West Africa," Ph.D. thesis, University of Oregon, 1983; G. Midiohouan, "Le Théâtre Négro-Africain d'Expression francaise," *Peuples Noires/Peuples Africains,* 31, 1983, pp. 54–78; J.M. Spronk, "Chaka and the Problem of Power in the French Theatre of Black Africa," *The French Review,* 57, 5, 1984, pp. 634–40; D.P. Kunene, "Shaka in the Literature of Southern Africa" in Burness (ed.), *Shaka, King of the Zulus in African Literature,* pp. 165–92; R.E. McDowell, "The Brief Search for an African Hero: The Chaka–Mzilikazi Story in the South African Novel," *Discourse,* 11, 1968; S. Gray, "Shaka as Literary Theme," *South African Journal of African Affairs,* 5, 1, 1975, pp. 66–70; B.V. Street, *The Savage in Literature: Representations of Primitive Society in English Fiction, 1858–1920,* London, Routledge & Kegan Paul, 1975; K. Ogunbesan, "A King for all Seasons: Chaka in African Literature," *Presence Africaine,* 88, 1973, pp. 197–217.

62. Burness (ed.), Shaka, *King of the Zulus in African Literature.*

63. Malaba, "Shaka as Literary Theme," p. 427.

64. *Ibid.*

65. J. Sévry, *Chaka Empereur des Zoulous: Histoire, Mythes et Légendes,* Paris, Editions l'Harmattan, 1991, p. 10. I am grateful to Jae Maingard for assistance in reading this text.

66. Wylie, "Who's Afraid of Shaka Zulu?"; "Autobiography as Alibi: History and Projection in Nathaniel Isaacs's Travels and Adventures in Eastern Africa (1836)," *Current Writing,* 3, 1991, pp. 71–90; "Textual Incest: Nathaniel Isaacs and the Development of the Shaka Myth," *History in Africa,* 19, 1992, pp. 411–33; "White Writers and Shaka Zulu," unpublished Ph.D. thesis, Rhodes University, 1995.

67. Novick, *That Noble Dream;* Saunders, *The Making of the South African Past,* see p. 2 in particular.

68. See, for example, B. Bozzoli and P. Delius, "Radical History and South African Society," introductory essay to J. Brown et al. (eds.), *History from South Africa: Alternative Visions and Practices,* Philadelphia, Temple University Press, 1991, in which the authors locate the roots of radical history in, among other origins, the writings of Sol T. Plaatje and S. Modiri Molema on Tswana history. Also see the criticisms of this essay which argue that the particular lineage for radical history claimed by Bozzoli and Delius is narrowly selective and highly exclusive. (See, in particular, W. Worger, "White Radical History in South Africa," and C. Saunders, "Radical History—the Wits Workshop Version—Reviewed," in the special "Perspectives" section on radical history, *South African Historical Journal,* 24, May 1991, pp. 145–53 and 160–65 respectively.)

69. Such a position ultimately underlies E. Hobsbawm and T. Ranger (eds.), *The Invention of Tradition,* Cambridge, Cambridge University Press, 1983, as well as much recent work on Inkatha's use of Zulu history; see note 31 above.

70. J.B. Wright, "Review," *South Africa International,* 19, 2, 1988, pp. 105–08, at p. 106.

71. For other early studies of images and perceptions of Africa see D. Hammond and A. Jablow, *The Africa That Never Was: Four Centuries of British Writing about Africa,* New York, Twayne, 1970; C. Allen (ed.), *Tales of the Dark Continent: Images of British Colonial Africa in the Twentieth Century,* London, Deutsch, 1979; M. van Wyk Smith, "The Origins of Some Victorian Images of Africa," *English in*

Africa, 6, 1, 1979, pp. 12–32. Also see the more literary discussion in E. Mphahlele, *The African Image,* London, Faber, 1962.

72. P.D. Curtin, *The Image of Africa: British Ideas and Action, 1780–1850,* Madison, University of Wisconsin Press, 1964, p. 479.

73. *Ibid.*

74. E. Said, *Orientalism,* New York, Pantheon Books, 1978.

75. R. Martin, "British Images of the Zulu, c.1820–1879," unpublished Ph.D. thesis, University of Cambridge, 1982, p. 16.

76. *Ibid.* It should be noted that Martin is sensitive to the extent to which a representer depends upon available cultural resources in constructing images.

77. Golan, *Inventing Shaka,* p. 5.

78. The key texts giving shape to this position are, of course, Hayden V. White's publications, *Metahistory,* Baltimore, Johns Hopkins University Press, 1973; *Tropics of Discourse,* Baltimore, Johns Hopkins University Press, 1978; and "The Question of Narrative in Contemporary Historical Theory," *History and Theory,* 23, 1, 1984, pp. 1–33; D. La Capra, *Rethinking Intellectual History: Texts, Contexts, Language,* New York, Ithaca, 1983; P. Ricoeur, *Time and Narrative,* Chicago, Chicago University Press, 1982. Also see D. Carroll, *The Subject in Question: The Languages of Theory and the Strategies of Fiction,* Chicago and London, Chicago University Press, 1982, esp. chaps. 5, 6.

79. The 1990 University of the Witwatersrand history workshop included a large number of "literary" contributions but little dialogue occurred between the historians and the literary scholars. For a discussion of this see the exchange of views on the conference by David Attwell and Isabel Hofmeyr in the journal *Pretexts,* 1990, 1991. See also the work of historians such as A. Ashforth, *The Politics of Official Discourse in Twentieth-Century South Africa,* Oxford, Clarendon Press, 1990; and C. Crais, *The Making of the Colonial Order: White Supremacy and Black Resistance in the Eastern Cape, 1770–1865,* Johannesburg, Witwatersrand University Press, 1992, on the relationship between texts, discourse, and power. In the study of representations of Shaka, the lead has been taken by the novelist Stephen Gray. See his "South African Fiction and a Case History Revisited: An Account of Research into Retellings of the John Ross Story of Early Natal," *Research in African Literatures,* 19, 4, 1988, pp. 455–76 and his novel, John Ross, *The True Story: A Novel,* Johannesburg, Penguin, 1987. Also see my discussion of Gray's project, "'An Appetite for the Past'"; and D. Golan, "Construction and Reconstruction of Zulu History," unpublished Ph.D. thesis, Hebrew University of Jerusalem, 1988, p. 5. Also see K. Barber and P.F. Moraes Farias (eds.), *Discourse and its Disguises: The Interpretation of African Oral Texts,* Birmingham, Birmingham University, 1989; and I. Hofmeyr, *We Spend our Years as a Tale That is Told: Oral Historical Narrative in a South African Chiefdom,* Johannesburg, Witwatersrand University Press, 1993, introduction.

80. White, *Metahistory; Tropics of Discourse; Content of Form,* Baltimore, Johns Hopkins University Press, 1987.

81. The use of the term "historiography" in this study intentionally plays into and seeks to explore the ambiguity in its common usage as both a historicized body of historical works and historical writing about such a body of historical works.

82. M. de Certeau, *The Writing of History,* New York, Columbia University Press, 1991. De Certeau interprets historical practice as a function of humankind's feelings of mourning, absence, and loss. I would add here the more commonplace feelings of nostalgia and the need for identity.

83. B. Anderson, *Imagined Communities: Reflections on the Origin and Spread of Nationalism,* London, Verso, 1983; L. Vail (ed.), *The Creation of Tribalism in Southern Africa,* London, James Currey, 1989; N. Thomas, "The Inversion of Tradition," *American Ethnologist,* 19, 2, 1992, pp. 213–32.

84. J.M. Philibert, "The Politics of Tradition: Towards a Generic Culture in Vanuatu," *Mankind,* 16, 1, 1986, pp. 1–12; Vail, *The Creation of Tribalism;* E. Hall, *Inventing the Barbarian: Greek Self-Definition through Tragedy,* Oxford, Clarendon Press, 1989; R. Keesing, "Creating the Past: Custom and Identity in the Contemporary Pacific," *The Contemporary Pacific,* 1, 1989, pp. 19–42; A. Hanson, "The Making of the Maori: Cultural Invention and its Logic," *American Anthropologist,* 91, 1990, pp. 890–902. See also an ancillary literature on the construction of custom, which includes among others, M. Chanock, *Custom and Social Order,* Cambridge, Cambridge University Press, 1987; S. Falk

Moore, *Social Facts and Fabrications: "Customary" Law on Kilimanjaro, 1880–1980*, Cambridge, Cambridge University Press, 1986.

85. Hobsbawm and Ranger (eds.), *The Invention of Tradition*, p. 4.

86. M. Foucault, *Power/Knowledge: Selected Interviews and Other Writings, 1972–1977*, ed. C. Gordon, New York, Pantheon Books, 1980, see esp. "Lecture One, 7 January, 1976," p. 81.

87. For a sophisticated discussion of the role of myths in history see R. Samuel and P. Thompson, "Introduction," in R. Samuel and P. Thompson, *The Myths We Live By*, London, Routledge, 1990, pp. 1–22.

88. See, for example, J. Clifford and G.E. Marcus, *Writing Culture: The Poetics and Politics of Ethnography*, Berkeley, Los Angeles, and London, University of California Press, 1986; J. Fabian, *Time and the Other: How Anthropology Makes its Object*, New York, Columbia University Press, 1983; H.L. Gates, Jr. (ed.), *"Race," Writing and Difference*, Chicago, Chicago University Press, 1986; H. Bhabha, *The Location of Culture*, London and New York, Routledge, 1994.

89. Said, *Orientalism*, p. 6.

90. Included here are the contributions to the special edition of *American Ethnologist* on the anthropology of colonialism which, on the whole, treat the category "colonizers" cautiously, but which are framed within the perspective of the colonizers defining and imposing culture on the colonized (*American Ethnologist*, 16, 4, 1989).

91. See, for example, D. Porter, "Orientalism and its Problems," in F. Barker et al. (eds.), *The Politics of Theory*, Colchester, University of Essex, 1983, p. 182.

92. The phrasing here is, of course, a play on Gayatri Chakravorty Spivak's article, "Can the Subaltern Speak," in C. Nelson and L. Grossberg (eds.), *Marxism and the Interpretation of Culture*, Urbana, University of Illinois Press, 1988, pp. 271–313.

93. J. Scott, *Domination and the Art of Resistance*, New Haven, Yale University Press, 1990.

94. In other words I question the usefulness of the concept of "a people without a history," and seek to raise questions about the notion of academic historians "giving" them a history. E. Wolf, *Europe and a People without a History*, Berkeley, University of California Press, 1982.

95. This understanding of hegemony draws on E. Laclau, *Politics and Ideology in Marxist Theory*, London, Verso, 1977.

96. I join Nicholas Thomas here in seeking to go beyond Bhabha's and Spivak's exclusion of the possibility of indigenous representations and agendas. Where Bhabha is concerned with the way in which denied knowledges enter the dominant discourse and estrange the basis of its authority, this study examines the way in which other knowledges were invited into the dominant discourse to constitute a basis of its authority (H. Bhabha, "Signs Taken for Wonders," *Critical Inquiry* I, 12, 1, 1985, p. 156). In contrast to Thomas, who only begins to explore the dichotomy of indigenous representations and their existence independent of colonialism, I probe the still more revisionist possibility that indigenous representations gave shape and content to colonial ones (N. Thomas, *Colonialism's Culture: Anthropology, Travel and Government*, Cambridge, Polity Press, 1994).

97. G. Prakash (ed.), *After Colonialism: Imperial Histories and Postcolonial Displacements*, Princeton, Princeton University Press, 1995, p. 6.

98. V. Mudimbe, *The Invention of Africa: Gnosis, Philosophy and the Order of Knowledge*, Bloomington and Indianapolis, Indiana University Press, 1988.

99. Thus where Mudimbe draws our attention to the extent to which "the explorers' text is not epistemologically inventive. Its follows a path prescribed by tradition," he refers to the eighteenth and nineteenth centuries' tradition of representations in the West. I would emphasize that the explorers' text also follows a path indicated by an indigenous "tradition."

100. For a discussion of this project see C. Miller, *Theories of Africans: Francophone Literature and Anthropology in Africa*, Chicago and London, Chicago University Press, 1990, introduction.

101. Studies that focus on such processes of colonial inscription include J. Comaroff and J. Comaroff, *Of Revelation and Revolution: Christianity, Colonialism and Consciousness in South Africa*, Chicago, Chicago University Press, 1991, esp. chap. 3; and C. Miller, *Blank Darkness: Africanist Discourse in French*, Chicago, Chicago University Press, 1985.

102. Miller, *Theories of Africans*, p. 296.

103. Golan, *Inventing Shaka*, pp. 35–50; J.Cobbing, "A Tainted Well: The Objectives, Historical

Fantasies and Working Methods of James Stuart, with Counter-Argument," *Journal of Natal and Zulu History,* 11, 1988, pp. 115–54.

104. See, for example, J.S.M Matsebula, *A History of Swaziland,* Cape Town, first publ. Penguin, 1972; Longman, 1988, p. 160. In suggesting that the idea of "cannibalism" has roots in African thought I question the perspective current that cannibalism was "an invention" of the West as the quintessential symbol of savagery (Comaroff and Comaroff, *Of Revelation and Revolution,* p. 123). I am not, however, suggesting that anthropophagy was common in early nineteenth-century Natal. I am arguing that the idea of *buzimuzimu* was current, and that it was counterposed to the idea of social order. My suggestion, then, is that the idea of cannibalism that appears in the writings of the colonizers has its origins as an idea in indigenous discourse.

105. The reference here is to the ethnophilosophy of the Belgian missionary Tempels, heralded by an earlier generation of Négritude scholars as the recovery of an indigenous Bantu philosophy, which Mudimbe critiques as but a more sophisticated and efficient means of civilizing and controlling Africans (Mudimbe, *Invention of Africa,* p. 138).

106. A. Apter, "Que Faire? Reconsidering Inventions of Africa," *Critical Inquiry,* 19, 1992, p. 97.

107. G. Dening, *Islands and Beaches: Discovering a Silent Land: Marquesas, 1774–1880,* Honolulu, University of Hawaii Press, 1980, p. 43.

108. G. Maré and G. Hamilton, *An Appetite for Power: Buthelezi's Inkatha and South Africa,* Johannesburg and Indianapolis, Ravan and Indiana University Press, 1987, p. 57; S. Marks, "Patriotism, Patriarchy and Purity: Natal and the Politics of Zulu Ethnic Consciousness," in Vail (ed.), *The Creation of Tribalism,* chap. 7.

109. In insisting on the naming of the "traditions" as histories and in referring to their canons, using the same language employed for their "western" counterparts, I am influenced by an exciting new body of literature on the nature of intellectual work within Africa, including most notably, D. W. Cohen and E.S. Atieno Odhiambo, Siaya: *The Historical Anthropology of an African Landscape,* London, James Currey, 1989; K.A. Appiah, "Out of Africa: Typologies of Nativism," *Yale Journal of Criticism,* 2, 1988, pp. 153–78; Miller, *Theories of Africans;* Mudimbe, *Invention of Africa.*

110. One exception here is the work of Daphna Golan which includes an analysis of the television series as an ideological text.

111. Such ideas are advanced persistently by Julian Cobbing and the supporters of his attack on the *mfecane.* See video of the 1991 Mfecane Aftermath Colloquium, "Natal Session," particularly the exchange between Alan Webster, Tim Stapleton, and Carolyn Hamilton.

112. My discussion of metaphor owes a great deal to stimulating discussions with JoAnne Brown, and draws heavily on the introduction to her study *The Definition of a Profession: The Authority of Metaphor in the History of Intelligence Testing, 1890–1930,* Princeton, Princeton University Press, 1992.

113. A. Ortony, "Why Metaphors are Necessary and Not Just Nice," *Educational Theory,* 25, 1, 1975, pp. 45–53.

114. M. Black, "More about Metaphor," *Dialectica,* 31, 3–4, 1977, pp. 431–57.

115. Brown, *The Definition of a Profession,* pp. 13–14.

116. E. Onuki-Tiernay, "Embedding and Transforming Polytropes: The Monkey as Self in Japanese Culture," in Fernandez (ed.), *Beyond Metaphor,* pp. 159–89.

117. Here I follow Onuki-Tiernay who points out that the monkey in Japanese culture is not ipso facto a metaphor, but becomes a particular kind of trope under particular circumstances in a particular context (Onuki-Tiernay, "Embedding and Transforming Polytropes").

118. Brown, *The Definition of a Profession,* p. 14.

119. N. Quinn, "The Cultural Basis of Metaphor," in Fernandez (ed.), *Beyond Metaphor,* pp. 56–93.

120. G. Lakoff and M. Johnson, *Metaphors We Live By,* Chicago, Chicago University Press, 1980.

121. Kunene, *Emperor Shaka,* pp. 176–77, also see p. 190.

122. For a thoughtful discussion of the necessity of continuing to work with the knowledge protocols of academic history, while recognizing the significance of antihistorical constructions of the past see D. Chakrabarty, "Postcoloniality and the Artifice of History: Who Speaks for 'Indian' Pasts?", *Representations,* 37, Winter 1992, pp. 1–23; A. Nandy, "History's Forgotten Doubles," *History and Theory,* 34, May 1995, pp. 44–66.

123. Dan Wylie's doctoral thesis, "White Writers and Shaka Zulu," offers such a genealogy of prominent published texts on Shaka.

Chapter Two

1. H.F. Fynn, *The Diary of Henry Francis Fynn,* ed. J. Stuart and D.M. Malcolm, Pietermaritzburg, Shuter & Shooter, 1950, see chaps. 1 and 2, and esp. p. 42. For background on Fynn's *Diary* see pp. 37–44, 143–4, 177–8.

2. See Fynn, *Diary,* pp. 51–53, p. 56, n. 1; J. King to the secretary for colonies, the earl of Bathurst, July 10, 1824, Cape Archives Depot (C.A.D.), Government House Archives (G.H.) 1/39, pp. 45–58; J. King, in *South African Commercial Advertiser,* July 11, 1826; for details of Farewell's engagement of King see Cape Archives, Notarial Protocols, Cape Districts (N.C.D.) 35/8, pp. 534–41. Owen's journal was edited and published as *Narrative of Voyages to Explore the Shores of Africa, Arabia and Madagascar,* London, Bentley, 1833, 2 vols. However, the publication also includes material drawn from other sources, is heavily edited, and cannot be treated as an accurate reflection of Owen's views in 1822. An account of Shaka, attributed to Farewell writing in 1825, is reproduced in Owen's text and must be treated with the same caution. It is most unlikely, for example, that Farewell would have referred to Shaka as "the king of Natal, and of the Hollontontes." One of Owen's officers, T. Boteler, also published an account of Owen's trip in 1835 (*Narrative of a Voyage of Discovery to Africa and Arabia, Performed in His Majesty's Ships Leven and Barracouta,* London, Bentley, 1835, 2 vols.). For some idea of what Owen's contemporary opinion of Shaka and the Zulu was like, see John Philip's report to acting colonial secretary, P.G. Brink, April 13, 1824 (Public Record Office [P.R.O.], Archives of the Colonial Office [C.O.] 48/62), believed to be based on Owen's information (see governor of the Cape, Lord Charles Somerset, to Bathurst, April 22, 1824 [G.H. 23/7, pp. 144–45]), in which Philip comments optimistically on the prospects for trade with the interior.

3. The precise nature of this setback in commercial terms is difficult to assess. The venture was well insured and substantial claims were made. Unfortunately, the extent of the final settlement is not known. In his letter to Somerset, May 1, 1824, Farewell noted that the earlier expedition "sustained a most considerable loss" (C.A.D., C.O. 211, pp. 222–25). However, it is clear that for his next expedition Farewell was obliged to seek other financial backing. See N.C.D. 35/9, pp. 67–75, 117–26, 144–49, 573–78, 585–89.

4. Farewell to Somerset, May 1, 1824 (C.O. 211, pp. 222–25; N.C.D. 35/9, pp. 573–78, 585–89). It is not clear from Farewell's letter who precisely "the natives" are, i.e. whether he means the Zulu authorities or the inhabitants of the bay area; for continued reports of Shaka's "friendly disposition" arriving at the Cape in this period see W.H. Lys, officer of health, to P.G. Brink, April 12, 1824 (P.R.O., C.O. 48/62).

5. Farewell to Somerset, September 6, 1824 (C.O. 211, pp. 650–51, 656–57).

6. Isaacs, *Travels and Adventures,* pp. 18, 22, 31; Fynn, *Diary,* pp. 110, 117.

7. For a detailed criticism of Julian Cobbing's claim that the Port Natal traders were slavers, and that all evidence of this aspect of their activities has been systematically excised from their accounts of this period, see Hamilton, "'The Character and Objects of Chaka'," pp. 42–53.

8. Lt. E. Hawes to C.R. Moorsam, commodore of the British fleet at the Cape, May 16, 1825 (C.O. 233, pp. 245–46). For the published report see the *Cape Town Gazette and African Advertiser,* June 4, 1825. Hawes' report was passed on to the Cape governor, Somerset (C.O. 233, p. 244). Note also, for example, that when Farewell's backers, Hoffman and Peterssen, lost contact with him as a result of the wreck of the *Julia* in late September 1824, they were dilatory in contacting the authorities, and once they did, expressed no alarm on behalf of the party at Port Natal. J. Hoffman and J.S. Peterssen to Moorsam, March 9, 1825 (C.O. 233, pp. 103–04). The authors of this letter comment that they returned from Natal because "the country and natives were different from what was told them." In the *Diary,* Fynn indicates that Peterssen was disappointed to find that Shaka's residence was not built out of ivory, and that (being corpulent and temperamental) he was not fitted for the rigors of Shaka's kingdom (chap. 5). Also see Moorsam's comments about their dilatoriness: Moorsam to Hoffman and Peterssen, March 17, 1825, encl. (N.C.D. 25/11, pp. 765–83).

9. Hawes to Moorsam, May 16, 1825 (C.O. 233, pp. 245–46). For the published report see the *Cape Town Gazette and African Advertiser,* June 4, 1825.

10. Isaacs, *Travels and Adventures*, pp. 15, 22, 24, 42, 52, 53, 71; also see King's comments, *South African Commercial Advertiser*, July 11, 1826; Farewell to Somerset, September 6, 1824 (C.O. 211, pp. 650–51); also see correspondence between the commander of the *Helicon* and the Cape administration regarding the first Zulu visitor to the Cape (C.O. 270, pp. 202–04).

11. Hoffman and Peterssen to Moorsam, March 9, 1825 (C.O. 233, pp. 103–04).

12. Hawes, *Cape Town Gazette*, June 4, 1825.

13. Hoffman and Peterssen to Moorsam, March 9, 1825 (C.O. 233, pp. 103–04); N.C.D. 35/11, pp. 765–83 and enclosures, 35/9, pp. 573–78.

14. King to Bathurst, July 10, 1824 (G.H. 1/39, pp. 45–58); Farewell to the editor, *South African Commercial Advertiser*, January 31, 1829.

15. Nonetheless, King's expedition was not heavily capitalized, and drew on credit as well as special concessions from the authorities. King to Somerset, August 9, 1825 (C.O. 3929, pp. 136–39); also the response from the colonial authorities, Sir Richard Plasket, chief secretary to the government, to King, August 12, 1825 (C.O. 4853, pp. 393, 409; also see C.O. 3929, pp. 184–85; 243, pp. 147–52; 235, pp. 511–12; 4853, p. 453; 293, pp. 1323–26).

16. King to Somerset, August 9, 1825 (C.O. 3929, pp. 136–39); W. Wilberforce Bird, comptroller customs, to Plasket, August 20, 1825 (C.O. 243, pp. 150–52).

17. Isaacs, *Travels and Adventures*, pp. 13, 18.

18. *Ibid.*, pp. 25, 60; also see Farewell's comments in the *South African Commercial Advertiser*, January 31, 1829; King to Bathurst, July 10, 1824 (G.H. 1/39, pp. 45–58). In fact, the building of a boat at Port Natal had been on King's agenda from the first, and to that end, he had taken with him to Port Natal the necessary tools and a shipwright.

19. Isaacs, *Travels and Adventures*, pp. 60, 64, 66.

20. *Cape Town Gazette and African Advertiser*, January 6, 1826.

21. A section of King's party, under Norton, the mate of the *Mary*, gave up the ship-building exercise, and in defiance of King, departed for the Cape in the wrecked ship's longboat. Those who remained behind began to find it impossible to obtain food or porters without invoking Shaka's name as a threat. Things became particularly severe in the period immediately prior to the traders' crops being ready for harvest. Isaacs, *Travels and Adventures*, pp. 27–28, 38, 41, 42, 47, 57, 64, 67–70; *Cape Town Gazette and African Advertiser*, January 6, 1826, and April 28, 1826; report of the mate of the late brig *Mary*, J.E. Norton, to Plasket, January 19, 1826 (C.O. 293, pp. 97–100).

22. Cobbing argues that the traders promoted a negative image of Shaka at the Cape in order to encourage British intervention in Natal in the form of colonization. His argument that two stereotypes—"depopulated Natal" and "Shaka-the-monster"—were designed to encourage settlement and British involvement in Natal is in itself not convincing. Both stereotypes can be seen as disincentives for colonization. A good or better case can be made to the effect that the very opposite stereotype—a stable and orderly Zulu society under the firm hand of a powerful king on the borders of the proposed colony and the existence of a plentiful supply of labor, preferably rendered docile by the conquering Zulu (especially in the face of the turbulent Cape frontier and that colony's labor problems)—would have constituted a significantly more powerful inducement to the British authorities. However, even had the traders wished to encourage settlement, they could not have argued that labor was plentiful, for it was not. Although he generalizes their source and timing, the images to which Cobbing refers arise out of this and a subsequent visit by King to the Cape.

23. Norton to Plasket, January 19, 1826 (C.O. 293, pp. 97–100); *Cape Town Gazette and African Advertiser*, April 28, 1826.

24. See the requests of C.H. Wehdemann, November 8, 1824 (C.O. 2659, pp. 693–94), granted November 9, 1824 (C.O. 2659, pp. 691–92, 695); see also C.O. 4851, p. 487; C.A.D., Archives of the Magistrate of Uitenhage (U.I.T.) 15/9, p. 247; and James Whitworth and Samuel Broadbent, March 4, 1825 (C.O. 230, pp. 375–78); and the response (C.O. 4852, p. 488), for permission to proceed to Natal.

25. *Cape Town Gazette and African Advertiser*, January 6 and April 28, 1826.

26. *South African Commercial Advertiser*, June 6, 1826.

27. In May, King attempted to negotiate the purchase of a schooner on a two-thirds mortgage. Pointing out that his finances were precarious, King sought colonial aid with the financing by stress-

ing that his object was to assist his wrecked crew or, failing aid, he requested the use of a government vessel. King was not allowed to bring ivory with him on the *Helicon* from Port Natal, despite Mrs. Farewell's request to the governor to allow an exception (King to Plasket, June 2, 1826, C.O. 293, pp. 619–22; Elizabeth Farewell to Somerset, December 27, 1825, C.O. 235, pp. 946–49). Among other things, King also heard at this time of the failure of another of his schemes (see G.H. 23/7, p. 401, concerning his lease on the Bird and Chaun islands). Note that the ordnance storekeeper at the Cape was pressing his backer Collison for debt settlement, while Collison himself was petitioning the lieutenant-governor of the Cape for relief (see C.O. 293, p. 1319; 219, pp. 1317–18).

28. C.A.D., C.O. 293/138.

29. *South African Commercial Advertiser,* June 11, 1826; note that this is the same description which is ascribed to Farewell in Bird (ed.), *Annals of Natal,* p. 93, and which was quoted in G. Thompson, *Travels and Adventures in Southern Africa,* vol. 1, London, H. Colburn, 1827, 2nd ed., Cape Town, Van Riebeeck Society, 1967, pp. 174–75.

30. On July 22, 1826 King, with the backing of one William Hollett, hired from John Thompson (Farewell's agent in the Cape) the *Anne,* and on the same day appointed Thompson his agent as well (N.C.D. 25/14, pp. 145–55, 156–59; 25/11, pp. 765–83).

31. B. Roberts, *The Zulu Kings,* London, Hamish Hamilton, 1974, p. 98.

32. Application by George Rennie and response (C.O. 293, pp. 911–12; 4895, pp. 60–61).

33. King to "T.," presumably Thompson, May 1827, published in the *Colonist,* January 3, 1828.

34. Isaacs, for example, was able to resume the collection of curiosities, an endeavor he had been obliged for some time to forgo because of the lack of trade goods (see *Travels and Adventures,* pp. 70–71).

35. Roberts, *The Zulu Kings,* pp. 99, 103–04. Roberts suggests that King wanted to take over Farewell's grant of land from Shaka, but cites no evidence for this. Note that Cobbing's treatment of the split is confined to a discussion of divisions on the eve of Shaka's assassination ("Grasping the Nettle: The Slave Trade and the Early Zulu," paper presented to the workshop on Natal and Zululand in the colonial and precolonial periods, University of Natal, Pietermaritzburg, 1990, p. 28).

36. Isaacs, *Travels and Adventures,* pp. 75–76.

37. Also see the report in the *South African Commercial Advertiser,* December 27, 1828.

38. See note 30 above.

39. J.K. Mallory, "Abnormal Waves on the South East Coast of South Africa," *International Hydrographic Review,* 51, 2, 1974, pp. 99–129. According to Ian Hunter of the Cape Town meteorological office freak waves occur in two places in the world, one of which is between Durban and Port Elizabeth. The waves are the result of a combination of three factors: low pressure systems causing stormy conditions; large waves emanating from the "Roaring Forties" near the Antarctic; and the south-flowing Agulhas current, added to the fact that the narrow Continental Shelf allows ships to sail very close to the continent (*Fifty/Fifty,* SABC TV, January 17, 1993).

40. King faced an added problem when his shipwright downed tools. For evidence of continued problems of supply, see the journey of "John Ross" to Delagoa Bay, and the traders' bartering for supplies with the *Buckbay Packet* (Isaacs, *Travels and Adventures,* pp. 101, 102, 117).

41. See John Cane's deposition, November 10, 1828, in which he asserts that Shaka "wished government to procure him a road that his people might come along with their sticks in their hands without assegaay or any other weapon to see the white people" and that Shaka said "he would send no more ivory by sea but would collect some and send them to Faka's kraal [en route to the Cape] . . . and deliver them to an officer who should be sent down and from whom he would expect a present in return . . ." (G.H. 19/3, pp. 388–415).

42. By this time, moreover, Fynn's family had set up base in Grahamstown.

43. Cobbing, "The Mfecane as Alibi," p. 509; "Grasping the Nettle," pp. 26–27.

44. Wright, "The Dynamics of Power and Conflict," p. 358.

45. See G.H. 19/3, pp. 473–75, 376–84.

46. See, for example, Fynn, *Diary,* p. 131.

47. Isaacs, *Travels and Adventures,* p. 71; King to "T.," presumably Thompson, May 27, 1827, published in the *South African Commercial Advertiser,* January 3, 1828.

48. King to "T.," presumably Thompson, published in the *South African Commercial Advertiser,* January 3, 1828.

49. King to J. van der Riet, civil commissioner, Uitenhage, May 10, 1828 (G.H. 19/3, pp. 30–33).

50. Richard Bourke to Lord Viscount Goderich, October 15, 1827 (G.H. 23/8, pp. 298–304).

51. By May 9, King had been in contact with military officials in Port Elizabeth from whom he would have learnt of this policy (see Commandant F. Evatt to Lieutenant-Colonel Somerset, May 9, 1828, G.H. 19/3, pp. 35–36).

52. See the discussion in Roberts, *The Zulu Kings,* pp. 129–36.

53. King to Van der Riet, May 10, 1828; see also the emphases on haste, and in particular on the urgency of the return of one of the chiefs in King's anxious communication to Van der Riet, May 24, 1828 (G.H. 19/3, pp. 39–42); Fynn, *Diary,* pp. 141, 153. Fynn subsequently made the same use of the hostage argument.

54. See C.O. 4888, p. 217; 4893, p. 249; 4895, pp. 312–13; D.P. Francis, port captain, to the acting secretary to government, Lieutenant-Colonel Bell, May 9, 1828 and May 23, 1828 (C.O. 359, pp. 191–92, 198–99); Evatt to Lieutenant-Colonel Somerset, May 9, 1828 (G.H. 19/3, pp. 35–36); *Colonist,* May, June 1828.

55. King to Bourke, June 6, 1828 (G.H. 19/3, pp. 48–53); King to Van der Riet, June 6, 1828 (G.H. 19/3, pp. 66–69); Van der Riet to Bell, June 7, 1828 (U.I.T. 15/12, pp. 45–47).

56. C.O. 4322, pp. 151–52. Nonetheless Bell took sufficient cognizance of the threat to have the possibility of registration carefully checked out for a loophole (see G.H. 19/3, p. 54).

57. Bell to Cloete, June 14, 1828 (C.O. 4893, pp. 255–357).

58. Minutes of the Cape Council of Advice, June 21, 1828 (A.C. 2, pp. 453–60); Major Dundas to Bourke, June 20, 1828 (G.H. 19/3, pp. 88–89).

59. See Somerset to Dundas, June 15, 1828 (C.A.D., Archives of the Magistrate of Albany [A.Y.] 8/79, pp. 193–96, 189–99); Rev. W.J. Shrewsbury to Somerset, June 12, 1828, Somerset to Bell, June 20, 1828 (G.H. 19/3, pp. 85–87); Dundas to Bourke, June 20, 1828 (G.H. 19/3, pp. 88–91); and deliberations of the Council of Advice in Cape Town, June 21, 1828 (G.H. 19/3, pp. 92–95); Bell to Dundas, June 21, 1828 (C.O. 4888, pp. 270–71); Cloete to Bell, June 27, 1828 (G.H. 19/3, pp. 96–103). Also see P.R.O., C.O. 48/124; G.H. 19/3, pp. 92–95; C.O. 4888, pp. 274–75.

60. Cloete to Bell, July 11, 1828 (G.H. 19/3, pp. 159–66). The colonial authorities were extremely suspicious of King and his motives in bringing the chiefs to the colony. They were also alert to the contradictions and shifts in the account of things that he promoted. See Van der Riet to Bell, June 7, 1828 (U.I.T. 15/12, pp. 45–47).

61. *Colonist,* May–July 1828.

62. King to Cloete, July 4, 1828 (G.H. 19/3, pp. 125–26); Cloete to King, July 4, 1828 (G.H. 19/3, pp. 126–27); Cloete to Bell, July 4, 1828 (G.H. 19/3, pp. 115–24); Cloete to King, July 5, 1828 (G.H. 19/3, pp. 167–68); King to Cloete, July 5, 1828 (G.H. 19/3, pp. 169–72); Cloete to King, July 10, 1828 (G.H. 19/3, pp. 174–77); Bell to King, July 11, 1828 (C.O. 4895, p. 336); Cloete to Bell, July 11, 1828 (G.H. 19/3, pp. 159–66); King to Cloete, presumably July 18, 1828 (G.H. 19/3, pp. 212–15); Cloete to King, July 18, 1828 (G.H. 19/3, p. 216); Frances to Bell, July 25, 1828 (G.H. 19/3, pp. 248–63); Cloete to Bell, July 29, 1828 (G.H. 19/3, pp. 258–63); King to Cloete, July 29, 1828 (G.H. 19/3, pp. 264–71); Cloete to Bell, July 18, 1828 (G.H. 19/3, pp. 198–203); Cloete to King, July 30, 1828 (G.H. 19/3, pp. 272–73); King to Cloete, July 30, 1828 (G.H. 19/3, pp. 274–81); also see C.O. 4894, pp. 18–19; G.H. 19/3, pp. 178–81; C.O. 4893, pp. 265–67, 291–92.

63. King to Cloete, July 11, 1828 (G.H. 19/3, pp. 178–81); King to Van der Riet, July 13, 1828 (G.H. 19/3, pp. 206–09).

64. *Colonist,* August 26, 1828.

65. *Ibid.*, August 19, 1828.

66. *Ibid.*

67. Thus it is clear that this reading of government documents and press reports of the period is very different from that of Roberts (*The Zulu Kings,* chaps. 2–6), whose account of wholesale panic at the Cape in response to scares about an invasion by Shaka is the root of Julian Cobbing's mistaken periodization of the image of Shaka. See note 22 above.

68. Isaacs, *Travels and Adventures*, p. 133; *South African Commercial Advertiser*, December 31, 1829.

69. Report of Sir Lowry Cole (G.H. 23/9, pp. 39–47).

70. *South African Commercial Advertiser*, November 15, 1828.

71. Cobbing, "The Mfecane as Alibi," pp. 512–13; "Grasping the Nettle," pp. 28–29.

72. See Farewell to Bell, February 19, 1829 (G.H. 19/3, pp. 579–80); Farewell to the chairman, Committee of the Commercial Exchange, Cape Town, March 3, 1829 (P.R.O., C.O. 48/133); S. Bannister to Bell, March 28, 1829 (C.O. 3941, pp. 403–04), and a host of other applications by Bannister. Note also the changed tenor of Farewell's communication to J. Barrow, of March 15, 1829 (P.R.O., C.O. 48/13).

73. Bell to Benjamin Green, August 22, 1828 (C.O. 4895, p. 350); Green to Bell, August 11, 1828 (C.O. 3937, pp. 323–24); Farewell to Bell, December 4, 1828 (C.O. 357, pp. 400–01).

74. *South African Commercial Advertiser*, December 27, 1828, January 31, 1829; Farewell's report (G.H. 23/9, pp. 39–47); G.H. 1/15, p. 665.

75. For a more detailed discussion of these political developments see Wright and Hamilton, "Traditions and Transformations."

76. Hamilton, "Ideology, Oral Traditions and the Struggle for Power," chaps. 4, 6, and 7.

77 See Fynn's comments on the condition of the royal house and the assassination of Shaka, *Diary*, pp. 156–57.

78. Hamilton, "Ideology, Oral Traditions and the Struggle for Power," chap. 5.

79. C. de B. Webb and J.B. Wright (eds.), *The James Stuart Archive of Recorded Oral Evidence Relating to the History of the Zulu and Neighbouring Peoples* (hereafter *JSA*), Pietermaritzburg and Durban, University of Natal Press and Killie Campbell Africana Library (KCAL), 4 vols., vol. 1, p. 118, Dinya.

80. Hamilton and Wright, "The Making of the *AmaLala*."

81. King to "T.," presumably Thompson, May 2, 1827, in the *Colonist*, January 3, 1828.

82. *JSA*, vol. 3, p. 15, Mbokodo.

83. See, for example, *JSA*, vol. 3, Mcotoyi, notably his narration of the story about Shaka directing people to sharpen their spears on the forehead of one Lucunge; even the testimony of Melapi, son of a *Lala* Shakan loyalist, Magaye, depicts Shaka in such terms. For the Qwabe view see the extensive discussion below of the testimony of Baleka (*JSA*, vol. 2, p. 232, Maquza; vol. 3, pp. 55–56, 65–67, Mcotoyi).

84. Fynn, *Diary*, pp. 60, 65–66, 130; Isaacs, *Travels and Adventures*, pp. 18, 19, 24–26, 32, 37, 41, 63, 67, 70, 78, 83, 89–90, 140.

85. Golan, *Inventing Shaka*, chap. 5; and her "The Life Story of King Shaka and Gender Tensions in the Zulu State," *History in Africa*, 17, 1990, pp. 95–111. In his Ph.D. thesis, on "Shaka as a Literary Theme," Malaba looks at the treatment of Shaka in praise poetry but not in historical narratives.

86. Golan, *Inventing Shaka*, p. 118.

87. Golan, "Gender Tensions," p. 95. Also see *Inventing Shaka*.

88. Golan, *Inventing Shaka*, pp. 120, 9.

89. H. Scheub, *The Xhosa Ntsomi*, Oxford, Oxford University Press, 1975.

90. Golan's work on the capacity of the life story of Shaka to reveal gender tensions in the Zulu state is challenging, but remains speculative in its current form because she has divorced the metaphorical from the historiographical. Golan needs, moreover, to take account of Hofmeyr's crucial points about differences in male and female storytelling, royal and commoner (Hofmeyr, "We Spend our Years").

91. For a discussion of the connection between myth in personal narrative and public tradition see Samuel and Thompson, *The Myths We Live By*, "Introduction," esp. p. 15.

92. To suggest, as I do here, that there may have been a dynamic form of history production in the nineteenth-century Zulu kingdom is not, however, to insist that it took the form of the particular mode of investigation and reconstruction that is typical in much of the modern world today. Indeed, as, for instance, the coming discussion of prophecy will make clear, the indigenous form of history production seems to have involved an entanglement of past, present, and future that is precisely the opposite of what modern history seeks to be.

93. This view of Zulu oral tradition is spelt out at length by Cobbing in a review of the *James Stuart Archive,* entitled "A Tainted Well. The Objectives, Historical Fantasies and Working Methods of James Stuart, with Counter-Argument," *Journal of Natal and Zulu History,* 11, 1988, pp. 115–54.

94. There has been a great deal of work done on how best to render oral narratives into written form. The performative aspects of oral narration are a crucial component of the text, as are pauses and tones. The oral narratives collected by James Stuart were recorded around the turn of the century and this kind of information was not included in his transcriptions. Its absence needs, however, to be noted. For a discussion of the kinds of meanings and information conveyed by these sorts of details see R. Bauman, *Story, Performance and Event: Contextual Studies of Oral Narrative,* Cambridge, Cambridge University Press, 1986; D. Tedlock, *The Spoken Word and the Work of Interpretation,* Philadelphia, University of Pennsylvania Press, 1983; D.W. Cohen, *Towards a Reconstructed Past: Historical Texts from Busoga, Uganda,* London, British Academy and Oxford University Press, 1986, introduction.

95. P.D. Curtin, "Field Techniques for Collecting and Processing Oral Data," *Journal of African History,* 9, 3, 1968, pp. 367–85; and his "Oral Tradition and African History," *Journal of the Folklore Institute,* 6, 1969, pp. 137–55; J. Vansina, *Oral Tradition: A Study in Historical Methodology,* Chicago, Aldine, 1965; and his *Oral Tradition as History,* Madison, University of Wisconsin Press, 1985; P. Thompson, *The Voice of the Past: Oral History,* Oxford, Oxford University Press, 1978; J. Miller (ed.), *The African Past Speaks: Essays on Oral Tradition and History,* Folkestone, Wm. Dawson & Sons, 1980; D. Henige, *Oral Historiography,* London, Longman, 1982. Also see D.W. Cohen, "The Undefining of Oral Tradition," *Ethnohistory,* 31, 1, 1989, pp. 9–17.

96. Close literary analysis of the collected transcriptions by James Stuart of oral traditions is a task that awaits sustained scholarly attention and would in all likelihood offer some qualification of these generalizations.

97. See Ruth Finnegan's *Oral Literature in Africa,* Oxford, Clarendon Press, 1970; her "A Note on Oral Tradition and Historiographical Evidence," *History and Theory,* 9, 2, 1971, pp. 195–201; her *Oral Poetry: Its Nature, Significance and Social Content,* Cambridge, Cambridge University Press, 1977; and her *Literacy and Orality: Studies in the Technology of Communication,* Oxford and New York, Basil Blackwell, 1988.

98. Hofmeyr, "We Spend our Years," p. 5.

99. Cobbing, "A Tainted Well," p. 150.

100. *Ibid.*

101. Hamilton, "Ideology, Oral Traditions and the Struggle for Power," chap. 3.

102. It is worth noting that Stuart recorded a wide selection of opinions on Shaka, ranging from the adulatory to the derogatory.

103. I. Hofmeyr, "'Wailing for Purity'—Oral Studies in Southern African Studies," paper presented to the *Journal of Southern African Studies* Twentieth Anniversary Conference, York University, September 1994, p. 12.

104. The focus here on the impact of political events is a product of the as yet limited information about black South African society in this period. To date, hardly any work has been done on, for instance, the traditions of storytelling that prevailed in the early nineteenth century. Such information, itself the object of an independent research project, would bring further nuances to the kind of discussion attempted here.

105. *JSA,* vol. 2, p. 247, Mayinga.

106. *Ibid.,* pp. 19, 22, 27, Mabonsa, pp. 70–71, Mageza, pp. 80, 93, Magidigidi, pp. 191–92, Mandhlakazi, p. 236, Maquza, pp. 250–51, 254, Mayinga, pp. 272, 279, 293, Maziyana, vol. 1, p. 6, Baleka, vol. 4, p. 218, Ndhlovu; Bryant, *Olden Times,* pp. 200, 391, 412, 413, 414, 494, 520, 632, 665, 667, 668–69; also see *JSA,* vol. 2, p. 111, Mahaya; Bryant, *Olden Times,* p. 107.

107. *JSA,* vol. 4, pp. 218, 219, Ndhlovu.

108. D. Rycroft and A. Ngcobo (eds.), *The Praises of Dingana,* Durban and Pietermaritzburg, KCAL and the University of Natal Press, 1988, p. 41. Note that this line does not occur in any of the other (later) versions reviewed in the book.

109. *JSA,* vol. 1, p. 6, Baleka; Rycroft and Ngcobo (eds.), *Praises,* pp. 97–98, 130. Also see the dis-

cussion of the denunciation of Shaka in versions of Dingane's praises in Malaba, "Shaka as Literary Theme," pp. 6–12.

110. Rycroft and Ngcobo (eds.), *Praises*, p. 17, and see lines 281–82 of Stuart's version of Dingane's praises and the discussion thereof on p. 171; Fynn, *Diary*, p. 157; Bryant, *Olden Times*, p. 667. It is interesting to note in this context Rycroft and Ngcobo's observation that eulogies concerning the "eating up" of enemies were a key element in the praises of the Zulu royalty (*Praises*, p. 29).

111. Bryant, *Olden Times*, pp. 398–99.

112. *JSA*, vol. 1, p. 243, Khumalo.

113. Report of the landdrost of Tugela, October 1839 (Bird [ed.], *Annals of Natal*, pp. 540–41), see also pp. 574–75, extract from A. Delegorgue's *Travels in Southern Africa*, trans. F. Webb, Pietermaritzburg and Durban, University of Natal Press and KCAL, 1990, vol. 1, chap. 13, copy of the Volksraad Proclamation issued by Pretorious on February 14, 1840; p. 376. Narrative by Daniel Pieter Bezuidenhout, published in *Orange Free State Monthly Magazine*, December 1879.

114. *JSA*, vol. 1, p. 196, Jantshi; Bryant, *Olden Times*, pp.43, 679; Adam Kuper raises the possibility that Mpande belonged to the left-hand (*ikhohlwa*) section of Senzangakhona's great house (A. Kuper, "The House and Zulu Political Structure in the Nineteenth Century," *Journal of African History*, 34, 1993, pp. 469–87). The *ikhohlwa* section was conventionally excluded from the succession and this may explain Mpande's survival.

115. R.C.A. Samuelson, *Long, Long Ago*, Durban, Knox, 1929, p. 216.

116. Rycroft and Ngcobo (eds.), *Praises*, p. 7. It is tempting to interpret the lines "Vezi, though people may die [their] eulogies will survive; These will remain and bring grief to them [*zibadabula*]; Remain and lament for them in the empty homes" of Dingane's eulogies which are ascribed to Magolwane, as a wry comment, through a play on the word *dabula*, on the capacity of eulogies to "cut" or "divide" both those who remember, and those who are remembered, by the poet who was both the author of the laudations in Dingane's time, and their refurbisher subsequently under Mpande.

117. *Ibid.*, pp. 39, 42, 99, 103–08, 139–40, 175, 227.

118. Bryant, *Olden Times*, p. 679; *JSA*, vol. 3, p. 243, Mmemi; *JSA*, vol. 2, pp. 204–05, Mangati. Kuper suggests that Gqugqu was born of a wife of Senzangakhona from the eGazini collateral of the Zulu, who probably constituted the "*unawekhohla* house" ("younger brother" house of the left-hand side) of Senzangakhona (Kuper, "The House"). The connections between his house and Senzangakhona's sister, Mawa, merit closer examination, and may throw light on the connection between Gqugqu's death and Mawa's flight.

119. Bryant, *Olden Times*, p. 44.

120. See the discussion in Rycroft and Ngcobo (eds.), *Praises*, p. 120; Mpande's testimony to the Volksraad in Pietermaritzburg, October 15, 1839 (Bird [ed.], *Annals of Natal*, p. 537).

121. Extract from Delegorgue's *Travels in Southern Africa*, chap. 13 (Bird [ed.], *Annals of Natal*, p. 553).

122. A footnote attributed to information supplied by Prof. L. Nyembezi, to E.H. Brookes and C. de B. Webb, *A History of Natal*, Pietermaritzburg, University of Natal Press, 1967, p. 94, notes: "Monase, Mbulazi's mother, had been one of Shaka's 'sisters'. When she became pregnant Shaka passed her on to his brother Mpande." See also KCAL, Stuart Papers (S.P.), file 9, item 51, p. 2, Socwatsha (March 29, 1914).

123. J. Guy, *The Destruction of the Zulu Kingdom*, London, Longmans, 1979, p. 13, notes that Mbuyazi was born in early 1830s.

124. Samuelson, *Long, Long Ago*, p. 218.

125. See "The Autobiography of Cetywayo" in Samuelson, *Long, Long Ago*, pp. 213–18.

126. Samuelson, *Long, Long, Ago*, pp. 220–21.

127. Guy, *Destruction of the Zulu Kingdom*, pp. 71, 72, 77.

128. For a detailed discussion of the Mandlakazi genealogy see Hamilton, "Ideology, Oral Traditions and the Struggle for Power," pp. 219–24.

129. Fuze, *The Black People and Whence they Came*, p. 177, editor's note 1; T. Cope, *Izibongo, Zulu Praise Poems*, Oxford, Oxford University Press, 1968, p. 200; Bryant, *Olden Times*, pp. 44–45.

130. See Bryant, *Dictionary*, p. 593; and his *The Zulu People: As They Were before the White Man Came*, Pietermaritzburg, Shuter & Shooter, 2nd ed., 1967, p. 519.

131. *JSA,* vol. 1, p. 96, Dinya, p. 307, Lunguza, vol. 4, p. 200, Ndhlovu; also see vol. 3, p. 206, Mkebeni.

132. *Ibid.*, vol. 4, pp. 198, 202, 203, 214, 215, 216, 222, 224, 227, 232, Ndhlovu. The story that Nandi was said to be dead and the birth of Shaka was concealed from Senzangakhona seems to be completely contradicted in another interview which appears in the published archive as Ndlovu's testimony, in which it is claimed that Nandi was *lobola*'d, married Senzangakhona, and went to live with him in the Zulu kingdom, leaving Shaka behind in the Langeni chiefdom (see p. 215). These claims are utterly at odds with the rest of Ndlovu's testimony, and do not accord with Ndlovu's argument as rehearsed by Stuart in the notes of his discussion with Ndukwana, which make it clear that both Stuart and Ndukwana understood Ndlovu to be claiming that Nandi and Senzangakhona never married (see p. 206). It is possible that the "marriage" version is an interpolation in the testimony of Ndlovu, of the testimony of another informant altogether.

133. *Ibid.*, pp. 198, 204, 205, 228, 229, Ndhlovu.

134. *Ibid.*, p. 219, Ndhlovu.

135. *Ibid.*, pp. 199, 232, Ndhlovu.

136. *Ibid.*, p. 39, Mruyi.

137. *Ibid.*, p. 217, Ndhlovu.

138. *Ibid.*, p. 206, Ndhlovu.

139. See, for example, *ibid.*, p. 39, Mruyi, and compare with pp. 211, 213, 224, 230, Ndhlovu.

140. *Ibid.*, pp. 36, 37, Mruyi; and p. 198, Ndhlovu.

141. *Ibid.*, p. 39, Mruyi.

142. *Ibid.*, pp. 200, 212, Ndhlovu. For Ndlovu's interest in Mbuyazi as the heir of Shaka, see his remarks on p. 198.

143. *Ibid.*, pp. 206, 207, Ndhlovu.

144. S. Marks, *Reluctant Rebellion: The 1906–8 Disturbances in Natal,* Oxford, Clarendon Press, 1970, pp. 228, 239.

145. *Ibid.*, pp. 229, 313, 315, 357. For her discussion of the role of Dinuzulu see chap. 10. The uSuthu were originally the supporters of Cetshwayo, and the name continued to be applied to the supporters of his descendants.

146. *JSA,* vol. 1, p. 188, Jantshi.

147. *Ibid.*, p. 177, Jantshi.

148. See Stuart's note, *ibid.*, vol. 4, p. 206, Ndhlovu.

149. *Ibid.*, vol. 1, pp. 178, 179, 188, 189, 191, 199, 200, Jantshi. On p. 179 Jantshi notes that illegitimate children were frequently referred to as "*itshaka.*"

150. *Ibid.*, pp. 181, 182, 199, Jantshi.

151. *Ibid.*, p. 187, Jantshi.

152. *Ibid.*, pp. 195, 196, 197, 201–02, Jantshi.

153. *Ibid.*, pp. 174, 180, Jantshi.

154. *Ibid.*, p. 175, Jantshi. Also see p. 180.

155. *Ibid.*, pp. 174, 175, 192, 193, 196, 197, 198, 200, Jantshi.

156. *Ibid.*, 174, 175, 176, 187, 189, 190, 197, 199, 201, Jantshi; *ibid.*, vol. 4, p. 206, Ndhlovu.

157. *Ibid.*, vol. 1, p. 5: Baleka noted that her account of Shaka's birth and accession was derived from her father. Note that on p. 4 Baleka observed that she heard most of her tales from Sixaba, her grandmother, called also Makokela, i.e. daughter of Kokela, brother of Mbengi, the Langeni chief. Her story is thus dominated by two orientations, the Langeni view of Shaka, and her status as a Qwabe.

158. *Ibid.*, p. 5, Baleka.

159. *Ibid.*, pp. 4, 6, 7, 8, Baleka.

160. *Ibid.*, pp. 4, 8, 10, Baleka.

161. *Ibid.*, pp. 7, 8, 9, 10, 11, 12, Baleka.

162. *Ibid.*, p. 12, Baleka.

163. *Ibid.*, p. 8, Baleka.

164. *Ibid.*

165. *Ibid.*, p. 188, Jantshi; *ibid.*, vol. 4, pp. 198, 214, 222, 232, Ndhlovu.

166. *Ibid.*, vol. 4, p. 232, Ndhlovu.

167. *Ibid.*, p. 232, Ndhlovu.

168. *Ibid.*, vol. 1, p. 178, Jantshi; *ibid.*, vol. 4, pp. 198, 202, 214, 221, Ndhlovu.

169. Oral productions were not confined to the inhabitants of the area between the Zulu king-dom and the Cape Colony, but prevailed on all the borders of the Zulu kingdom, and in the regions beyond those borders. Exploration of all those views of Shaka is a huge task, well beyond the scope of this study. This section focuses on the border region south of the Zulu kingdom because develop-ments in that area were germane to the creation of Cape opinion regarding Shaka.

170. See Cape Archives, Zululand Province (Z.P.) 1/1/33 and 1/1/36; C.O. 234, pp. 270–71, 672–87, 691; 233, pp. 400–05; 287, pp. 204–18, 224–25, 285–303; 333, pp. 18–21, 39; 2692, pp. 923–40; 48887, pp. 341–44.

171. W.M. Mackay to the chief secretary of government, August 8, 1827 (C.O. 2693, pp 783–94).

172. Minutes of the Council of Advice, August 23, 1827 (A.C. 2, pp. 55–59).

173. Somerset to Bourke, August 31, 1827 (C.O. 2693, pp. 833–35).

174. C.O. 2693, pp. 837–46.

175. "Some Account of Mr. Farewell's settlement at Port Natal, and of a visit to Chaka, King of the Zoolas" (from an anonymous article in the *South African Commercial Advertiser,* July 18, 1826), in Thompson, *Travels and Adventures,* p. 248. The argument developed in this section of chapter 2 about the existence of webs of ideas about Shaka criss-crossing between colonial and indigenous societies on the frontier complements Martin Legassick's view of the frontier as characterized by similar webs of social and economic relations, constituting a single interwoven social entity (M. Legassick, "The Frontier Tradition in South African Historiography", in S. Marks and A. Atmore (eds.), *Economy and Society in Pre-Industrial South Africa,* London, Longman, 1980, pp. 44–79).

176. See, for example, the lieutenant-governor of the Cape, General Richard Bourke, to Lord Vis-count Goderich, October 15, 1827 (G.H. 23/8, pp. 298–304).

177. Cobbing, "The Mfecane as Alibi," p. 509.

178. For critiques of the web of conspiracy posited by Cobbing, see essays by Eldredge and Peires, and the contextualizing essay by Wright in Hamilton (ed.), *The Mfecane Aftermath.*

179. Malaba, "Shaka as Literary Theme," part 1 and chap. 3.

180. See, for example, the speech by King Zwelithini, given at the launch of C. Ballard's book *The House of Shaka,* December 9, 1988, in which the king attributed the invention of the image of Shaka as a bloodthirsty tyrant to A.T. Bryant.

Chapter Three

1. In Somerset Maugham, *Maugham's Choice of Kipling's Best,* New York, Doubleday & Co., 1953, pp. 162–92, this quotation p. 169.

2. Wylie, "White Writers and Shaka Zulu," esp. chap. 2.

3. British Parliamentary Papers (BPP), Colonies, Africa 30, Natal, facsimile reproductions pro-duced by Irish University Press, Shannon, 1971, c.1137, "Statement by Zulu messengers Sidindi and Komesiwebu, June 9th, 1873," pp. 24–25.

4. BPP, c.1137, "Report of the Expedition Sent to Install Cetshwayo as King of the Zulus," p. 11.

5. T. Ranger, *Dance and Society in Eastern Africa, 1890–1970: The Beni Ngoma,* Berkeley and Los Angeles, University of California Press, 1975, pp. 166–67; T. Ranger, "The Invention of Tradition in Colonial Africa," in E. Hobsbawm and T. Ranger (eds.), *The Invention of Tradition,* Cambridge, Cam-bridge University Press, 1983, pp. 211–62; Jean Comaroff and John Comaroff, *Ethnography and the Historical Imagination,* Boulder, San Francisco, and Oxford, Westview Press, 1992, p. 4; D. James, "'I Dress in this Fashion': Transformations in Sotho Dress and Women's Lives in a Sekhukhuneland Vil-lage, South Africa," in H. Hendrickson (ed.), *Clothing and Difference: Embodied Identities in Colonial and Post-Colonial Africa,* Durham, NC, Duke University Press, 1996; H. Hendrickson, "Historical Idioms of Identity Representation among the OvoHerero in Southern Africa," unpublished Ph.D. thesis, New York University, 1992.

6. Comaroff and Comaroff, *Of Revelation and Revolution,* p. 4.

7. See, for example, D.M. Anderson and D.H. Johnson (eds.), *The Predictable Past: Prophets and Prophecy in Eastern Africa,* London, James Currey, 1994.

8. C. Ballard, *John Dunn: The Great White Chief of Zululand,* Johannesburg, Ad Donker, 1985, p. 100.

9. BPP, c.1137, "Statement by Zulu messengers 'Umrabalala, Gwaisa and Hlabemcitsha', on 26 February, 1873," statement signed by W. Harding (chief justice), D. Erskine (colonial secretary), J. Ayliff (treasurer), M.H. Gallwey (H.M.'s attorney-general), and T. Shepstone (secretary for native affairs), p. 22.

10. BPP, c.1137, "Statement of Zulu messengers Sidindi and Komesiwebu, June 9th, 1873," pp. 24–25. The question arises as to whether this document is an accurate reflection of the Zulu envoys' orally delivered message. In the discussion below of Zulu rulers' rationales, I marshal the evidence that leads me to think that it is. In addition it should be noted that the written statement was translated by W.D. Wheelwright, and attested to by the resident magistrate, J. Bird, and bears the "marks" of the two messengers. See also "Message from Cetshwayo and Mpande," December 27, 1870 (Natal Archives Depot, Secretary for Native Affairs Papers [SNA] 1/7/6, p. 138) in which the Zulu rulers stated that they looked to the government as "protectors of the house of Chaka"; see also "Message from Cetshwayo," February 29, 1876, in which Cetshwayo represented himself as "a child of the Natal Government, having been placed by it at the head of the Zulu nation" (SNA 1/7/6, p. 244). The reading and interpretation of the texts of the messengers poses complex problems: the very notion of "messenger" is imprecise. We know very little about the way that these messengers were briefed at the royal Zulu end, nor do we know by whom they were briefed. It seems that they were envoys (Stuart's informant Socwatsha used the term *amanxusa,* the modern sense of which is members of a commission of inquiry: KCAL, Stuart Papers [S.P.] file 9, item 51, p. 4), i.e. representatives who could be cross-questioned after delivering their messages and who could draw on their own understandings of the situations in hand to further explicate matters. Likewise, the circumstances of the delivery of the message, its reception and transcription are not known. Close examination of the language of the messages and their various contexts, which would go some way to answering these kinds of questions, merits a study in its own right.

11. "Report of the Expedition", p. 7. The account of the installation rendered here is as seen through Shepstone's eyes and is drawn from his official report. In order to achieve a critical perspective on his version of events I have also used accounts published in the Natal press (see, for example, the *Natal Mercury,* September 4, September 9, and September 11, 1873; *Natal Colonist,* September 23, 1873; *Natal Witness,* September 23, 1873; *Times of Natal,* September 23, 1873) as well as John Dunn's account in D.F.C. Moodie, *The History of the Battles and Adventures of the British, the Boers and the Zulus in Southern Africa from the Time of Pharoah Necho to 1880,* vol. 2, Cape Town, Murray & St. Leger, 1888, pp. 476-77; and S.P. file 9, item 51, testimony of Socwatsha.

12. The major exception is C.T. Binns' well-researched but unannotated early work, *The Last Zulu King: The Life and Death of Cetshwayo,* London, Longmans, 1963, which contains a detailed description of the installation, but offers little analysis.

13. J. Guy, *The Heretic: A Study of the Life of John William Colenso, 1814–1883,* Johannesburg and Pietermaritzburg, Ravan and University of Natal Press, 1983, p. 223.

14. "Report of the Expedition," p. 9.

15. R.L. Cope, "Shepstone and Cetshwayo, 1873–1879," unpublished M.A. thesis, University of Natal, 1967, p. 57.

16. For an account of this ceremony see Binns, The Last Zulu King, pp. 62–63.

17. "Report of the Expedition," pp. 10–11.

18. *Ibid.,* p. 11.

19. *Ibid.,* p. 12.

20. See, for example, S.P. file 9, item 51, p. 34, for Socwatsha's discussion of Shaka's foresight, as well as the references to Shaka's death-bed prophecies in chapter 2 above.

21. For Cetshwayo's version see C. de B. Webb and J.B. Wright, *A Zulu King Speaks: Statements Made by Cetshwayo kaMpande on the History and Customs of his People,* Pietermaritzburg and Durban, University of Natal Press and KCAL, 1978, p. 18.

22. "Report of the Expedition," pp. 14–15. Shepstone's report does not clarify what the "theory" was.

23. G. Dominy, "Thomas Baines: the McGonagall of Shepstone's 1873 Zululand Expedition," in M. Comrie (comp.), "Notes and Queries", *Natalia*, December 21, 1991, pp. 75–79.

24. "Report of the Expedition," p. 16.

25. *Ibid.*

26. Binns, *The Last Zulu King*, p. 72.

27. "Report of the Expedition," p. 16.

28. Webb and Wright, *A Zulu King Speaks*, p. 18. This account was published in *Macmillan's Magazine*, February 1880, as a narrative "taken down from the lips of Cetywayo," by Captain J. Ruscombe Poole, the officer in charge of the Zulu king in captivity. It was translated by the official interpreter, W.H. Longcast. As Poole became a close friend of Cetshwayo it is probable that he sought accurately to reflect the king's view, but the text must be treated with reservations concerning the possibility that it may have mutated in transcription and translation. In his letter to the governor of the Cape, Sir Hercules Robinson, Cetshwayo confirmed that Shepstone was invited to officiate at the coronation because the Zulu thought of themselves "not without or outside the English nation, but within the English nation" (Webb and Wright, *A Zulu King Speaks*, p. 45). The content of this letter was probably affected by Cetshwayo's straitened circumstances as a British prisoner needing, at the time of writing, to demonstrate his loyalty to the crown. See also the testimony of Ndukwana (*JSA*, vol. 4, p. 275), who declared that "Somsewu had expressed himself thus, the whites had never as a matter of fact governed Zululand."

29. "Report of the Expedition," p. 17.

30. BPP, c.1342-1 "Further Correspondence Relating to the Colonies and States of South Africa (Natal)," Lieutenant-Governor Sir H. Bulwer to the earl of Carnarvon, September 7, 1875, encl. copy of a letter Bishop Schreuder to SNA Sir Theophilus Shepstone, August 20, 1875, pp. 30–35.

31. My analysis of the Zulu leaders' reasons for inviting Shepstone to the ceremony, and Shepstone's reasons for accepting, is in broad agreement with that of Etherington, but through its focus on Shaka offers a different reading of the significance of the logics at play in the installation (N. Etherington, "Anglo-Zulu Relations, 1856–1878," in A. Duminy and C. Ballard (eds.), *The Anglo-Zulu War: New Perspectives*, Pietermaritzburg, University of Natal Press, 1981, pp. 30–31).

32. BPP, c.1137, message by Sidinda and Komesiwebu, June 9, 1873, pp. 24–25.

33. SNA 1/7/6, message from Cetshwayo, November 11, 1875, p. 237; SNA 1/7/6, John Dunn to Shepstone, April 20, 1876, p. 250, both cited in Cope, "Shepstone and Cetshwayo," pp. 110 and 121 respectively.

34. *The Transvaal Advocate*, February 25, 1873, quoted in *Natal Witness*, March 11, 1873, cited in Cope, "Shepstone and Cetshwayo," p. 45.

35. BPP, c.1137, written copy of Zulu messengers responding to query about the Boers being asked to crown Cetshwayo, May 3, 1873, pp. 89–90.

36. See, for example, *JSA*, vol. 3, p. 105, Mgidhlana.

37. *Ibid.*, vol. 4, p. 109, Mtshayankomo. *Ukugodhla*—to hold back, to reserve. Also see J. Stuart, *uKulumetule*, London, Longmans, Green & Co., 1925, chap. 29.

38. J. Laband, *Rope of Sand: The Rise and Fall of the Zulu Kingdom in the Nineteenth Century*, Johannesburg, Jonathan Ball, 1995, p. 148.

39. Laband notes that Hamu was in fact the first son born to Mpande. His mother was Nozibhuku, daughter of Sothondose of the Nxumalo people, who was the brother of Monase, Mbuyazi's mother. Sothondose and Monase both fled into Natal in 1857, and were harbored there along with two sons of Mpande and potential rivals to Cetshwayo, Mkhungo and Sikhotha: *ibid.*, pp. 147, 149.

40. *JSA*, vol. 4, pp. 110, 118, quotation p. 117, Mtshayankomo.

41. Webb and Wright, *A Zulu King Speaks*, "Cetshwayo's Letter to the Governor," p. 43. For further discussion of the royal *bayete* see p. 97 below.

42. Webb and Wright, *A Zulu King Speaks*, p. 80. See also p. 41.

43. *JSA*, vol. 4. Mtshayankomo's testimony was the basis for the account in J. Stuart, *uHlangakula*, London, Longmans, Green & Co., 1924, chap. 20.

44. In his account Shepstone claimed that Masiphula died before the party reached emLam-

bongwenya, while Mtshayankomo has him alive for Shepstone's arrival at emLambongwenya. Mtshayankomo was present at emLambongwenya at the time and, as the son of Mpande's leading *imbongi*, was likely to have been aware of developments within royal circles. At least two possible explanations present themselves: that Shepstone was implicated in Masiphula's death and chose to distance himself from Masiphula in his report by saying that Masiphula had died before he arrived at Cetshwayo's *ikhanda* (military establishment); or that the confrontation described by Mtshayankomo actually happened outside emLambongwenya, at, for example, the *emakhosini*. It is also possible that Mtshayankomo's account of the confrontation is a dramatized, personalized version of tensions between Shepstone and the Masiphula faction.

45. *JSA*, vol. 4, p. 127, Mtshayankomo.

46. *Ibid.*, p. 109, Mtshayankomo.

47. *Ibid.*

48. *Ibid.*, p. 126, Mtshayankomo. See also the account of Cetshwayo's installation by one of the girls in his *isigodlo*, in which mention is made of tensions within the Zulu kingdom on the eve of the first ceremony: P. Dlamini (H. Filter [comp.] and S. Bourquin [trans. and ed.]), *Paulina Dlamini: Servant of Two Kings*, Durban and Pietermaritzburg, KCAL and University of Natal Press, 1986, pp. 28, 30.

49. *JSA*, vol. 4, p. 126, Mtshayankomo.

50. *Ibid.*, p. 127, Mtshayankomo. See also *Natal Mercury*, July 31, 1873 for reports of conflict between Cetshwayo and Hamu.

51. Binns, *The Last Zulu King*, p. 61 (based on J. Dunn, *Cetywayo and the Three Generals*, Pietermaritzburg, Natal Print & Publishing Co., 1886) noted a tension at the preemptive ceremony between Cetshwayo and factions under Hamu, Mnyamana, and Ziwedu. Also see S.P. file 9, item 51, Socwatsha, March 29, 1914. Socwatsha related how Shepstone insisted on being shown Cetshwayo's "younger brother" before the installation. Eventually Zibhebhu was produced and it was explained that he was not a son of Mpande but belonged to a collateral house.

52. Paulina Dlamini, by way of contrast, claimed that Masiphula was poisoned on Cetshwayo's orders because the king feared that he was "savagely incompassionate" (Dlamini, *Servant of Two Kings*, p. 61).

53. Note the cautious inquiries made by the *Natal Mercury* special correspondent among local missionaries (*Natal Mercury*, September 23, 1873).

54. A hint that Shepstone may have contemplated installing Hamu, or that at least the promotion of another candidate was seen to be a matter of concern for Cetshwayo, is contained in a poem about the ceremony written by the artist Thomas Baines, a member of Shepstone's "coronation" party. On Shepstone passing Hamu's residence, Baines has Cetshwayo send a messenger to Shepstone urging his "father" not to stop there for "that place was unlucky to all my family and twill be the same to me I fear" (Dominy, "Thomas Baines," p. 78). On August 12, 1873, the *Natal Mercury* correspondent, presumably Thomas Baines, accompanying the "coronation" expedition reported a widespread rumor that Shepstone was expected to install a rival claimant, "Umbelaas" (Mbuyazi). Also see *Natal Mercury*, September 4, 1873, for an account of a visit by Hamu and Ziwedu to Shepstone's camp on August 22, 1873. Unfortunately the report does not offer any explanation for the visit.

55. S.P. file 9, item 51, p. 4, Socwatsha.

56. "Report of the Expedition," p. 7.

57. SNA 1/7/6, Shepstone, memorandum, March 3, 1873. Quoted in Etherington, "Anglo-Zulu Relations," p. 30.

58. Guy, *Heretic*, p. 223.

59. W.R. Guest, *Langalibalele: The Crisis in Natal, 1873–1875*, Durban, Department of History and Political Science, University of Natal, 1976, pp. 28–30, 36–37.

60. "Report of the Expedition," p. 82.

61. Laband, *Rope of Sand*, p. 180.

62. R. Cope, "Political Power within the Zulu Kingdom and the 'Coronation Laws' of 1873," *Journal of Natal and Zulu History*, 8, 1985, pp. 11–31.

63. *Ibid.*, p. 15. See also the comments of the *Natal Mercury's* special correspondent noting that the "coronation laws" effectively established the king's monopoly over the ivory trade, as well as

enforcing status distinctions between the elite and commoners within the kingdom (*Natal Mercury,* September 23, 1873).

64. SNA 1/8/1, letterbook, T. Shepstone, "Report on the Native Population of Natal," September 20, 1851.

65. Quoted in R.E. Gordon, *Shepstone: The Role of the Family in the History of South Africa, 1820–1900,* Cape Town, A.A. Balkema, 1968, p. 131.

66. For a penetrating analysis of the significance of polygamy and *lobolo* in homestead production, and the impact of the *rentier* faction see H. Slater, "The Changing Pattern of Economic Relationships in Rural Natal, 1838–1914," in S. Marks and A. Atmore (eds.), *Economy and Society in Pre-Industrial South Africa,* Harlow, Longman, 1980, pp. 148–70; and H. Slater, "Land, Labour and Capital in Natal: The Natal Land and Colonisation Company, 1860–1948," *Journal of African History,* 16, 2, 1975, pp. 257–83.

67. Shepstone, cited in N. Etherington, *Preachers, Peasants and Politics: South East Africa: African Christian Communities in Natal, Pondoland, and Zululand,* London, Royal Historical Society, 1978, p. 15.

68. J. Guy, "The Role of Colonial Officials in the Destruction of the Zulu Kingdom," in Duminy and Ballard (eds.), *The Anglo-Zulu War,* p. 154. The governor of Natal assumed the role of supreme chief over Natal Africans, and he could use this position to appoint chiefs and thereby check the power of hereditary ones.

69. For Natal settler attitudes to Shepstone see, for example, *Natal Mercury,* January 1, 1857, September 24, 1857, October 1, 1857.

70. D. Welsh, *The Roots of Segregation: Native Policy in Colonial Natal, 1845–1910,* Cape Town, Oxford University Press, 1971, p. 22.

71. Shepstone, cited in Etherington, *Preachers,* p. 15.

72. Wright, "The Dynamics of Power and Conflict," p. 106.

73. Enclosures in dispatch no.34, Scott to Newcastle, February 26, 1864, published in *Correspondence Relating to Granting to Natives in Natal of Documentary Tribal Titles to Land,* Sessional Papers nos. 22 and 23 of the Natal Legislative Council, 1890, and as far as can be ascertained, first published in the report of the Cape government commission in 1883.

74. Wright, "The Dynamics of Power and Conflict", p. 107.

75. Enclosures, item 29, p. 610.

76. The "driven-by Shaka" motif is a trope that occurs in recorded African oral tradition. See *JSA,* vol. 4, pp. 279, 285 (recorded in *isiZulu* in Stuart's notes), Ndukwana, but also see p. 326 where Ndukwana says that Shaka did not scatter the nations but unified them. This then raises the issue of the extent of Stuart's interpolations in the traditions. See *JSA,* vol. 4, Ndongeni where the phrase "driven by Tshaka" occurs in a paraphrased version of Ndongeni's testimony. While the phrase would seem to be Stuart's, Shaka-as-disperser is the substance of, and not an overlay on, whole testimonies. See, for example, *JSA,* vol. 4, testimony of Mqaikana. Also see *JSA,* vol. 1, p. 5, Baleka, p. 183, Jantshi, p. 298, Lunguza. This suggests that we need to take seriously, but not uncritically, Shepstone's statement that "The above short sketches were written down from the lips of the narrators, and, as near as possible, in their words" (p. 153).

77. See, for example, Enclosures, items 5, p. 604, 29, p. 609, 57, p. 615.

78. *Ibid.,* item 43, p. 613. Also see Natal Archives Depot, Shepstone Papers (Sh.P.), A96, vol. 90, "General Historical," p. 11; "The Zulus", *Cape Monthly Magazine,* 11, 1875, pp. 95–101.

79. See, for example, *JSA,* vol. 4, p. 5, Mqaikana; vol. 3, pp 26–27, Mbovu; vol. 3, p. 81, Melapi; vol. 2, pp. 14–15, 24, 31, Mabonsa; vol. 2, p. 113, Magidigidi; vol. 2, p. 85, Mahaya; vol. 2, p. 202, Mangati; vol. 2, p. 277, Maziyana; vol. 1, p. 90, Dabula; vol. 1, p. 201, Jantshi; vol. 1, pp. 302, 336, Lunguza.

80. Enclosures, p. 622.

81. R. Godlonton, *A Narrative of the Irruption of the Kaffir Hordes,* Grahamstown, Meurant & Godlonton, 1836.

82. Enclosures, p. 626.

83. Comaroff and Comaroff, *Of Revelation and Revolution,* p. 169.

84. See above, chapter 2. The documenter of the oral accounts discussed in chapter 2, James Stu-

art, was, following Shepstone, centrally concerned with the figure of Shaka, and brought a Shepstonian conception of Shaka to bear in his recording exercise. But it is a central contention of this study that Stuart was further possessed of a philosophy regarding the collection of oral data that obliged him to record that material in words as close to the originals as he could manage. To argue this is, as will be seen later, not to suggest that Stuart did not leave his imprint on the materials he recorded. It is, however, to claim that the variety and detail of information about Shaka that characterizes the texts he recorded had logics of their own, consistent with the life situations and histories of the informants, which were manifestly not Stuart's invention.

85. It should be borne in mind that Shepstone was raised in the Eastern Cape and entered the colonial service at a very early age. He spoke the Xhosa language fluently as a boy and was, from early on, familiar with the norms and practices of African society. These personal factors are part explanation for this recourse to an African model of government.

86. For an interesting comparative account see Thomas, *Colonialism's Culture,* esp. chap. 5.

87. T. Carlyle, *On Heroes, Hero Worship, and the Heroic in History,* Berkeley, Los Angeles, and Oxford, University of California Press, 1993, introduction by Michael K. Goldberg, ed. Michael K. Goldberg, J. Bratton, and M. Engel, first publ. 1841.

88. Sh.P. vol. 76, p. 15. Also see vol. 82, "Historical Notes," p. 24, and "Powers of Chiefs," p. 136.

89. Golan, *Inventing Shaka,* p. 45.

90. See also Sh.P. vol. 79, pp. 17–18.

91. S.P. file 66, item 8, p. 4, Socwatsha.

92. BPP, c.1137, "Memorandum by the Secretary for Native Affairs, June 11th, 1873," p. 25.

93. *Ibid.*

94. Etherington, "Anglo-Zulu Relations," p. 19.

95. Other subsequent accounts of the 1861 encounter provide circumstantial evidence of recognition of the basic elements of Shepstone's memorandum and the messengers' statements. See, for example, Cetshwayo's letter to Sir Hercules Robinson, governor of the Cape, March 29, 1881, in Webb and Wright, *A Zulu King Speaks,* p. 43, where Cetshwayo's account of the 1873 ceremony records that Shepstone, on that occasion, received the *bayete* salute, thereby suggesting that he might well have been considered to be entitled to it twelve years earlier. Also see S.P. file 19, KCM 23467 (20030), "Results of Inquiries Made of Zulus as to Sir Theophilus Shepstone Having Been Regarded by the Zulu Nation as Representing Tshaka."

96. Hamilton, "Authoring Shaka," pp. 264–73.

97. My list is not exhaustive, but illustrative of the range of available narratives. See also R. Cope's review of Mpande's and Cetshwayo's messages in 1857–60 to Shepstone to visit the Zulu kingdom ("Shepstone and Cetshwayo," pp. 6–7).

98. See *JSA* vol. 4, p. 62, testimony of Mtshapi for a claim that Cetshwayo was pointed out by Mpande to "the white people [who] cut a distinguishing mark on his ear." Also see testimony of Makuza who talks about the Boers making an ear notch (*ibid.*, vol. 2, p. 165).

99. Quoted in Etherington, "Anglo-Zulu Relations," p. 16.

100. Guy, *Heretic,* p. 88; Etherington, "Anglo-Zulu Relations," p. 16.

101. Brooks and Webb, *History of Natal,* p. 95, information attributed to Professor L. Nyembezi. Also see S.P. file 9, item 51, p. 2, Socwatsha (March 29, 1914).

102. *JSA,* vol. 4, p. 301, Ndukwana.

103. "Memorandum," p. 25.

104. "Report of the Expedition," p. 4.

105. *Ibid.*, pp. 4, 5, 6.

106. SNA 1/7/6, message from Cetshwayo, February 29, 1876, p. 244.

107. "Memorandum," p. 26. See also Sh.P. vol. 30, Shepstone to Frere, August 1, 1877 (I am grateful to Richard Cope for giving me access to his notes of these correspondences). See also Sh.P., box 7, letterbook 2, Shepstone to Frere, June 20, 1877, where he claims that by virtue of the 1861 nomination he has the legal standing of the king's father.

108. Lazarus Xaba, interviewed by James Stuart, quoted in Gordon, *Shepstone,* p. 179. Also see p. 165.

109. A. McClintock, *Imperial Leather: Race, Gender and Sexuality in the Colonial Context*, New York, Routledge, 1995, pp. 250–51.

110. Guy, *Heretic*, p. 198; N. Etherington, *Rider Haggard*, Boston, Twayne Publishers, 1984, p. 3. Also see Frances Colenso (alias Atherton Wylde), *My Chief and I*, London, Chapman & Hall, 1880, pp. 68–71.

111. Welsh, *Roots of Segregation*, pp. 20–21.

112. Laband claims that "Somtsewu" is a hybrid word derived from isiZulu, siXhosa, and seSotho, literally meaning "father of the white man," that is, a pioneer (*Rope of Sand*, chap. 12, n. 18).

113. For instances in which white writers report Cetshwayo describing himself as a "child" and the British rulers as parents see Sh.P. vol. 34, Shepstone to Herbert, October 5, 1877. For recorded reports from African commentators using a similar discourse, see SN6, report of Lazarus Xaba and Sabulawu, November 3, 1877. I am grateful to Richard Cope for providing me with his notes of this correspondence.

114. Guy, *Heretic*, p. 85.

115. Comaroff and Comaroff, *Of Revelation and Revolution*, p.14, emphases in the original.

116. *Ibid.*, p. 171.

117. This is a vast topic for research beyond the scope of this study. A useful starting point is provided by McClintock, *Imperial Leather*, chap. 6.

118. Welsh, *Roots of Segregation*, p. 172.

119. Comaroff and Comaroff, *Of Revelation and Revolution*, p. 116.

120. Bird (ed.), *The Annals of Natal*.

121. Sh.P. vol. 86, letter by J. Bird, Pietermaritzburg, August 1, 1885 to Shepstone.

122. J.W. Colenso, "First Steps of the Zulu Mission," in J.W. Colenso, *Bringing Forth the Light*, ed. Ruth Edgecombe, Pietermaritzburg and Durban, University of Natal Press and KCAL, 1982, pp. 74–75.

123. Also see the similar argument made in Frances E. Colenso and A. Durnford, *History of the Zulu War and its Origins*, London, Chapman & Hall, 1880, p. 14, in which the authors note in defense of the Zulu system of political authority that "to rule a nation without any assistance in the form of gaol or fetters, capital punishment must needs be resorted to rather more frequently than in our country where, indeed, it is not long since we hung a man for stealing a sheep, and for other acts far short of murder."

124. R. Thornton, "This Dying Out Race: W.H.I. Bleek's Approach to the Languages of South Africa," *Social Dynamics*, 9, 2, 1, 1983, pp. 1–10.

125. The main studies of the Langalibalele affair on which I have relied are Colenso and Durnford, *History of the Zulu War*; Guest, *Langalibalele*; Norman Herd, *The Bent Pine: The Trial of Chief Langalibalele*, Johannesburg, Ravan, 1976; J. Wright and A. Manson, *The Hlubi Chiefdom in Zululand–Natal: A History*, Ladysmith Historical Society, Ladysmith, 1983; Guy, *Heretic*.

126. Wright and Manson, *The Hlubi Chiefdom*, pp. 65–66.

127. Guy, *Heretic*, p. 202.

128. Wright and Manson, *The Hlubi Chiefdom*, p. 73.

129. BPP, c.1025, no. 45, enc. 48.

130. Wynn Rees (ed.), *Colenso Letters from Natal*, Pietermaritzburg, Shuter & Shooter, 1958, p. 330.

131. For the rift between Colenso and Shepstone, and Colenso's campaign on behalf of Langalibalele, I have relied on Guy, *Heretic*, chap. 13, as well as Rees (ed.), *Letters from Natal*, part 3; Guest, *Langalibalele*, chap. 5; Herd, *The Bent Pine*, chaps. 5, 6, 7, and 8.

132. The argument here draws heavily on Guy, *Heretic*, chap. 13.

133. See Rees (ed.), *Letters from Natal*, pp. 309–10.

134. For a discussion of Carnarvon's confederation plans, and the role envisaged therein for Shepstone, see Guy, *Destruction of the Zulu Kingdom*, pp. 44–46.

135. See, for example, Shepstone's address to the Royal Colonial Institute, London, published in the *Cape Monthly Magazine*, 11, 1875, pp. 95–101.

136. "Cetshwayo's letter to the Governor of the Cape, 29 March, 1881," in Webb and Wright, *A Zulu King Speaks*, pp. 49–50.

137. Colenso, series 1, p. 81, reprinting a message from Cetshwayo to Bulwer in BPP, c.2000, quoted in Guy, *Destruction of the Zulu Kingdom*, p. 47.

138. Also see Colenso's comments on the significance of the "drilled" Zulu army in C. Vijn, *Cetshwayo's Dutchman: Being the Private Journal of a White Trader in Zululand during the British Invasion,* trans. from the Dutch and ed. J.W. Colenso, first publ. London, Longmans, Green & Co., 1880, repr. New York, Negro Universities Press, 1969, p. 112, as well as the quotes Colenso cites on p. 154.

139. BPP, c.2318, p. 214.

140. BPP, c.2381, p. 183.

141. BPP, c.2260, p. 25. Richard Cope's 1995 article lends detailed support to the argument developed first in earlier versions of this chapter regarding the timing of and motivation for Frere's discrediting of Cetshwayo through reference to the despotism of Shaka. Cope notes perceptively the extent to which Frere based his characterization of the Zulu monarch on missionary accounts of the time (R.L. Cope, "Written in Characters of Blood? The Reign of King Cetshwayo kaMpande 1872–1879," *Journal of African History*, 36, 1995, pp. 247–69).

142. Quoted in Guy, *Heretic*, p. 269.

143. *Ibid.*, p. 263.

144. Sir Garnet Wolseley, *The South Africa Journal of Sir Garnet Wolseley, 1879–1880,* ed. A. Preston, Cape Town, A.A. Balkema, 1973, entry for July 19, 1879, p. 59.

145. *Ibid.*, entry for June 21, 1879, p. 40.

146. This discussion of the post-war settlement draws on Guy, *Destruction of the Zulu Kingdom,* chap. 5.

147. Sitimela claimed to be a grandson of Dingiswayo. See H.R. Haggard, *Cetywayo and his White Neighbours,* 3rd ed., London, Trübner & Co., 1890, first publ. London, Trübner, 1882, pp. 39–41.

148. On Osborn see Guy, *Destruction of the Zulu Kingdom,* pp. 82–83.

149. Frances S. Colenso to Harriette Colenso, late 1888, in Rees (ed.), *Letters from Natal,* p. 423.

150. BPP, c.5331, encl. in 13, "Memorandum by Sir Theophilus Shepstone," August 12, 1887, p. 31.

151. Quoted in Guy, *Heretic*, p. 303.

152. Guy, "Colonial Officials," p. 155.

153. Wolseley, *South African Journal,* entry for August 8, 1879, p. 78.

154. See Guy's discussion, *Destruction of the Zulu Kingdom,* p. 160.

155. BPP, c.3466, p. 158, encl., Osborn to Bulwer, December 28, 1882, reply by Ntshingwayo, p. 287.

156. KCAL, Colenso Papers (C.P.), "The Course of Political Events in Zululand, from October, 1881, to 16 June, 1883. Official, Colonial and Zulu Statements," p. 436.

157. BPP, c.3616, encl., Sir T. Shepstone to the governor of Natal, Sir Henry Bulwer, February 27, 1883, "Report of the Re-installation of Cetshwayo," pp. 40–42.

158. *Ibid.*, p. 45.

159. *Ibid.*, p. 46.

160. Frances S. Colenso to Mrs Lyell, January 13, 1883, in Rees (ed.), *Letters from Natal,* p. 369.

161. "Report of the Re-installation," p. 49.

162. "Political Events," p. 353b.

163. Binns, *The Last Zulu King,* appendix c.

164. BPP, c.3466, p. 79, encl. report by Bulwer, quoted in Guy, *Destruction of the Zulu Kingdom,* p. 157.

165. Stuart, *uKulumetule,* pp. 179–80.

166. BPP, encl. 2 in 37, p. 64, governor, Sir Arthur Havelock, to Dinuzulu and Ndabuko.

167. Martin, "British Images of the Zulu," chap. 6.

168. A.B. Fynney, "The Rise and Fall of the Zulu Nation", in his *Zululand and the Zulus,* Pietermaritzburg, Horne Bros., 1884, repr. Pretoria, State Library, 1967, p. 1.

169. See, for example, H.H. Parr, *A Sketch of the Kafir and Zulu Wars: Guadana to Isandlwana,* London, Kegan Paul, 1880; W.E. Montague, *Campaigning in South Africa: Reminiscences of an Officer in 1879,* London, W. Blackwood & Sons, 1880; W. Ashe and E.V.W. Edgell, *The Story of the Zulu Campaign,* London, Low, Marshe, Searle & Rivington, 1880.

170. Quoted in Martin, "British Images of the Zulu," p. 287.

171. See, for example, F.W. Chesson, *The War in Zululand: A Brief Review of Sir Bartle Frere's Policy*, London, King, 1879. Also see *The Aborigines Friend*, 1879 (pamphlet).

172. Vijn, *Cetshwayo's Dutchman*, preface by Colenso, pp. vii–viii. See also Frances S. Colenso to Mrs Lyell, January 19, 1879; January 1, 1882; March 14, 1882, all in Rees (ed.), *Letters from Natal*, pp. 340, 359, 363.

173. Colenso and Durnford, *History of the Zulu War*, p. 9.

174. H.E. Colenso, "Zululand: Past and Present," lecture given to the members in the Memorial Hall, October 1, 1890, and published in the *Journal of the Manchester Geographical Society*, 1890, p. 5.

175. "The Transvaal," *Macmillan's Magazine*, 36, May 1877, pp. 71–79; "A Zulu War Dance," *Gentleman's Magazine*, 243, July 1877, pp. 94–107; D.S. Higgins, *Rider Haggard: The Great Storyteller*, London, Cassell, 1981, p. 20; "A Visit to the Chief Secocoeni", *Gentleman's Magazine*, 243, September 1877, pp. 302–18.

176. Haggard, *Cetywayo*, p. 12.

177. *Ibid.*, p. 52.

178. *Ibid.*, pp. 3, 4, 21.

179. *Ibid.*, pp. 5, 13, 14, 18, 19, 23, 35, 54.

180. Wolseley, quoted in *ibid.*, p. 35.

181. *Ibid.*, p. 54.

182. *Ibid.*, p. 56.

183. *Ibid.*, p. xlviii. Also see pp. 45–46, where Haggard noted: "It must be remembered that when once they have found their master, there exists no more law-abiding people in the world than the Zulu, provided that they are ruled firmly, and above all, justly."

184. *Ibid.*, p. liii.

185. *Ibid.*, 3rd ed., p. liii.

186. *Ibid.*, pp. xiii, xiv, xxix.

187. *The South African*, September 28, November 9, 1882.

189. H.R. Haggard, *The Witch's Head*, London, Spencer Blackett, 1884, p. 182.

189. Higgins, *The Great Storyteller*, London, Cassell, 1981, p. 22.

190. Ibid., pp. 70, 71, 115; P.B. Ellis, *H. Rider Haggard: A Voice from the Infinite*, London and Henley, Routledge & Kegan Paul, 1978, pp. 96–97.

191. H. Rider Haggard, *King Solomon's Mines*, London, Cassell, 1885.

192. Ellis, *A Voice from the Infinite*, p. 1.

193. *Ibid.*, p. 101.

194. *Ibid.*, p. 102.

195. *Ibid.*, p. 104.

196. *King Solomon's Mines* is set somewhere north of Zulu country and the Kukuanas are depicted as a branch of the Zulus (p. 251). Their society is imagined in terms of a host of very "Zulu" social and political institutions, and demonstrates features strongly akin to the practice of *ukuhlonipha*, the giving of the *bayete* salute, and so on. Haggard mentions the similarity in the introduction, saying he wishes he could go into the differences, but that he cannot.

197. Etherington, *Rider Haggard*, p. 44.

198. D. Bunn, "Embodying Africa: Description, Ideology, Imperialism, and the Colonial Romance," unpublished Ph.D. thesis, Northwestern University, 1987, p. iv.

199. *Ibid.*, pp. 204–05.

200. Etherington, *Rider Haggard*, p. 104.

201. H.R. Haggard, *She*, in *Three Adventure Novels of H. Rider Haggard*, New York, Dover Publications, 1951, first publ. London, Longmans, Green & Co., 1887, p. 134.

202. McClintock, *Imperial Leather*, p. 247.

203. Quoted in M. Cohen, *Rider Haggard: His Life and Works*, London, Hutchinson, 1960, p. 187.

204. In fact, the real Umslopogaas on whom this character was modeled was Shepstone's head attendant, and a son of the Swazi king, Mswati II. H.R. Haggard, *Nada the Lily*, London, Longmans, 1882, pp. ix, 47.

205. *Ibid.*, pp. 52–53.

206. *Ibid.*, p. 179.

207. *Illustrated London News,* January 2–March 7, 1892.

208. *New York Herald,* January 3–May 1, 1892.

209. For an interesting discussion of the transition in late Victorian male culture from filiation to affiliation as rehearsed in Haggard's spell in the colonial administration and of the reinvention of the patriarch in the colonies, see McClintock, *Imperial Leather,* chap. 6.

210. Haggard, *Nada,* dedication, p. v.

211. Shepstone to Haggard, July 13, 1892, quoted in H.R. Haggard, *Days of my Life,* ed. C.J. Longman, London and New York, Longmans, Green & Co., 1926, 2 vols., vol. 2, p. 23.

212. Haggard, *Nada,* p. 254.

213. *Ibid.*, pp. 1, 6.

214. *Ibid.*, editor's (i.e. Haggard's) note, p. 5 and p. 161; *Days of my Life,* vol. 2, p. 18.

215. Haggard, *Nada,* p. ix.

216. *Ibid.*, editor's (i.e. Haggard's) note, p. 5.

217. McClintock, *Imperial Leather,* p. 245.

218. N. Etherington, "South African Origins of Rider Haggard's Early African Romances," *Notes and Queries,* 24, 1977, pp. 436–38; Haggard, *Days of my Life,* vol. 1, pp. 56, 76; Ellis, *A Voice from the Infinite,* pp. 37, 43; Higgins, *The Great Storyteller,* pp. 18, 19, 22–23, 74, 99.

219. Fynney, *Zululand and the Zulus,* pp. 4, 5.

220. *Ibid.*, p. 7.

221. *Ibid.*, p. 9.

222. *Ibid.*, p. 11.

223. D. Leslie, *Among the Zulus and Amatongas,* Glasgow and Edinburgh, Edmonston & Douglas, 1875, republ. New York, Negro Universities Press, 1961; Bird (ed.), *Annals of Natal;* Higgins, *The Great Storyteller,* p. 131.

224. Quoted in Higgins, *The Great Storyteller,* p. 71.

225. Haggard, *Days of my Life,* vol. 1, p. 242.

226. Etherington, *Rider Haggard,* p. 113.

227. Haggard, *Days of my Life,* vol. 1, pp. 206–08; Higgins, *The Great Storyteller,* pp. 83, 181; *The Spectator,* 58, October 1885; Ellis, *A Voice from the Infinite,* pp. 101–02, 108, 117. For a discussion of the sales of Haggard's books, see Cohen, *Life and Works,* pp. 231–38; Bunn, "Embodying Africa," pp. 158–60; Etherington, *Rider Haggard,* pp. 56–57.

228. Ellis, *A Voice from the Infinite,* pp. 152–53, 158, 160.

229. *Ibid.*, pp. 179–81; Etherington, *Rider Haggard,* pp. 115–16; Cohen, *Life and Works,* pp. 230–31.

230. Cohen, *Life and Works,* p. 230.

231. S. Gray and T. Couzens, "Printers and Other Devils: The Texts of Sol. T. Plaatje," *Research in African Literatures,* 9, 2, 1978, pp. 198–215; Malaba, "Shaka as Literary Theme," chap. 5.

232. D. Wylie, "A Dangerous Admiration: E.A. Ritter's *Shaka Zulu,*" *South African Historical Journal,* 22, 1993, pp. 98–118; H. Kucklick, *The Savage Within: The Social History of British Anthropology, 1885–1945,* Cambridge, Cambridge University Press, 1991, p. 65; Haggard, *Days of my Life,* vol. 2, p. 121; Higgins, *The Great Storyteller,* p. 228.

233. Quoted in W. Katz, *Rider Haggard and the Fiction of Empire: A Critical Study of British Imperial Fiction,* Cambridge, Cambridge University Press, 1987, p. 1.

234. Cohen, *Life and Works,* p. 229.

235. Haggard, *Cetywayo,* p. xi.

236. *Ibid.*, p. xiii.

237. Haggard, *Nada,* pp. 9–10.

238. *Ibid.*, p. 181, also see p. 10.

239. *Ibid.*, p. 86.

240. M. Cohen (ed.), *Rudyard Kipling to Rider Haggard: The Record of a Friendship,* London, Hutchinson, 1965, p. 69.

241. E. Stokes, "Kipling's Imperialism", in John Gross (ed.), *The Age of Kipling,* New York, Simon & Schuster, 1972, pp. 90–98, this quotation p. 93.

242. Kipling, "The Man Who Would Be King," p. 185.

243. Dening, *Islands and Beaches,* p. 186.

244. The Comaroffs do allow that "some of the ways of Africans interpolated themselves, again detached and transformed, into the habitus of the missionaries," but the point is not developed, nor are the processes by which this might have happened explored in depth (Comaroff and Comaroff, *Of Revelation and Revolution,* p. 18).

Chapter Four

1. For a detailed discussion of Stuart's early career in Eshowe see Hamilton, "Authoring Shaka," pp. 367–75.

2. S.P. file 8, item KCM 1865c, James Stuart to his mother, June 23 (*sic*), 1893.

3. As the *Natal Mercury* described him, June 26, 1893. On the memorial see Sh.P. vol. 88, "Memorial Subscription List."

4. See *Natal Mercury,* April 1, 1892. Also see *Natal Mercury,* January 29, 1892.

5. *Natal Mercury,* April 1, 1892.

6. See *Natal Witness,* October 11, 1893, editorial; *Times of Natal,* October 12, 1893, editorial.

7. My discussion of Moor draws heavily on Uma Shashikant Dhupelia's unpublished M.A. thesis, "Frederick Robert Moor and Native Affairs in the Colony of Natal 1893–1903," University of Durban-Westville, 1980.

8. *Ibid.,* pp. 39–40.

9. Marks, *Reluctant Rebellion,* p. 98.

10. *Ibid.,* p. 101.

11. This title was later changed to commissioner for native affairs.

12. For a detailed discussion of the development of Stuart's interest in African institutions in the late 1890s see Hamilton, "Authoring Shaka," pp. 382–86.

13. S.P. file 8, KCM 1865.

14. Dhupelia, "Moor," pp. 62–63.

15. *Natal Mercury,* June 6, 1900.

16. Matsebula, *History of Swaziland,* p. 157; Duphelia, "Moor," p. 79.

17. A. Odendaal, *Vukani Bantu! The Beginnings of Black Protest Politics in South Africa to 1912,* Cape Town, David Philip, 1984, p. 310, n. 143.

18. S.P. file 8, item KCM 1865f, Stuart (Ladysmith) to his mother, November 1900.

19. I have not as yet been able to establish when and how Ndukwana kaMbengwana came into Stuart's service. Stuart's first interview with Ndukwana occurred in October 1897. The location of this interview is not given, but in 1897 Stuart was posted to Ingwavuma (*JSA,* vol. 4, p. 263). Stuart's notes include another interview with Ndukwana in July 1900 at Impendhle and in August at Howick (*ibid.,* p. 269, Ndukwana). Ndukwana gave Stuart substantial testimony of his own and was present at a large numbers of interviews with other informants recorded by Stuart. Stuart discussed the individual testimonies with him, and used him to locate further informants. Ndukwana was, in a number of ways, clearly very influential in the development of Stuart's understanding of the region's history. It is possible that Ndukwana was Stuart's *induna,* but this requires further substantiation.

20. *JSA,* vol. 1, p. 223, John Khumalo commenting on Johannes Khumalo. *Ibid.,* pp. 213–14, Johannes Khumalo. Also see S.M. Meintjes, "Edendale 1850–1906: A Case Study of Rural Transformation and Class Formation in an African Mission in Natal," unpublished Ph.D. thesis, University of London, 1988, p. 354.

21. *JSA,* vol. 1, pp. 215–16, 222, 223. For a detailed discussion of the position of the Natal *amakholwa* see Meintjes, "Edendale," chaps. 10, 11, and 12.

22. *JSA,* vol. 1, p. 221.

23. *JSA,* vol. 1, p. 247, Khumalo.

24. *JSA,* vol. 1, ed's. note 67, p. 270.

25. *JSA,* vol. 1, p. 230, Khumalo.

26. For a detailed discussion of the inadequacies of native policy and administration leading up to the situation that prevailed in 1900, see J. Lambert, "Africans in Natal, 1880–1899: Continuity, Change and Crisis in a Rural Society", unpublished Ph.D. thesis, University of South Africa, 1986, chap. 10.

27. *Inkanyiso,* May 5, 1892, letter from "Philanthropist."

28. Odendaal, *Vukani Bantu,* p. 59.

29. *JSA,* vol. 1, p. 232, Khumalo (my emphasis).

30. *Ibid.,* p. 233, Khumalo.

31. Odendaal, *Vukani Bantu,* p. 60.

32. S.P. file 8, item 1865h, Stuart (Durban) to his mother, April 5, 1901.

33. SNA 1/4/14 C43/05, November 8, 1905 and SNA 1/4/14 C43/05, minute, MNA *c.*November 8, 1905, both cited in Marks, *Reluctant Rebellion,* pp. 173–74.

34. S.P. file 8, item KCM 1865, Stuart to his mother, December 1900. In 1903, in conversation with one Mnguni, Stuart posited that a "study of the general life, customs, habits and character of the native races [confined for practical reasons] . . . to a particular national organisation, viz. the Zulu" was necessary to be in a position to "approach still nearer to the main object in view . . . the building up of all into one organised body-politic" (KCM23511, file 30 [ii]). Precisely what Stuart means by "all" (all the inhabitants of Natal, black and white? all Zulu speakers?) is not clear. Nonetheless, the comment does raise the possibility that Stuart's "Idea" was not simply the collection of information, but its collection for a larger purpose, that of the "building up of one organised body-politic." The rest of this chapter suggests something slightly different, i.e. that Stuart's larger purposes were the continued separation of Africans and Europeans and the protection of "tribal" institutions, at least in part to secure continued control over the African population. I am grateful to Stephen Ramsay for drawing my attention to the interview with Mnguni.

35. This letter was written four years after Stuart began to record African oral histories.

36. S.P. file 8, item KCM 1865h, Stuart (Durban) to his mother, April 5, 1901.

37. Duphelia, "Moor," p. 138.

38. *Ibid.,* pp. 205–06.

39. *Ibid.,* p. 209.

40. S.P. file 40, item xx, KCM 23774, handwritten script by Stuart entitled "Observations by the Acting Assistant Magistrate, Durban on the *Labour Question* as existing in Durban," dated April 13, 1902.

41. *Ibid.*

42. Duphelia, "Moor," p. 209.

43. *Blue Book,* Native Affairs, Annual Reports, 1904, p. 77.

44. D. Hemson, "Class Consciousness and Migrant Labour: Dockworkers in Durban," unpublished Ph.D. thesis, University of Warwick, 1979, p. 114; P. la Hausse, "The Struggle for the City: Alcohol, the Ematsheni and Popular Culture in Durban, 1902–1936," unpublished M.A. thesis, University of Cape Town, 1984, p. 38.

45. See *JSA,* vol. 3, pp. 23–24, Mbovu, February 9, 1903, discussion with Mbovu, Jantshi, and Ndukwana on the land question, and discussion with Ndukwana about African resistance.

46. *Ibid.,* vol. 1, p. 93, Dhlozi.

47. Hamilton, "Authoring Shaka," chap. 8.

48. S.P. file 42, item ii (emphasis in the original). Also see item xliii for further insights into Stuart's campaign for the preservation of knowledge of native custom.

49. For discussion on the way in which western urges to mastery were the drives that established the "native question" as a problem to be solved through the generation of knowledge and expertise of a particular kind see Ashforth, *The Politics of Official Discourse,* introduction.

50. *JSA,* vol. 4, pp. 354–83, Ndukwana.

51. *Ibid.,* vol. 1, pp. 174–202, Jantshi.

52. Jantshi's account of the life of Shaka is discussed in detail in chapter 2 above.

53. *JSA,* vol. 1, p. 188, Jantshi.

54. *Ibid.,* p. 189, Jantshi.

55. This impression is borne out by a comparison of the testimony of Jantshi with a statement on *togt* labor which Stuart in his capacity as magistrate took down in April 1902 (S.P. file 40, item 19).

56. *JSA*, vol. 4, Ndhlovu. Ndlovu's testimony on Shaka is discussed more fully in chapter 2 above.

57. January 7 and 8, 1903 (S.P. file 14); January 1, 1903 *(izibongo)*, January 8, 1903. Ndukwana was present when both Mhuyi and Jantshi spoke. Both interviews were recorded in the first person (JSA, vol. 4, pp. 36–39, Mruyi).

58. May 28, 1903 (typescript in S.P. file 14, Ndukwana present).

59. *JSA*, vol. 2, p. 80, Magidi.

60. July 8, 1903 (*ibid.*, pp. 47–48, Madikane).

61. August 15, 16, 17, and 30, 1903 (*ibid.*, pp. 49–52, Madikane).

62. February 7, 8, 9, 1904 (*ibid.*, vol. 3, pp. 23–31, Mbovu).

63. August 7 and 29, October 16 and 25, November 10 and 13, 1904 (*ibid.*, vol. 4, pp. 31, 34–38, 41–45, Mbovu.)

64. *Ibid.*, vol. 3, p. 100, Meseni.

65. *Ibid.*, pp. 238–72, Mmemi.

66. *Ibid.*, vol. 2, pp. 232–37, Maquza.

67. April 18, 19, and 21, 1905. Also present Socwatsha, Mkotana, Mgqibelo kaSokwebula, and Nduna (*ibid.*, vol. 3, pp. 210–18, Mkehlengana, and pp. 222–27, Mkotana).

68. *Ibid.*, vol. 2, pp. 264–301, Maziyana.

69. *Ibid.*, vol. 3, pp. 53–67, Mcotoyi.

70. *Ibid.*, pp. 72–94, Melapi.

71. *Ibid.*, vol. 2, pp. 83–97, Magidigidi.

72. May 26, 27, 28, and 29, June 27 and 28, July 11 and 12, 1905 (*ibid.*, pp. 52–62, Madikane).

73. *Ibid.*, pp. 246–59, Mayinga.

74. S.P. file 52, p. 7, June 21, 1903.

75. *JSA*, vol. 4, p. 206, Ndhlovu.

76. See S.P. file 52, item 1, KCM 24148, "Tshaka: a short account of his life, character and reign, preceded as introduction thereto, by remarks on the early history of the Zulu and Mtetwa tribes" (February 22, 1903), in which Stuart discusses his research methods, including his comparative examination of the "recognised authorities," as well as the importance of "independently enquiring of the natives themselves for such facts as tend to bring about more exact knowledge" (p. 1).

77. Stuart's copy of Isaacs, *Travels and Adventures,* vol. 1, pp. 66, 324. Held at KCAL.

78. See *JSA*, vol. 1, pp. 39, 57, 62, 63, 75, 103, 164, 167, 194, 220, 226, 237, 326, 330, 337; vol. 2, pp. 408, 413.

79. Stuart's copy of Isaacs, *Travels and Adventures,* vol. 1, p. 350.

80. E.B. Tylor, *Primitive Culture: Researches into the Development of Mythology, Religion, Language, Art and Custom,* London, John Murray, 1903, 2 vols., 4th ed., first publ. 1871.

81. S.P. file 49, item 14.

82. *Ibid.*

83. S.P. uncataloged manuscripts, "Extracts 1–7."

84. S.P. file 49, item 13, KCM 24069.

85. Emphasis in the original.

86. S.P. file 31, item xvi, KCM 23543. This document is a rough draft. I have not as yet been able to establish whether Stuart did indeed submit a memorandum, and, if he did, to what extent it differed from this draft.

87. S.P. file 31, item 16, pp. 1–2, 3, 15, 24.

88. Kucklick, *The Savage Within,* p. 46.

89. H. Kucklick, "Contested Monuments: The Politics of Archaeology in Southern Africa," in G. Stocking (ed.), *Colonial Situations,* Madison, University of Wisconsin Press, 1991, pp. 145–46.

90. S.P. file 52, item i, KCM 24148.

91. S.P. file 52, items 3 and 4.

92. S.P. file 52, item 7.

93. S.P. file 53, item 2, pp. 4, 5.

94. S.P. file 52, item 1, p. 1.

95. S.P. file 52, item 2, KCM 24149, p. 26.

96. For example, the doggerel "You are looking at the earwax of a dog"; "Pierced by an Ntungwa stick," which Stuart included in the draft came from his interviews with Ndlovu the previous year (*JSA*, vol. 4, pp. 199, 200).

97. S.P. file 52, item 1, p. 3.

98. Stuart, *Studies in Zulu Law and Custom*, Durban, n.p., printed by Robinson & Co. (probably 1903) (hereafter *Marriage*), p. 5.

99. *Ibid.*, p. 14.

100. *Blue Book*, Native Affairs, p. 78.

101. Stuart, *Marriage*, p. 20.

102. *Ibid.*, p. 21.

103. *Ibid.*, p. 20.

104. S.P. file 52, item i, pp. 2–3, "Early History of the Tribes of Zululand."

105. S.P. file 48, item 2.

106. S.P. file 49, item 13, p. 8.

107. *Ibid.*

108. Cobbing, "A Tainted Well."

109. S.P. file 40, items 2 and 13.

110. S.P. file 10; file 49, item 35; file 40, item 4.

111. S.P. file 44, KCM 23879.

112. J. Stuart, *The Conjunctive and Subjunctive Methods of Writing Zulu*, Durban, n.p., 1906, p. 11.

113. *Ibid.*, p. 5.

114. The disjunctive method also suited Stuart's own notation style. When Stuart took notes, he did so in a mixture of English and *isiZulu* to which the disjunctive method lent itself better.

115. On the shift from orality to literacy see J. Goody, *Interface between the Written and the Oral*, Oxford, Oxford University Press, 1987. Much has been written, in other contexts, about the loss of the voice expression, the performance component, and their meanings, in the move from a spoken text to a written one. That literature brings useful perspectives to bear in the assessment of the traditions recorded by Stuart. Stuart, himself a performer in his role as a practising *imbongi*, is likely to have been, to a degree, alert to such points, and indeed, this is borne out by his decision to record his praising orally. However sensitive to such issues he may have been, these performative aspects and the oral character of the accounts are lost in his records, leaving little trace. The absence must be noted.

116. Isabel Hofmeyr has taken the lead in bringing this work to the attention of South African scholars who use oral materials. See her *We Spend Our Years as a Tale That Is Told*.

117. E.A. Havelock, *Prologue to Greek Literacy*, Cincinnati, University of Cincinnati Press, 1971, p. 52.

118. Quoted in Brookes and Webb, *History of Natal*, p. 213.

119. Ashforth, *The Politics of Official Discourse*, p. 34.

120. S.P. file 2, KCM 1046, February 29, 1904, typescript of Stuart's submission to the commission, entitled "What Then Is To Be Done?", p. 4.

121. *Ibid.*, pp. 4–6.

122. *Ibid.*, pp. 3, 7, 9–10, 11; file 6, KCM 23464, pp. 7–9.

123. S.P. file 6, KCM 23464, typescript of Stuart's examination, pp. 4–5.

124. *Ibid.*, p. 5.

125. *Ibid.*

126. S.P. file 2, KCM 1046, p. 2.

127. S.P. file 6, KCM 23464, p. 12.

128. *Ibid.*, pp. 18–19.

129. See *Ibid.*, typescript of Stuart's examination, p. 6.

130. The most comprehensive account of this uprising is Shula Marks' study *Reluctant Rebellion*.

131. J. Stuart, *A History of the Zulu Rebellion, 1906, and of Dinuzulu's Arrest, Trial and Expatriation*, London, Macmillan & Co., 1913.

132. *Ibid.*, p. 22.

133. *Ibid.*, p. 136, and "Replies to Criticisms," on pp. 522–27.

134. S.P. file 2, KCM 1046, typescript dated September 6, 1911.

135. *Ibid.*

136. Stuart, *Zulu Rebellion,* p. 531 (emphasis in the original).

137. *Ibid.*, p. 536.

138. *Ibid.*

139. Ashforth, *The Politics of Official Discourse,* p. 1.

140. Stuart, *Zulu Rebellion,* p. 536.

141. S.P. file 19, p. 172, copy of letter from A.J. Shepstone to Rider Haggard, December 30, 1911 (original letter in NAD, Pietermaritzburg).

142. Gordon, *Shepstone,* p. 256.

143. Haggard, *Days of my Life,* pp. 62, 68.

144. S.P. file 19, pp. 173–74, copy of letter from A.J. Shepstone to Rider Haggard, December 30, 1911 (original letter in NAD, Pietermaritzburg).

145. *Ibid.*, pp. 176–77.

146. *Ibid.*, p. 175.

147. S.P. file 19, copy of a letter from H. Rider Haggard to Arthur Shepstone, January 23, 1912.

148. S.P. file 19, KCM 23467, pp. 183–85.

149. S.P. file 19, James Stuart's notes on Sir Theophilus Shepstone.

150. Lilias Rider Haggard, *The Cloak That I Left: A Biography of the Author Henry Rider Haggard, KBE, by his Daughter Lilias Rider Haggard,* London, Hodder & Stoughton, 1951, p. 210.

151. See dedication in the front of H. Rider Haggard's *Child of Storm,* London, Longmans, 1913, in which the author refers to Stuart's comments.

152. Cohen, *Life and Works,* p. 204.

153. Haggard, *The Cloak That I Left,* pp. 51, 64, 85, 110–11, 223. My account of Haggard's Natal and Zululand visit in 1914 and his interaction with Stuart and Socwatsha is largely drawn from this source.

154. *Ibid.*, p. 224. The morning after their arrival at the Residency at Eshowe, Haggard's daughter records, the party "walked over to the site of a kraal called Jazi, meaning Finished, or Finished with Joy. An old native led him [Haggard] to a place in the middle of a patch of mealies whose growth was weak and thin, for there stood the large hut where died the last of the Zulu kings—Cetywayo" (*Ibid.*, p. 233).

155. H.R. Haggard, *Finished,* London, Macdonald, 1962, first publ. 1917, p. 23.

156. D.S. Higgins (ed.), *The Private Diaries of Sir Rider Haggard, 1914–1925,* London, Cassell, 1980, p. 7.

157. S.P. file 2, KCM 1046, "European Civilization from the Uncivilized Native's point of View."

158. S.P. file 2, KCM 1046; file 31, item 7.

159. S.P. file 40, item 7.

160. *Natal Mercury,* July 10, 1946; S.P. file 10, item 7.

161. S.P. file 48, item 10.

162. J. Stuart, *uTulasizwe,* 1923; *uHlangakula,* 1924; *uBaxoxele,* 1924; *uKulumetule,* 1925; *uVusezakiti,* 1926, all London, Longmans, Green & Co.

163. *Native Teacher's Journal,* 4, 1, 1923, pp. 43–44 (extract in S.P. file 48, item 6).

164. Rycroft and Ngcobo, *Praises,* pp. xii, 44; Malaba, "Shaka as Literary Theme," pp. 228–41; E. Gunner, "*Ukubonga nezibongo:* Zulu Praising and Praises," unpublished Ph.D. thesis, University of London, 1984.

165. Rycroft and Ngcobo, *Praises,* p. 45.

166. S.P. unaccessioned manuscript, proof copies of *Tulasizwe* (1936) and *Vusezakithi* (1938).

167. La Hausse, "Two Zulu Nationalists," pp. 125–29, 136–37.

168. See Malaba, "Shaka as Literary Theme," chap. 3, esp. pp. 238–40.

169. Golan, *Inventing Shaka,* p. 60.

170. Stuart, *uKulumetule,* p. 94. Also see his comments S.P. file 60, item 4.

171. Stuart, *uKulumetule,* discussion of Magolwane, chap. 17.

172. Golan, *Inventing Shaka,* pp. 59–61.
173. *The Times,* May 17, 1944.
174. S.P. file 42, item ii.
175. S.P. file 40, item xi; also see file 42, item vi, for Stuart on the subject of rights for Africans.
176. Ashforth, *The Politics of Official Discourse,* p. 5.
177. See his comments, S.P. file 42, item vi.
178. S.P. file 42, item xxi.
179. Cited in La Hausse, "Two Zulu Nationalists," p. 16.
180. Marks, "Patriotism, Patriarchy and Purity," p. 220.
181. S.P. file 42, item xxiv.
182. Kucklick, *The Savage Within,* p. 253.

Chapter Five

1. A. Costa, "Custom and Commonsense: The Zulu Royal Family Succession Dispute of the 1940s," paper presented to the seminar of the Institute for Advanced Social Research, University of the Witwatersrand, 1996.

2. A. Costa, "Two Bulls in the Herd: The Royal Succession Dispute of the 1940s," B.A. Honours report, University of the Witwatersrand, 1995, p. 19.

3. Sarah Gertrude Millin quoted in Wylie, "White Writers and Shaka Zulu," p. 216.

4. Wylie, "White Writers," p. 217.

5. See Marks, *Ambiguities of Dependence;* N. Cope, "The Zulu Petit Bourgeoisie and Zulu Nationalism in the 1920s: Origins of Inkatha," *Journal of Southern African Studies,* 16, 3, 1990, pp. 431–51.

6. Cope, *To Bind the Nation.*

7. "Two Zulu Nationalists."

8. Cope, *To Bind the Nation,* p. 255.

9. La Hausse, "Two Zulu Nationalists," p. 29.

10. For close analyses of the effects of white writings on these early Zulu nationalist texts see Golan, *Inventing Shaka,* pp. 87–91, and La Hausse, "Two Zulu Nationalists," chap. 3.

11. For a detailed discussion of this text see Golan, *Inventing Shaka,* pp. 96–102.

12. Inkatha's use of history has been extensively written about: see Golan, "Zulu Past"; and Forsyth, "The Past in Service of the Present."

13. *Shaka Zulu Souvenir Brochure,* Johannesburg, 1986, p. 3.

14. See for example, *Weekly Mail,* October 31–November 6, 1986; *Sunday Star,* October 12, 1986; *Style,* February 1987; *Star,* October 4, 1986.

15. *Souvenir Brochure,* p. 3.

16. *New York Times,* November 2, 1987; *Cape Times,* July 16, 1986; *Star,* October 4, 1986; *Sunday Star,* October 12, 1986; *Star,* October 10, 1986.

17. *Hartford Courant,* February 28, 1987; *Star Telegram,* February 22, 1987; *Houston Chronicle,* March 8–14, 1987; *San Francisco Chronicle, Datebook Television,* undated clipping, Harmony Gold publicity package; *New York City Tribune,* March 2, 1987.

18. *Drum,* January 1987.

19. *Weekly Mail,* October 9–16, 1986.

20. *Star,* October 9, 1986.

21. Fynn, *Diary;* Isaacs, *Travels and Adventures,* pp. vi–xvii; Bird (ed.), *Annals of Natal;* Roberts, *The Zulu Kings;* Du Buisson, *The White Man Cometh,* pp. 3–5, 35, 36–39.

22. *Star,* October 4, 1986; *Style,* November 1986; *Houston Chronicle,* March 8–14, 1987; Harmony Gold publicity flyer, n.d.; *Souvenir Brochure,* pp. 4, 6–7, 12, 14, 22, 25; C. Burgess, "Shaka Zulu: The Aftermath," *South Africa Today,* 3, 2, 1987; for a discussion of the authenticity of the weaponry used, see the *Historical Firearms Society of South Africa Newsletter,* 34, 1985.

23. *Houston Chronicle,* March 8–14, 1987; *United States Anti-Apartheid Newsletter,* 3, 1, 1988. On the making of local films and attempts to hide their origins, see the article by John Hookham in the *Weekly Mail,* May 13–19, 1988, and the reply by film-maker Chris Davies in the *Weekly Mail,* May 27–June 2, 1988.

24. The phrase is D.W. Cohen's, drawn from his original position paper, "The Production of History," prepared for the Fifth International Roundtable in Anthropology and History, Paris, 1986.

25. *Beacon Journal,* October 8, 1987.

26. My discussion with Faure at his home in Florida, South Africa, 1990; telephone interview with Faure, April 2, 1988.

27. Sinclair was fired when he refused to follow editing instructions from the American distributors, Harmony Gold (*Style,* November 1986). These conclusions are based on an article in the *Cape Times,* July 16, 1986; a telephone interview with Faure, April 2, 1988; and a reading of Sinclair's publication in German of *Shaka Zulu* (Munich, 1986) based on his script. I am grateful to Anja Baumhof for assistance with the translation of key passages from Sinclair's German text into English.

28. Telephone interview with Faure, April 2, 1988.

29. K. Tomaselli et al., *Myth, Race and Power: South Africans Imaged on Film and TV,* Cape Town, Anthropos, 1986, p. 43.

30. Telephone interview with Faure, April 2, 1988.

31. Isaacs, *Travels and Adventures;* also see the discussion of Isaacs above. Ritter, *Shaka Zulu.*

32. *Drum,* January 1987; *Weekly Mail,* November 21–27, 1986.

33. Isaacs, *Travels and Adventures,* pp. xi–xii; for background on Fynn and Isaacs see Roberts, *The Zulu Kings.*

34. Ritter, *Shaka Zulu,* pp. 3–14.

35. *Souvenir Brochure,* pp. 2–14.

36. *Ibid.,* p. 15.

37. K. Tomaselli, "Camera, Colour and Racism in *Shaka Zulu,*" *History News,* 30, November 1987, pp. 9–11.

38. *Style,* November 1986.

39. *Ibid.*

40. *Star,* September 29, 1986; *Souvenir Brochure,* p. 6.

41. *Style,* November 1986; *Star,* September 29, 1986.

42. Harmony Gold publicity flyer, n.d. On the riskiness of the venture also see *Electronic Media,* September 22, 1986.

43. *Style,* November 1986.

44. J. Saul and S. Gelb, *The Crisis in South Africa,* New York, Monthly Review Press, 1986, p. 214; *Star,* December 23, 1985.

45. Saul and Gelb, *The Crisis in South Africa,* p. 222.

46. *Beacon Journal,* October 8, 1987.

47. *Race Relations Survey 1985,* Johannesburg, 1985, p. 460.

48. See I. Wilkins and J. Strydom, *The Super-Afrikaners: Inside the Afrikaner Broederbond,* Johannesburg, Jonathan Ball, 1978; P. Crankshaw, A. Williams, and G. Hayman, "To Educate, Entertain and Inform: The Meyer Commission into TV," *SAFTTA Journal,* 3, 1983, pp. 20–27; G. Hayman and R. Tomaselli, "Technology in the Service of Ideology: The First 50 Years of Broadcasting in South Africa," in K. Tomaselli et al. (eds.), *Addressing the Nation: Studies in South African Media,* vol. 1, Johannesburg, R. Lyon, 1986.

49. *Weekly Mail,* November 21–27, 1986; *Star,* October 1, 1986. For Faure on the role of television in influencing racial attitudes see the interview with Faure, *New York Daily News,* October 6, 1987; and the interview with Faure and actor Henry Cele, *Houston Chronicle,* March 8–14, 1987.

50. *Star,* September 29, 1986. In eighteen American cities *Shaka Zulu* delivered higher ratings than the local stations' 8 p.m. films. In Baltimore *Shaka Zulu* gave WBFF-TV the highest rating and share in the M-F 8 p.m. movies, with an average increase of over 300 percent. Harmony Gold publication "*Shaka Zulu* vs. M-F O'clock Movies," n.d. These figures are based on Nielsen and Arbitron ratings.

51. Interview with Faure and Cele, *Daily News,* October 6, 1987.

52. *Ibid.*

53. *Washington Post TV Week,* November 1–7, 1987; *Beacon Journal,* October 8, 1987; *Daily News,* October 6, 1987. The series was also promoted as educational material in the United States. *Harmony Gold News,* n.d.; *New York City Tribune,* March 2, 1987; *Sunday Republican,* March 1, 1987.

54. The phrase is Shula Marks', coined to express the tensions at the heart of politics in apartheid South Africa, and to describe the political activity of leadership figures in South Africa who negotiated a precarious course between traditionalism and modernism, action and restraint, the imperatives of the South African state and the expectations of black South Africans: Marks, *Ambiguities of Dependence,* p. 6.

55. Maré and Hamilton, *An Appetite for Power,* pp. 1, 173; see also the *Guardian,* July 6, 1987; *Star,* September 30, 1986, October 4, 1987.

56. Interview with Faure, *Hartford Courant,* February 28, 1987.

57. Maré and Hamilton, *An Appetite for Power,* p. 6.

58. J. Wright and G. Maré, "The Splice of Coincidence," *Sunday Tribune,* December 7, 1986.

59. Maré and Hamilton, *An Appetite for Power,* pp. 3, 164.

60. Interview with Faure, *Daily News,* October 6, 1987.

61. *Drum,* January 1987. Also see *Sunday Tribune,* December 21, 1986.

62. *Star,* October 4, 1986; *Sunday Star,* October 12, 1986; *Souvenir Brochure,* p. 12; interview with Faure, *Houston Chronicle,* March 8–14, 1987; *Guardian,* July 6, 1987.

63. *Drum,* January 1987.

64. G. Buthelezi, *Power is Ours,* New York, Books in Focus, 1984.

65. Marks, *Ambiguities of Dependence,* conclusion.

66. *Ibid.,* p. 123.

67. Tomaselli, "Camera, Colour and Racism," pp. 9–11.

68. Fax, Errard Sullivan, manager of Shakaland, to C.A. Hamilton, January 25, 1992.

69. Shakaland staff were unable to provide a detailed visitor profile. Director Barry Leitch estimated that, excluding the high numbers of local visitors that came in school parties, the number of foreign tourists slightly exceeded that of locals. He noted further that the local component was growing steadily, and expected it to equal the foreign component in the very near future. While large numbers of black schoolchildren visited the resort, only a small—but steadily increasing—proportion of black guests stayed in the luxury accommodation.

70. *The Motorist,* first quarter, 1989, p. 4.

71. *Weekend Getaway,* October 1989, p. 76.

72. Siobhan O'Reagain in *Weekend Getaway,* October 1989.

73. *Ibid.*

74. In his article "Mickey Mouse History: Portraying the Past at Disney World" (*Radical History Review,* 32, 1985, pp. 33–57), Michael Wallace remarks on a similar attention to detail in Disneyland, which he ascribes to Disney's cinematic roots (see p. 38).

75. In October 1991 a deluxe double room cost R390.00 (about $180) per night, meals and "cultural experience" included. Day trips—the "Nandi experience" which offered a "two hour sampler of Zulu tradition which included Ngoma dancing and lunch"—cost around R60.00 (about $20.00) per person, with significantly reduced rates for school trips and other large parties.

76. Leitch noted that Shakaland was launched into "the slipstream" of the television series, and that following the series, the name Shakaland provided "an instantly powerful image" (interview with Leitch, February 25, 1992).

77. In fact, Shakaland was not the site of either the original Great Kraal or even the miniseries' Great Kraal. That was fired in the final flaming scene of the film. It was, as we have noted, the set of the smaller residence inhabited in the film by Shaka's father, Senzangakhona, while the Mhlathuze Lake is a dam constructed in the mid-1980s, which was not a feature of the landscape in Shakan times.

78. A similar "cultural experience" was also on offer at Phumangena, outside Johannesburg, which drew an equally favorable response from its visitors. Its popularity was such that minibus taxi drivers from the townships of Seboxeng and Mamelodi offered associations and other groups, including Sotho-speaking women's clubs, special rates for day trips. All aspects of Phumangena were imported from KwaZulu and modeled on Shakaland, down to the staff, many of whom were related to the staff at Shakaland. Sotho-speaking visitors to Phumangena expressed interest in visiting Shakaland, which they perceived to be superior to Phumangena, but noted that it was "too far" and "more expensive," as well as expressing concern about venturing into a Zulu-speaking area.

79. *Your Family,* March 1989.

80. Interview with Leitch, February 25, 1992.

81. Interview with Leitch, February 25, 1992.

82. Interview with Leitch, February 25, 1992.

83. Assessing audience response to an exhibit such as Shakaland poses tremendous difficulties. In addition to the use of visitor statistics, the evaluation of its reception was based on overheard audience comments and responses actively elicited in conversation with other visitors by myself and three other anthropologists who accompanied me on a trip. I have also used reviews by travel writers and interviews with travel agents.

84. For a more detailed discussion of the popular appetite in South Africa for a revised history, and the role played by the Reader's Digest in identifying and meeting this need, see L. Witz and C. Hamilton, "Reaping the Whirlwind: The *Reader's Digest Illustrated History of South Africa* and Changing Popular Perceptions of History," *South African Historical Journal,* May 1991, pp. 185–202.

85. Wallace, "Mickey Mouse History," p. 33.

86. There were few sites in South Africa where this was happening, a notable exception being the "Art and Ambiguity" exhibition hosted by the increasingly politically and socially aware Johannesburg Art Gallery. Reviewing the exhibition, prominent critic Barry Ronge noted that it "opens another avenue along which we can see what Martin Luther King called 'the content of our character' which will inevitably define our future" (*Sunday Times,* December 8, 1991).

87. *Weekend Getaway,* October 1989, p. 76.

88. R. Rosenzweig, "American Heritage," in Susan Porter Benson, Stephen Breier, and Roy Rosenzweig (eds.), *Presenting the Past: Essays on History and the Public,* Philadelphia, Temple University Press, 1986, p. 47.

89. At this time the Africana Museum in Johannesburg approached both the present author and the University of the Witwatersrand's history workshop for assistance in reconceptualizing their displays. The despair of educators concerning the inappropriateness of present history curricula and the absence of suitable materials for teaching beyond the curricula was also evident at the teaching workshop section of the colloquium on the *mfecane* debate held in September 1991 at Wits University.

90. Ford and Rockefeller, for example, were among the first creators of museum villages in the United States (see Benson et al. (eds.), *Presenting the Past,* p. 146).

91. Interview with Leitch, February 25, 1992.

92. Letter, Fiona Small to Rotary Club president, January 22, 1990.

93. Interview with Leitch, February 25, 1992.

94. Interview with Leitch, February 25, 1992.

95. *Masikanda* is a modern urban musical form, while *ngoma* is a rural dance style that has its roots in first fruits ceremonies.

96. The demonstrator was a spear-maker by trade before coming to Shakaland to practice his craft.

97. There was no attempt to suggest that a genuine consultation was taking place. Indeed, in response to subsequent questioning, the adviser noted that the man who acted as the *sangoma* was not a real practitioner. By comparison, the entrepreneurs behind commercial Haitian voodoo shows which are "acted" for audiences claim that on some occasions real possession occurs in the course of a show. See Alan Goldberg, "Identity and Experience in Haitian Voodoo Shows," *Annals of Tourism Research,* 10, 1983, pp. 479–97.

98. U. Eco, *Travels in Hyper Reality,* San Diego, Harcourt Brace, Jovanovich, 1990.

99. *The Motorist,* first quarter, 1989, p. 5.

100. *Ibid.,* pp. 4–5.

101. The closest parallel to this to be found elsewhere are the refurbished ghost towns in the United States. Noting that in these towns tourists get fleeced just like the cowboys of yesteryear, Eco comments, ". . . since the theatricality is explicit, the hallucination operates in making the visitors take part in the scene and thus become participants in that commercial fair that is apparently an element of the fiction, but in fact represents the substantial aim of the whole imitative machine" (*Travels in Hyper Reality,* pp. 42–43). A key difference in Shakaland is that the commercial basis of the enterprise was obscured.

102. D. MacCannell, "Staged Authenticity: Arrangements of Social Space in Tourist Settings," *American Journal of Sociology,* 79, 1973, pp. 589–603; E.C. Fine and J.H. Speer, "Tour Guide Performances as Sight Sacralization," *Annals of Tourism Research,* 12, 1985, pp. 73–95.

103. Fine and Speer, "Tour Guide Performances," p. 82.

104. V. Turner, *The Ritual Process: Structure and Anti-Structure,* Chicago, Aldine, 1969, p. 129.

105. I. Karp and C. Kratz, "The Fate of Tippoo's Tiger: A Critical Account of Ethnographic Display," paper presented to the anthropology department, Northwestern University, 1992, p. 8.

106. It has been argued in relation to the fissured nature of the relationship between history and memory in American life that the repairing of this fracture through the enhancing of people's ability to imagine and create a different future through the re-use of history is a major goal of public history (Benson et al. (eds.), *Presenting the Past,* p. 6).

107. In these respects, Shakaland functioned in a manner similar to "an invented tradition." See E. Hobsbawm, "Introduction: Inventing Traditions," in Hobsbawm and Ranger (eds.), *The Invention of Tradition,* p. 9.

108. The distinction is made in Karp and Kratz, "The Fate of Tippoo's Tiger," p. 2.

109. I. Karp, C.M. Kreamer, and S.D. Lavine (eds.), *Museums and Communities: The Politics of Public Culture,* Washington, Smithsonian Institution Press, 1992, p. 6.

110. I. Karp, "On Civil Society and Social Identity," in Karp et al. (eds.), *Museums and Communities,* p. 19.

111. Interview with Leitch, February 25, 1992.

112. Interview with Leitch, February 25, 1992.

113. At Phumangena, the guide described the Great Hut as the venue of all important discussions in the homestead, and as the site for conflict resolution. He went on to say that when labor disputes broke out in the resort between the workers and the manager, discussions would convene in the Great Hut.

114. E. Preston-Whyte, "The Real Zulu?", paper presented to a special panel on Shakaland at the Association for Anthropology in Southern Africa Annual Meeting, 1992.

115. King Goodwill Zwelithini, quoted in the *Weekly Mail,* December 19, 1991–January 2, 1992.

116. Shaka Day speech, King Goodwill Zwelithini, Eshowe, 1991.

117. Both quotes from the *Weekly Mail,* August 30–September 5, 1991.

118. Quoted in the *Weekly Mail,* May 30–June 6, 1991.

119. "Faith in Fakes" was the original English title of Eco's essay on exhibitions in the United States in his *Travels in Hyper Reality,* cited earlier in this chapter.

120. *Weekend Getaway,* October 1989, p. 75.

121. C. Geertz, *Works and Lives: The Anthropologist as Author,* Stanford, Stanford University Press, 1988.

Chapter Six

1. D.W. Cohen, *The Combing of History,* Chicago, Chicago University Press, 1994, chap. 1.

2. T. Lodge, "South Africa: Democracy and Development in Post-Apartheid South Africa," unpublished paper presented to the Institute for Advanced Social Research, University of the Witwatersrand, 1994.

3. Z.S.T. Skweyiya, "Chieftaincy, the Ethnic Question and the Democratisation Process in South Africa", Community Law Centre Occasional Paper Series, University of the Western Cape, 1993, p. 1.

4. *Negotiation News,* December 15, 1993. I am grateful to Elsabe Wessels for this reference.

5. See Buthelezi quoted in M. Massing, "The Chief," *New York Review of Books,* February 12, 1987.

6. See, for example, Wright and Hamilton, "Traditions and Transformations," pp. 49–82; Hamilton, "Ideology, Oral Traditions and the Struggle for Power."

7. Cited in Malaba, "Shaka as Literary Theme," p. 53.

8. *Ibid.,* p. 55.

9. Malaba notes that Shaka's praises express feelings of insecurity prevalent in Shakan times (*ibid.*).

10. Hamilton (ed.), *The Mfecane Aftermath.*

11. Wright, "The Dynamics of Power and Conflict," p. 71.

12. *JSA,* vol. 1, p. 201, Jantshi.

13. *Ibid.,* vol. 3, p. 161, Mkando.

14. *Ibid.,* vol. 2, p. 15, Mabonsa. For details on Mahlaphahlapha see *ibid.,* vol. 1, p. 299, Lunguza; Bryant, *Olden Times,* pp. 58, 347; and Bryant, *History of the Zulu,* p. 37.

15. A.Kuper, "Cannibals, Beasts and Twins," in A. Kuper, *South Africa and the Anthropologist,* London and New York, Routledge & Kegan Paul, 1987, pp. 167–96.

16. See, for example, Matsebula, *History of Swaziland,* p. 160.

17. "Cannibals. There used to be a saying as the sun was setting, 'Oh! It is going to be devoured by cannibals', for the impression was that cannibals lived to the west" (*JSA,* vol. 1, p. 34, Baleni). See vol. 3, pp. 26–27, Mbovu; vol. 3, p. 81, Melapi. For a claim that cannibals were to be found among the upcountry Ntuli see vol. 1, p. 126, Dunjwa. Also see vol. 1, p. 301, Lunguza. For "cannibal" attacks reported on Hlubi and Tshabalala, and by the Radebe, see vol. 2, pp. 14–14, Mabonsa.

18. *Ibid.,* vol. 1, p. 60, Bazley; vol. 1, p. 90, Dabula.

19. *Ibid.,* vol. 1, p. 302, Lunguza; vol. 2, p. 24, Mabonsa, vol. 2, p. 202, Mangati.

20. *Ibid.,* vol. 1, p. 90, Dabula, p. 201, Jantshi.

21. *Ibid.,* p. 54, Bazley.

22. *Ibid.,* vol. 2, p. 277, Maziyana.

23. *Ibid.,* vol. 1, p. 201, Jantshi.

24. *Ibid.,* p. 56, Bazley.

25. *Ibid.,* vol. 2, p. 31, Mabonsa.

26. *Ibid.,* pp. 85, 87, Magidigidi; Bryant, *Olden Times,* p. 271.

27. D. Coplan, *In the Time of Cannibals: The Word Music of South Africa's Basotho Migrants,* Chicago, Chicago University Press, 1995, p. 1.

28. *JSA,* vol. 3, testimony of Mbovu kaNdengezi contained within that of Mbovu kaMtshumayeli, p. 29.

29. See Mamdani's discussion of hostel dwellers' use of tradition and rural ideas of discipline in the face of mounting political violence in the early 1990s (*Citizen and Subject,* pp. 276–84).

30. This was recognized at the 1994 history workshop's History Teachers' Conference which solicited for its proceedings a paper on "Precolonial Democracy."

Bibliography

Published

Allen, C. (ed.), *Tales of the Dark Continent: Images of British Colonial Africa in the Twentieth Century,* London, Deutsch, 1979.

Alpers, E.A., "State, Merchant Capital and Gender Relations in Southern Mozambique to the End of the Nineteenth Century: Some Tentative Hypotheses," *African Economic History,* 13, 1984, pp. 22–55.

Anderson, B., *Imagined Communities: Reflections on the Origin and Spread of Nationalism,* London and New York, Verso, 1983 and 1986.

Anderson, D.M. and D.H. Johnson (eds.), *The Predictable Past: Prophets and Prophecy in Eastern Africa,* London, James Currey, 1994.

Angas, G.F., *The Kafirs of Natal,* first publ. London, Hogarth, 1849; republ. Cape Town, A.A. Balkema, 1974.

Appiah, K.A., "Out of Africa: Typologies of Nativism," *Yale Journal of Criticism,* 2, 1988, pp. 153–78.

Apter, A., "Que Faire? Reconsidering Inventions of Africa," *Critical Inquiry,* 19, 1992, pp. 87–104.

Ashe, W. and E.V.W. Edgell, *The Story of the Zulu Campaign,* London, Low, Marshe, Searle & Rivington, 1880.

Ashforth, A., *The Politics of Official Discourse in Twentieth-Century South Africa,* Oxford, Clarendon Press, 1990.

Attwell, D., "Mofolo's *Chaka* and the Bambata Rebellion," *Research into African Literatures,* 18, 1, Spring 1987, pp. 51–70.

Ayliff, J., "History of the Abambo," *Gazette,* Butterworth, 1912.

Badian, S., *La Mort de Chaka,* Paris, Presence Africaine, 1972.

Ballard, C., *John Dunn: The Great White Chief of Zululand,* Johannesburg, Ad Donker, 1985.

Ballard, C., *The House of Shaka: The Zulu Monarchy Illustrated,* Durban, Emoyeni Books, 1988.

Barber, K. and P.F. Moraes Farias (eds.), *Discourse and its Disguises: The Interpretation of African Oral Texts,* Birmingham, University of Birmingham, 1989.

Barker, F. et al. (eds.), *The Politics of Theory,* Colchester, University of Essex, 1983.

Barter, C., *Stray Memories of Natal and Zululand,* Pietermaritzburg, Munro Bros., 1897.

Bauman, R., *Story, Performance and Event: Contextual Studies of Oral Narrative,* Cambridge, Cambridge University Press, 1986.

Becker, P., *Path of Blood,* London, Longmans, 1962.

Becker, P., *Rule of Fear,* London, Longmans, 1964.

Benham, M.S., *Henry Callaway, First Bishop for Kaffraria: His Life-History and Work: A Memoir,* ed. Rev. Canon Benham, London and New York, Macmillan & Co., 1896.

Benson, S.P., S. Breier, and R. Rozenzweig (eds.), *Presenting the Past: Essays on History and the Public,* Philadelphia, Temple University Press, 1986.

Bhabha, H., "Of Mimicry and Man: The Ambivalence of Colonial Discourse," *October,* 29, 1984, pp. 125–33.

Bhabha, H., "Signs Taken for Wonders," *Critical Inquiry,* 12, 1, 1985, pp. 144–65.

Bhabha, H., *The Location of Culture*, London and New York, Routledge, 1994.

Binns, C.T., *The Last Zulu King: The Life and Death of Cetshwayo*, London, Longmans, 1963.

Binns, C.T., *Dinuzulu*, London, Longmans, 1968.

Bird, J. (ed.), *The Annals of Natal: 1495–1945*, vol. 1, Pietermaritzburg, P. Davis & Sons, 1888; repr. Cape Town, Struik, 1965.

Black, M., "More About Metaphor," *Dialectica*, 31, 3–4, 1977, pp. 431–57.

Blair, D., "The Shaka Theme in Dramatic Literature in French in West Africa," *African Studies*, 33, 3, 1974, pp. 113–41.

Blue Book, Native Affairs, Annual Reports, government publication, 1904.

Bond, G., *Chaka the Terrible*, London, Arco Publications, 1961; reissued as James Langa, *Shaka*, Salisbury, Longmans, 1982.

Bonner, P., *Kings, Commoners and Concessionaires: The Evolution and Dissolution of the Nineteenth-Century Swazi State*, Cambridge and Johannesburg, Cambridge University Press and Ravan, 1983.

Bonner, P. et al. (eds.), *Holding their Ground: Class, Locality and Culture in Nineteenth and Twentieth Century South Africa*, Johannesburg, University of the Witwatersrand Press, 1989.

Boteler, T., *Narrative of a Voyage of Discovery to Africa and Arabia, Performed in His Majesty's Ships Leven and Barracouta from 1821–1826, under the Command of Capt. F.W. Owen, R.N. By Capt. Thomas Boteler*, 2. vols., London, R. Bentley, 1835.

Bozzoli, B., "The Discourses of Myth and the Myth of Discourse," *South African Historical Journal*, 26, 1992, pp. 191–97.

Bozzoli, B. and P. Delius, "Radical History and South African Society," in Brown et al. (eds.), *History from South Africa*, pp. 3–25; first published in *Radical History Review*, 46, 7, 1990, pp. 13–45.

Brookes, E., *History of Native Policy*, Pretoria, J. L. van Schaik, 1927.

Brookes E.H. and C. de B. Webb, *A History of Natal*, Pietermaritzburg, University of Natal Press, 1967.

Brown, J., *The Definition of a Profession: The Authority of Metaphor in the History of Intelligence Testing, 1890–1930*, Princeton, Princeton University Press, 1992.

Brown, J. et al. (eds.), *History from South Africa: Alternative Visions and Practices*, Philadelphia, Temple University Press, 1991.

Brown, S. (ed.), *The Pressures of the Text: Orality, Texts and the Telling of Tales*, Birmingham University African Studies Series, no.4, Centre for West African Studies, 1995.

Bryant, A.T., "A Sketch of the Origin and Early History of the Zulu People," in *A Zulu–English Dictionary*, Pietermaritzburg, P. Davis & Sons, 1905.

Bryant, A.T., "The Origin of the Zulus," *Native Teacher's Journal*, 1, 1, 1919, pp. 9–16.

Bryant, A.T., *Olden Times in Zululand and Natal*, London, Longmans, 1929.

Bryant, A.T., *A History of the Zulu and Neighbouring Tribes*, Cape Town, Struik, 1964.

Bryant, A.T., *The Zulu People: As They Were before the White Man Came*, Pietermaritzburg, Shuter & Shooter, 2nd ed., 1967.

Burgess, C., "Shaka Zulu: The Aftermath," *Southern Africa Today*, 3, 2, 1987, pp. 32–34.

Burness, D. *Shaka, King of the Zulus in African Literature*, Washington, Three Continents Press, 1976.

Buthelezi, G. *Power is Ours*, New York, Books in Focus, 1984.

Callaway, H., *Nursery Tales, Traditions and Histories of the Zulu*, Pietermaritzburg, Davis, and Springvale, 1868.

Callaway, H., *The Religious System of the AmaZulu*, Pietermaritzburg, Davis, and Springvale, 1870.

Callinicos, L., "The People's Past: Towards Transforming the Present," in B. Bozzoli (ed.), *Class, Community and Conflict*, Johannesburg, Ravan, 1987, pp. 44–64.

Campbell, E., "Ricksha Boy," *Natal Verse*, n.p., 1921.

Campbell, R., "The Flaming Terrapin," in G. Butler (ed.), *A Book of South African Verse*, Cape Town, Oxford University Press, first publ. 1959; republ. 1963.

Carlyle, T., *On Heroes, Hero Worship, and the Heroic in History*, Los Angeles and Oxford, University of California Press, 1993, ed. Michael K. Goldberg, J. Bratton, and M. Engel, introduction by Michael Goldberg; first publ. 1841.

Carroll, D., *The Subject in Question: The Languages of Theory and the Strategies of Fiction*, Chicago and London, Chicago University Press, 1982.

Chakrabarty, D., "Postcoloniality and the Artifice of History: Who Speaks for 'Indian' Pasts?" *Representations,* 37, Winter 1992, pp. 1–23.

Chanock, M., *Custom and Social Order,* Cambridge, Cambridge University Press, 1987.

Chase, J.C. (ed.), *The Natal Papers,* first publ. Grahamstown, Godlonton, 1883; republ. Cape Town, Struik, 1968.

Chesson, F.W., *The War in Zululand: A Brief Review of Sir Bartle Frere's Policy,* London, King, 1879.

Clifford, J., *The Predicament of Culture: Twentieth-Century Ethnography, Literature and Art,* Cambridge, MA, Harvard University Press, 1988.

Clifford, J. and G.E. Marcus, *Writing Culture: The Poetics and Politics of Ethnography,* Berkeley, Los Angeles, and London, University of California Press, 1986.

Cobbing, J., "The Mfecane as Alibi: Thoughts on Dithakong and Mbolompo," *Journal of African History,* 29, 1988, pp. 487–519.

Cobbing, J., "A Tainted Well. The Objectives, Historical Fantasies and Working Methods of James Stuart, with Counter-Argument," *Journal of Natal and Zulu History,* 11, 1988, pp. 115–54.

Cobbing, J., "Grasping the Nettle: The Slave Trade and the Early Zulu," paper presented to the workshop on Natal and Zululand in the colonial and precolonial periods, University of Natal, Pietermaritzburg, 1990, and published as Conference Proceedings in 1991.

Cohen, D., *Shaka, King of the Zulus,* New York, Doubleday & Co., 1973.

Cohen, D.W., *Towards a Reconstructed Past: Historical Texts from Busoga, Uganda,* London, British Academy and Oxford University Press, 1986.

Cohen, D.W., "The Undefining of Oral Tradition," *Ethnohistory,* 36, 1, 1989, pp. 9–17.

Cohen, D.W., *The Combing of History,* Chicago, Chicago University Press, 1994.

Cohen, D.W., and E.S. Atieno Odhiambo, *Siaya: The Historical Anthropology of an African Landscape,* London, James Currey, 1989.

Cohen, M., *Rider Haggard: His Life and Works,* London, Hutchinson, 1960.

Cohen, M. (ed.), *Rudyard Kipling to Rider Haggard: The Record of a Friendship,* London, Hutchinson, 1965.

Colenso, F. (alias Atherton Wylde), *My Chief and I,* London, Chapman & Hall, 1880.

Colenso, F.E. and E. Durnford, *History of the Zulu War and its Origins,* London, Chapman & Hall, 1880.

Colenso, H.E., "Zululand: Past and Present," *Journal of the Manchester Geographical Society,* 1890.

Colenso, J.W., *Bringing Forth the Light,* ed. Ruth Edgecombe, Pietermaritzburg and Durban, University of Natal Press and KCAL, 1982.

Comaroff, J., "Images of Empire, Contests of Conscience: Models of Colonial Domination in South Africa," *American Ethnologist,* 16, 4, 1989, pp. 661–85.

Comaroff, J. and J. Comaroff, *Of Revelation and Revolution: Christianity, Colonialism and Consciousness in South Africa,* vol. 1, Chicago, Chicago University Press, 1991.

Comaroff, J. and J. Comaroff, *Ethnography and the Historical Imagination,* Boulder, San Francisco, and Oxford, Westview Press, 1992.

Cope, N., "The Zulu Petit Bourgeoisie and Zulu Nationalism in the 1920s: Origins of Inkatha," *Journal of Southern African Studies,* 16, 3, 1990, pp. 431–51.

Cope, N., *To Bind the Nation: Solomon kaDinuzulu and Zulu Nationalism,* Pietermaritzburg, University of Natal Press, 1993.

Cope, R., "The History of Land Occupation in South Africa–Myth and Reality," *Some Basic Issues,* Johannesburg, Independent Teachers' Centre, 1981, pp. 9–23.

Cope, R., "Political Power within the Zulu Kingdom and the 'Coronation Laws' of 1873," *Journal of Natal and Zulu History,* 8, 1985, pp. 11–31.

Cope, R.L., "Written in Characters of Blood? The Reign of King Cetshwayo kaMpande 1872–1879," *Journal of African History,* 36, 1995, pp. 247–69.

Cope, T., *Izibongo, Zulu Praise Poems,* Oxford, Oxford University Press, 1968.

Coplan, D., *In the Time of Cannibals: The Word Music of South Africa's Basotho Migrants,* Chicago, Chicago University Press, 1995.

Cory, G.E., *The Rise of South Africa,* London, Longmans, 1910–30, 5 vols.

Cowley, C., *Kwa-Zulu: Queen Mkabi's Story,* Cape Town, Struik, 1966.

Crais, C., *The Making of the Colonial Order: White Supremacy and Black Resistance in the Eastern Cape, 1770–1815,* Johannesburg, Witwatersrand University Press, 1992.

Crankshaw, P., A. Williams, and G. Hayman, "To Educate, Entertain and Inform: The Meyer Commission into TV," *SAFTTA Journal,* 3, 1983.

Curtin, P.D., *The Image of Africa: British Ideas and Action, 1780–1850,* Madison, University of Wisconsin Press, 1964.

Curtin, P.D., "Field Techniques for Collecting and Processing Oral Data," *Journal of African History,* 9, 3, 1968, pp. 367–83.

Curtin, P.D., "Oral Tradition and African History," *Journal of the Folklore Institute,* 6, 1969, pp. 137–55.

Daniel, J.B. McI., "A Geographical Survey of Pre-Shakan Zululand," *South African Geographical Journal,* 55, 1, 1973, pp. 23–31.

Darlow, D.J., *African Heroes: Ntsikana, Tshaka, Khama and Moshoeshoe,* Lovedale, Lovedale Press, 1936.

Davis, S., *Apartheid's Rebels: Inside South Africa's Hidden War,* New Haven and London, Yale University Press, 1987.

De Certeau, M., *The Writing of History,* trans. T. Conlay, New York, Columbia University Press, 1991, first publ. in French, 1975.

De Kiewiet, C.W., *The Imperial Factor in South Africa: A Study in Politics and Economics,* London, Cambridge University Press, 1937.

Delegorgue, A., *Travels in Southern Africa,* trans. F. Webb, vol. 1, Pietermaritzburg and Durban, University of Natal Press and KCAL, 1990.

Dening, G., *Islands and Beaches: Discourses on a Silent Land: Marquesas 1774–1880,* Honolulu, University Press of Hawaii, 1980.

Dhlomo, H.I.E., *Valley of a Thousand Hills,* Durban, Knox, 1941.

Dhlomo, R.R.R., *UShaka,* Pietermaritzburg, Shuter & Shooter, 1936.

Dlamini, P. (H. Filter [comp.] and S. Bourquin [trans. and ed.]), *Paulina Dlamini: Servant of Two Kings,* Durban and Pietermaritzburg, KCAL and University of Natal Press, 1986.

Dominy, G., "Thomas Baines: The McGonagall of Shepstone's 1873 Zululand Expedition," in M. Comrie (comp.), "Notes and Queries," *Natalia,* December 21, 1991, pp. 75–79.

Dube, J.L., *Insila kaTshaka,* Mariannhill, Mariannhill Mission Press, 1932, trans. J. Boxwell as *Jeqe, the Body Servant of Shaka,* Lovedale, Lovedale Press, 1957.

Du Buisson, L., *The White Man Cometh,* Johannesburg, Jonathan Ball, 1987.

Duminy, A. and C. Ballard (eds.), *The Anglo-Zulu War: New Perspectives,* Pietermaritzburg, University of Natal Press, 1981.

Duminy, A. and B. Guest (eds.), *Natal and Zululand: From Earliest Times to 1910: A New History,* Pietermaritzburg, University of Natal Press and Shuter & Shooter, 1989.

Dunn, J., *Cetywayo and the Three Generals,* Pietermaritzburg, Natal Print & Publishing Co., 1886.

Eco, U., *Travels in Hyper Reality,* San Diego, Harcourt Brace Jovanovich, 1990; first publ. in Italian, 1976.

Eldredge, E., "Sources of Conflict in Southern Africa, c. 1800–1830: The 'Mfecane' Reconsidered," *Journal of African History,* 33, 1992, pp. 1–36.

Eldredge, E., and F. Morton (eds.), *Slavery in South Africa: Captive Labor on the Dutch Frontier,* Boulder, Westview Press, 1994.

Ellis, P.B., *H. Rider Haggard: A Voice from the Infinite,* London and Henley, Routledge & Kegan Paul, 1978.

Etherington, N., "South African Origins of Rider Haggard's Early African Romances," *Notes and Queries,* 24, 1977, pp. 436–38.

Etherington, N., *Preachers, Peasants and Politics: South East Africa: African Christian Communities in Natal, Pondoland, and Zululand,* London, Royal Historical Society, 1978.

Etherington, N., "Anglo-Zulu Relations, 1856–1878," in Duminy and Ballard (eds.), *The Anglo-Zulu War,* pp. 13–57.

Etherington, N., *Rider Haggard,* Boston, Twayne Publishers, 1984.

Etherington, N., "Shrinking the Zulu," *Southern African Review of Books,* September–October 1992, p. 12.

Evans, M.S., *The Native Problem in Natal,* Durban, P. Davis & Sons, 1906.

Evans, M.S., *Black and White in South Africa: A Study in Sociology*, London, Longmans, Green & Co., 1911.

Fabian, J., *Time and the Other: How Anthropology Makes its Object*, New York, Columbia University Press, 1983.

Fabian, J., *Power and Performance*, Madison, Wisconsin University Press, 1990.

Fall, M., *Chaka ou le Roi Visionnaire*, Dakar, Abidjan, Lomé, Les Nouvelles Editions Africaines, 1984.

Feierman, S., *Peasant Intellectuals: Anthropology and History in Tanzania*, Madison, University of Wisconsin Press, 1990.

Fernandez, J.W., "The Shaka Complex," *Transition*, 29, 1967, pp. 11–14.

Fernandez, J. (ed.), *Beyond Metaphor: The Theory of Tropes in Anthropology*, Stanford, Stanford University Press, 1991.

Fine, E.C. and J.H. Speer, "Tour Guide Performances as Sight Sacralization," *Annals of Tourism Research*, 12, 1985, pp. 73–95.

Finnegan, R., *Oral Literature in Africa*, Oxford, Clarendon Press, 1970.

Finnegan, R., "A Note on Oral Tradition and Historiographical Evidence," *History and Theory*, 9, 2, 1971, pp. 195–201.

Finnegan, R., *Oral Poetry: Its Nature, Significance and Social Content*, Cambridge, Cambridge University Press, 1977.

Finnegan, R., *Literacy and Orality: Studies in the Technology of Communication*, Oxford and New York, Basil Blackwell, 1988.

Forsyth, P., "The Past in Service of the Present: The Political Use of History by Chief A.N.M.G. Buthelezi, 1951–91," *South African Historical Journal*, 26, 1992, pp. 74–92.

Foucault, M., *Power/Knowledge: Selected Interviews and Other Writings, 1972–1977*, ed. C. Gordon, New York, Pantheon Books, 1980.

Fourie, P., *Tsjaka*, Johannesburg, Perskor, 1976, trans. Sheila Gilham as *Shaka*, Cape Town, Longman, 1976.

Freund, B., "Radical History Writing and the South African Context," *South African Historical Journal*, 24, 1991, pp. 154–59.

Friedman, F.L., D.M. Malcolm, and J.M. Sikakana (eds.), *Zulu Horizons*, Johannesburg, Witwatersrand University Press, 1962; repr. 1973.

Fritschi, G., *Africa and Gutenberg: Exploring Oral Structures in the Modern African Novel*, European University Studies, No. 9, Peter Lang, Bern, 1983.

Fuze, M.M., *The Black People and Whence They Came: A Zulu View*, first publ. privately in isiZulu as *Abantu Abamnyama*, Pietermaritzburg, 1922; and republ. in English, trans. H.C. Lugg, ed. A.T. Cope, Pietermaritzburg and Durban, University of Natal Press and KCAL, 1979; repr. 1982.

Fynn, H.F., *The Diary of Henry Francis Fynn*, ed. J. Stuart and D.M. Malcolm, Pietermaritzburg, Shuter & Shooter, 1950.

Fynney, A.B. "The Rise and Fall of the Zulu Nation" in A.B. Fynney, *Zululand and the Zulus*, Pietermaritzburg, Horne Bros., 1884; repr. Pretoria, State Library, 1967.

Gardiner, A., *Narrative of a Journey to the Zoolu Country*, first publ. London, 1836; republ. Cape Town, Struik, 1966.

Gates, H.L., Jr. (ed.), *"Race," Writing and Difference*, Chicago, Chicago University Press, 1986.

Geertz, C., *Works and Lives: The Anthropologist as Author*, Stanford, Stanford University Press, 1988.

Gérard, A., "Relire Chaka," *Politique Africaine*, 13, March 1984, pp. 8–20.

Gluckman, M., "Analysis of a Social System in Modern Zululand," part B, *Bantu Studies*, 14, 1940, pp. 147–74.

Gluckman, M., "The Kingdom of the Zulu in South Africa," in M. Fortes and E. Evans-Pritchard (eds.), *African Political Systems*, London, Oxford University Press, 1940, pp. 25–55.

Gluckman, M., "The Individual in a Social Framework: The Rise of King Shaka of Zululand," *Journal of African Studies*, 1, 2, 1974, pp. 113–44.

Godlonton, R., *A Narrative of the Irruption of the Kaffir Hordes*, Grahamstown, Meurant & Godlonton, 1836.

Golan, D., "The Life Story of King Shaka and Gender Tensions in the Zulu State," *History in Africa*, 17, 1990, pp. 95–111.

Golan, D., "Inkatha and its Use of the Zulu Past," *History in Africa*, 18, 1991, pp. 113–26.

Golan, D., *Inventing Shaka: Using History in the Construction of Zulu Nationalism*, Boulder and London, Lynne Rienner, 1994.

Goldberg, A., "Identity and Experience in Haitian Voodoo Shows," *Annals of Tourism Research*, 10, 1983, pp. 479–97.

Goody, J., *Interface between the Written and the Oral*, Oxford, Oxford University Press, 1987.

Gordon, R.E., *Shepstone: The Role of the Family in the History of South Africa, 1820–1900*, Cape Town, A.A. Balkema, 1968.

Goro-X, S., *Shaka–A Drama*, Johannesburg, Juta, 1940.

Gray, S., "Shaka as Literary Theme," *South African Journal of African Affairs*, 5, 1, 1975, pp. 66–70.

Gray, S., *John Ross, the True Story: A Novel*, Johannesburg, Penguin, 1987.

Gray, S., "South African Fiction and a Case History Revisited: An Account of Research into Retellings of the John Ross Story of Early Natal," *Research in African Literatures*, 19, 4, 1988, pp. 455–76.

Gray, S. and T. Couzens, "Printers and Other Devils: The Texts of Sol. T. Plaatje," *Research in African Literatures*, 9, 2, 1978, pp. 198–215.

Gray, S. and C. Skotnes, *The Assassination of Shaka*, Johannesburg, McGraw-Hill, 1974.

Gross, J. (ed.), *The Age of Kipling*, New York, Simon & Schuster, 1972.

Grundlingh, A.M., "George Orwell's 'Nineteen Eighty-Four': Some Reflections on its Relevance to the Study of History in South Africa," *Kleio*, 16, 1984, pp. 20–33.

Guest, W.R., *Langalibalele: The Crisis in Natal, 1873–1875*, Durban, Department of History and Political Science, University of Natal, Durban, 1976.

Guy, J., "Ecological Factors in the Rise of Shaka and the Zulu Kingdom," in Marks and Atmore (eds.), *Economy and Society*, pp. 102–19.

Guy, J., "The Role of Colonial Officials in the Destruction of the Zulu Kingdom," in Duminy and Ballard (eds.), *The Anglo-Zulu War*, pp. 148–74.

Guy, J., *The Destruction of the Zulu Kingdom*, first publ. London, Longmans, 1979; republ. Johannesburg, Ravan, 1982.

Guy, J., *The Heretic: A Study of the Life of John William Colenso, 1814–1883*, Pietermaritzburg and Johannesburg, University of Natal Press and Ravan, 1983.

Haggard, H.R., *Nada the Lily*, London, Longmans, 1882.

Haggard, H.R., *Allan Quatermain*, London, Longmans, 1887.

Haggard, H.R., *The Witch's Head*, London, Spencer Blackett, 1884.

Haggard, H.R., *King Solomon's Mines*, London, Cassell, 1885.

Haggard, H.R., *Allan's Wife*, serialized in *Macmillan's Magazine*, vol. 53, February 1886.

Haggard, H.R., *Cetywayo and his White Neighbours*, first publ. London, Trübner, 1882; ed. with new material, 1888; 3rd ed., London, Trübner & Co., 1890.

Haggard, H.R., *Remarks on Recent Events in Zululand, Natal and the Transvaal*, London, Kegan Paul, Trench, Trübner & Co., 1900.

Haggard, H.R., *Child of Storm*, London, Longmans, 1913.

Haggard, H.R., *She*, in *Three Adventure Novels of H. Rider Haggard*, New York, Dover Publications, 1951; first publ. London, Longmans, Green, 1887.

Haggard, H.R., *Days of my Life*, ed. C.J. Longman, London and New York, Longmans, Green & Co., 1926, 2 vols.

Haggard, H.R., *Finished*, London, Macdonald, 1962; first publ. 1917.

Haggard, L.R., *The Cloak that I Left: A Biography of the Author Henry Rider Haggard, KBE, by his Daughter Lilias Rider Haggard*, London, Hodder & Stroughton, 1951.

Hall, E., *Inventing the Barbarian: Greek Self-Definition through Tragedy*, Oxford, Clarendon Press, 1989.

Hall, M., "Dendroclimatology, Rainfall and Human Adaptation in the Later Iron Age of Natal and Zululand," *Annals of the Natal Museum*, 22, 3, 1976, pp. 693–703.

Hamilton, C.A., "Ideology and Oral Traditions: Listening to the 'Voices from Below'," *History in Africa*, 14, 1987, pp. 67–86.

Hamilton, C.A., "'An Appetite for the Past': The Re-creation of Shaka and the Crisis in Popular Historical Consciousness," *South African Historical Journal*, 22, 1990, pp. 141–57.

Hamilton, C.A., "'The Character and Objects of Chaka': A Reconsideration of the Making of Shaka as 'Mfecane' Motor," *Journal of African History,* 33, 1992, pp. 37–63.

Hamilton, C.A. (ed.), *The Mfecane Aftermath,* Johannesburg and Pietermaritzburg, Witwatersrand University Press and University of Natal Press, 1995.

Hamilton, C.A. and J.B. Wright, "The Making of the *AmaLala*: Ethnicity, Ideology and Relations of Subordination in a Precolonial Context," *South African Historical Journal,* 22, 1990, pp. 3–23.

Hammond, D. and A. Jablow, *The Africa that Never Was: Four Centuries of British Writing about Africa,* New York, Twayne, 1970.

Hanson, A., "The Making of the Maori: Cultural Invention and its Logic," *American Anthropologist,* 91, 1990, pp. 890–902.

Harries, P., "Slavery, Social Incorporation and Surplus Extraction: The Nature of Free and Unfree Labour in South-East Africa," *Journal of African History,* 22, 1981, pp. 309–30.

Havelock, E.A., *Prologue to Greek Literacy,* Cincinnati, University of Cincinnati Press, 1971.

Hayman, G. and R. Tomaselli, "Technology in the Service of Ideology: The First 50 Years of Broadcasting in South Africa," in K. Tomaselli et al. (eds.), *Addressing the Nation: Studies in South African Media,* vol. 1, Johannesburg, R. Lyon, 1986.

Henige, D., *Oral Historiography,* London, Longman, 1982.

Herd, N., *The Bent Pine: The Trial of Chief Langalibalele,* Johannesburg, Ravan, 1976.

Higgins, D.S. (ed.), *The Private Diaries of Sir Rider Haggard, 1914–1925,* London, Cassell, 1980.

Higgins, D.S., *Rider Haggard: The Great Storyteller,* London, Cassell, 1981.

Higham, J. et al., *History: The Development of Historical Studies in the United States,* Princeton, Prentice-Hall, 1965.

Hobsbawm, E. and T. Ranger (eds.), *The Invention of Tradition,* Cambridge, CUP, 1983.

Hofmeyr, I., *We Spend our Years as a Tale that is Told: Oral Historical Narrative in a South African Chiefdom,* Johannesburg, Witwatersrand University Press, 1993.

Holden, W.C., *The Past and Future of the Kaffir Races,* London, publ. for the author, printed by William Nichols, 1866; republ. Cape Town, Struik, 1963.

Isaacs, N., *Travels and Adventures in Eastern Africa,* first publ. London, E. Churton, 1836; republ. Cape Town, Van Riebeeck Society for the Publication of South African Historical Documents, 1937, and Cape Town, Struik, ed. L. Herrman and P. Kirby, 1970.

James, D.,"'I Dress in this Fashion': Transformations in Sotho Dress and Women's Lives in a Sekhukhuneland Village, South Africa", in H. Hendrickson (ed.), *Clothing and Difference: Embodied Identities in Colonial and Post-Colonial Africa,* Durham, NC, Duke University Press, 1996, pp. 34–65.

Junod, H., *Life of a South African Tribe,* London, Macmillan, 1927, 2 vols.

Karp, I., "Other Cultures and Museum Perspectives," in I. Karp and S. Lavine (eds.), *Exhibiting Cultures: The Poetics and Politics of Museum Display,* Washington, Smithsonian Institution Press, 1991.

Karp, I., "On Civil Society and Social Identity," in Karp et al. (eds.), *Museums and Communities,* pp. 19–33.

Karp, I., C.M. Kreamer, and S. Lavine (eds.), *Museums and Communities: The Politics of Public Culture,* Washington, Smithsonian Institution Press, 1992.

Katz, W., *Rider Haggard and the Fiction of Empire: A Critical Study of British Imperial Fiction,* Cambridge, Cambridge University Press, 1987.

Keesing, R., "Creating the Past: Custom and Identity in the Contemporary Pacific," *The Contemporary Pacific,* 1, 1989, pp. 19–42.

Kipling, R., "The Man Who Would Be King," in W. Somerset Maugham, *Maugham's Choice of Kipling's Best,* New York, Doubleday & Co., 1953, pp. 162–92.

Krige, E.J., *The Social System of the Zulus,* first publ. London, Longmans, Green & Co., 1936; republ. Pietermaritzburg, Shuter & Shooter, 1950.

Krikler, J., "Waiting for the Historians," *Southern African Review of Books,* 3, 6, August–October, 1990, pp. 16–17.

Kotze, D.A., *African Politics in South Africa, 1964–1974: Parties and Issues,* Pretoria, J.L. van Schaik, 1975.

Kucklick, H. "Contested Monuments: The Politics of Archaeology in Southern Africa," in G. Stocking (ed.), *Colonial Situations,* Madison, University of Wisconsin Press, 1991.

Kucklick, H., *The Savage Within: The Social History of British Anthropology, 1885–1945,* Cambridge, Cambridge University Press, 1991.

Kunene, D.P., "Shaka in the Literature of Southern Africa," in Burness, D. (ed.), *Shaka, King of the Zulus in African Literature,* pp. 165–92.

Kunene, M., *Emperor Shaka the Great: A Zulu Epic,* London, Heinemann, 1979.

Kunene, M., *Anthem of the Decades,* London, Heinemann, 1981.

Kuper, A., *South Africa and the Anthropologist,* London and New York, Routledge & Kegan Paul, 1987.

Kuper, A. "The House and Zulu Political Structure in the Nineteenth Century," *Journal of African History,* 34, 1993, pp. 469–87.

Laband, J., *Rope of Sand: The Rise and Fall of the Zulu Kingdom in the Nineteenth Century,* Johannesburg, Jonathan Ball, 1995.

Laband, J. and J.B. Wright, *King Cetshwayo kaMpande,* Pietermaritzburg and Durban, University of Natal Press and KCAL, 1980.

Laclau, E., *Politics and Ideology in Marxist Theory,* London, Verso, 1977.

La Capra, D., *Rethinking Intellectual History: Texts, Contexts, Language,* New York, Ithaca, 1983.

Lakoff, G. and M. Johnson, *Metaphors We Live By,* Chicago, Chicago University Press, 1980.

Lamula, P. *UZulukaMalandela,* Durban, Native Church Press, 1924.

Legassick, M., "The Frontier Tradition in South African Historiography," in Marks and Atmore (eds.), *Economy and Society,* pp. 44–79.

Leslie, D. *Among the Zulus and Amatongas,* Glasgow and Edinburgh, Edmonston & Douglas, 1875; republ. New York, Negro Universities Press, 1961.

MacCannell, D., "Staged Authenticity: Arrangements of Social Space in Tourist Settings," *American Journal of Sociology,* 79, 1973, pp. 589–603.

MacCannell, D., "Reconstructed Ethnicity: Tourism and Cultural Identity in Third World Communities," *Annals of Tourism Research,* 1984, pp. 375–91.

Mack, J., *Zulus,* Morristown, Silver Burdett & Co., 1981.

Macmillan, W.M., *Bantu, Boer and Briton,* London, Cambridge University Press, 1929.

Malaba, M.Z., "Super Shaka: Mazisi Kunene's *Emperor Shaka the Great," Research in African Literatures,* 19, 4, 1988, pp. 477–88.

Mallory, J.K., "Abnormal Waves on the South East Coast of South Africa," *International Hydrographic Review,* 51, 2, 1974, pp. 99–129.

Mamdani, M., *Citizen and Subject: Contemporary Africa and the Legacy of Late Colonialism,* Cape Town and Princeton, David Philip and Princeton University Press, 1996.

Maphalala, S., "The Black Man's Interpretation of South African History," paper presented at the University of Stellenbosch, October 14, 1981, publ. as Series B, no. 36, University of Zululand, 1983.

Maré, G., *Brothers Born of Warrior Blood: Politics and Ethnicity in South Africa,* Johannesburg, Ravan, 1992.

Maré, G. and C. Hamilton, *An Appetite for Power: Buthelezi's Inkatha and South Africa,* Johannesburg and Indianapolis, Ravan Press and Indiana University Press, 1987.

Marks, S., *Reluctant Rebellion: The 1906–8 Disturbances in Natal,* Oxford, Clarendon Press, 1970.

Marks, S., "South Africa: The Myth of the Empty Land," *History Today,* January 1980, pp. 8–12.

Marks, S., *The Ambiguities of Dependence in South Africa,* Johannesburg and Baltimore, Ravan and Johns Hopkins University Press, 1986.

Marks, S., "The Historiography of South Africa: Recent Developments," in B. Jewsiewicki and D. Newbury (eds.), *African Historiographies: What History for Which Africa?* Beverly Hills, London, and New Delhi, Sage, 1986, pp. 165–76.

Marks, S., "Patriotism, Patriarchy and Purity: Natal and the Politics of Zulu Ethnic Consciousness," in Vail (ed.), *The Creation of Tribalism,* pp. 215–40.

Marks, S. and A. Atmore (eds.), *Economy and Society in Pre-Industrial South Africa,* Harlow, Longman, 1980.

Matsebula, J.S.M., *A History of Swaziland,* Cape Town, Longman Penguin, 1988; first publ. Penguin, 1972.

Mbatha, S.B.L., *Nawe Mbopha kaSithayi*, Pietermaritzburg, Shuter & Shooter, 1971.

McClintock, A., *Imperial Leather: Race, Gender and Sexuality in the Colonial Context*, New York, Routledge, 1995.

McDowell, R.E., "The Brief Search for an African Hero: The Chaka–Mzilikazi Story in the South African Novel," *Discourse*, 11, 1968.

McMenemy, N., *Assegaai!* New York, Saturday Review Press, 1973.

Midiohouan, G., "Le Théâtre Négro-Africain d'Expression Francaise," *Peuples Noires/Peuples Africains*, 31, January–February 1983, pp. 54–78.

Miller, C., *Blank Darkness: Africanist Discourse in French*, Chicago, Chicago University Press, 1985.

Miller, C., *Theories of Africans: Francophone Literature and Anthropology in Africa*, Chicago and London, Chicago University Press, 1990.

Miller, J. (ed.), *The African Past Speaks: Essays on Oral Tradition and History*, Folkestone, Wm. Dawson & Sons, 1980.

Mncwango, L.L.J., *Ngezeni?* Pietermaritzburg, Shuter & Shooter, 1977; first publ. 1959.

Modum, E., "Le Mythe de Chaka," *Ethiopiques*, 14, 1978, pp. 49–58.

Mofolo, T., *Chaka*, Morija, Morija Sesuto Book Depot, 1925; first publ. in English trans. F.H. Dutton, London, Oxford University Press, 1931; publ. in French in 1940; republ. in English, London, Ibadan, and Narobi, Heinemann, 1981, with a new introduction by Daniel Kunene.

Molema, S.M., *The Bantu Past and Present*, Cape Town, Struik, 1963; first publ. Edinburgh, W. Green, 1920.

Montague, W.E., *Campaigning in South Africa: Reminiscences of an Officer in 1879*, London, W. Blackwood & Sons, 1880.

Moodie, D.F.C., *The History of the Battles and Adventures of the British, the Boers and the Zulus in Southern Africa from the Time of Pharaoh Necho to 1880*, vol. 2, Cape Town, Murray & St. Leger, 1888.

Moore, S.F., *Social Facts and Fabrications: "Customary" Law on Kilimanjaro, 1880–1980*, Cambridge, Cambridge University Press, 1986.

Morris, D., *The Washing of Spears*, London, Cape Publishing, 1966.

Moustapha, B., *Le Commandant Chaka*, Paris, Hatier, 1981.

Mphahlele, E., *The African Image*, London, Faber, 1962.

Msimang, C.T., "The Image of Shaka," in M. Macnamara (ed.), *World Views*, Pretoria, J.L. van Schaik, 1980, pp. 91–97.

Mtshali, O., "The Birth of Shaka," in *Sounds of a Cowhide Drum*, New York, Third Press, 1972.

Mudimbe, V., *The Invention of Africa: Gnosis, Philosophy and the Order of Knowledge*, Bloomington and Indianapolis, Indiana University Press, 1988.

Mulikita, F.M., *Shaka Zulu*, Lusaka, Longmans, 1967.

Murray, B.K., *Wits, the Early Years*, Johannesburg, Witwatersrand University Press, 1982.

Mzala, *Gatsha Buthelezi: Chief with a Double Agenda*, London, Zed Books, 1988.

Nandy, A., "History's Forgotten Doubles," *History and Theory*, 34, May 1995, pp. 44–66.

Nelson, C. and L. Grossberg (eds.), *Marxism and the Interpretation of Culture*, Urbana, University of Illinois Press, 1988.

Nenekhaly-Camara, C., *Amazoulou*, Honfleur, J.P. Oswald, 1970.

Ngubane, J., "Shaka's Social, Political and Military Ideas," in Burness (ed.), *Shaka, King of the Zulus in African Literature*, pp. 127–64.

Niane, D., *Chaka*, Honfleur, J.P. Oswald, 1971.

Nora, P. (ed.), *Les Lieux de Mémoire, III: Les France*, Paris, Gallimard, 1993, 3 vols.

Novick, P., *That Noble Dream: The "Objectivity Question" and the American Historical Profession*, Cambridge, Cambridge University Press, 1988.

Ntuli, F.L., *Umbuso kaShaka*, Mariannhill, Mariannhill Mission Press, 1954.

Odendaal, A., *Vukani Bantu! The Beginnings of Black Protest Politics in South Africa to 1912*, Cape Town, David Philip, 1984.

Ogunbesan, K., "A King for all Seasons: Chaka in African Literature," *Presence Africaine*, 88, 1973, pp. 197–217.

Omer-Cooper, J.D., *The Zulu Aftermath: A Nineteenth Century Revolution in Bantu Africa*, London, Longmans, Green & Co., 1966; repr. 1971.

Omer-Cooper, J., "The Mfecane Defended," *Southern African Review of Books,* July–October 1991, pp. 12–16.

Ong, W., *Ramus, Method and the Decay of Dialogue,* Cambridge, MA, Harvard University Press, 1958.

Ong, W., *The Presence of the Word,* New York, Simon & Schuster, Clarion Books, 1970; first publ. 1967.

Ong, W., "I See What You Say," in W. Ong, *Interfaces of the Word,* Ithaca, Cornell University Press, 1977.

Onuki-Tiernay, E., "Embedding and Transforming Polytropes: The Monkey as Self in Japanese Culture," in Fernandez (ed.), *Beyond Metaphor,* pp. 159–89.

Ortony, A., "Why Metaphors are Necessary and Not Just Nice," *Educational Theory,* 25, 1, 1975, pp. 45–53.

Owen, F., *The Diary of the Rev. Francis Owen,* first publ. 1838; republ. Cape Town, Van Riebeeck Society, 1926.

Owen, W.F.W., *Narrative of Voyages to Explore the Shores of Africa, Arabia and Madagascar,* London, Bentley, 1833, 2 vols.

Ozick, C., "Metaphor and Memory," in C. Ozick, *Metaphor and Memory,* New York, Vintage, 1991.

Parr, H.H., *A Sketch of the Kafir and Zulu Wars: Guadana to Isandlwana,* London, Kegan Paul, 1880.

Philibert, J.M., "The Politics of Tradition: Towards a Generic Culture in Vanuatu," *Mankind,* 16, 1, 1986, pp. 1–12.

Plant, R., *The Zulu in Three Tenses, Being a Forecast of the Zulu's Future in the Light of his Past and Present,* Pietermaritzburg, P. Davis & Sons, 1905.

Porter, D., "Orientalism and its Problems," in Barker et al. (eds.), *The Politics of Theory,* pp. 179–93.

Prakash, G. (ed.), *After Colonialism: Imperial Histories and Postcolonial Displacements,* Princeton, Princeton University Press, 1995.

Preston-Whyte, E. and J. Thorpe, "Ways of Seeing, Ways of Buying: Images of Tourist Art and Culture Expression in Contemporary Beadwork," in A. Nettleton and D. Hammond-Tooke (eds.), *African Art in Southern Africa: From Tradition to Township,* Johannesburg, Ad Donker, 1989, pp. 123–51.

Price, S., *Primitive Art in Civilized Places,* Chicago, Chicago University Press, 1989.

Prince, F.T., "Chaka," in *Poems,* London, Faber & Faber, 1938; republ. in *The Doors of Stone,* London, Rupert Hart Davis, 1963.

Quinn, N., "The Cultural Basis of Metaphor," in Fernandez (ed.), *Beyond Metaphor,* pp. 56–93.

Race Relations Survey 1985, Johannesburg, 1985.

Ranger, T., *Dance and Society in Eastern Africa, 1890–1970: The Beni Ngoma,* Berkeley and Los Angeles, University of California Press, 1975.

Ranger, T., "The Invention of Tradition in Colonial Africa," in Hobsbawm and Ranger (eds.), *The Invention of Tradition,* pp. 211–62.

Raum, J., "Historical Concepts and the Evolutionary Interpretation of the Emergence of States: The Case of the Zulu Reconsidered Yet Again," *Zeitschrift für Ethnologie,* 114, 1989, pp. 125–38.

Reed, J. and C. Wake, *Senghor: Selected Poems,* New York, Atheneum, 1969.

Rees, W. (ed.), *Colenso Letters from Natal,* Pietermaritzburg, Shuter & Shooter, 1958.

Ricoeur, P., *Time and Narrative,* trans. from the French by K. McLaughlin and B. Pellamer, Chicago, Chicago University Press, 1984.

Ridehalgh, A., "Some Recent Francophone Versions of the Shaka Story," *Research in African Literatures,* 22, 2, Summer 1991, pp. 135–52.

Ritter, E.A., *Shaka Zulu: The Rise of the Zulu Empire,* first publ. London, Longmans, Green, 1955; republ. Middlesex, Penguin, 1978, and London, Viking, 1985.

Roberts, B., *The Zulu Kings,* London, Hamish Hamilton, 1974.

Rosenzweig, R., "American Heritage," in Benson et al. (eds.), *Presenting the Past.*

Rycroft, D. and A. Ngcobo (eds.), *The Praises of Dingana,* Durban and Pietermaritzburg, KCAL and the University of Natal Press, 1988.

Said, E., *Orientalism,* New York, Pantheon Books, 1978.

Samuel, R. and P. Thompson, *The Myths We Live By,* London, Routledge, 1990.

Samuelson, R.C.A., *Long, Long Ago,* Durban, Knox, 1929.

Sandison, A., *The Wheel of Empire,* London, Macmillan, 1967.

Sandison, A., "A Matter of Vision: Rudyard Kipling and Rider Haggard" in Gross (ed), *The Age of Kipling,* pp. 128–34.

Saul, J. and S. Gelb, *The Crisis in South Africa,* New York, Monthly Review Press, 1986.

Saunders, C., *The Making of the South African Past,* Cape Town, David Philip, 1988.

Saunders, C., "Radical History–the Wits Workshop Version–Reviewed," *South African Historical Journal,* 24, 1991, pp. 160–65.

Saunders, C., "Pre-Cobbing Mfecane Historiography," in Hamilton (ed.), *The Mfecane Aftermath,* pp. 21–34.

Scheub, H., *The Xhosa Ntsomi,* Oxford, Oxford University Press, 1975.

Schoeman, P.J., *Phampatha: The Beloved of King Shaka,* Cape Town, Howard Timmins, 1983.

Scott, J., *Weapons of the Weak: Everyday Forms of Peasant Resistance,* London, Yale University Press, 1985.

Scott, J., *Domination and the Art of Resistance,* New Haven, Yale University Press, 1990.

Scully, W.C., *Poems,* London, T. Fischer Unwin, 1892.

Senghor, L.S., *Selected Poems,* London, Oxford University Press, 1964.

Sévry, J., *Chaka Empereur des Zoulous: Histoire, Mythes et Légendes,* Paris, Editions l'Harmattan, 1991.

Shooter, J., *The Kafirs of Natal and the Zulu Country,* first publ. London, E. Stanford, 1857; repr. New York, Negro Universities Press, 1960.

Sinclair, J., *Shaka Zulu,* Munich, n.p., 1986.

Slater, H., "Land, Labour and Capital in Natal: The Natal Land and Colonisation Company, 1860–1948," *Journal of African History,* 16, 2, 1975, pp. 257–83.

Slater, H., "The Changing Pattern of Economic Relationships in Rural Natal, 1838–1914," in Marks and Atmore (eds.), *Economy and Society,* pp. 148–70.

Smith, A., "The Trade of Delagoa Bay as a Factor in Nguni Politics, 1750–1835," in L. Thompson (ed.), *African Societies in Southern Africa,* London, Heinemann, 1969, pp. 171–89.

Smith, K., *The Changing Past: Trends in South African Historical Writing,* Johannesburg, Southern Book Publishers, 1988.

Sontag, S. (ed.), *A Roland Barthes Reader,* London, Vintage Press, 1993.

Spivak, G.C., "Can the Subaltern Speak," in Nelson and Grossberg (eds.), *Marxism and the Interpretation of Culture,* pp 271–313.

Spooner, B., "Weavers and Dealers: Authenticity and Oriental Carpets," in A. Appadurai (ed.), *The Social Life of Things: Commodities in Cultural Perspective,* Cambridge, Cambridge University Press, 1988, pp. 195–235.

Spronk, J.M., "Chaka and the Problem of Power in the French Theatre of Black Africa," *The French Review,* 57, 5, April 1984, pp. 634–40.

Stanley, D., and P. Vennem, *Shaka, King of the Zulus,* New York, Morrow Junior Books, 1988.

Stokes, E., "Kipling's Imperialism," in Gross (ed.), *The Age of Kipling,* pp. 90–98.

Stow, G.W., *The Native Races of South Africa,* ed. for publication by G. Theal after the author's death, first publ. London, Swann Sonneschein, 1905; repr. Cape Town, Struik, 1964.

Street, B.V., *The Savage in Literature: Representations of Primitive Society in English Fiction, 1858–1920,* London, Routledge & Kegan Paul, 1975.

Stuart, E., *I Remember,* Pietermaritzburg, private publication, 1984.

Stuart, J., *Studies in Zulu Law and Custom,* Durban, n.p., printed by Robinson & Co. (probably 1903).

Stuart, J., *The Conjunctive and Subjunctive Methods of Writing Zulu,* Durban, n.p., 1906.

Stuart, J. (ed.), *Zulu Orthography,* Durban, n.p., printed by Robinson & Co., 1907.

Stuart, J., *A History of the Zulu Rebellion, 1906, and of Dinuzulu's Arrest, Trial and Expatriation,* London, Macmillan & Co., 1913.

Stuart, J., *uTulasizwe,* London, Longmans, Green & Co., 1923.

Stuart, J., *uHlangakula,* London, Longmans, Green & Co., 1924.

Stuart, J., *uBaxoxele,* London, Longmans, Green & Co., 1924.

Stuart, J., *uKulumetule,* London, Longmans, Green & Co., 1925.

Stuart, J., *uVusezakiti,* London, Longmans, Green & Co., 1926.

Stuart, P.A., *An African Attila: Tales of the Zulu Reign of Terror,* London, T. Fischer Unwin, 1927.

Summary of the Report of the Commission for the Socio-Economic Development of the Bantu Areas within the Union of South Africa, Pretoria, Government Printer, 1955.

Taylor, R., "Is Radical History 'White'?," *South African Historical Journal,* 27, 1992, pp. 259–61.

Tedlock, D., *The Spoken Word and the Work of Interpretation,* Philadelphia, University of Pennsylvania Press, 1983.

Theal, G.M., *The Republic of Natal,* Cape Town, Solomon, 1886.

Theal, G.M., *South Africa,* London, Fischer & Unwin, 1894.

Theal, G.M., *History of South Africa,* London, Allen & Unwin, 1900, 11 vols.

Theal, G.M., *History of South Africa from 1795–1828,* London, Allen & Unwin, 1903.

Theal, G.M. (ed), *Records of South East Africa,* London, vols. 2, 4, first printed for the government of the Cape Colony, 1903; repr. Cape Town, Struik, 1964.

Thomas, N., "The Inversion of Tradition," *American Ethnologist,* 19, 2, 1992, pp. 213–32.

Thomas, N., *Colonialism's Culture: Anthropology, Travel and Government,* Cambridge, Polity Press, 1994.

Thompson, G., *Travels and Adventures in Southern Africa,* London, H. Colburn, 1827; facsimile repr., ed. V.S. Forbes, Cape Town, Africana Connoisseurs Press, 1962; repr. Cape Town, Van Riebeeck Society, 1967–68, 2 vols.

Thompson, L. (ed.), *African Societies in Southern Africa,* London, Heinemann, 1969.

Thompson, L., "Co-operation and Conflict: The Zulu Kingdom and Natal," in M. Wilson and L. Thompson (eds.), *A History of South Africa to 1870,* Cape Town, David Philip, 1982, pp. 334–90.

Thompson, P., *The Voice of the Past: Oral History,* Oxford, Oxford University Press, 1978.

Thornton, R., "This Dying Out Race: W.H.I. Bleek's Approach to the Languages of South Africa," *Social Dynamics,* 9, 2, 1, 1983, pp. 1–10.

Tomaselli, K. et al., *Myth, Race and Power: South Africans Imaged on Film and TV,* Cape Town, Anthropos, 1986.

Tomaselli, K., "Camera, Colour and Racism in *Shaka Zulu,*" *History News,* 30, November 1987.

Turner, V., *The Ritual Process: Structure and Anti-Structure,* Chicago, Aldine, 1969.

Tylor, E.B., *Primitive Cultures, Researches into the Development of Mythology, Philosophy, Religion, Language, Art and Custom,* London, John Murray, 1903, 2 vols., 4th ed.; first publ. 1871.

U Tam'si, T., *Légendes Africaines,* Paris, Seghers, 1967–68.

Vail, L. (ed.), *The Creation of Tribalism in Southern Africa,* London, Berkeley, and Los Angeles, James Currey and University of California Press, 1989.

Van Coller, P.P.R., *Die Swart Attila—Verhale van Shaka,* Pretoria, APB, 1946.

Van den Berghe, P., "Tourism and Recreated Ethnicities," *Annals of Tourism Research,* 1984, pp. 343–52.

Van Jaarsveld, F.A., *The Afrikaner's Interpretation of South African History,* Cape Town, Simondium, 1964.

Van Jaarsveld, F., *From Van Riebeeck to Vorster, 1652–1974: An Introduction to the History of the Republic of South Africa,* Johannesburg, Perskor, 1975.

Van Jaarsveld, F.A., *Omstrede Suid-Afrikaanse Verlede: Geskiedenisideologie en die Historiese Skuldvraagstuk,* Johannesburg and Cape Town, Struik, 1984.

Vansina, J., *Oral Tradition: A Study in Historical Methodology,* Chicago, Aldine, 1965.

Vansina, J., *Oral Tradition as History,* Madison, University of Wisconsin Press, 1985.

Van Warmelo, N.J., *Preliminary Survey of the Bantu Tribes of South Africa,* Ethnological Publications, Pretoria, Government Printer, 1935.

Van Warmelo, N.J., *A History of Matiwane and the amaNgwane,* Ethnological Publications, Pretoria, Government Printer, 1938.

Van Warmelo, N.J., "Shaka's Grave at Stanger," *African Studies,* 2, 1942, pp. 108–12.

Van Wyk Smith, M., "The Origins of Some Victorian Images of Africa," *English in Africa,* 6, 1, 1979, pp. 12–32.

Vijn, C., *Cetshwayo's Dutchman, Being the Private Journal of a White Trader in Zululand during the British Invasion,* trans. from the Dutch and ed. J.W. Colenso, first publ. London, Longmans, Green & Co., 1880; repr. New York, Negro Universities Press, 1969.

Vilakazi, B.W., *Inkondlo kaZulu,* first publ. 1935, trans. into English by F.L. Friedman, D.M. Malcolm, and J.H. Sikakana (eds.) as *Zulu Horizons,* Johannesburg, Witwatersrand University Press, 1962; repr. 1973.

Walker, E., *History of South Africa,* London, Longmans, 1928.

Wallace, M., "Mickey Mouse History: Portraying the Past at Disney World," *Radical History Review,* 32, 1985, pp. 33–57.

Walters, E.V., *Terror and Resistance: A Study of Political Violence with Case Studies of Some Primitive African Communities,* New York, Oxford University Press, 1969.

Watt, E., *Febana,* London, Davies, 1962.

Webb, C. de B. and J.B. Wright (eds.), *The James Stuart Archive of Recorded Oral Evidence Relating to the History of the Zulu and Neighbouring Peoples [JSA],* Pietermaritzburg and Durban, University of Natal Press and KCAL, 1976–86, 4 vols., proceeding.

Webb, C. de B. and J. B. Wright, *A Zulu King Speaks: Statements made by Cetshwayo kaMpande on the History and Customs of his People,* Pietermaritzburg and Durban, University of Natal Press and KCAL, 1978.

Welsh, D. *The Roots of Segregation: Native Policy in Colonial Natal, 1845–1910,* Cape Town, Oxford University Press, 1971.

West, R., *The Diamonds and the Necklace: A South African Journey,* London, Hodder & Stoughton, 1989.

White, H.V., *Metahistory,* Baltimore, Johns Hopkins University Press, 1973.

White, H.V., *Tropics of Discourse,* Baltimore, Johns Hopkins University Press, 1978.

White, H.V., "The Question of Narrative in Contemporary Historical Theory," *History and Theory,* 23, 1, 1984, pp. 1–33.

White, H.V., *Content of the Form,* Baltimore, Johns Hopkins University Press, 1987.

Wilkins, I. and J. Strydom, *The Super-Afrikaners: Inside the Afrikaner Broederbond,* Johannesburg, Jonathan Ball, 1978.

Wilmsen, E. and P. McAllister (eds.), *The Politics of Difference: Ethnic Premises in a World of Power,* Chicago and London, Chicago University Press, 1996.

Wilson, M., *Divine Kings and the "Breath of Men,"* Cambridge, Cambridge University Press, 1959.

Witz, L. and C.A. Hamilton, "Reaping the Whirlwind: The *Reader's Digest Illustrated History of South Africa* and Changing Popular Perceptions of History," *South African Historical Journal,* May 1991, pp. 185–202.

Wolf, E., *Europe and a People without a History,* Berkeley, University of California Press, 1982.

Wolseley, G., *The South African Journal of Sir Garnet Wolseley, 1879–1880,* ed. A. Preston, Cape Town, A.A. Balkema, 1973.

Worger, W., "Clothing Dry Bones: The Myth of Shaka," *Journal of African Studies,* 6, 3, 1979, pp. 144–58.

Worger, W., "White Radical History in South Africa," *South African Historical Journal,* 24, May 1991, pp. 145–53.

Worger, W., "'White' Radical History: A Response," *South African Historical Journal,* 27, 1992, pp. 262–63.

Wright, H.M., *The Burden of the Present: Liberal–Radical Controversy over Southern African History,* Cape Town, David Philip, 1977.

Wright, J.B., "Pre-Shakan Age-Group Formation among the Northern Nguni," *Natalia,* 8, 1978, pp. 23–29.

Wright, J.B., "Politics, Ideology and the Invention of the Nguni," in T. Lodge (ed.), *Resistance and Ideology in Settler Societies,* vol. 4, Johannesburg, Ravan Press, 1986, pp. 96–118.

Wright, J.B., "Review," *South Africa International,* 19, 2, 1988, pp. 105–08.

Wright, J.B., "Political Mythology and the Making of Natal's Mfecane," *Canadian Journal of African Studies,* 23, 2, 1989, pp. 272–91.

Wright, J.B., "A.T. Bryant and the 'Wars of Shaka'," *History in Africa,* 18, 1991, pp. 409–25.

Wright, J.B. and C.A. Hamilton, "Traditions and Transformations: The Phongolo–Mzimkhulu Region in the Late Eighteenth and Early Nineteenth Centuries," in Duminy and Guest (eds.), *Natal and Zululand.*

Wright, J. and A. Manson, *The Hlubi Chiefdom,* Ladysmith, Ladysmith Historical Society, 1983.

Wright, J. and A. Mazel, "Controlling the Past in the Museums of Natal and KwaZulu," *Critical Arts,* 5, 3, 1991, pp. 59–77.

Wylie, D., "Autobiography as an Alibi: History and Projection in Nathaniel Isaacs's *Travels and Adventures in Eastern Africa* (1836)," *Current Writing,* 3, 1991, pp. 71–90.

Wylie, D., "Who's Afraid of Shaka Zulu?," *Southern African Review of Books,* May–June 1991, pp. 8–9.

Wylie, D., "Textual Incest: Nathaniel Isaacs and the Development of the Shaka Myth," *History in Africa,* 19, 1992, pp. 411–33.

Wylie, D., "A Dangerous Admiration: E.A. Ritter's *Shaka Zulu,*" *South African Historical Journal,* 22, 1993, pp. 98–118.

Zinsou, S.A., *On Joue la Comédie,* Lomé, Haho Haarkem, 1975.

Zondi, E., *Ukufa KukaShaka,* Johannesburg, Witwatersrand University Press, 1960; repr. 1976.

Unpublished

Bunn, D., "Embodying Africa: Description, Ideology, Imperialism, and the Colonial Romance," Ph.D. thesis, Northwestern University, 1987.

Cobbing, J., "The Case against the Mfecane," seminar paper, University of Cape Town, 1983; in a revised form, "The Case against the Mfecane," seminar paper, University of the Witwatersrand, 1984.

Cobbing, J., "The Myth of the Mfecane," seminar paper, University of Durban-Westville, 1987.

Cobbing, J., "Jettisoning the Mfecane (with Perestroika)," seminar paper, presented together with J.B. Wright's "Political Mythology and the Making of Natal's Mfecane," to an African Studies Institute Seminar entitled "The Mfecane: Beginning the Inquest," University of the Witwaters-rand, 1988.

Cohen, D.W., "The Production of History," paper prepared for the Fifth International Roundtable in Anthropology and History, Paris, 1986.

Cope, N., "The Zulu Royal Family under the South African Government, 1910–1930: Solomon kaDinuzulu, Inkatha and Zulu Nationalism," Ph.D. thesis, University of Natal, 1986.

Cope, R., "Shepstone and Cetshwayo, 1873–1879," M.A. thesis, University of Natal, 1967.

Costa, A. "Two Bulls in the Herd: The Royal Succession Dispute of the 1940s," B.A. Honours report, University of the Witwatersrand, 1995.

Costa, A. "Custom and Commonsense: The Zulu Royal Family Succession Dispute of the 1940s," paper presented to the seminar of the Institute for Advanced Social Research, University of the Witwatersrand, 1996.

De Kiewiet, C.W., "Government, Colonists, Missionaries, Natives on the North-Eastern Frontier and Beyond, 1832–46," M.A. thesis, University of the Witwatersrand, 1925.

Dhupelia, U.S., "Frederick Robert Moor and Native Affairs in the Colony of Natal 1893–1903," M.A. thesis, University of Durban-Westville, 1980.

Forsyth, P., "Inkatha's Use of History," M.A. thesis, University of Natal, Pietermaritzburg, 1990.

Gewald, J.B, "Untapped Sources: Slave Exports from Southern and Central Namibia up to the Mid-Nineteenth Century," paper presented at the colloquium "The Mfecane Aftermath: Towards a New Paradigm," University of the Witwatersrand, 1991.

Golan, D., "Construction and Reconstruction in Zulu History," Ph.D. thesis, Hebrew University of Jerusalem, 1988.

Gorham, C., "'A Blind Darkness': Knowledge, Trade and the Myth of 1824: The Trading Settlement of Port Natal as Gateway to the 'Mfecane',", paper presented at the colloquium "The Mfecane Aftermath: Towards a New Paradigm," University of the Witwatersrand, 1991.

Gunner, E., "*Ukubonga Nezibongo:* Zulu Praising and Praises," Ph.D. thesis, University of London, 1984.

Guy, J., "Cattle Keeping in Zululand," paper presented to the Language and History in Africa Seminar, School of Oriental and African Studies (SOAS), University of London, 1971.

Hamilton, C.A., "Ideology, Oral Traditions and the Struggle for Power in the Early Zulu Kingdom," M.A. thesis, University of the Witwatersrand, 1986.

Hamilton, C.A., "The Production of Shaka and 'the Weighing of Evidence only Procurable in Prejudiced Channels'," paper presented to the Conference on Enlightenment and Emancipation, Durban, 1989.

Hamilton, C.A. "Authoring Shaka: Models, Metaphors and Historiography," Ph.D. thesis, Johns Hopkins University, 1993.

Harries, P., "Imagery, Symbolism and Tradition in a South African Bantustan: Gatsha Buthelezi, Inkatha and Zulu History," Department of History, University of Cape Town, 1987.

Hedges, D.W., "Trade and Politics in Southern Mozambique and Zululand in the Eighteenth and Early Nineteenth Centuries," Ph.D. thesis, SOAS, University of London, 1978.

Hemson, D. "Class Consciousness and Migrant Labour: Dockworkers in Durban," Ph.D. thesis, University of Warwick, 1979.

Hendrickson, H., "Historical Idioms of Identity Representation among the OvoHerero in Southern Africa," Ph.D. thesis, New York University, 1992.

Hofmeyr, I., "We Spend our Years as a Tale that is Told: Oral Storytelling, Literacy and Historical Narrative in the Changing Context of a Transvaal Chiefdom," Ph.D. thesis, University of the Witwatersrand, 1991.

Hofmeyr, I., "'Wailing for Purity'–Oral Studies in Southern African Studies," paper presented to the *Journal of Southern African Studies* Twentieth Anniversary Conference, York University, September 1994.

Karp, I. and C. Kratz, "The Fate of Tipoo's Tiger: A Critical Account of Ethnographic Display," paper presented to the Anthropology Department, Northwestern University, 1992.

La Hausse P., "Ethnicity and History in the Careers of Two Zulu Nationalists: Petros Lamula (c.1881–1948) and Lymon Maling (1899–c.1936)," Ph.D. thesis, University of the Witwatersrand, 1993.

La Hausse, P., "The Struggle for the City: Alcohol, the *Ematsheni* and Popular Culture in Durban, 1902–1936," M.A. thesis, University of Cape Town, 1984.

Lambert, J., "Africans in Natal, 1880–1899: Continuity, Change and Crisis in a Rural Society," Ph.D. thesis, University of South Africa, 1986.

Lambourne, B., "A Chip off the Old Block: Early Ghoya History and the Emergence of Moletsane's Taung," paper presented at the colloquium "The Mfecane Aftermath: Towards a New Paradigm," University of the Witwatersrand, 1991.

Lodge, T. "South Africa: Democracy and Development in Post-Apartheid South Africa," paper presented to the Institute for Advanced Social Research, University of the Witwatersrand, 1994.

Malaba, M.Z., "Shaka as Literary Theme," Ph.D. thesis, York University, 1986.

Maré, G., "The Past, The Present and Negotiation Politics: The Role of Inkatha," paper presented at the Africa Seminar, University of Cape Town, 1989.

Martin, R., "British Images of the Zulu, c.1820–1879," Ph.D. thesis, University of Cambridge, 1982.

Meintjes, S.M., "Edendale 1850–1906: A Case Study of Rural Transformation and Class Formation in an African Mission in Natal," Ph.D. thesis, University of London, 1988.

Mothlabi, M.B.G., "The Theory and Practice of Black Resistance to Apartheid: A Social–Ethical Analysis of the Internal Struggle for Political and Social Change," Ph.D. thesis, Boston University, 1980.

N'Diaye, I., "Théâtre et Société en Afrique Noire 'Francophone'," Ph.D. thesis, Université Cheikh Anta Diop, Dakar, 1979.

Preston-Whyte, E., "Trading Networks and Money-Making at a 'Traditional Zulu' Market," paper delivered at the University of Cape Town, n.d.

Preston-Whyte, E., "The Real Zulu?," paper presented to a special panel on Shakaland, at the Association for Anthropology in Southern Africa, Annual Meeting, 1992.

Rasool, C., "Going Back to our Roots: Aspects of Marxist and Radical Thought and Politics in South Africa, 1930–1960," M.A. thesis, Northwestern University, 1987.

Richner, J., "The Withering Away of the 'Lifaqane': Or a Change in Paradigm," B.A. Honours essay, Rhodes University, 1988.

Richner, J., "Eastern Frontier Slaving and its Extension into the Transorangia and Natal, 1770–1843," paper presented at the colloquium "The Mfecane Aftermath: Towards a New Paradigm," University of the Witwatersrand, 1991.

Skweyiya, Z.S.T. "Chieftaincy, the Ethnic Question and the Democratisation Process in South Africa," Community Law Centre Occasional Paper Series, University of the Western Cape, 1993.

Slater, H., "Transitions in the Political Economy of South-East Africa," D.Phil. thesis, Sussex University, 1976.

Smith, A., "The Struggle for Control of Southern Mozambique, 1720–1835," Ph.D. thesis, University of California, Los Angeles, 1970.

Spronk, J.M., "The Shaka Theme in the Francophone Theatre of West Africa," Ph.D. thesis, University of Oregon, 1983.

Webb, C. de B., "Of Orthodoxy, Heresy and the Difaqane," paper presented to the Teachers' Conference on African History, University of the Witwatersrand, Johannesburg, 1974.

Webb, C. de B., "Environment and History: The Northern Nguni Example," paper presented at the Conference on the History of the Transkei and Ciskei, Rhodes University, Grahamstown, 1983.

Webster, A., "An Examination of the 'Fingo Emancipation' of 1835," paper presented at the African Studies Seminar, University of Cape Town, 1990.

Webster, A., "Unmasking the Fingo: the War of 1835 Revisited," paper presented at the colloquium "The Mfecane Aftermath: Towards a New Paradigm," University of the Witwatersrand, 1991.

Wright, J.B., "Political Mythology and the Making of Natal's Mfecane," seminar paper, presented together with J. Cobbing's "Jettisoning the Mfecane," to an African Studies Institute seminar entitled "The Mfecane: Beginning the Inquest," University of the Witwatersrand, 1988.

Wright, J.B., "The Dynamics of Power and Conflict in the Thukela–Mzimkhulu Region in the Late Eighteenth and Early Nineteenth Centuries: A Critical Reconstruction," Ph.D. thesis, University of the Witwatersrand, 1990.

Wylie, D., "White Writers and Shaka Zulu," Ph.D. thesis, Rhodes University, 1995.

Archival references

Cape Archives Depot, Archives of the Magistrate of Albany (A.Y.) 8/79
Cape Archives Depot, Archives of the Magistrate of Uitengage (U.I.T.) 15/9, 15/12
Cape Archives Depot, Government House Archives (G.H.) 1/15, 1/39, 19/3, 23/7, 23/8, 23/9
Cape Archives Depot, Minutes of the Cape Council of Advice (A.C.) 2
Cape Archives Depot, Notarial Division, Cape Districts (N.C.D.) 25/11, 25/14, 35/8, 35/9, 35/11
Cape Archives Depot, Zululand Province (Z.P.) 1/1/33 1/1/36
Killie Campbell Africana Library, Colenso Papers (C.P.)
Killie Campbell Africana Library, Stuart Papers (S.P.)
Natal Archives Depot, Fynn Papers.
Natal Archives Depot, Shepstone Papers (Sh.P.)
Public Record Office (P.R.O.), Archives of the Colonial Office (C.O.) 48/13, 48/62, 48/124, 48/133 211, 219, 230, 233, 234, 235, 243, 287, 270, 293, 293/138, 333, 357, 359, 2659, 2692, 2693, 3929, 3937, 3941, 4322, 4851, 4852, 4853, 4888, 4893, 4894, 4895, 48887

Periodicals and newspapers

Azalea promotions flyer issued on behalf of the Tourist Association of Natal and Kwazulu, n.d.
Beacon Journal
Cape Times
Cape Monthly Magazine
Cape Town Gazette and African Advertiser
Daily News
Drum
Electronic Media
Financial Times
Gentleman's Magazine
Grahamstown Journal
Guardian
Harmony Gold News
Hartford Courant
Historical Firearms Society of South Africa Newsletter
Houston Chronicle
Ilanga
Ilanga lase Natal

Illustrated London News
Imvo Zabantsundu
Injula
Inkanyiso
Leadership
Leselinyana La Lesotho
London Quarterly Review
Macmillan's Magazine
Natal Adverstiser
Natal Mercury
Natal Witness Echo
Negotiation News
New African
New Nation
New York City Tribune
New York Daily News
New York Herald
New York Review of Books
New York Times
Orange Free State Monthly Magazine
Personality
San Francisco Chronicle
Shaka Zulu Souvenir Brochure, Johannesburg, 1986
South African Commercial Advertiser
Sowetan
Star
Star Telegram
Star Weekend
Style
Sunday Independent
Sunday Republican
Sunday Telegraph
Sunday Star
Sunday Times
Sunday Tribune
The Citizen
The Colonist
The Independent on Sunday
The Motorist
The South African
The Times Higher Education Supplement
Time
United States Anti-Apartheid Newsletter
Vrye Weekblad
Washington Post
Weekend Getaway
Weekly Mail
Your Family

Films
Amazulu, People of the Sky
Bantu Tribes of South Africa
Cesar's World (Zulu)
Encyclopedia Cinematographica (Zulu)

Fifty/Fifty
Mfecane Aftermath Colloquium, video series
Shaka Zulu
Zulu
Zulu Dawn

Interviews
William C. Faure, interview, Florida, South Africa, 1980
William C. Faure, telephone interview, April 2, 1988
Barry Leitch, telephone interview, February 25, 1992

Speeches
King Goodwill Zwelithini, speech at the launch of C. Ballard's *The House of Shaka,* Hulett Country Club, December 9, 1988
King Goodwill Zwelithini, Shaka Day speech, Eshowe, September 24, 1991
King Goodwill Zwelithini, Shaka Day speech, Stanger, September 26, 1992
King Goodwill Zwelithini, Shaka Day speech, KwaMashu, September 27, 1992
M.G. Buthelezi, "The Bias of Historical Analysis," opening address of the Anglo-Zulu War Centenary, University of Natal, Durban, February 7, 1979
M.G. Buthelezi, Shaka Day speech, Ngoye, November 4, 1984
M.G. Buthelezi, Shaka Day speech, Stanger, September 21, 1991
Oscar Dhlomo, Shaka Day speech, Stanger, 1978

Index

Mnkabayi 56, 122
Mnyamana kaNgqengelele 83–4
Mofolo, Thomas 20, 121
Monase 57, 97
Moor, Frederick Robert 131, 133, 139–40, 154
Moshoeshoe 85, 212
Mpande 56–8, 63, 72–3, 75, 80–5, 94–7, 105, 112, 134; buck omen 81, 83–4; nomination of Cetshwayo as his heir 75, 94–6
Mpitikazi 64–6, 68
Mthonga 85
Mtshayankomo kaMagolwana 81, 83–4
Mudimbe, Valentin 28–9
Mudli 61–2, 66–8, 143
Nandi 59, 62–5, 67, 123
Natal Mercury 11, 131
Natal Native Congress 133, 135–6, 148
Natal Witness 131, 139–40
native administration 25; after Shepstone 131–3, 135, 138–40, 156–7, 160; after Union 169; Shakan principles of Shepstonian system 4, 34, 72–129, 131–2, 168, 206, 210, 213–14
native policy: after Union 158–9, 168, 170–1; in 1879 58; Shepstonian thinking 74, 88, 108, 120–1, 126, 130, 206; Stuart's vision of 137–8, 141, 148–9, 154–5, 165–6; under Moor 53, 131–3, 139
native question 17, 142, 149, 159–60, 165
Ndabuko 110
Ndlovu kaThimuni 59–68, 143–4, 147, 157, 181
Ndukwana kaMbengwana 60, 133, 136–8, 142, 147, 246 n.19
Ngcobo, A. 56, 162–3
Ngwabi 58–9
Ngwenya, Kaiser 173
Nongila 62–4, 66–8
Ntshingwayo kaMahole 83, 108
Nyembezi, C.L.S. 162
Nzibe 58, 82, 94
Omer-Cooper, John 18
oral traditions 34, 47, 50–4, 59, 62, 70–1, 118, 127, 146–7, 166, 174, 176, 178
orthography, Zulu 151, 154, 162, 166
Osborn, Melmoth 107–8, 116, 122, 132
Owen, W.F.W. 37, 228 n.2
Oxford History of South Africa, The 18
paternalism 90, 97, 104–5, 163
Pine, *Sir* Benjamin 88, 103–4
Plaatje, Sol. T. 125

praise poems 21, 50, 55–7, 70–1, 143, 162–3, 210
Quinn, Naomi 33–4
Qwabe (chiefdom) 50, 54, 65–7, 143
Ranger, Terence 25, 73
Retief, Piet 54, 57
Ritter, Ernst A. 20, 121, 125, 169–70, 178
Roberts, Brian 40
Rycroft, D. 56–7, 162–3
Said, Edward 23, 27–8, 30
Samuelson, S.O. 131, 133, 150
Saunders, C.R. 132
segregation, ideology and policy of 3, 142, 158, 165, 168–70, 213–14
Senzangakhona 1, 60–4, 66–8, 82
Sévry, Jean 21–2, 24, 26, 30
Shaka: African oral accounts of 17, 21, 31, 36–7, 47–8, 51, 54–5, 60–70, 92, 121, 176, 206, 210; as depicted by academics 12–24, 30; as depicted by colonial officials 4–5, 14, 29–31, 45, 206, *see also* Stuart, James; as depicted by early settlers 16–17, 22, 30, 36–48, 70–2, 90–2, 113, 206; as depicted by missionaries 17, 23–4, 30, 90, 92; as depicted by travelers 17, 22–4, 30–1, 69–70; as depicted in television series 6, 9, 25, 31, 171–187, 189 *see also Shaka Zulu (television series)*; as metaphor 6, 32–5, 52, 68–9, 111, 128, 168–205, 214; birth and accession 60–4, 66–8, 143; image as used in present-day politics 1–3, 8–12, 23, 26, 30–1, 35, 171, 209, 213–14; in literature 5, 20–2, 26, 30–1, 72, 114, 116–25, 127, 169–70, 176–8, 206, *see also Haggard, Henry Rider*; influence of succession disputes on 55–9; rebellion against 49–50, 54, 65; relationship with Cape authorities 43–6, 80; rise to power 48–9, 91; rule 49–50, 63, 209–10
Shaka Day 1–2, 6, 10–11, 15, 30, 185
Shaka Zulu (television series) 6, 9, 25, 30–1, 171–90, 207, 214; criticism of 173–5, 178–9, 182–7, 199; production costs 171, 180; story of 171–2
Shakaland (holiday resort) 6, 9, 25, 31, 171, 187–205, 207, 214; criticism of 199–205; cultural experience 190–9; description of 188–91
Shepstone, Arthur 160
Shepstone, Henrique 108
Shepstone, John 108, 150, 155, 160
Shepstone, Theophilus 130–1, 134, 143, 160–1, 169–70, 181, 184, 206, 214; and

land for Africans 88–90, 108; and native
administration 4–5, 72–129, 156, 168;
assumption of Shaka's mantle 28, 73–6,
80, 89–90, 94–8, 102–3, 116, 119, 128,
160, 167, 206–7; at installation of
Cetshwayo 72–88, 90, 93–4, 97–8,
105–6, 128; at nomination of Cetshwayo
as Mpande's heir 75, 95–6, 119, 127; at
restoration of Cetshwayo 108–11; attempts to preserve Zulu customs 74–5,
88–90, 98, 131; his view of Shaka and
Zulu system 91–3, 101, 106, 111–12,
116, 121, 125, 127, 156; souring relationship with Cetshwayo 104–6, 108
Sigujana 63
Sipika 60–1, 66–9
slave trade 38, 42, 175
Sojiyisa 58–9
Solomon kaDinuzulu 169–70
Somtsewu *see* Shepstone, Theophilus
South African Broadcasting Corporation
171, 176–7, 180–1, 184, 186
South African Commercial Advertiser 40, 43,
46, 69–70, 144
South African Native Affairs Commission
(1903–5) 154–6
sovereignty 4, 73, 92, 97–101, 103–4, 117,
119, 121, 166, 214
Stuart, James 4–5, 14, 29, 52–5, 60–5, 70,
125, 130–70, 178, 181, 207, 214; and
Zulu orthography 151, 154, 166, 207;
and Bambatha rebellion 157; belief in
tribal system 139, 156; criticism 144,
152–4, 163–7; Fynn's influence and *Diary*
144, 164; Haggard's influence on 125,
160–1; his 'Idea' 137–8, 141–2, 144–5,
166; his view of Shaka 142, 144, 146–50,

155–6, 162, 166; interviews on Shaka
142–4, 206, 210; James Stuart Archive 14,
70, 125, 150–2, 207; relationship with
Natal Native Congress 133, 135–6; re-
search among documentary sources
143–4, 147; Shepstone's influence on
130–1, 134–5, 156, 206
Theal, George McCall 16
Thimuni 60–2, 64, 66–8
Thompson, George 69–70
Togt Labour Amendment Act of 1902 140
Van Warmelo, N.J. 18, 168
Vansina, Jan 52, 207
Vye Weekblad 3, 8
Walker, Eric 16
Walters, E.V. 18
Weekly Mail 11, 173
Werner, Alice 161–2
White, Hayden 24
Wolseley, *Sir* Garnet 104, 106, 108,
114–15
Worger, William 16, 19–20
Wright, John 13–16, 22–23, 42, 90–1, 102,
207, 211
Wylie, Dan 16, 21, 23, 30, 169
Zibhebhu kaMaphitha 58–9, 62, 106–7, 110
Zondi, P.E. 3
Zulu, *Prince* Sifiso 2
Zulu civil war (1856) 57
Zulu civil war (1881) 107, 128
Zulu in literature, the 112–21; *see also names
of individual authors*
Zulu militarism 3, 10, 12, 30, 33, 202–3
Zulu nationalism 1–3, 5, 8–10, 13, 17–18,
30, 62, 169–70, 184, 203, 214
Zwelithini, *King* Goodwill 1–2, 10–11, 185,
203